Ferruccio Busoni

"A Musical Ishmael"

Della Couling

THE SCARECROW PRESS, INC.
Lanham, Maryland • Toronto • Oxford
2005

SCARECROW PRESS, INC.

Published in the United States of America
by Scarecrow Press, Inc.
A wholly owned subsidary of
The Rowman & Littlefield Publishing Group, Inc.
4501 Forbes Boulevard, Suite 200, Lanham, Maryland 20706
www.scarecrowpress.com

PO Box 317
Oxford
OX2 9RU, UK

British Library Cataloguing in Publication Information Available

Library of Congress Cataloging-in-Publication Data

Couling, Della.
  Ferruccio Busoni : "a musical Ishmael" / Della Couling.
    p. cm.
  Includes bibliographical references (p.   ) and index.
  ISBN 0-8108-5142-3 (hardcover : alk. paper)
  1. Busoni, Ferruccio, 1866–1924. 2. Composers—Biography. I. Title.
ML410.B98C74 2005
780'.92—dc22

                                        2004010740

∞™ The paper used in this publication meets the minimum requirements of
American National Standard for Information Sciences—Permanence of Paper
for Printed Library Materials, ANSI/NISO Z39.48-1992.
Manufactured in the United States of America.

To K. J.
Best of teachers, kindest of friends. Another purveyor of the broader picture.

~

Contents

~

Acknowledgments

My first thanks are due to the music department of the State Library in Berlin, in particular to Dr. Jutta Theurich, Dr. Uta Hertin-Loeser, and Dr. Helmut Hell, who all helped me in different ways to explore the enormous treasure chest of Busoniana the library contains; to the staff of the Centro Busoni in Empoli; to the special collections reading room in the Helsinki University Library; and to the music library of King's College, Cambridge. Dr. Marlies Ebert of the photographic collection department of the Stiftung Stadtmuseum Berlin deserves special gratitude for her efforts in tracking down a photograph of the Viktoria-Luise-Platz at a time when the Stiftung was in the process of moving to new premises. Dr. Martina Weindel has been a generous and hospitable colleague. Professor Marc-André Roberge patiently answered questions and generously forwarded articles that proved useful. Professor Larry Sitsky provided useful details on Busoni and Egon Petri. The publisher Dr. Ursula Müller-Speiser kindly provided a copy of Claudia Feldhege's *Ferruccio Busoni als Librettist*. Special thanks are due to my old friend and walking encyclopedia Dieter Kranz, not only for providing a room in Berlin during my many weeklong visits to the state library, but for his great hospitality, generosity, and encouragement. I owe a particular debt of gratitude to my daughter, Antonia Couling-Dinis, for casting a meticulous editorial eye on the manuscript at proof stage, and for her loving support. Thanks too to Bruce Phillips of Scarecrow Press for his belief in the book and constant support.

Photographs

x ⁓ Photographs

~

Introduction

It was Busoni's friend, the Anglo-Dutch composer Bernard van Dieren, who astutely dubbed him "a musical Ishmael." The Ishmael of the Old Testament, Abraham's son by the Egyptian handmaid Hagar, was never fully recognized by his father's tribe, particularly after the birth of Isaac, Abraham's legitimate heir. Ishmael wandered far, was difficult, but nevertheless, according to later legend, is considered the founder of several of the Arab peoples. Busoni was born, somewhat less colorfully, of a Tuscan father and an Italo-German mother; although he spent the greater portion of his life in German-speaking countries, in fact settling in Berlin at the age of twenty-eight, he never felt truly at home in either Germany or Italy—nor anywhere else, for that matter.

It was prophesied to Hagar that Ishmael would be "a wild man: his hand will be against every man," which was certainly not the case for Busoni. Nevertheless, owing to his feelings of rootlessness, and of being condemned for much of his time to the exhausting strains of a peripatetic life as a concert pianist, which he hated and resented more and more the older he grew, he certainly had a very aggressive, often malicious streak. The malice was often defused by his startling thunder-clap laugh—itself often a sign of repressed aggression. And Busoni never suffered fools gladly. He had scant respect for most of his fellow musicians—at least, off the concert platform—as few could begin to share his wide-ranging interests, and therefore most proved dull traveling companions. His early experiences made him supremely self-centered, at times to a quite callous degree, yet his generosity could be magnificent, particularly to his composition pupils, many of whom he taught gratis, and to other composers. In his series of concerts of contemporary music in the first years of the twentieth century in Berlin, he not only introduced foreign composers—such as Elgar, Saint-Saëns, Sibelius, Delius, Debussy, Franck, and many others—to German audiences, but initially financed these concerts out of his own pocket. Busoni longed to belong to Italy, but became too German to tolerate what he perceived as Italy's shortcomings, which made his criticisms of Italy particularly harsh, "almost like the bitterness of a betrayed lover," as his friend and pupil Guido Guerrini put it, in his own rather idiosyncratic study of his onetime teacher. But Busoni's lifestyle made him a cosmopolitan, and his character and personal history made him an instinctive despiser of nationalism.

Busoni did not found a race, but he most certainly did found a musical dynasty: many were the composers and other artists and thinkers who owed a tremendous debt not only to Busoni's teaching of composition and piano playing, but to his attitude to the whole of intellectual and artistic life, which he was always keen to pass on to his pupils. Edgard Varèse, Kurt Weill, Arnold Schoenberg, Egon Petri, and Bernard van Dieren are just some of the many who remained deeply in his debt. His openness to all musical styles, past, present, and future, inspired many, but also drew the fire of Hans Pfitzner, among others, who, like conservatives throughout history, saw openmindedness and a willingness to entertain new ideas and question old ones as a personal threat. Today, particularly in the light of recent technology, Busoni's ideas on the division of the scale, what is and is not music, and many other aspects of composition are not only easier to accept, but in many cases familiar practice—and prove just how prescient he was.

Where opera is concerned, Busoni rather willfully turned his back on the undeniable achievements of his fellow countryman and coeval Giacomo Puccini (he found *Madame Butterfly* "indecent"), and tended to look down on Verdi too until that chastening experience in 1894 of hearing the great man's last work, *Falstaff*. Busoni's ideas on what opera should be were rigid, even dictatorial in many ways. For him, music in opera should be used only to convey what cannot be conveyed in any other way, Mozart's *The Magic Flute* being the perfect example. Simply putting a play to music was anathema to him, and the many examples of this being churned out today, consisting in effect of orchestral music in the pit and recitative on stage, would have attracted his vehement scorn. In this attitude to the stage he proved himself a true descendant of *commedia dell'arte*, with its distancing from "reality" and emotion, what Bertolt Brecht was later to call the "alienation effect" (*Verfremdungseffekt*)—here Busoni's famous pupil Kurt Weill was certainly the conduit between Busoni and Brecht. But Busoni would recognize many of his theories in other modern operas today, with their use of a wide variety of instruments and musical styles, free play of ideas, and recruitment of the full panoply of modern technology. Not one of his operas is realistic in any meaningful sense, yet they are full of meaning: his bitterly ironic contempt for war and nationalism in *Arlecchino* is as relevant today as when the opera was written, during the carnage of the First World War. And his *Doktor Faust* contains a heartfelt warning for those who wish to hear.

Busoni's instrumental music is instantly recognizable: sonorous, cerebral, intense. It was said of him that he had no small talk, and the same could be said for his music: he is very much a musicians' musician. Likewise his piano playing had, owing to his intelligence and erudition, a dimension lacking in the mere virtuoso performance. He would often write to his wife after having played for friends that he had played a particular piece better than ever before—reaching the core of the music's meaning was more important to him than the acclaim of a large audience, most of whom he heartily despised. Even today, his name is revered by cognoscenti such as Alfred Brendel. It is a great pity that the relatively few recordings he made are not very satisfactory in giving a true idea of his great talent; he hated recording, and in the recording studio could never relax and give of his best.

Soon after his death in 1924, Europe entered the dark night of Fascism that only ended in flames two decades later. No wonder this free spirit and great cosmopolitan was airbrushed out of the picture. There was no place for him, alive or dead, during that period of rabid nationalism. To the Germans he was a foreigner, to the Italians a distant figure who had turned his back on his native land. It was only in the last two decades of the twentieth century that Busoni finally started to emerge from the shadows again, and take his place as one of the groundbreaking figures in musical history.

But Busoni's fascination does not end there: from the age of eight, he entered the world of the child prodigy, peddled around Europe by his ambitious father, robbed of a childhood, impelled to precocious maturity. In this volume, for the first time, his many letters to his parents—as a child, he traveled mostly with his father, from his late teens, often alone—are dealt with in depth. They give us a unique inside view of this life from the child's viewpoint. They also offer a melancholy picture of a child who, knowingly and competently, was more or less in charge of this circus by the age of nine, writing to his mother on the finances of the operation, what items of wardrobe he needed urgently, future plans, and much else. (The admirably indefatigable and competent Dr. Martina Weindel is now editing and annotating all Busoni's letters to his parents, to be published shortly.) That childhood largely explains the man and the Faustian struggles that finally left him exhausted: the struggle between the Italian and the German, the performing musician and the composer, the ever-curious polymath chained to the discipline of the piano—unlike that secret rival he constantly measured himself against, the Olympian Goethe, who chose the relative obscurity of Weimar as the ideal base from which to explore his many interests in peace. It was no accident that for his greatest work, Busoni, like Goethe, turned to Faust for his theme—*Doktor Faust* is a profoundly autobiographical and also a prophetic work. The fruit of Busoni's wide-ranging studies in philosophy, religion, and world literature, and of his own experience, it offers a bleak picture, in spite of the desperate optimism of its closing scene.

Since Busoni's death in 1924, there has only been one full biography: that by Edward Dent, published in 1933, and reprinted in 1966, 1974, and 1982. Although a masterly and highly readable work, it contains errors and suffers from many restrictions, chief among them the fact that Busoni's widow, although she greatly assisted Dent in his task, also exercised censorship on quite a massive scale. Dent concentrated far more on Busoni the musician than Busoni the man—let alone Busoni the child—and having been long under Busoni's spell, he had his own personal reasons for presenting him in a purely positive light. In the seventy years since Dent's book was published, much more material has become available: letters, journals, and biographies of many who swam into Busoni's orbit, offering an oblique view, also often a less partisan view, unhampered by the restraints under which Dent suffered. Nevertheless, Dent's book is one main pillar on which any new biography must rest. Another is Antony Beaumont's masterly study, *Busoni the Composer*, and the same writer's *Ferruccio Busoni: Selected Letters*, which Beaumont himself translated into English. Equally important is Sergio Sablich's study *Busoni*, which, like Beaumont's, consists of a brief biography and then an exhaustive study of Busoni's work; Sablich has also published an Italian edition of Beaumont's selection of Busoni's letters, but Sablich's edition is much fuller and, of course, has the added advantage that the Italian letters in the selection are given in the original language. Two further indispensable pillars are Marc-André Roberge's heroic achievement *Ferruccio Busoni: A Bio-Bibliography* and Larry Sitsky's admirably lucid *Busoni and the Piano*. Without all these, this book could not have been written. Dr. Martina Weindel has also contributed greatly to Busoni scholarship, having already published a new, exhaustively annotated edition of Busoni's seminal work, *Entwurf einer neuen Ästhetik der Tonkunst* (Sketch of a New Aesthetic of Music); another volume features Busoni's correspondence with Gottfried Galston and, yet another, the complete extant collection of Busoni's letters to Henri, Katharina, and Egon Petri. As stated above, Dr. Weindel is now working on an edition of Busoni's letters to his parents. It can only be hoped that Dr. Weindel will then turn her attention to Busoni's letters to his wife. A selection of these letters was published under the editorship of Friedrich Knapp in 1935 (English translation by Rosamond Ley, 1938), but the selection begins in 1895, well after Busoni's marriage. Knapp coyly gives his reason for this decision as: "The earlier letters were all of a private character," and states that the excisions in the letters in his selection are all of personal matter. As Busoni's wife was still alive at the time, this was an inevitable decision. Busoni engendered enormous loyalty among his circle, many of whom misguidedly accorded him an almost godlike status. I have nevertheless attempted to offer as rounded an impression as possible—often in his own words—of a more than usually complex genius. In particular in the Busoni Nachlass collection in the State Library in Berlin, but elsewhere too, there is now so much material that the most difficult choice was often what to leave out, if this book was to be kept to a reasonable length. All translations, unless otherwise stated, are my own.

Introductory Remarks to Notes Sections

Most letters quoted from are in the Busoni Nachlass in the State Library in Berlin. Therefore "StBB Bus. Nachl. 933" refers to the Staatsbibliothek Berlin Busoni Nachlass 933. "MW" refers to Martina Weindel, ed., *Ferruccio Busoni: Briefe an Henri, Katharina und Egon Petri*. "FB" refers to Ferruccio Busoni.

CHAPTER ONE

~

Early Childhood

I was baptized with the names of Ferruccio Dante Michelangelo Benvenuto, and my father (without knowing it) followed the theory of old Shandy who assigned to the name an influence on the abilities of the bearer. A heavy responsibility which I lightened for myself by striking out the three great Tuscan artists and only keeping the name Ferruccio.

—Ferruccio Busoni, *Two Autobiographical Fragments*

Empoli is a small town on the Arno, on the wide plain running between Florence and Pisa, but the charm of most Tuscan towns has largely eluded it. (It also suffered severe bomb damage during World War II.) From the railway station, facing a dusty square, the straight and nondescript Via Roma leads to another square, today called the Piazza della Vittoria; in the nineteenth century it was an unpaved area known as the Campaccio and used as a horse market. At the entrance to this square, on the corner, is a church, and on its side wall we see the name of Busoni for the first time, on a memorial plaque for a former mayor of the town, one Luigi Busoni, who died at the age of eighty on January 29, 1837. No more is known of this particular Busoni, but the name was and still is a relatively common one in Empoli and its immediate surroundings (there were twenty-three in the local telephone directory in the late 1990s).

1

In the Piazza della Vittoria there is another plaque, on the wall of number 16, commemorating the birth of a musician whose importance in musical history is only now beginning to be fully appreciated. In this modest three-story house, on April 1, 1866, Ferruccio Dante Michelangelo Benvenuto Busoni was born, his name a typically flamboyant gesture on the part of his father, Ferdinando, containing as it does more than a whiff of bet-hedging paternal ambition.

Ferdinando had himself been born in Empoli in 1834, but his son's birth in the town was a close-cut thing. Until a few days prior to the birth Ferdinando and his wife, the pianist Anna Weiss-Busoni, had been in Rome, where she had been performing. Nevertheless, driven by some primitive dynastic instinct ("the near prospect of the genealogical event," as his son dryly put it[1]), when the birth became imminent Ferdinando had dragged his wife the two hundred miles—presumably by road: the railway was still not fully integrated at that time—to his sisters' house in Empoli, in order that their child could be born in his father's native town.

There was little in Ferdinando's background to justify this drastic maneuver—indeed not even the Tuscan lineage so heavily hinted at in his infant son's full name. According to Ferruccio's account, one Ferdinando Busoni had emigrated from Corsica in the late eighteenth century and settled at Spicchio, a village near Empoli—which would indicate that all subsequent Busonis in the region stem from him. Until the advent of the railway, most goods in Tuscany traveled to the Mediterranean seaports by barge, along the Arno. That particular Ferdinando, with the energy and industry of the immigrant, became a prosperous barge owner, but died relatively young—it was suspected, of a contagious disease. In the Italy of that time, this meant that the entire contents of his family's home were burned, which left the widow and her three sons destitute. They moved to Empoli. The sons had fortunately inherited their father's zest and business sense, and soon prospered as felt hatmakers.

The second son, Giovanni Battista, married Anna Bini, daughter of a local market gardener, who gave him six sons and three daughters. Tragedy struck this branch of the family, too, when Giovanni Battista died in 1860, soon followed by his wife. And once more, the Busonis rolled up their sleeves and fought back—all except the eldest son, Ferdinando, who had left the town behind him some years before.

From a very young age Ferdinando had gone his own way, and balked at joining the rest of this industrious family in hat making. He preferred to spend his time reading; he had also soon discovered a gift for music and learned to play the clarinet. A passion for dog and horse racing, developed early on, further distanced him from the rest of the family—and indeed from respectable small-town life. His music teacher at Empoli, Gaetano Fabiani, was the leader of the town band and a pillar of the community. He and Ferdinando quarreled, and, in 1854, at the age of twenty, the latter left Empoli and joined the Banda Carini at the coastal town of Livorno (Leghorn), some forty miles west of Empoli.

For several years Ferdinando flourished as a traveling virtuoso clarinetist, having served an apprenticeship as first clarinet with more than one minor provincial orchestra, and even a term as professor of the clarinet in the Istituto Musicale at Novara for five months in 1862, all of which indicates remarkable talent in someone who was virtually self-taught. He moved on from each position after a very short time, however, usually following a clash of temperaments or on the excuse of ill health. This soon settled into the pattern that would continue for the rest of his life. Irascible, impatient, capricious, dogged by dyspepsia and other ills, many of them doubtless psychosomatic, Ferdinando turned to the nomadic life as the only existence feasible for him.

In spring 1865 his wanderings led him to Trieste, where, in his second concert, he was partnered by a young local pianist, Anna Weiss. It was that common phenomenon, the attraction of opposites, with music the linking current. Ferdinando was at thirty-one a romantic, dashing figure, with a considerable reputation as a ladies' man. Anna had led a strictly controlled, sheltered life. She fell in love with him at first sight and now, aged thirty-two, had enough strength of will to stick up for what she wanted.

Anna's father, Josef Ferdinand Weiss, was of Bavarian stock but born (in 1799) and educated in Ljubljana (Laibach—then part of the Austro-Hungarian Empire). His father, a painter and gilder, left his son to his own devices at thirteen by finding him employment as ship's boy on a vessel plying the Levant. By the age of thirty, however, Josef was settled in Trieste (then also under Austrian rule), and employed by a firm of Hamburg grain merchants, Alexander and Christian Schröder, whom he served well for the rest of his active life. He soon attained a position of considerable respectability in Trieste, which enabled him to marry a young Italian lady of good family, Carolina de Candido, originally from Friuli, to the north of Trieste. The couple had three children, a son and two daughters. Anna, the elder daughter, was born in 1833. In Trieste, Josef Weiss, or "Sor Giuseppe Weiss," as he was known, became completely Italianized—Italian being the dominant culture—and moved exclusively in Italian circles.

The children spoke the local Trieste dialect at home, but received a good Italian education. Anna, a serious young lady, also read French literature and spoke a rather stilted German, though apparently she always had difficulty writing it. She inherited her father's robust constitution (he died at the age of ninety-three, scarcely having known a day's illness in his life), unlike the rest of the family: his wife died young; at twenty their son became insane and spent the remaining twenty-eight years of his life in an asylum; and the younger daughter Mina married, but died of consumption in 1870, leaving two daughters, Ersilia and Carolina, who were to become Ferruccio's first playmates

Anna Weiss showed exceptional musical gifts at an early age, and was given every encouragement. She not only studied the piano, but was given lessons in composition. For a time her teacher was the Neapolitan composer Luigi Ricci (1805–1859), who had settled in Trieste and who became a notorious footnote in musical history by marrying one of the twin sisters of the great soprano Teresa Stolz (later to become Verdi's mistress), while apparently continuing to enjoy the favors of the other twin. He and his composer brother, Federico (1809–1877), collaborated in several operas, the most famous being *Crispino e la comara*, to a libretto by Francesco Maria Piave, which premiered in Venice in 1850. They now belong to the vast army of once popular but now largely forgotten nineteenth-century opera composers.

Anna gave her first public concert at the age of fourteen, playing a fantasia by Sigismond Thalberg. A few months later she gave another concert, this time including a fantasia she herself had composed. Soon after, she began taking lessons from the Austrian pianist Ferdinand Carl Lickl (1803–1864), which greatly improved her technique. As she was a young lady of good family, in Italy it was considered not quite respectable for her to make a career as a concert pianist, but she nevertheless performed frequently in public, often at charity concerts, either with orchestra or as a solo recitalist. In 1855 she even gave three concerts in Vienna. She also gave lessons to other young ladies, being considered of unimpeachable character. She was pious, and had the blinkered, overprotected artistic tastes of a young lady of her time; her horizons remained narrow.

Her repertoire also remained restricted: Mozart's Concerto in D Minor (no. 20, K. 466) and Weber's E-Flat Concerto, and in solo recitals the operatic fantasies of Thalberg and Liszt, but she was highly thought of by critics and public alike, their opinion possibly influenced by her beauty.

And it was her beauty that first attracted the flashy Ferdinando. Her father shrewdly gauged her suitor's measure and forbade him the house—always a fatal parental strategy: within a few weeks of their first meeting they were married. Anna, meek and sensitive, with a religious fervor subsequently verging on mania, was soon completely dominated by her willful and overbearing husband, her only refuge a dutiful self-sacrifice fueled by her intense piety. In her son Ferruccio she was to find an outlet for the boundless, submissive love that, she must soon have realized in her heart, was wasted on Ferdinando.

Ferdinando had his shrewd side; he rapidly saw the commercial advantages of their union, changed their name to Weiss-Busoni, reckoning that his wife's surname contributed a more solid, Germanic ring, and carted her off on an extensive Italian tour as his tame accompanist. Anna soon became pregnant, which failed to slow down the pace of their performing schedule. In Rome, around the end of February 1866, she played privately for Liszt, and on March 25 performed in public there for the last time before Ferruccio's birth. (Busoni was once asked when he appeared on stage for the first time, and answered jokingly, "Eight days before I was born!") And so, in the house of Ferdinando's sisters in Empoli, "surrounded by a great tribe of relatives," Ferruccio was born on Easter Sunday, April 1, 1866.

After eight months, the longest continuous period he ever spent in Empoli, the child was taken to his maternal grandfather's home in Trieste, where he was left, with a nurse, while his parents resumed their nomadic life. Old Giuseppe Weiss had been a widower for some years and, although strict toward his daughters, was now under the thumb of his housekeeper, Matilde, who was also his mistress, and a hated figure in the family. It was not the best of households for a young child, but fortunately Anna's now married sister, Mina Grusovin (who had only three years left to live), took over much of Ferruccio's early upbringing, together with that of her two daughters, Ersilia and Carolina, to whom Ferruccio remained devoted throughout his life.

This rather unsatisfactory situation lasted, interspersed with short visits from the parents, for over a year, after which the Weiss-Busonis picked up their son again. They had been extending their travels beyond Italy to include southern Styria in Austria, Stuttgart in Germany, and Nancy in northern France, but the goal, as for many a musical performer of the time, was Paris, where they arrived in December 1868. Their first appearance was at a New Year's Eve entertainment at the home of one M. Kugelmann, proprietor of the newspaper Le Gaulois. This led to other private concerts, then public concerts, and resounding success, either playing together or with others. By spring 1869 they were being described as "decidedly the heroes of the musical season." Ferdinando concentrated more on concerts in private houses, while Anna shone in public concerts, to great public and critical acclaim: "Under her steely touch the pianoforte sings, shudders, and becomes a complete orchestra in itself," wrote the critic of L'Art musical on April 8, 1869. "In the Schumann Quintet she showed a loftiness of style and brilliance of execution one would never have believed possible from the hands of a mere woman." (The reviewer had obviously never encountered the playing of that other mere woman, Clara Schumann, who had frequently played in Paris—the first time in 1832, when she was thirteen.)

The Busonis resolved to settle in Paris. It was a very busy time for them both, particularly for Anna, who now had to look after a lively toddler as well as prepare for concerts. But it was a happy time for her, as is evident in her letters to her niece Ersilia in Trieste, which are full of Ferruccio. "You should see him at the pianoforte," she wrote[2] at the beginning of 1869, "and how prettily he puts those dear little hands on the keyboard. He tries to imitate me, lifts his head and says 'What a lovely thing Daddy's playing!' . . . He makes himself understood charmingly in French, and in the street everybody stops to look at him; you hear the ladies say 'Isn't he lovely? Isn't he charming? What a beautiful

boy!' May God make him good and studious, then he will be a consolation to me." A year later Ferruccio, not yet four years old, was already
having piano and violin lessons from his mother, as was also gushingly
relayed to Trieste.

The family's happy and successful stay in Paris was about to come to
an end, however. By early 1870 it was clear that war between France
and Germany was imminent. The leaders of both countries had been
whipping up a public mood of hysterical aggression for some time, each
waiting for the other to throw a lighted match into the powder keg.
The Busonis, made nervous by the threat of war, felt constrained to
abandon their flourishing dual career in the French capital and retreat
to Trieste, well before the inevitable war finally erupted in mid-July.

Ferdinando immediately resumed his nomadic lifestyle, while Ferruccio and Anna went to stay briefly with the Grusovins. Anna then
joined her husband, and they played at Gorizia, Abano, and Recoaro,
but she soon returned to Trieste, as she could not bear to be parted from
her son. (Anna's sister Mina Grusovin died some time during this year,
and the Busonis' return to Trieste probably had something to do with
this.) All three Busonis spent part of the summer at Abano, near Padua,
where Ferdinando tried the mud baths for his chronic dyspepsia. By
spring 1871 it was decided that Ferdinando was to continue traveling
alone, while Anna returned to the parental home in Trieste and built
up a modest career giving private piano lessons. The full ramifications
behind this decision are unknown, but it is safe to assume that it was
largely to Ferdinando's advantage: he was feckless, used to having his
own way, and the bonds of family life were proving little to his taste, although certainly the peripatetic life would have been very unsuitable
for a small child. To be a virtuoso musician inevitably involved travel,
then as now, and even a large city like Paris would eventually have
proved insufficient to provide enough work. We can only speculate on
more personal reasons: perhaps Ferdinando had fallen out of love with
Anna as quickly as he had fallen in love with her. Over the six years of
their marriage so far, the basic relationship seems to have been that he
was too good for her, and the best she could do for him was to submit
to his will, earn money, and look after the child. Perhaps the trauma of
childbirth had triggered an antipathy to sexual activity in her, which
would create strains on the marital relationship. Whatever the truth,

the return to Trieste meant the end of their life as a married couple, except for relatively brief periods, until approaching old age—and firm
action on their son's part—threw them together again on a permanent
basis.

In the first year of this separated existence, Ferdinando did not
travel far from Trieste, and returned periodically, but he was away for
nearly the whole of 1872 (rather curious in an age of developing rail
networks). His wife and child were left in a household governed by the
dreaded housekeeper Matilde, who acted true to type as the "serva
padrona," bullying the old man, openly disrespectful to Anna, and always trying to cause mischief. In this tense and unpleasant atmosphere
Ferruccio, under the concentrated tuition of his mother, not only developed in his musical studies but also became uncannily mature for his
years. Anna was stuck in a very unpleasant and humiliating situation—
humiliating, too, in that her father chose to believe he had been right
to disapprove of Ferdinando, and that her return to the paternal roof
was ample proof of this. We can be sure that she saw her child as a companion in adversity and confided in him as they huddled together amid
the storms. Ferdinando in his turn was quite uninhibited in running the
old man down, so that, as Ferruccio confessed, it was only much later
that he was able himself to draw up a truer picture of his grandfather.
(There is some evidence that Weiss was not all bellowing bluster: in a
letter[3] to Ferdinando of April 23, 1872, Anna relates that her father
"said to me that he has the sweet sound of your clarinet always in his
ears.") But nevertheless, how the situation directly impinged on the
child helped lay the foundations for a dark strain of melancholy and
bitterness that colored the rest of his life.

The precocity the situation engendered was already evident in Ferruccio's first extant letter to his father, dated February 1870, when they
had just left Paris and he was not yet four years old. These early letters
were dictated more or less by his mother, as is revealed two and a half
years later in a letter dated August 1872, which, Ferruccio wrote, was
written all by himself. But even those first letters were written in a
hand not at all childish, the characters joined, sloping forcefully forward, fluid and strangely authoritative. The handwriting is also quite
distinct from his mother's (they often wrote to Ferdinando in the same
letter).

The child, not surprisingly, was used by the mother as a medium for blatant emotional blackmail. On February 28, 1870, in that first letter, he writes:

My dearest Daddy [Mio amatissimo babbo],
Thank you for the pieces of music you have sent. I promise to study them as you wish, to give you pleasure, as soon as I have finished some other little pieces I have already started. I wish so much to see you, as also does my good Mamma, but our desire is, somehow or other, not to leave you alone any more. Mamma will write to you at greater length tomorrow. Know meanwhile that we are well thanks to the grace of God and your constant prayers.[4]

And later, in 1870 or 1871 (the letter is undated), the four-year-old is writing: "Things at home are going very badly. Write to me soon, if you can't now, then write to me when you can. The women in the house are still annoying as usual."[5]

By the time Ferruccio was in his sixth year, it was becoming obvious to the parents that they had something extraordinary on their hands. Apart from his normal schooling, he was continuing his musical studies with an enthusiasm constantly stoked by his mother. His half of a letter of January 22, 1872 (Anna's half is dated January 24), although written under maternal guidance, nevertheless gives an accurate idea of his daily routine:

My dear good Daddy [Mio caro buon babbo],
Here I am again to spend some time with you to tell you how grateful I am for your words of affection. I think of you all the time, my dear Daddy, and it would take too long to do justice to my thoughts. Now, having come home from school, with my good Mamma I have had my piano lesson which lasted a good hour, then I did my homework, and so I thought to dedicate to you too a part of the evening, thinking that it will not be displeasing to you to read what I have written. I am happy at your musical triumphs, and echo the general applause.
As Mamma has been very pleased with me lately regarding my studies, she wanted to reward me, and gave me Czerny's piano method, and also a piece for four hands, and one for two hands. I study piano every day for one hour with my Mamma, and work hard at my violin lessons. I hope to do myself honor with my studies, and so to make myself dearer to my beloved parents. I kiss you with all my heart and sign myself your affectionate son Ferruccio.[6]

And in her half of the letter, Anna writes, among other things: "May the saints protect your steps and bless you for my consolation. . . . I tell you again I want to do everything possible to make myself your worthy companion to shine at your side. I still study every hour I can and deprive myself of everything to succeed in my intention." This was to a husband she had not seen for several months, and to whom she sent whatever she could of her earnings as a piano teacher. (A letter of February 16, 1872, written by Ferruccio but quite obviously dictated by his mother, ends, "I pray every evening and morning to our Holy and dearest Mother to help us and protect us and see to it that we can rejoin you to live in blessed peace.")[7] On average, one of these two-hander letters a week went from Trieste to wherever Ferdinando happened to be, and—to do him justice—most of the time he was an equally faithful correspondent, as far as can be judged from the letters sent to him. No letters from Ferdinando survive from this period, not even the newspaper cuttings on his performances he apparently often enclosed with his letters, which makes it very difficult to track down his movements.

One peculiar feature in Ferruccio's contributions to these early letters is his use of the semicolon; uncommon enough among letter writers in general, it is quite extraordinary in a small child. Obviously inserted under Anna's tuition, it became a very frequent form of punctuation in his letters for the rest of his life. The letter-writing habit also lasted, and turned Busoni into one of the most prolific letter writers in musical history.

From a distance, Ferdinando also did his best to lick his son into the required shape, eliciting this in a contrite letter on March 3, 1872, from a child approaching his sixth birthday: "You are quite right that last time my writing was worse than usual, but from now on I really want to correct myself of this ugly fault. I intend to make every possible effort to satisfy you." (Anna's handwriting in the same letter to her "amatissimo Nando" is far less legible, and Ferdinando's was always atrocious.)

Anna made periodic efforts to change their situation, which was causing her understandable distress. Ferdinando had obviously been complaining about the loneliness and trials of his peripatetic life, but argued (logically) thàt it would be too expensive for the three of them to travel together. "I too am tired enough of this sort of life," Anna had written on February 7, 1872, in answer to a letter recounting his success at a concert in Ferrara. But, she continues, they need money, and Ferruccio must have a settled existence—not because any child needs security, but because he must not be distracted from his lessons, "which he learns with so much love and diligence." She suggests that when Ferdinando is in Florence, he "should try (if Princess Margherita is there) to get me given the title of chamber pianist to her, and perhaps with some influence you could obtain some little pension for me or an assured position." She would be more than willing to leave Trieste, "and never come back again to this home of mine where I have also suffered so much."[8] It is almost comic to imagine Ferdinando's chances of success in the kind of delicate, not to say obsequious, diplomacy such a gambit would entail. Nevertheless, it is a pity Princess Margherita of Savoy was not applied to. She was already in a position of some power, having married her cousin Umberto, the future King Umberto I, in 1868 and given birth to Victor Emmanuel a year later. Although still very young—she was only twenty-one at this time—unlike her rather oafish husband she already had a reputation as a patron of the arts, particularly music, and in 1880 was to give the young Puccini crucial financial support.

But for the Busoni household, nothing altered for the time being, although the future was taking on an outline. On August 11, 1872, the six-year-old wrote his father: "In piano I'm now doing the two-handed exercises by Diabelli. In violin on Wednesday I shall start to do some sonatinas."[9] At the end of the letter come those significant words: "This letter I wrote all by myself." It was the beginning of his taking control, not only of his own life, but also of his parents'. On October 21, 1872, in a letter in which Anna expressed disquiet that the last letter she had received from Ferdinando was dated October 13, Ferruccio writes in his half: "As Mamma has told me you have bought a beautiful dog for me, I can't wait to get it! I hope it will be as faithful and intelligent as poor Fede [his first dog, recently deceased]. I would like you to write me soon, and not just to find out about the dog."[10]

The end of the situation in Trieste was dramatic, and had something of E. T. A. Hoffmann about it—the German Romantic writer of grotesque and surreal tales Busoni was drawn to, significantly, time and again in later life. Busoni related the incident in the second of his "Two Autobiographical Fragments" written in 1909.[11] (He dates it late 1872, but it must in fact have been January 1873, as Anna wrote to him in a seven-page letter bearing the date December 29, 1872, at the beginning and January 3, 1873, at the end, "Mio amatissimo Nando, I am writing unfortunately at the end of the year! I say unfortunately, because in a few days a year will have passed since you left, I say unfortunately, because a year ago we were still together, and had spent so nicely the end and the start [of the year] at Monfalcone."[12] She had to wait to send the letter because she did not know his address in Pisa, where he was playing at the time.)

One evening, it must have been in the autumn of 1872 [sic], remains unforgettable. We were still living alone [that is, without his father] in Trieste, my mother and I, when she took me on that memorable evening to a *Teatro Meccanico* which . . . was to be found somewhat outside the town; at the crossing of the Via del Torrente and the Corsìa del Stadion. In this theatre—it was much more like a barracks—scenes were performed, acted by puppets that moved by means of an internal mechanism without help from visible wires. One scene made a lively impression on me, namely when one of the figures drank a bottle of wine in such a way that one saw the contents get less and the liquid gradually pass into the puppet's mouth until the bottle was finally empty. After the performance we went quietly home, without fear and without hope, in that stage of melancholy indifference that is frequently to be found in small Italian families; especially if something rather out of the common has been enjoyed and now one's thoughts turn again to everyday monotony.

We had gone about fifty steps when a *Signor* stood in our way. He was very imposing in appearance and wore a great beard divided into two points, and something like a pair of top boots that reached to his knees. He led a very well-behaved, pleasant-looking poodle on a steel chain, as if it were a wild animal, and the man's whole bearing had something of a master of the horse, or an animal tamer, about it. My mother greeted him, a little moved and a little embarrassed. The gentleman embraced me and called me "Ferruccio" many times in a voice charged with emotion and excitement. From these signs and from the recollection they awoke in me—kept alive through pictures and letters—I recognized my father. He had come back unexpectedly. I had a feeling that this surprise held the promise of I know not what festivity. That smile between emotion and uncertainty froze on my mother's lips and I experienced a little storm in my heart that was an invisible but perhaps much stronger reflection of that smile.

My life changed completely after that evening.

The vividness of the description, written four decades later, betrays the incident's deep significance in Busoni's life.

From this distance in time, and in the absence of Ferdinando's own account, we can only conjecture on what drove him, after two years, to return—albeit briefly—to family life. During the longer than usual silence Anna had complained of in the letter of October 21, 1872, perhaps Ferdinando had already been wrestling with a decision. Whatever the truth, once back in Trieste, he put his back into bringing the situation around, as Busoni relates further in his "Two Autobiographical Fragments." "My father at once took energetic measures in order to remove my mother from the house of that 'murderer of a father' [assassino di suo padre], as my father was wont to express himself regarding his father-in-law. Two rooms were rented on the Via Geppa, opposite the Turkish consulate."[13] (The daughter of the Turkish consul, a little girl of around his age, was also the first young lady to touch his heart—from the window they exchanged what Busoni called "my first gallant glances,"[14] which his father soon put a stop to.)

Ferdinando rapidly set to work giving the child intensive and systematic instruction in piano playing, in stark contrast to the cozy methods of the mother, which consisted of popular classics scaled down for parlor performance, often in four-handed versions, such as those published by Anton Diabelli, very popular at the time.

My father, who understood little about piano-playing and was uncertain regarding rhythm too, made up for these deficiencies by a quite indescribable energy, strictness and punctiliousness, being capable of sitting beside me for four hours a day and supervising every note and every finger. As far as he was concerned there was no escape, no rest, no conceivable inattention. The only pauses were provoked by outbreaks of his terrible hot temper, resulting in some boxed ears, copious tears, threats, black prophecies and reproaches. All these ended with ultimate reconciliations, paternal emotion, and the assurances that he wanted nothing but the best for me—to begin anew the following day.[15]

One might well wonder what Ferdinando was doing taking the child's piano playing in hand; perhaps he considered Anna too mild and softhearted for the task. Whatever the truth, Ferdinando was definitely in a hurry, and his draconian methods paid off: within the year Ferruccio

made his public debut as a pianist, appearing with his parents at a concert of the Schiller-Verein in Trieste on November 24, 1873, playing the
first movement of Mozart's Sonata in C Major, "The Poor Orphan" and
"Soldier's March" from Schumann's *Album für die Jugend*, and Muzio
Clementi's Fourth Sonatina in F Major. "We wanted to leave to last the
seven-year-old boy Ferruccio Weiss-Busoni, who was performing in public for the first time," wrote the *Corriere di Trieste* on November 27,

> arousing a real feeling of astonishment and admiration. This truly phe-
> nomenal little boy played from memory on the piano with his little
> hands pieces by Mozart and Schumann, which are not accessible to
> every grown-up pianist, with a confidence, and precision in tempi, be-
> yond all praise. The little Weiss-Busoni must without doubt be endowed
> with natural talent; but his precocious musical culture also to a great ex-
> tent reflects honor on his distinguished and gifted mother, who with a
> very special intuition has been able to guide his exceptional aptitude.

Doubtless owing to local pride, for once Anna got more credit than
Ferdinando.

Five months later, on March 26, 1874, Ferruccio gave his first solo
concert, playing two Handel fugues in C Major, Schumann's "Knecht
Ruprecht" (again from the *Album für die Jugend*), and a theme with
variations by Johann Nepomuk Hummel.

He had already begun composing, too, these early works copied, or
possibly written down in the first place, by his father. The first extant
composition is a Canzone in C Major for Piano (BV 1), written in June
1873, followed by a Berceuse in C Major for Piano (BV 2), also dated
June 1873. The majority of the early compositions are, for reasons any
beginner can readily understand, in C Major. They are, as Edward Dent
opined, "entirely childish in material and expression, but they show a
clear and well-defined sense of musical form—the best promise for the
future. They show too how his ear must have been perpetually haunted
by the sound of his father's clarinet."[16] A "Marcia funebre " in C Minor
(BV 9), written in February 1874, in memory of his aunt Mina Grusovin, conforms to this description, with a simple melody in the bass, variations in the treble, and a return to the melody at the end. A "Canzone
del Cacciatore" (Hunter's Song) in C Major (BV 12) of the same year
quite cleverly imitates a hunting horn, but is otherwise unremarkable—
except, of course, for the fact that it was written by an eight-year-old.

It is ironic that flawed, flamboyant Ferdinando probably gave his son more than the selfless and pious Anna, for all her more solid musical learning and his lack of it. Living on his wits had conditioned Ferdinando to enter worlds, on a musical version of foraging expeditions, of which Anna remained essentially ignorant to her dying day. Ferdinando's own musical taste and repertoire were in general what today might be called "easy listening": transcriptions of popular operatic arias, virtuoso show pieces for the clarinet, and suchlike. Nevertheless, his showman instincts were astute enough to home in on exactly the right path for his gifted son: the study of Bach's works. It was something his son never ceased to marvel at—and to be grateful for. "I have to thank my father for the good fortune that he kept me strictly to the study of Bach in my childhood," wrote Busoni in 1923, in an epilogue to his complete edition of Bach's Piano Works,

> and that in a country in which the master was rated little higher than a Carl Czerny. My father was a simple virtuoso on the clarinet, who liked to play fantasias on *Il Trovatore* and the *Carnival of Venice*; he was a man of incomplete musical education, an Italian and a cultivator of the *bel canto*. How did such a man in his ambition for his son's career come to hit upon the very thing that was right? I can only compare it to a mysterious revelation. In this way he educated me to be a "German" musician and showed me the path that I never entirely deserted, though at the same time I never cast off the Latin qualities given me by nature.

(Ironically, it is the "German" musician speaking here.)

Ferdinando did not stay in Trieste all the time that year; periodically he would go off on a concert tour, usually taking the poodle Nanni with him, to Ferruccio's anguish. He demonstrated a precociously shrewd assessment of his father's character in one finger-wagging letter: "Next time tell me a little more about Nanni and please don't tell me lies because I love her very much and if you have given her away then just tell me, I prefer that to your saying you haven't."[17] Nanni returned to Trieste with Ferdinando. (Nanni had replaced Fede, his first dog, in Ferruccio's affections. Dogs were often to play a large part in his life; their unquestioning devotion was very necessary to him, and their often comic ways appealed to his quirky sense of humor.)

Harsh though Ferdinando was in his teaching methods, now that father and son were together more, a companionable, jokey relationship developed between them that was to remain: in December 1874 Ferruccio signed off one letter to his father, who was away on tour, "Your son Francesco Aldighieri Buonarotti Cellini [his own spellings of the other names of his namesakes] and Grandi buchi ["Big holes"—the meaning of *busoni* in Triestino dialect]."[18]

From the age of six, Ferruccio attended school in Trieste for his general education. In addition to the usual subjects, he was learning German and Latin, and continuing to take violin lessons from one Professor Cappelletti: he was not allowed to miss this lesson, even to go to his cousin Ersilia's birthday party. As Busoni often sadly remarked later, "I never had a childhood."

In January 1875 Ferruccio performed in another concert in Trieste, and in May, now aged nine, he played Mozart's Concerto in C Minor, No. 24 (K. 491) at the Schiller-Verein, with his father conducting. But in the autumn of that year, Ferdinando decided the time was ripe for his child prodigy to attack the musical Everest of Vienna, and, after a farewell concert, in which Ferruccio also played some of his own compositions, father and son set off. If Paris attracted the virtuosi, Vienna had that and more: it had been—and still was—the home of some of Europe's greatest composers. It says much for Ferdinando's supreme confidence in his son's talents that he was eager to present him to these Titans.

The long-suffering Anna was left behind in Trieste, with Nanni, earning money to finance the venture.

Notes

1. Busoni, "Two Autobiographical Fragments," in *The Essence of Music*, p. 55.

2. This letter is quoted in Edward Dent, *Ferruccio Busoni: A Biography* (London: Eulenburg Books, 1974; first published London: Oxford University Press, 1933), p. 10. Its present whereabouts is unknown.

3. Letter from Anna Weiss-Busoni to Ferdinando Busoni, April 23, 1871, StBB Bus. Nachl. 965.

4. Letter from FB to Ferdinando Busoni, February 28, 1870, StBB Bus. Nachl. 943.

5. Letter from FB to Ferdinando Busoni, late 1870 or early 1871, StBB Bus. Nachl. 947.

6. Letter from FB to Ferdinando Busoni, January 24, 1872, StBB Bus. Nachl. 960.

7. Letter from FB to Ferdinando Busoni, February 16, 1872, StBB Bus. Nachl. 962.

8. Letter from Anna Busoni to Ferdinando Busoni, February 7, 1872, StBB Bus. Nachl. 961.

9. Letter from FB to Ferdinando Busoni, August 11, 1872, StBB Bus. Nachl. 972.

10. Letter from FB to Ferdinando Busoni, October 21, 1872, StBB Bus. Nachl. 974.

11. Busoni, "Two Autobiographical Fragments," pp. 57ff.

12. Letter from FB and Anna Busoni to Ferdinando Busoni, December 29, 1872, to January 1, 1873. FB one page, Anna six. Anna dates her section December 29, 1872 (beginning), and January 3, 1873 (end); FB dates his section January 1, 1873, StBB Bus. Nachl. 976.

13. Busoni, "Two Autobiographical Fragments," pp. 58–59.

14. Busoni, "Two Autobiographical Fragments," p. 59.

15. Busoni, "Two Autobiographical Fragments," p. 59.

16. Dent, *Ferruccio Busoni*, p. 16.

17. Letter from FB to Ferdinando Busoni, n.d. (early 1873), StBB Bus. Nachl. 978.

18. Letter from FB to Ferdinando Busoni, December 1874, StBB Bus. Nachl. 980.

~

CHAPTER TWO

Vienna Debut, Touring, First Compositions

It was a daring risk to bring the child to Vienna, certainly, but a well-calculated one; Ferdinando had honed and polished his product, and was now determined to sell it hard. In the autumn of 1875, when father and son entered the Archduke Charles Hotel (also a calculated risk, given their by no means affluent condition—it was the city's most prestigious address for visitors), Vienna was at one of its many musical high points. In September, Gustav Mahler and Hugo Wolf had just entered the Conservatory of the *Gesellschaft der Musikfreunde*, at which Anton Bruckner, among others, taught. (On February 20, 1876, a few months after the Busonis's arrival, Bruckner conducted the premiere of the second version of his Second Symphony for the *Gesellschaft der Musikfreunde*.) In September the conductor Hans Richter (1843–1916), following a triumphant Viennese debut, had taken over as chief conductor of the Hofoper (court opera) in Vienna and director of the Philharmonic Concerts, a post he was to retain for the next twenty-three years. A friend of Wagner and exponent of his works, in 1876 Richter was to conduct the first performance of the entire *Ring* cycle in Bayreuth. He was subsequently to cause the teenage Busoni much grief.

In October, Bizet's *Carmen* received its Viennese premiere at the Hofoper. In November, the Hofoper also saw the Viennese premiere of

Wagner's *Tannhäuser*, in a version supervised by Wagner himself, followed by *Lohengrin* on December 15, again supervised and conducted by the composer. And there was Brahms. Brahms had settled in Vienna in 1863 and was now the leading musical personality in the city, not only as composer but also as conductor and general organizer of musical events. Liszt, whom Busoni had first encountered in utero in Rome, was a frequent visitor to the city, although the two were not to meet there for another year.

Politically, Austria was stable. Having kept out of the Franco-Prussian war, the Austro-Hungarian Empire was quiet on more or less all fronts, in spite of that perennial, trouble in the Balkans, which again erupted in 1875, and the odd bout of saber-rattling over the fence by the Emperor Franz Josef, which his politicians always managed to contain.

Ferdinando Busoni's plan was to introduce his son not only as pianist, but also as composer and improviser, and he himself had brought his clarinet. His optimism is startling, particularly as, according to his son, "he understood not a word of German."[1] The plan, drawn up after Ferdinando took (or rejected) advice from various quarters, included entering Ferruccio as a pupil at the conservatory to continue his piano studies. Ferruccio was accepted to the conservatory, as far as we can gather from his account to his mother, after a series of competitive tests: on the first day he was made to play eight of J. B. Cramer's *Studies for the Pianoforte*, which he did better than other pupils "who had already had five or six lessons." On the second day he was given study number 19, "which is a bit difficult"; the third day a trill study, also by Cramer.[2] Josef Hellmesberger (1828–1893), the violinist and director of the conservatory, suggested that Ferruccio also study composition, but Ferdinando thought him still too young—or this did not fit in with his own ambitions.

Ferruccio himself was not very satisfied with the structure of piano lessons at the conservatory:

> The Conservatory is three times a week and they only examine me once or twice at most (a week). So you can see that if it weren't for Papa I would gain rather little and instead of making progress I would go backwards. The Cramer studies are quite easy for me and now that they are

making me do the Clementi sonata we are not even going beyond them. For this year studies are quite easy for me and I could have gone into the third [year], especially as Epstein [Julius Epstein, head of piano classes at the Conservatoire from 1867 to 1901] had said that if it were not for my lack of physical strength he would have put me in the final class. So I will have to stay at the Conservatory for five years.[3]

Word of the arrival of father and son in the city had certainly traveled rapidly upward, as on October 19 they received six hundred florins from the Empress Elisabeth, though only after the bearer (*porgitore*) of the money had thoroughly gone into their affairs and even invited them to spend a few hours in his home. Reporting on it to Anna next day,[4] Ferruccio gives a complete breakdown of what the money would be spent on:

Papa paid the rent of thirty-four florins, plus he paid back twenty-five florins that he had borrowed lately. He bought me a pair of boots for seven florins, then a shirt, two florins, four florins for mending to the tailor, three florins thirty-three p[?] of linen which comes in all to seventy-six florins. There you have the exact sum. Papa has to pay the German teacher, the piano. Meanwhile God has helped us and will always help us. I need a winter suit, tomorrow Papa is having me measured and he'll pay for it later.

These letters to his mother reveal the extent to which the nine-year-old was already not only fully conversant with the practicalities of life, but more and more taking charge. "Papa received your ten florins," he wrote in late October. "Papa will earn fifty florins on 20 November, and as the rent is due on the 22nd it will all be just in time. . . . But because of this we shall have to be without money because those of yesterday [presumably Anna's ten florins] we have spent to pay for the dinners we have eaten on account."[5]

Ferdinando's plans for concerts, both for himself and for his son, did not always come off. Often, financial catastrophe was averted only by the cash infusions from Trieste. The concert of November 20 Ferdinando was to have played in at the Künstler-Abend (Artists' Evening)—and earned that much-needed fifty florins—and the one the following evening in which father and son were to have played together at the Nobles' Club were both postponed, provoking a bout of ill humor in Ferdinando, "not without reason," as Ferruccio wrote to his mother, as they had counted on the money for the next month's expenses.[6]

In the same letter Ferruccio tries not very tactfully to persuade his mother to join them, using the argument that she could give lessons, and that she could play a Henry Litolff piece with orchestra "or something" and make a great effect, "because the most stupid people (as I saw the other evening, a violinist who was playing out of tune and his sister pianist who was pathetic) make the greatest effect and are applauded to the skies. But you want to stay on in Trieste." This makes it clear that the decision to remain in Trieste was Anna's (unless, of course, this was merely the version fed to the child); but she knew the advantages of a sure and steady income, however modest, and stayed put. For the first few months, other than Anna's contributions, their only income was from rich patrons.

At this age Ferruccio, with his big hazel eyes and wavy hair, was an enchanting sight, packaged in velvet suits, often with a lace collar. More important still: he was manifestly a highly talented musician. Nevertheless, his father had to work hard, spending long hours on what is now known as "networking," sometimes in ways that were a humiliating nightmare to the child. Ferdinando's very first target was the legendary Russian pianist and composer Anton Rubinstein (1829–1894), who was also staying at the Archduke Charles,

> to whom my father found the opportunity to present me and "have me heard" [*farmi sentire*], as he was wont to express it. This "let him hear" [*fagli sentire*] still rings horribly in my ears. There was no one whom my father might run into in the street or coffee house, who was not told of "his son"—which then concluded by his taking the stranger back and bursting into the room dragging his new acquaintance behind him and flinging the horrible "*fagli sentire*" in my face![7]

According to his son, however, Ferdinando nearly always managed to scupper any advantages of these encounters by quickly becoming disenchanted and finally heaping opprobrium on the unfortunate strangers if they did not immediately prove useful to his purpose.

Rich patrons were indispensable, but the rich have many distractions; they spend long periods out of town, forgetting promises made when the recipient of those promises is no longer frequently before them, and they can also be capricious, as Ferruccio was to experience, to his frustration and shame, until he was in his twenties. And the vivid memory of those impromptu *fagli sentire* auditions left a residue of disgust that tainted his attitude toward public performance for the rest of his life. But of all those dragged along to "hear him play," a few remained faithful, in their fashion, and for many years provided a lifeline for him to continue studying, playing, and composing. Of these, the most reliable were the Gomperz family, a well-known focus of intellectual and artistic life in Vienna, and generous patrons.

Theodor von Gomperz (1832–1912) was an eminent philosopher and classical scholar born in Brno, in what is now the Czech Republic. When the Busonis first met him he was teaching classical philology at the university in Vienna. His brother Julius, a successful industrialist and keen follower of the arts, had in 1867 married the contralto Karoline Bettelheim (1845–1926), who retired from a short but successful operatic career on her marriage, though she continued to give recitals; she had herself begun her musical career while still a child, as a pianist (taught by Karl Goldmark). There were also two Gomperz sisters: Josefine (Frau von Wertheimstein) and Sophie (Baronin von Todesco). They were all to prove generous supporters of Ferruccio's talents. It is not known exactly how the contact with the Gomperz family was made in the autumn of 1875, but they swiftly took Ferruccio over, the Baronin von Todesco providing him with a tutor for German and general subjects; Julius and Karoline von Gomperz, who were childless, even offered to adopt him.

The child's imagination was fed by frequent visits to theater, opera, and concerts. By the time he left Trieste, he had written some thirty musical works, mainly for piano, and two for clarinet and piano. Although remarkable as the product of such a young child, they inevitably reflect the influences available to him at that point: mainly Carl Czerny's studies and exercises, written expressly for learners, and the Diabelli anthologies that Ferruccio had played with his mother in four-handed versions. His repertoire had been broadened for his concerts in Trieste, and by the introduction to Bach's keyboard works, but by bringing his son to Vienna, Ferdinando now exposed him to the finest flowerings of European music, past and present, on a vast scale, and the child voraciously absorbed all he could.

With the little firsthand information available, mostly in the form of letters from Ferruccio himself to his parents—some eighty are still extant from the ages of four to eighteen—and from Anna and Ferdinando, plus Busoni's "Two Autobiographical Fragments" written when he was in his forties, much of his early life, influences, and formation of character must remain conjecture. Anna, in her loneliness in Trieste, had treated him more as an adult companion than a small son, and other than with his Grusovin cousins, he played relatively little with other children: from a very young age, he was made to realize that music always came before childish pleasures. Undoubtedly, he was quite remarkably intelligent, and because of high parental expectations and stern training, he not only "put away childish things" at an age when most children are only beginning to discover them, but developed extraordinary self-assurance that could scarcely help tipping over into self-centeredness.

From the outset in Vienna, therefore, Ferruccio cast a cool eye even on the giants, and was unafraid of giving an independent opinion. In the letter of November 20, 1875, to his mother he had commented: "The other evening I heard Brahms; but I didn't like him at all, but I did like his compositions; for example I liked the quartet very much [C Minor Piano Quartet, op. 60—this was the Viennese premiere]. . . . The other day I showed my score to the professor of harmony, who said it was very well done."[8] This score was an overture that remained a fragment of 158 bars; its main significance is that it was Busoni's first work scored for orchestra, although inevitably the musical language is cruder than in his works for piano of this period.

Giacomo Meyerbeer's opera *Dinorah* received a mixed review: "I didn't like the performance much but the production was done realistically. In the second act, when the bridge breaks, a whole cataract of real water burst over the stage so that what was ruined really seemed so. The other evening I bought some more works for piano and voice. . . . I have twelve now."[9] Ferruccio's father had also bought him the scores of several Mozart operas and of Beethoven's *Missa Solemnis*, as rewards for his diligence, and he was composing in every spare moment. Already a voracious reader—a habit that remained throughout his life—in that first autumn in Vienna he was asking his mother to send him Jules Verne's *The Adventures of Captain Hatteras*, in the same edition as the other Verne novels he already had at home, specified the budding bibliophile.[10]

It was only on February 8, 1876, four months after their arrival, that Ferruccio finally played for the first time in public in Vienna, in the Bösendorfer Saal, in a concert that also featured the twenty-year-old future conductor Arthur Nikisch on the violin. (Nikisch was later to become a good friend.) The program included Haydn's D Major Trio, a Mozart rondo, a theme and variations by Hummel, and ended with five piano pieces by Busoni himself. The concert attracted serious press attention, including that of the formidable critic and musicologist Eduard Hanslick (1825–1904), who gave this assessment of Busoni's own works, in his usual high-flown prose:

> They reveal the same robust musical feeling as we enjoyed in his playing; no precocious sentimentality or studied bizarrerie, but naive enjoyment of music making, in lively figuration and little combinatorial arts. Nothing operatic or dancelike, more a remarkably serious, masculine mind, which indicates a dedicated study of Bach. The pieces are all short, as befits a still fledgling talent, short and good, but not so good as to lead one to suspect the aid of a master. The authenticity of the compositions is for me beyond doubt, since I gave the child at the piano various themes that he immediately developed with a free imagination in the same severe style.[11]

But the excitement and strain of these months in Vienna—certainly not helped by having that first concert put off from November to February—proved too much for a child of not yet ten, no matter how gifted and eager to learn. After the concert he fell ill, and was taken back to Trieste by his father to recover, which he soon did in the reassuring calm of something approaching a family home, and his mother's presence.

On March 8, 1876, Busoni began writing a diary. It is an interesting glimpse into the mind of a child who is nevertheless, by nature, totally in thrall to music, like the young Mozart. (It was noted of him that as a child, sophisticated concepts such as the fugue and counterpoint did not need to be explained to him—he knew them instinctively.) The diary, written in a stilted, self-conscious Italian, begins:

> I am still between waking and sleeping. Confused sounds reach my ear, and waking up almost completely I hear words spoken in German.

". . . noch etwas zu warten" [wait a little longer]. They come from the mouth of my mother, who receives from the person to whom the words are addressed "jo, scho guat" [yes, all right], also in German, in reply. Then a door slams loudly.

"Mamma" I begin to shout. And she says "yes, dear" but doesn't move. I wait a moment then repeat impatiently "Mamma." "What do you want?" —"Is my tea made?" "Yes, right away, do you want to put your jacket on?"—"Yes."

And then finally that long-awaited mother arrives and helps me put on my jacket. Soon after she returns with the tea, accompanied by my dog Nanni, who was and still is faithful. She puts her front paws on my bed to wish me good morning, waiting for caresses from me with which I am not sparing. Having finished the tea I ask Mamma for manuscript paper and a pencil so I can compose.

I try to write a fugue with my left hand; I succeed and I have a lot of inspiration; but after one page it disappears.

So I put paper and pencil aside and begin to get dressed. Meanwhile three hours have passed and now the cathedral clock strikes eleven. I have finished dressing and prepare to try out at the piano what I have composed.

It's not bad, eh! eh! but it could go better, this fugue. The servant girl who has meanwhile come to clean the room, accustomed to the merry and light music of Strauss, stops her ears and, aping my music, really does take flight [prende la fuga—fuga also means "fugue"].[12]

In June the family went to Gmunden on the Traunsee in Austria, about forty miles east of Salzburg, mainly for the sake of Ferruccio's health. But composing was not neglected. From Vienna, Karoline von Gomperz recommended one Johann Evangelist Habert, the cathedral choirmaster in Gmunden, to tutor him in counterpoint. The Hungarian composer Karl Goldmark (1830–1915), Karoline's former piano teacher, also gave him composition lessons. There was assorted royalty, including the exiled Queen of Hanover, and the Archduchess Elisabeth, staying in the vicinity, and no opportunity was lost to play to them in semiprivate concerts, to help pay for this extended "holiday."

All three Busonis returned to Vienna in the autumn, again staying at the Archduke Charles Hotel. Ferruccio gave no public concerts that winter, concentrating on his studies, and the family relied mainly on the Gomperz family to support them. To further his son's career, Ferdinando had always been diligent in wresting testimonials on Ferruccio's talents from all and sundry. According to Edward Dent, Busoni's first biographer, Ferdinando failed with Franz Liszt, who was in Vienna in March 1877 for the commemoration of the fiftieth anniversary of Beethoven's death: Liszt said he never wrote testimonials "on principle." But at some stage something must have been obtained in writing from Liszt, as Ferruccio includes him soon after in lists of people from whom he has obtained a testimonial. Whatever the truth, through the intermediary of Karoline von Gomperz, who was a friend of the great man, Liszt did write to Anna asking her to bring Ferruccio to play to him. No record survives of the meeting between these two giants of the pianoforte, one, at sixty-five, coming to the end of his career, the other, at ten, just beginning. Although very different in character, the two had much in common. Both were groomed by ambitious fathers and began their public careers at a very young age; both uneasily combined public performance and the more private world of composition, both wrote piano transcriptions of Bach's organ works and were greatly in debt to the earlier composer, and both were tireless and generous promoters of the music of others.

In May 1877 Ferruccio caught diphtheria, necessitating another period of recuperation in Gmunden. In the autumn the family returned to Vienna yet again, where the boy gave another public concert, in a program that included Bach's Chromatic Fantasia and Fugue. He continued his studies at the conservatory, making good progress but pestered by the attentions of the older girl pupils, who kept trying to kiss him, as he indignantly wrote to his cousin Ersilia.

Ferdinando managed to obtain a testimonial for Ferruccio from Franz von Suppé (1819–1895), a composer now remembered chiefly for his overtures to *Poet and Peasant*, *Light Cavalry*, and *Morning, Noon and Night in Vienna*, but in his lifetime a successful composer of operas and operettas. Von Suppé, distantly related to Gaetano Donizetti, was born in Split, in Croatia. His mother was Viennese, making him another Italo-German (though in his case of distant Belgian descent—hence the name), and he may have felt on this ground alone a certain kinship with his young colleague. That autumn also saw Ferruccio's first published work (thanks to Franz von Suppé's recommendation), his recently composed *Five Pieces for Piano* (BV 71), with the publisher August Cranz. It is here that we begin to hear the personal voice of Busoni: a particular sonority and fluidity that hint distantly at the minimalism of the late twentieth century. Influences were, of course, also obvious—of Schumann in number 3, a Minuet in F Major, and quite decidedly of Bach in number 4, an Etude in C Minor, which is nevertheless written with very assured panache.

Anton Rubinstein was also successfully petitioned by Ferdinando, but his contribution, dated February 6, 1878, was double-edged: "The young Ferruccio Busoni has a very remarkable talent both as performer and composer—in my opinion he should work very seriously at his music, and have the means to enable him not to have to play in public to earn his livelihood."[13]

In February 1878 the doctor treating the child advised he should be removed from Vienna, but the family stayed on. One problem was the bill at the Archduke Charles and Ferdinando's debts everywhere else. Eventually the Baronin von Todesco stumped up, and in July they were able to leave. That summer they gave concerts in Baden and in Vöslau, and in October went to Graz, in Styria, southeast Austria. Ferdinando (Dent thinks it could have been Ferruccio himself) saw to it that the testimonials from Rubinstein and others were printed in the local papers, so that on their arrival in the city the twelve-year-old was interviewed and profiled by the press, providing plenty of advance publicity for his first concert. The composer Wilhelm Kienzl (1857–1941), who had just returned to his hometown of Graz after studying in Leipzig, came under the child's spell and devoted much time and effort to furthering his career. He was not alone: there was already Luigi Cimoso, a pianist and teacher, son of a Trieste musical family who were close friends of Anna's. The young Cimoso called Ferruccio his "Wolfgangerl," in allusion to the young Mozart, and provided him with much-needed support and advice from afar. (It is typical of Ferdinando's insouciant insensitivity that in answer to a letter from Cimoso containing practical suggestions, written while the Busonis were still in Vienna, Ferdinando suggests that Cimoso should try to get money for the Busonis from Cimoso's own pupils!)

Then there was the twenty-year-old journalist and poet Otto von Kapff (1856–ca. 1920), Prussian by birth (from Königsberg in East Prussia, now Kaliningrad) but Viennese by choice, who took up Ferruccio's

cause. He saw and heard Ferruccio in Graz in November, and wrote expressing a wish to meet him. The twelve-year-old reacted with self-
assured aplomb, putting off the first meeting twice, as he was busy
preparing further concerts. Von Kapff, ugly and unprepossessing, came
to nurture a humble love for the beautiful and talented child that developed into a lifelong devotion verging on obsession. Letters to and
from von Kapff provide useful insights into Ferruccio's character and
into the family's life and travels during this period. Starting in late
1878, soon after that first meeting, with Ferruccio addressing his admirer as "Lieber Herr Kapff," by the end of the year there had been a
swift progression through "Lieber Herr Otto" to "Lieber Otto," with the
occasional bluff "Lieber Kapff" when "business matters" needed to be
discussed. For some reason, Ferruccio's letters to von Kapff in the first
year of their friendship are all in Anna's handwriting, a fact we should
take care not to interpret using the psychoanalytical tools of our own
age, particularly given Anna's mind-set. Von Kapff also sent Ferruccio
poems of his own, which Ferruccio set to music—if he thought they
were good enough. Ferruccio seems to have had some instinctive understanding of von Kapff's feelings for him, and although he kept him
at a distance, he also flirtatiously teased him on occasion, with the innocent, wayward cruelty of the pubescent.

In Graz Ferruccio attended the local school, studying mainstream
subjects. It was a rare chance to mix with other children again. By now
his German was fluent, although still imperfect. But the family only
stayed in Graz two months, still undecided on where to settle. Luigi
Cimoso wrote from Trieste suggesting Florence, Trieste itself (to which
Ferdinando was vehemently opposed), even Naples.

In early December they were in the Carinthian town of Klagenfurt,
where the family gave two concerts. It was part of the show that
Ferruccio would improvise on themes suggested by the audience—some
of them stupid, as he wrote to von Kapff after the second concert on
December 9. "I was given three themes by one and the same gentleman, each more stupid than the last. I chose the best and improvised
badly on it. It is as if you were given a stupid subject for a poem and had
to make a good poem out of it. The thing is impossible."[14] Having been
"groomed for stardom" from such a young age, and largely kept away
from other children, a few traits had been allowed to develop in him

that are usually knocked out or at least kept in check by the brutal democracy of the playground. These included an intolerance of what he considered stupidity, particularly in musical matters. He remained generous and loving to the end of his life, but his character was shot through with the odd seam of acid, laid down too perhaps by the unnatural strains of those formative years, that caused him at times to inflict enormous hurt.

The family traveled on to Italy: to Bolzano, Trento, Arco, Rovereto, and Trieste. In Trento in December he played three times in two weeks, to full houses, and at least one member of the audience, a Professor Bazzicotti, earned his gratitude by giving him a Rossini tune to improvise on.

Ferruccio's health continued to suffer from this hectic life, and illness was frequent. Ferdinando's talent for rubbing people the wrong way—and into debt—was a further irritant and source of nervous strain: many concerts were either cancelled or a financial disaster, always, according to Ferdinando, thanks to someone else's iniquitous behavior. Ferruccio was often so weak he could not sit at the piano for more than half an hour at a time. As Anna was actually writing his letters to von Kapff, what is allegedly Ferruccio's account of the cause of one bout of illness, in a letter from Klagenfurt of March 29, 1879,[15] may have been "edited":

> Let me assure you at the outset that this illness did not arise from overexertion or excitement (something I never feel); now I'll tell you the cause: everybody thought I had a weak constitution and advised Papa to strengthen me up somehow. As he had heard so much about indoor gymnastics he had the idea of giving it a try. For the first few days it seemed to be helping a little but unfortunately the gym teacher was careless enough to make me lie on the floor after having got hot from the exercises, and I inhaled the colder air; this brought on a catarrh, from which I am still suffering.

Klagenfurt became one of several backwaters the family found themselves stranded in, usually through lack of funds, and these places left a nightmarish impression on Ferruccio. To illustrate this, Edward Dent gave a dramatic (and dramatized) account of an incident occurring years later in Hamburg, when Busoni was dining with colleagues, during rehearsals for his opera *Die Brautwahl*. The name of Klagenfurt was mentioned (it means "ford of wailing"), at which he groaned and was obviously made uneasy by the memory. "I was there with my parents; I was twelve years old; I was a wonder-child, and everything turned on me. We were in a hotel there and had to stay for three months, because we had no money and could not pay the bill."[16]

He continued to compose: a four-part mass, various works for piano, a clarinet solo, and in Klagenfurt in April he had begun a setting of the German Romantic poet Ludwig Uhland's well-known ballad "Des Sängers Fluch" (The Minstrel's Curse), for solo voice and orchestra (based on his setting for alto and piano written in November the year before).[17]

Ferruccio spent his thirteenth birthday on April 1, 1879, in bed, resting: in the preceding three months, he had given twelve concerts. Ferdinando wrote a birthday poem, the last line of which is comically self-revealing:

> Garlands and gifts may April shower on thee,
> Most glorious boast of various Harmony!
> Heaven grant thee health and laurels ever new,
> The crown of fame and heaps of money too.
> [Edward Dent's translation][18]

Writing to von Kapff two days later,[19] Ferruccio lists his birthday presents: twenty-eight books in all, mainly novels, from Berthold Auerbach to Jules Verne. On April 11, it is back to business.[20] "Papa did get the money but nothing yet from Herr Tandler [an impresario]." Without Tandler's contribution, the letter goes on, it would be impossible to go to Milan, as that trip would cost at least 150 florins. It is in this letter that Ferruccio (or Anna) gives von Kapff a potted biography, intended to be passed on to one Elise Polko in Leipzig, a well-known literary figure of the time specializing in sentimental fictionalized lives of the great composers, who, von Kapff thinks, might be able to help him.

> I was born on 1 April 1866 and am therefore thirteen years old, have already played before great personages, such as, at the Austrian court, before the Emperor of Brazil, Queen of Hanover, Archduchess Elisabeth, and have also been examined by several leading artistic-musical figures,

such as, for example, Liszt, Rubinstein, Brahms, Goldmark, etc., everywhere with great applause; have given in all around 50–60 concerts, the first of which at 7 years of age.

Von Kapff was instructed to tell Fräulein Polko that Ferruccio had written 150 pieces, "including four string quartets, four piano sonatas, a concerto, a Mass, a rather large (seventy–eighty pages) score." Of these, fifty to sixty works were to be considered good and free of mistakes (*gut und fehlerfrei*) and therefore ready for publication. The main purpose behind all this was to find somewhere—someone—to offer tuition. Leipzig was considered, but the climate thought too harsh.

Following the usual pattern, the family was able to leave Klagenfurt thanks only to a collection raised by Wilhelm Kienzl, and at the beginning of June they moved to Cilli, a small resort town in Hesse. Here they remained for the summer and autumn of 1879, their stay also financed largely by Kienzl's collection, plus the continuing generosity of Frau von Wertheimstein and the proceeds of one or two concerts. In Cilli Ferruccio kept himself feverishly busy, practicing, composing, but also exploring areas where his parents almost certainly had no interest in pushing him. He began (in German) a novel set in Cilli "in 1237" that, not surprisingly, given its ambitions, its author's age, and all the other demands on his energies, did not get far.

Ferruccio's letters to von Kapff were, as always, largely taken up with business. On June 4,[21] he writes:

One concert is already over, the second is on Saturday and we are hoping for splendid results, as I earned great applause in the first.

We are staying the whole summer in Cilli until September and we have found a very nice place to live, meadows and fields and forest; really poetic, the way you like it, outside the town and . . . at a cheap price! That's the main thing. . . . So our address from Sunday on is Oberlandhof, Villa Wartold (Cilli). This also holds for the impresario, if he wants to speak to me. "Des Sängers Fluch" (my composition) has already been published [in the piano version]. I'll be sending you three copies very soon, one for you, 1 for Frau E. Polko, one for the director of the *Musikzeitung* in Vienna where something, as you write me, is to appear on me. I have now composed new things, in all two male choruses and a string quartet [all now lost], since I have been in Cilli. . . . I still don't know whether you were pleased that I had set your two poems to music;

I have written to you repeatedly about it and received no response. I have sent Dr. Hausegger [Friedrich von Hausegger (1837–1899), critic and musicologist] and Director Swoboda a copy of "Des Sängers Fluch," I expect a small report on it in the [Grazer] Tagespost [by Wilhelm Kienzl] and didn't want to send anyone else the composition before the review had appeared. How can that be brought about?

Von Kapff was still trying to interest the impresario Tandler in the child. On June 7,[22] Ferruccio was writing again to von Kapff regarding Tandler, "On behalf of my father you are to tell him" that Ferruccio could offer twenty different programs, for eight thousand florins, that is, four hundred florins per concert, plus travel costs. The following passage was underlined: "Papa doesn't want me to undergo an examination for the impresario either; I have gone through these, in front of greater personages . . . and Papa can show him the testimonials of these great artists (such as Rubinstein, Liszt, Suppé, Willmers, Brahms, Goldmark, etc.) and does not want me to tire myself out again." Ferruccio enclosed four copies of "Des Sängers Fluch" and added that should Herr Tandler be willing to act as his impresario for this tour, "I should be prepared to allow him a third of the price." In spite of the references to his father— possibly strategic, to add weight to his arguments—it is obvious from these letters alone to what extent the thirteen-year-old was making decisions on his career and, by the same token, to what extent his parents were failing in the task.

In spite of all the letters to and from von Kapff of this summer, including the suggestion (which was accepted) of dedicating the published version of Ferruccio's setting of von Kapff's poem "Lied der Klage"[23] (Mourning Song) to Elise Polko, for the moment plans of studying in Leipzig, or anywhere, came to nothing. (Of Busoni's settings of von Kapff's poems, only "Lied der Klage" was published, and a "Frühlingslied" [Spring Song] for four male voices still exists in manuscript; the rest have disappeared.) At the end of June the printers were only waiting for Elise Polko's written consent before going ahead with printing copies, but there had been no news from von Kapff. "What has happened? For God's sake don't be untrue to me. Your eternally loving friend, Ferruccio."[24] In August, although there had still been no response from Elise Polko, lighter matters were also dealt with. Von Kapff had sent Ferruccio a photograph: "From your picture I see you are letting your hair grow long. I on the other hand have had my hair cut very short, a greater advantage during the summer heat."[25] Later in August Ferruccio sent some brief instructions to von Kapff scribbled on his own visiting card, which bore the name "Ferruccio Benvenuto Busoni."[26]

On August 30 he wrote:[27]

> I am completely recovered now, and live here very comfortably with my dear parents, compose masses of music and with some success. Financial matters aren't too bad either, and as for now everything is fine, we have to prepare ourselves about plans for the future. I am also looking forward to seeing you soon in Graz, with your long hair, which however, to be honest, doesn't suit you as much as short hair. I'm curious to learn the judgment you will pronounce on my hair! I already had photographs taken in Trento and Bolzano but unfortunately do not have a copy to send you, and I also had a portrait made with short hair two years ago which looks very similar to now and which I shall show you when we meet shortly. Professor Hausegger was very kind to express himself so favorably about me and I can be quite proud of his judgment! I should like to see Graz, described so beautifully to me [by von Kapff?] from a distance too or better still looking down from the Schlossberg during a beautiful sunset, walking arm in arm with you, how lovely that would be.

On September 8 Ferruccio was briefly in Graz for a concert, sending a short note to von Kapff on yet another visiting card: "I'm now in Graz and awaiting you soon in my apartment, Hotel Erzherzog Johann."[28] Then it was back to Cilli, where the family was still on November 1, not knowing if a planned performance of Ferruccio's *Stabat Mater* in Graz was going to take place. Ferruccio had written to von Kapff, to one Herr Jonas, and to Tandler, but received no answers from any of them:

> What should and can this mean!!!?!! I have everything already prepared, have written out fourteen copies of the roles of the *Stabat Mater*, have even set a German text under it, have prepared Herr Prager's violin part, so nothing is missing from *my* side. . . . So please be so good and go to Tandler and see if he has set the date of the concert at least.[29]

Two days later Ferruccio wrote that he would be in Graz that week, "to see to the singers."[30] "Where Jonas is concerned, I haven't rejected his suggestion, but offered a sum which is in correct proportion to the heavy expenses of the journey. Why doesn't he answer? If he pays the sum suggested, I am prepared to travel with him."

At thirteen, Ferruccio's days as a Wunderkind were numbered. Given his enormous talent as a pianist, it is surprising that more was not made of him during the five years since his first appearance on the concert platform. He had performed only in the relatively small area of Austria, southern Germany, and northern Italy, and even in this area not always in first-class venues. Compared with the steady upward progression and enormous international resonance of other Wunderkinder, such as Mozart or Liszt, it was not much of a triumph. The latter two had also been driven by paternal ambition, but Mozart and Liszt *pères* came from musically sophisticated backgrounds, and were far more self-controlled and single-minded than Ferdinando in their management of their sons' talents. It is impossible at this distance in time to pinpoint the reasons for Ferruccio's relative lack of success as a child prodigy, but a careful reading of the dozens of letters that passed between Anna, Ferdinando, and Ferruccio leads one to conclude that Ferdinando's volatile nature militated against the child's advancement, and also prevented—for whatever muddled reasons—the logical step of applying to and remaining with an established impresario to mastermind his career. Busoni himself states that his father was a very bad financial manager, but given Ferdinando's nature it is difficult to imagine any agent lasting long. As the family letters, and those to von Kapff, Kienzl, and others, make poignantly clear, Ferruccio himself realized early on that he had to take charge, but of course he lacked the necessary experience, turning to anyone who showed himself a friend in largely fruitless attempts to make progress, always with the danger hovering that at any moment Ferdinando would torpedo any enterprise, as he had torpedoed his own professional advancement.

From an early age too, Ferruccio saw himself primarily as a composer, the piano playing a money-making distraction. This conflict of interests, with his playing forever associated in his mind with the humiliations of that *fagli sentire*, formed the nucleus of the dilemma that was to hang unresolved like a dark cloud over his whole life.

On November 23, in Graz, Ferruccio finally conducted his *Stabat Mater*, written for two sopranos, alto, tenor, two basses, and string quartet.

Remarkable achievement though it was for a thirteen-year-old, not even the faithful Kienzl could pronounce it an unqualified success: in his review he mentions its lack of logical construction, among other things. (No copies of the work have survived.) What it did demonstrate to the citizens of Graz was that they had a very gifted young composer in their midst, sorely in need of intensive tuition. For the next two years, Ferruccio was to enjoy not only first-class tuition in composition, but the nearest he was to come in his early years to a settled existence.

Notes

1. Busoni, "Two Autobiographical Fragments," p. 59.
2. Letter from FB to Anna Weiss-Busoni, October 9, 1875, StBB Bus. Nachl. 985.
3. Letter from FB to Anna Weiss-Busoni, n.d., ca. October 25, 1875, StBB Bus. Nachl. 982.
4. Letter from FB to Anna Weiss-Busoni, October 20, 1875, StBB Bus. Nachl. 986.
5. Letter from FB to Anna Weiss-Busoni, n.d., autumn 1875, StBB Bus. Nachl. 984.
6. Letter from FB to Anna Weiss-Busoni, November 20, 1875, StBB Bus. Nachl. 987.
7. Busoni, "Two Autobiographical Fragments," p. 91.
8. Letter from FB to Anna Weiss-Busoni, November 20, 1875, StBB Bus. Nachl. 987.
9. Letter from FB to Anna Weiss-Busoni, n.d., ca. October 25, 1875 (see note 3), StBB Bus. Nachl. 982.
10. Letter from FB to Anna Weiss-Busoni, n.d., ca. October–November 1875, StBB Bus. Nachl. 989.
11. Eduard Hanslick, Neue Freie Presse, ca. February 9, 1876.
12. "Rivista Giornaliera," March 8, 1876, StBB Bus. Nachl. CI 162. This is contained in a small notebook that also contains a poem by Ferruccio on his father's name day (written out by Anna?), "written at the age of 7 years in Trieste" and another, "written on 15 August 1873 in Triest at the age of 7 years," and some other poems. The notebook also contains a rather sententious "Allegory" (with four footnotes!), recounting a story of the goddess Euterpe, one of the Muses, who had a ruby stone (footnote 2 explains that this refers to [Anton] Rubinstein). The diary itself ends with two lines written on a fresh verso page, suggesting that no more was written.
13. Quoted in Dent, Ferruccio Busoni.

14. Letter from FB to Otto von Kapff, December 10, 1878, StBB Bus. Nachl. 573.
15. Letter from FB to Otto von Kapff, March 29, 1879, StBB Bus. Nachl. 578.
16. Dent, *Ferruccio Busoni*, pp. 33–34.
17. Alto and Piano version: BV 98; Alto and Orchestra version: BV 98a.
18. Dent, *Ferruccio Busoni*, pp. 30–31. The original Italian reads:

> April fiorisca e Te ghirlande e doni,
> Canto glorioso dei Diversi Suoni.
> Salute il ciel ti dia e freschi Allori,
> Denaro in quantità e Sommi Onori.

19. Letter from FB to Otto von Kapff, April 3, 1879, StBB Bus. Nachl. 579.
20. Letter from FB to Otto von Kapff, April 11, 1879, StBB Bus. Nachl. 580.
21. Letter from FB to Otto von Kapff, June 4, 1879, StBB Bus. Nachl. 585.
22. Letter from FB to Otto von Kapff, June 7, 1879, StBB Bus. Nachl. 586.
23. BV 94, published by August Cranz, Hamburg, in 1879 (Roberge gives 1878).
24. Letter from FB to Otto von Kapff, June 29, 1879, StBB Bus. Nachl. 590.
25. Letter from FB to Otto von Kapff, August 11, 1879, StBB Bus. Nachl. 591.
26. Note from FB to Otto von Kapff, August 19, 1879, StBB Bus. Nachl. 592.
27. Letter from FB to Otto von Kapff, August 30, 1879, StBB Bus. Nachl. 593.
28. Note from FB to Otto von Kapff, September 8, 1879, StBB Bus. Nachl. 598.
29. Letter from FB to Otto von Kapff, November 1, 1879, StBB Bus. Nachl. 596.
30. Letter from FB to Otto von Kapff, November 3, 1879, StBB Bus. Nachl. 597.

CHAPTER THREE

~

Graz, Trieste, Frohnleiten, Vienna: November 1879 to November 1886

Through his father, the young Busoni had acquired a basic grounding in musical theory (his mother only ever taught him piano), and there had been the lessons at the conservatory in Vienna, and elsewhere, but these were in relatively short bursts. Given the child's natural abilities, these lessons had provided him with adequate tools for composing works, some of which were thought good enough to be published: other than the *Five Pieces for Piano*, there had been an Ave Maria Antiphon for Voice and Piano (BV 67, written in October 1877), the setting for Contralto and Piano of Otto von Kapff's "Lied der Klage" (BV 94, October 1878), and the setting for Alto and Piano of Ludwig Uhland's "Des Sängers Fluch" (BV 98, November 1878), all published by August Cranz in 1879. (The orchestrated versions of the two poems have remained unpublished.) Nevertheless, the need for systematic tuition at an advanced level was becoming more and more urgent. Various teachers had been tried over the years, only to be found wanting by Ferdinando, for whom, apparently, no teacher was good enough for his son. There is the story, possibly apocryphal, that first appeared in Melanie Mayer's recollections[1] of Busoni, published after Busoni's death, and was taken up by Edward Dent, according to which the irascible Ferdinando, after a few trial lessons, would always eventually say, "Ick nehmen mio bambino wieder weg" (I take *mio bambino* away again) and flounce out, dragging his unfortunate bambino behind him. Mayer wrote her recollections some fifty years after the event, so that we can take her not very credible, comic, stage-Italian's attempt at German with a pinch of salt. Apocryphal or not, the end result was always the same. It may also have been that Ferdinando, the notoriously bad money manager, often was unable to pay the fees.

As Wilhelm Kienzl recalled,[2]

> The young lad had at that time [1879] already composed 130 [*sic*] pieces, most of them in polyphonic style, including a string quartet, although he had not enjoyed any systematic tuition. He played some of these for me. He also improvised in an astonishing manner on themes I gave him. Sitting at the piano he was inspired to the most profound seriousness and totally absorbed in his task. Then, a child once more, he would leap around the room and play ball games. Furthermore, Ferruccio was then already completely fluent in three languages and had an almost adult, fully "developed" handwriting.

Kienzl kept interest in Ferruccio alive in Graz by writing reviews of his published compositions in the local press, helping to bring about the *Stabat Mater* performance. He also made it known that the family was to settle in the city, with Anna offering piano lessons (Ferdinando likewise, although at a more elementary level). But most importantly, Kienzl was the intermediary leading to the ideal composition teacher for Ferruccio, Dr. Wilhelm Mayer, a man whose urbanity and track record alike were manifestly enough to cow Ferdinando into silence.

Mayer (1831–1898) was born in Prague. Like his father, he studied law and for several years held various posts in the Austro-Hungarian civil service, while composing music under the pseudonym of W. A. (as in Wolfgang Amadeus) Rémy. In 1861 he made the decision to devote himself entirely to music, and settled in Graz, first as a conductor, then as a teacher of composition. He was an outstanding teacher, albeit vehemently outspoken in his likes and (more particularly) dislikes: regarding the two giants of the time, he loathed Wagner from start to finish and was not that keen on Brahms either.

Mayer's reputation as a teacher extended throughout Europe; the list of those drawn to Graz to study under him includes Friedrich von

Hausegger, Emil Nikolaus von Reznicek, and Felix Weingartner. Mayer's own compositions, which comprised five symphonies, an orchestral fantasy, and a wealth of *Lieder*, chamber music, and other works, have long since fallen into oblivion. Even in his lifetime, it was more his teaching that earned him praise, culminating in the Emperor Franz Josef awarding him the Knight's Cross of the Franz-Josef Order for his achievements in twenty-five years of teaching in Graz—a unique distinction for a private music teacher.

Kienzl had also been a pupil of this excellent man, and introduced Ferruccio to Mayer, his lively and cordial wife, and his daughter Melanie. Melanie Mayer was a few years older than Ferruccio; she became a good friend, a useful instructor in the social graces, and an intelligent and witty discussion partner, a role that continued in epistolary form for several years after. The Mayer household also offered a happy, relaxed, and settled home environment, with a lot of lighthearted fun and banter, embellished by Frau Mayer's excellent cooking. It was probably in this cultured and stimulating atmosphere that Ferruccio first became acquainted in depth with the writings of the German Romantics, in particular Ludwig Tieck, Clemens Brentano, and E. T. A. Hoffmann—the latter's grotesque and fantastic world becoming a lasting influence and inspiration and indeed providing the theme for one of Busoni's operas.

Mayer was probably skeptical when first confronted with what looked like the standard-model child prodigy, with his curls, beautiful face, and velvet suit—although now entering his teens, Ferruccio was still, like Dickens's Infant Phenomenon in *Nicholas Nickleby*, dressed as a much younger child by his parents, with an eye to the box office. Mayer soon recognized Ferruccio's serious sense of purpose, however, and they got down to work together, setting a punishing pace.

Although Mayer was surprised at the knowledge the child already had, he insisted on starting at the beginning and going through the whole of his composition course in meticulous detail, from basic rudiments through harmony, counterpoint, and fugue to instrumentation. (When Ferruccio left Graz fifteen months later, in April 1881, he had accomplished what usually took Mayer's pupils two years—all the more remarkable, given his age.)

Mayer was one of those rare teachers able to teach holistically: whatever he taught, whether relating to particular composers, or to the development of musical theory, or any other aspect of what he thought it important for his students to acquire, was presented against the historical, cultural, and musical background of the time and not just as a series of abstract facts. This was all delivered with great wit and comic asides, but also with veneration and unabashed love for great art—Mozart occupying pride of place. As Busoni described it in the *Allgemeine Musikzeitung* on the occasion of Mayer's death in 1898:[3]

> Even though—owing to his age and the limited sphere he belonged to— he was unable to approve of everything the new age produced, even though as a peaceful citizen of his own ideal artistic world he no longer wished to participate in the battles being fought outside—it was a great love, a limitless veneration, an unshakeable belief that inspired him and which he deposited in the minds and hearts of his pupils forever as his legacy: admiration for the genius of Wolfgang Amadeus Mozart. When he pronounced this name, then his lively features took on the expression of an almost paternal familiarity and joy. . . . Next to Mozart, Bach occupied the highest place in his heart, and he was inexhaustible in the dissection, explanation and poetical interpretation of the Preludes and Fugues from the Well-Tempered Clavier. Thus he described the four first Preludes as the "four elements," water, fire, earth and air; the theme of the C-sharp Major Fugue he dubbed the butterfly, that settles on a flower and—sated—zigzags off. The great B-flat Minor Fugue from Volume 2 was for him "Cologne Cathedral," because of its aspiring construction and the "filigree work," which he compared with the ornamentation of the Gothic style.
>
> Full of homely humor is the image he created of the theme of the E-Flat Fugue, which, "like a rocket" shoots up quick as lightning, falls slowly to earth and (in the diminished seventh intervals at the end) "leaves a stench behind."

The influence of this remarkable man not only permeated Busoni's musical awareness for the rest of his life, but continued in Busoni's own composition pupils, for whom Busoni was to be an equally inspiring teacher. Mayer not only was painstakingly thorough in every aspect of music, but insisted that any serious composer should also possess a broad cultural grounding—a concept that fell, in Ferruccio's case, on soil more than ready to receive it. Throughout his life Ferruccio read voraciously, on every conceivable subject; his library was to become vast and eclectic. In all the cities of the world he played in, he immediately sought out the bookshops, the secondhand bookshops in particular, which he trawled again and again on subsequent visits (a maneuver any bibliophile will recognize).

In Graz, the Busoni family was as usual in financial difficulties. They had found accommodation in a cheap hotel on the outskirts of the town, which was particularly uncomfortable in winter. The story goes that often Ferruccio wrote up his exercises in bed, as they could not afford heating. Concerts, to refill the coffers, were few and far between. (It is not known how successful the parents were in finding piano pupils.)

That faithful friend von Kapff had moved from Graz to Vienna during the first half of 1880 and become engaged to the feminist writer Franziska Essenther. By the autumn he was married, but the marriage was not to bring him much happiness and ended after eight years. His effusive attachment to Ferruccio continued unabated, and from Vienna he wrote plaintive letters, mainly on his constant tribulations. Reading of his difficulties with the newspapers, whom he was trying to interest on Ferruccio's behalf, the latter reacted in October 1880 with the rather startling sentiment,

> These people are all canaille, and deserve to be thoroughly thrashed. But things here are not like in Italy where a pig of an editor like that or anyone similar would be attacked from behind when out on a walk by a couple of vagabonds, thrown to the ground, and possibly have his nose burned with a lighted cigar or he would be thoroughly thrashed. That recently happened to one of my friends in Italy.[4]

This is teenage bravado certainly, though we will never know what exactly triggered it. What the letter does show is that, as usual, Ferruccio had to rely on fragmented, uncoordinated efforts for the furtherance of his career, so that this outburst could merely have been the product of frustration.

Ferruccio worked hard in Graz at his studies, even during the two weeks in the summer of 1880 when the Mayers were away on holiday. He also managed, in spite of poverty, to go to the opera (possibly he obtained free tickets via Kienzl). Graz, the second city of Austria, was—and still is—an important cultural center, with a fine opera house and several theaters. It is far enough away from Vienna to lead an independent life. (One famous example: in 1906 Richard Strauss's Salome was to have its Austrian premiere there, conducted by the composer, the opera having been banned in Vienna by the aptly named Cardinal Piffl.) For the young Busoni, it was an ideal setting for those fifteen months of study: it offered a high cultural standard, but few of the pressures of the capital, where he would have been constantly measured against—and competing with—world-class musicians.

When Ferruccio left Graz in April 1881, he took with him an elaborate certificate proving that he had completed the course, and—more importantly—a book of 430 folio pages[5] in his own hand, containing a complete treatise on composition, a record of all he had learned from Mayer: not only music theory, but also the history of music, with examples of styles ranging from the medieval to the modern.

Ferruccio's course with Mayer had ended in March; his friends arranged a concert for him in April as a send-off, at which he played Schumann's A Minor Concerto and Beethoven's Sonata Opus 111. Some of his own recent compositions were also on the program: a C Major String Quartet (BV 177, composed two months previously, unpublished), a Prelude and Fugue for Piano (BV 178, manuscript now lost), and a setting in German of Psalm 67 for Chorus and Orchestra (BV 174a, composed late the previous year, unpublished, arranged from a setting of the same text for Chorus and Piano, BV 174). Most of his early compositions remain unpublished, and the manuscripts of several are now lost. The bulk of those still extant are in the Berlin State Library. The few works published between 1878 and 1882 by Cranz or Lucca are all either for solo piano or voice and piano, as indeed were most of his compositions before he studied with Wilhelm Mayer; a Concerto in D Minor for Piano and String Quartet (BV 80) written in 1878 was published in 1987, edited by the pianist and Busoni scholar Larry Sitsky. The *Stabat Mater* had been so far Busoni's only completed work for orchestra; in view of the technical shortcomings of the work pointed out by Kienzl, it is possible that Busoni himself later destroyed it.

From Graz, Ferruccio and his mother returned to Trieste, to her father's house, where their board and lodging were paid for by Anna's labors as a piano teacher. They lived in some poverty, as any extra money earned had to be sent to Ferdinando, who was touring the Styrian spas, and later Italy, with his clarinet, but as usual not earning enough to keep himself in the style he considered his due. Ferruccio kept busy composing, practicing, and drawing architectural views of Trieste—a favorite pastime, for which he had considerable talent. (As in Graz, any ideas of regular school attendance seemed to have been abandoned.) In May he wrote Twenty-four Preludes for Piano (BV 181). They are all short—with a total playing time of roughly forty-five minutes—and quite remarkable in their sophisticated assurance. They also require virtuosic skill from the performer. Like Bach, and like Chopin, whom he was consciously emulating here, Busoni wrote them in a sequence using all the keys. There is an exuberant breadth of styles and influences.

He had also started on a requiem mass, and his frequent letters to his father contain ongoing reports on its progress. These letters to an absent parent, resumed after a break of five years, during which the three of them had been together most of the time, now betray a keen adolescent wit, not only in Busoni's self-mockery when describing his own work, but also in his depictions of others, plus his shrewd assessments of other composers' work. On June 7 he writes:[6] "I begin my letter with some good news: the 'Tuba mirum' of the Requiem was finished 3 days ago, and I have also begun the full score, of which I have written a few pages." There follows a breakdown of how Busoni intends to continue, which is not very enlightening:

cres.	Tuba mirum spagens sonum	
Trumpets	Per sepulcra regionum	
Dim	Coget omnes ante thronum.	
	Mors stupebit et natura	
Mysterious	Cum resurget creatura	4 solo
theme	Judicanti responsura	voices
	Liber scriptus proferetur	Bass and tenor
agitato	In quo totum continetur	soloists,
	Unde mundus judicetur.	then chorus
Reprise of	Judex ergo cum sedebit	
verse I	Quidquid latet apparebit	then
	Nil inultum remanebit.	dim.

Quid sum miser tum dicturus
pp   Quem patronum rogaturus
theme of the   Cum vix justus sit securus.
Which had not yet been given to the voices.

Yesterday I had lunch at Cimoso's. I ate well. After lunch Bianchini[7] came. I played him my newly published fugue [Prelude and Fugue in A Minor for Organ (BV 157), written in 1880 and published by Cranz in 1881] which he liked very much, so much so that he wanted to hear it a second time. He found it *masterly*. Then he wanted to let me hear a sonata of his for piano and violin, and as Luigi said he had not studied it, I offered to play it myself at sight, which surprised them very much, and even more so as I read it very well. Bianchini was beside himself and kissed me several times and told me he wanted to dedicate to me the very next piece he composed. Then I played them *my* sonata [Sonata in F Minor for Piano (BV 164), unpublished], which in general they liked very much. Bianchini assured Luigi that today only Rubinstein could write such a work. And Luigi turned to me saying: You see, you see, you are already beginning to enter the ranks of such people. I write you all this because I know that it will please you and not out of pride or arrogance. Anyway, you know my character better than I do.

Bianchini recently composed a *Requiem*, various parts of which he let me hear. The Tuba mirum is the best of all the pieces and I like it rather more than Verdi's, although it doesn't achieve the grandiosity, or rather the charlatanism, of the latter. That always reminds me of a battlefield and the signals the soldiers give one another to warn of the enemy's attack. I am glad *my* idea "persuaded" you.

Bianchini comes in for some rough treatment from his younger colleague in a letter written three days later, on June 10:[8]

Babbo Caro! [in large, ornate Gothic script]
This morning I received the letter you wrote me from Neuhaus, and that gave me a lot of pleasure. I am replying straight away since you want that; and I too amuse myself in writing to you although I do not have any news. Our life is not bursting with variety. The only variation is the passage from good weather to rain. Today we are in stage II, i.e., rain. We don't go to the theater since the main ones are closed, and at the Politeama there are "I Phoites" which is synonymous with bullshit [*fotte*]. Excuse the term. Moreover we don't have the means to procure these su-

perfluous entertainments, in fact Mamma has asked me to express to you her regret at not being able to help you at the moment, as she cannot send money as she hasn't even paid the month's rent to Grandfather yet.

She would like to send you 2,000 florins if she could do so, but she promises to send you everything she can as soon as she gets the month's payment from Signora Finzi.

You want me to keep you merry, and how do you expect me to do that if at this moment I am writing a Requiem?

Further on, he turns to a new work of Bianchini's:

His sonata for violin has no clear form, or rather an obscure form, or *little* form, which means no form. It starts not knowing where it's going to end, and ends not knowing where it began.

This sonata consists of:

A 1st movement which should be classical but which unfortunately loses its way and resembles more a labyrinth than the 1st movement of a sonata. There follows a minuet which out of eccentricity lacks a trio. Then an adagio, poetical rather (as we artists are poetic!) but which through too much exuberance of poetry, in fact lacks imagination and is two and a half miles long, or longer than Meo's shirt [inordinately spun out].

—In the finale Bianchini goes into a frenzy, or as you would say, *takes his hat* [takes offence] and tries to become clever and full of dash. It gives me the impression of someone who wants to show he has mastered running up stairs, and who accidentally breaks his neck before he has been able to prove his ability.

—His preludes that he played to me are all at the level of those you possess for clarinet; only the title is changed: here one can read:

"Pure sentiments"

"Ecstasy"

"*The shepherdess lost and found*"

"Passionate melody"

"Morning song," etc.

I too want to try to compose a piece entitled *Bianchini the poetic, or ecstasy in music in all its stages*. This will need a prelude as introduction: *The fantasy, the genius, the dash, the delirium. True, pure and authentic sentiments of Pietro Bianchini, magister musicae. Set to music according to the theory of the above maestro, by F. B. Busoni*. These pieces will be composed for piccolo, double bassoon, and bass drum with cymbals and triangles ad libitum, which means you can play, you can also refrain.

I read over the last few days a wonderful humorous novella by Barrili, *The Queen of Spades*, that Ersilia gave me. A certain Baron Frauenthal falls in love with a playing card, and the book starts as a maker of play-ing cards receives a letter from this Baron, in which he is asked if he knows the original on the card. The subject is quite interesting, as also the three main characters, a "painter who has gone astray" and becomes fixated on the color yellow, a clerk who becomes a poet, and a music teacher who wants untempered or primitive tuning restored.

Grandfather is as usual still lively, today I went with him to the count-ing house, where he introduced me to Cristiano [*sic*] Schröder [old Weiss's employer] who was very pleased to see me. Grandfather is fully recovered and still makes his little jokes at table. And when Mamma says to him: You know, Papa, for us [*per noi*, "in our view"] you should go to bed; he replies: I am not going to bed for you, I'm going to bed for me. And as he always drinks undiluted wine he says "Give me wine," he takes wine, "and now give me water" and takes the wine flask from the other side and pours for himself.

Ferruccio's letters to his father also illustrate that intimate bond, forged not only by the natural child-parent relationship but also by the shared musical background, that persisted between all three Busonis. Busoni was a true son of Italy in his unquestioning allegiance to his parents, and with them too at that point in his life he could share his musical thought unguardedly, as with no other. Communication with others was always vital to him. At this age, sharing musical gossip and having an audience for his exuberant wit was enough. With adolescence and early adult-hood, inevitably his parents proved inadequate: his mother's narrow piety and, as he later realized, his father's indifference to any aspect of his son's life that held no advantages for him stifled true intimacy.

But in 1881, and in Trieste, *faute de mieux*, he was happy to write long letters to his father as light relief from composing and piano practice. His mind was bursting with ideas, such as those in Barrili's *Queen of Spades*: a surreal theme with a dash of menace, an atmosphere the young Busoni was already drawn to, and to which he frequently returned. Per-haps he already sensed the nightmarish aspects of his own life.

In the letters written during that summer in Trieste, the underlying frustration of the gifted fifteen-year-old is evident. Time and again, what seemed like a clear path to artistic success was willfully ignored or blocked by his father. It is painful to contemplate what Busoni's life and career might have been had he indeed been adopted at nine in Vienna by Julius and Karoline von Gomperz, impossible though that idea was: understandably, both parents, for their own not always laudable reasons, would never have contemplated letting him go. He made some musical friends in Trieste, such as Pietro Bianchini, with whom he conversed on equal terms, in spite of the thirty-eight-year age difference, and there was always Luigi Cimoso, but Trieste was a musical backwater.

In October, Ferruccio gave a concert in the town, then set off with his parents for a tour of Italy: in November and December he gave two concerts in Milan, to sparse audiences. Italians at that time were not great concertgoers, and the concert halls were often badly heated. The boy's pale and haggard appearance was commented on. In January 1882, in Bergamo, he played for the first time his *Una festa di villaggio: Six Character Pieces for Piano* (BV 185), completed the month before. (The work was published by the Milanese firm of Lucca in the same year, and republished in 1926 by Ricordi.) It clearly shows the progress achieved thanks to Mayer's tuition. It starts assertively with the piano loudly "ringing" the church bell to summon the village to the *festa*, a short melody jauntily elaborated on. The subsequent movements, Triumphal march, In church, The fair, Dance, and Night, are programmatic and yet abstract. What is startling here is that the impression, typical of most of Busoni's subsequent work, is already given of a highly sophisticated mind thinking private musical thoughts aloud, which makes any hearing of his work like eavesdropping on a very intimate experience. This work also exudes secure self-confidence.

After Bergamo, five concerts were given during the early part of 1882 in Bologna, a town that proved more appreciative than others in northern Italy: in March the Accademia Filarmonica (now the Conservatorio G. B. Martini) conferred its diploma for composition on Ferruccio. The examination consisted of the composition of a four-part fugue on a given theme, for voices.[9] At fifteen Ferruccio was the second-youngest composer to be admitted a member of the academy; the youngest had been the fourteen-year-old Mozart in 1770. The diploma was accompanied by a letter referring to this fact:

> Remember, o young artist, that in the hall in which you have enthused a select audience with your playing, and in which you have composed the pieces of the Maestro examination, here too, at a tender age, the

immortal Mozart underwent his examination to obtain in this Academy the same rank that you too have achieved. May this serve you as spur and encouragement to continue in the career you have embarked upon, which must lead you to fame.[10]

In April the whole family returned to Ferdinando's hometown of Empoli, and gave a typical concert consisting of duets by Ferdinando and Anna of fantasias on famous opera melodies, and works by Liszt and Adolfo Fumagalli (1828–1856) played by Ferruccio, with the now almost obligatory *Improvvisazione* by Ferruccio in the middle, during which Ferdinando would walk around the auditorium collecting themes from the audience. The town responded by presenting Ferruccio with a gold medal. In May Ferruccio and his parents were in Pisa, then in early summer in the villa of one of Ferdinando's brothers in San Giusto, just outside Empoli.

In August Ferruccio arrived in Arezzo, where the "anniversary" was being celebrated of Guido d'Arezzo (ca. 990–1050), the musical theorist and one-time monk (also known as Guido Monaco), to whom we owe the system of modern musical notation. There was an exhibition of pianos and the unveiling of a monument to Guido, for which Arrigo Boito had written the verses for an anthem and march set to music by Luigi Mancinelli (1848–1921), then director of the Accademia in Bologna and chief conductor of the town's Teatro Comunale, who was possibly responsible for Ferruccio's presence in Arezzo. Here Busoni first met Boito. (Boito was also engaged at the time in the very ticklish task of persuading Verdi out of retirement to write *Otello*, to Boito's libretto, an enterprise that went through agonizing stops and starts, and in the summer of 1882 was still tantalizingly uncertain, in spite of covert assistance from Verdi's wife and from Ricordi, his publisher. Boito was also to write the libretto for Verdi's next and final opera, *Falstaff*.)

Boito (1842–1918), composer, librettist, poet, journalist, had been an active member of the *Scapigliatura* (literally "dishevelled"), a movement bent on reforming and revitalizing artistic life in Italy, and had been an ardent supporter of Garibaldi in his struggle for Italian unity. As a composer, Boito is remembered today chiefly for his opera *Mefistofele* and a second opera, *Nerone*, which he worked and worried at for many years, and which was finally first performed posthumously in 1924.

Boito demonstrated great kindness and encouragement to his young colleague, for which Busoni remained grateful. The latter was engaged for three weeks in September as demonstrator of the pianos in the exhibition, and Boito allowed him access to rehearsals of his *Mefistofele* in the town, during which, as Busoni himself recalled in an obituary notice in the *Neue Zürcher Zeitung* in June 1918,[11] he

> got to know the opera by heart, became an enthusiastic admirer of it and of the composer. Boito—cultured, engaging, simple—took an interest in me in the most kindly way. It was thanks to him that the following winter [March 22, 1883] in Bologna Mancinelli had a sizeable cantata of mine (for soloists, chorus and orchestra) performed. I shall never forget that, much later, Boito was annoyed that I had devoted too much time to the piano, too little to composition. In this interpretation of my artistic duty he stood almost alone, and I understood this reproach as the most splendid praise, and it served me as the most conducive encouragement.

Another artist who allowed himself, through an eclectic intellectual curiosity, to be led off in too many directions, Boito was possibly trying to warn Busoni against making the same mistake. In early August the younger composer had written a setting (BV 192, the cantata alluded to above, unpublished), for soloists, chorus, and orchestra, of *Il sabato del villaggio* (Village Sabbath), the most well-known poem by the greatest of the Italian Romantic poets, Giacomo Leopardi. Busoni showed the piece to Boito, who urged him to continue setting Leopardi's poems to music—he commented on the "admirable exuberance of rhythm"[12] and melodic flow of Busoni's setting— reasoning that Leopardi would provide the right inspiration. But in spite of Busoni's growing admiration for the great poet's work, there were no further settings of his poems, indeed, very few settings at all in Italian from now on.

That autumn, again in Empoli, Ferruccio wrote what was in effect a begging letter to Giovannina Lucca, the Milan music publisher, to whom he had offered some of his works. Although she sent back a letter praising the compositions, she had rejected them for publication. In a letter dated October 24[13] he tried again, this time putting his cards on the table: he needed the money, as his plan was to return to Vienna: "Your negative response destroys my plan and forces me to remain for an indeterminate and *perhaps not brief* period in places in which I shall not be able to achieve my aim and where I shall be forced to lose precious time, the more so at such a young age as mine." What he needed was time to study, in order to progress, in order to be able to write a work for the opera house. Signora Lucca relented and published *Una festa di villaggio* by the end of the year, plus Busoni's Twenty-Four Preludes for Piano (BV 181), written in May 1881. Where the money went remains a mystery, and another year was to pass before Ferruccio returned to Vienna. (Although grateful to Signora Lucca, he was sharply defensive regarding his artistic integrity; he informed her early the next year that he was going to change the second movement of his *Una festa di villaggio*, an idea she disapproved of. On May 4, 1883,[14] he wrote: "I do not know why it *displeases* you that I intend to change the 2nd piece of the 'Festa di Villaggio.' Correcting one's own compositions has always seemed to me the proof of progress, and for me *progressing* has never been a cause for *displeasure*." She need not lose money at it, he goes on, because she could sell remaining stocks of the old edition, then for a new edition sell the old "Marcia" as a separate piece. With a youthful lack of tact—not to mention blithe ignorance of the realities of publishing—he explains that he made this change "acknowledging the truth of the old adage; *to err is human, but to persist in error is irrational. Whether leaving things as they are* will or will not be artistically an evil we should leave to the judgment of *those more competent.*" As the publisher and friend of Verdi, among others, and a genial woman with a good sense of humor, she found it easy to forgive him, and was probably amused. But she did not accept the "Marcia": it was published in late 1883 by Carlo Schmidl—another old friend—in Trieste, as *Marcia di paesani e contadine* [March for Countrymen and Peasant Women] for Piano [BV 193].)

In Bologna, on March 22, 1883, Ferruccio's cantata setting of Leopardi's *Il sabato del villaggio* was performed at the Teatro Comunale, conducted by Luigi Mancinelli. The performance was repeated a few days later, this time conducted by Ferruccio. Then it was back to Trieste. Ferruccio returned in some triumph: news of his concert successes had preceded him, and he was greeted as a celebrity—in spite of which, his family's life continued in the usual chaotic muddle. In July father and son were in the Austrian spa of Bad Mark Tüffer, hoping to pay their way by giving concerts to the guests. This was a disastrous failure, and a humiliating begging letter had to be sent via an old family friend, Antonio Zampieri (ca. 1850–1919), conductor and musicologist, founder of the Trieste Municipal Orchestra, to the latter's rich friend Leone Segrè. Ferdinando asks for a loan, for Ferruccio's "artistic needs"; the real need, as Ferruccio subsequently told Zampieri,[15] was considerably more basic: "I know that Papa sent you a letter to forward to Sig. Segrè. The need, however, is much more urgent than we believed a few days ago. For several days (it is hard for me to have to tell you this) we have been unable to pay for food, and the landlord wants the rooms free by Saturday. I don't know where to turn, and I assure you neither of us is at fault at all in this matter." They were threatened with the gravest consequences if two hundred florins were not found by the Saturday. As usual, Ferdinando, Micawber-like, escaped the situation by the skin of his teeth, thanks to the generosity of others, who responded for his son's sake. The effect of the constant humiliation of these situations on Ferruccio can easily be imagined: his letter to Zampieri telling the truth was the only way in this particular case that he could retain any self-respect.

In the autumn there were financially more successful concerts, first in Laibach (now Ljubljana), where Ferruccio also continued work on a Symphonic Suite (BV 201) begun that summer. They then went on to Graz, where he continued work on the suite. He was full of plans and ideas: he wrote to Michele Buono (1826–1892), poet and editor of a literary journal in Trieste, L'Arte, asking him to write the Italian libretto for an opera based on the Danish playwright Henrik Hertz's King René's Daughter, which Ferruccio wanted to submit for a competition in Vienna. The plan came to nothing, as, in spite of sending three letters to Buono, Busoni did not even receive a reply to the request.

Then, on October 10, traveling directly from Graz, father and son arrived for another onslaught on Vienna,[16] staying first at the Archduke Charles yet again, then hiring a room at forty-five florins a month and a piano at ten florins. (From Graz, Anna had returned alone to Trieste.) They were hoping to consolidate Ferruccio's reputation in Vienna as pianist and composer. This was to prove no easy task: a child prodigy is one thing; a seventeen-year-old pianist, no matter how gifted, is merely yet another recruit in the legion of concert performers vying for space. But Ferruccio was determined to fight hard: the very day of their arrival, he sought out the music publisher and agent Albert Gutmann to sound out the possibility of a performance at one of Hans Richter's Philharmonic concerts of the symphonic suite he had been working on over recent months.

The next day a chapter began in the young Busoni's life that caused him much grief and through which he learned some bitter lessons. He went to see Hans Richter himself. Was Gutmann's judgment on his chances negative, or was the agent's advice simply ignored? Although in later life Busoni did use agents, he never got out of the habit of acting over their heads, conditioned as he was since early youth to believe that he alone was capable of making the important decisions.

Hans Richter (see chapter 2, p. 19), friend not only of Wagner but also of Brahms and Bruckner, among others, was one of the conductors of the time who helped to achieve full recognition and prominence for the conductor's art, and was therefore also a valuable friend and ally for any composer. Although he was still only forty, his international reputation was already assured. He lived in the remote suburb of Döbling and was not at home (officially or otherwise is not known) when Ferruccio arrived that autumn day. Only at the sixth attempt was the young man allowed in to see a rather frosty Richter, who did, however, consent to let Ferruccio play his suite to him, whereupon Richter became generally enthusiastic and offered constructive advice, which Ferruccio acted on. In a possibly embellished account relayed to Anna on October 14[17] Ferruccio reported:

> He had scarcely heard the Preludio when he exclaimed: "Bravo! If all the movements are like this, I shall perform it at once." More than anything he was surprised—as he himself said—by the *allegro fugato*, however he found the *menuetto* weak (that is, weak compared with the magnificence of the other movements) regarding which he advised me—either to change it so that it became less long-winded, or to simply leave it out. I confess that, on hearing the whole Suite afterwards, I was persuaded of this.

(As Ferruccio reported it, Richter commented that Italian and English composers were doing more interesting work at the moment than young Germans, "who waste their time imitating Wagner.") Richter told him the full orchestral score must be ready by November 13 to be tried out before the committee, whose consent was needed for the work to be included in the coming season of concerts. Richter also remarked that if the work were a success it would be performed at one of his annual London concerts, a prominent feature of the London calendar since 1879. At a more immediate level, he offered Ferruccio free tickets for the theater and concerts.

In late November Ferruccio was told the trial run-through would be put off to January 1884, then played in a concert the following month if accepted. He showed the work to Brahms, who said he would go to the trial, which in January was postponed again; at the end of March Richter told him it was too late to try it out, but that he would do his best for it in the next season. Next season it was to be the same story, perhaps not helped by Ferruccio's (understandable) siege tactics in his efforts to pin Richter down. Finally it was tried out on October 4, 1884—and the orchestra (which had the final say) rejected it, by a majority of one vote. Ferruccio had only the bitter satisfaction of hearing it performed: flouting the rule that the composer should not be present at a trial orchestral run-through, he had crept unnoticed into the gallery.

He had placed all his hopes in a public performance of the work in Vienna, to establish his reputation as a composer, and this was a bitter blow, though it did nothing to damage his confidence in his own powers. It is a remarkably mature and forceful work, in five movements. In its final version, published four years later, in 1888, by C. F. Kahnt in Leipzig, the Präludium is sonorous, idiosyncratic, and full of the strong, urgent rhythms that typified much of Ferruccio's later orchestral work. The Gavotte has a dry, elegant, almost Rossini-esque wit, with a lot of solo work for the woodwind; the Gigue has a macabre, almost demonic quality; and the Langsames intermezzo and the final Allegro fugato betray a strident virility. The work had real merits from the outset, as is evidenced by the serious interest in it shown by Brahms and Richter, but Busoni was now learning that merit alone was no guarantee of success in a highly competitive field.

Back in autumn 1883, however, he was still optimistic, in spite of all. On October 17 he wrote to Anna[18] of a meeting with the violinist and composer Josef Hellmesberger Jr. (1855–1907):

> Hellmesberger received me with his famous forced smile, still chic, still elegant, smart, with kind words on his lips and a *je ne sais quoi* that does not inspire confidence. He told me I should go back and see him some

morning, and I shall keep to his advice. Door [Anton Door, 1822–1919, pianist and since 1869 professor at the conservatory] was with him, who on seeing me made a *really ugly grimace*. They chatted together while a pupil was playing, and every now and again they raised their heads and tapped their feet to make her play *in time*. . . . I have taken advantage of my free ticket to the theater to see *Don Giovanni* and *Il Rapimento* [sic] *del Seraglio*. Both operas have stunned me; the one through its power, the other through its inimitable grace: and through the force of expression with the simplest harmonic and instrumental means. . . . Yesterday I was again at the Flamms' and played them various things (they have a good Streicher piano), among them my *Studio-Fuga* [no. 5 of the 6 *Etudes* (BV 203), dedicated to Brahms and published by Gutmann in Vienna that year] and the *Schumann Toccata*, which astounded them. I managed the Toccata very well. The Flamms are very fond of me and treat me quite kindly, taking a keen interest in my affairs.

There were other setbacks: the Flamms, old friends and patrons whom Ferruccio had met on his first stay in Vienna as a child in 1875, did initially receive him with great friendliness and listen to his music, but after a few weeks Frau Flamm wrote that her husband had forbidden him to come to the house anymore, as their daughter, Paula, was growing up and his visits might compromise her chances of an advantageous marriage. His stunning good looks were obviously seen as posing a risk not worth running. This was doubly sad, as Paula was also quite an accomplished pianist.

In November Ferruccio met his old friend Otto von Kapff and his wife, "who is older and *much uglier* than he is, otherwise very nice."[19] Other old Viennese friends disappointed him. Perhaps they were unwilling to digest the fact that he was now his own man, less prepared to take their advice unquestioningly. The Baronin von Todesco in particular incensed him by recommending lessons with Theodor Leschetizky (1830–1915), the great Polish pianist and composer, now famous only as teacher of some of the greatest pianists of the age, such as Ignacy Paderewski, Artur Schnabel, and Benno Moiseiwitsch. The baronin compounded the offence by making her recommendation on the advice of her lady companion, who said Ferruccio "thumped," her authority for passing judgment on his playing being a father and brother who claimed to be pianists: "The father too old and weak to shine, contents

himself by playing in society some easy pieces and some passages from
difficult pieces by Chopin and swears he heard them from Chopin himself thus and thus, [played] in this way."[20] (Ferruccio is similarly
scathing about the brother.) Ferruccio's brusque rejection of the baronin's advice was forgiven to the extent that she allowed him one
hundred florins a month (and she ordered a dozen shirts for him) after
hearing him at a concert on November 30. Neither Richter, nor
Hanslick, nor Brahms came to the concert, but Leschetizky did, and
spoke very well of Ferruccio.[21] Ferruccio played Beethoven's Sonata
Opus 111, Bach's Italian Concerto, some Schumann, Chopin, and
Liszt, plus some of his own work—a mammoth program that set the
pattern for subsequent performances. This first concert was well received by the critics, who made up for their mildness, however, at subsequent concerts. Ferruccio had been bedridden just before the concert
with a bad cold, caught apparently waiting outside the dressing room
after a concert given by the Spanish violin virtuoso and composer
Pablo Sarasate (1844–1908), a performer Busoni was often to tour with
in later years.

Two days after his own concert, Busoni was at the Philharmonie for
the premiere of Brahms's Symphony no. 3.[22] At some time during late
1884 Ferruccio performed in public his Six Etudes for Piano (BV 203),
written in 1883. While each étude has its own mood, the general impression is of exuberance—in fact, four are marked allegro, with various modifications, and the last is a scherzo in 4/4. (The second, Allegro moderato, in 12/8, a stately, staccato dance, contains a short phrase
used years later in Busoni's great Piano Concerto.) All these études demand assured musicianship and technical skill: number 4, aptly marked
"Allegro vivace assai e con fuoco," has left-hand scale passages rushing
up and down at great speed, joined by resounding chords—creating
that particularly sonorous sound that makes Busoni's work easily recognizable. Number 5, a fugue, allegro giusto, lets us know through its
technical skill how much Busoni has absorbed of Bach, while retaining
his own voice. Number 6, scherzo, a march marked "Vivacissimo, energico, feroce," is a young man's show of strength, full of pounding resonance, ending in hammer blows in deafening chords.

Ferruccio got rid of some of his annoyance at setbacks and humiliations suffered in Vienna by writing satirical letters to the Mayers on

musical life in the Austrian capital, drawing appreciative replies from his old teacher, who, apart from enjoying Busoni's wit, was glad to find his own decision to avoid Vienna justified:[23] "Your portrayal of Viennese music and musical conditions is glorious. Not for anything in the world would I live among that brimstone mob [Schwefelbande]. . . . I'd rather remain a despised provincial."

In January 1884 Ferruccio had composed Variations and Fugue on Chopin's Prelude in C Minor, op. 28, no. 20 (BV 213), which he premiered in Vienna exactly one year later and which was subsequently published by Breitkopf und Härtel. Still a popular piece on the concert platform and in the recording studio, albeit not one to be attempted by the fainthearted, it is a lengthy work, consisting of eighteen variations plus a four-voice fugue and extended coda, of quite fiendish intricacy, full of exciting, highly complicated rhythms. After the theme is stated, Busoni indulges in every ingenious pianistic device, to brilliant effect, constantly returning to Chopin's original five-note opening phrase. The coda is grandly Lisztian. In 1922 Busoni wrote a shorter, revised version of these variations (BV 213a). (Rachmaninov was another composer drawn to write variations on the same prelude, in 1903.)

Letters to Trieste give us some idea not only of what Busoni was doing, seeing, and hearing, but of musical life in Vienna at the time, dominated as it was by the war between the Wagnerians and their opponents. "Brahms too has his party," he wrote, "and the Slavs and the Germans have constant battles. So everyone is fighting, like cat and dog."[24] The same letter contains a comic description of a performance by Arthur Friedheim (1859–1932), who seems to have taken on some of his master Liszt's characteristics to the point of parody:

[He] has long hair and a mien between the severe and the bored. When he plays he comes out and bows in such a way that his hair covers his whole face, then he throws his head back to reorder his tresses. Then he sits down with a great frown, and throws himself backward, waiting for the audience to fall silent. Finally he seizes the keys, "like a wild beast seizing its prey," as Hanslick says. But the best thing is to watch him during the orchestral tutti. This gives him the chance to show off his whole act [mimica]. He examines his nails, observes the audience, passes his hands through his hair and similar nonsense.

The unfortunate Friedheim nevertheless offered Ferruccio a useful lesson on how not to behave on the concert platform.

Rubinstein gave a series of four concerts in Vienna that winter, all of which Busoni attended. At the first, in February, Rubinstein played thirty pieces, "among them three sonatas, one by Schumann and two by Beethoven. Rubinstein is undeniably the first among living pianists, but even he is not perfect."[25] Busoni paid Rubinstein a brief visit on February 15; the older man had no time to listen to a recent sonata by his young colleague, but accepted the dedication. (This work, a Sonata in F Minor (BV 204), was not published until 1983, by Breitkopf und Härtel.)

In March Ferruccio gave two more concerts; the last of which, on March 28, went "quite well,"[26] he wrote to Trieste, and the next evening he was invited to take part "in a concert for charity [*benefi-cenza*], where I played without being benefited"[27]—that is, without fee. There had been yet another contretemps with the Baronin von Todesco, but she had come to his March 28 concert, which was in fact a great public success; and he was presented with a laurel wreath. She was obviously impressed and pacified. He visited her on March 31, and she gave him his monthly one hundred florins, plus ten for theater visits, and asked him what clothing he was in need of, so that she could get him some as a birthday present on April 1. She invited him to come often, saying, "If I just had *some idea* of what steps we should take now!"[28] Busoni promised to go again soon to discuss the matter. It was at this time that Richter had informed him that it was now too late to try out his suite, but promised to try it out next season. Writing to his mother,[29] Busoni tried to be philosophical about it, but admitted that his main reason for coming to Vienna had failed. But the next day would be his eighteenth birthday:

Evviva! (*Chorus offstage*) Evviva! (Echo comes back:) Evviva! (Distant voices:) Evviva! (All:) Eternal God! The curtain falls after the eighteenth act. Applause.

Eighteenth Act
The scene is the first of April, a desk, a bed with a Ferruccio in it, and a Bösendorfer piano. To the left another bed with Busoni *père*. Everyone asleep.

Scene One
Ferruccio (waking up): Mamma—coffee!
Father: Evviva Ferruccio! (Wakes up)
Ferruccio: Evviva! make the coffee!
Father: (gets up grumbling) Richter! Richter! You've let me down as well. Enough! I knew it would happen. Baroness! Baroness! We have to settle accounts. And that Filtsch. If he speaks to me I'll tell him—but he doesn't have the nerve, because one look from me was enough, he realized who he had to deal with. They ought to come here—if they deigned to. I'd give them a piece of my mind. I've got it all off pat. I've had it up to here. (Grabs the coffee pot.)
Ferruccio (still half asleep): Is the coffee ready?
(Someone knocks at the door)
Father: Herein!
As the door slowly opens the curtain falls.

There you have a rough idea of how my birthday began, and that's how every day has begun—for some time.

Cara Mamma, I know that for my birthday you wish me a thousand wonderful things, happiness and pleasures, and I hope to be able to share them with you and *il buon babbo*, whom I love just as much—when he's not grumbling.

Busoni began writing articles for the Trieste newspaper *L'Indipendente*, under the anagrammatic pseudonym of Bruno Fioresucci, in a straightforward style full of lucid critical sense. During 1884 Busoni wrote eight articles on musical life in Vienna, plus three on the Trieste premiere of Bizet's *Carmen*, a six-part series in 1885 entitled On Musical Intelligence, and many others, attesting to a remarkably acute and mature intelligence. (Later, between August and October 1886, he was to write a three-part essay on the condition of music in Italy for the *Grazer Tagespost*—see p. 72 below.)

But in Vienna in his late teens, all this theoretical work was not only useful in sorting out his own ideas, it was also a cry for help, a call to the outside world, part of a desire to engage in dialogue, somehow to get through what he was trying to say at the piano and through his compositions. Seldom finding satisfactory dialogue partners in his early years unfortunately led to a monologue mind-set in Busoni. As with his lack of a normal schooling as a child, his lack of a prolonged period at a conservatory, involving daily contact with other students, who, as his peers, would have challenged his thinking, accentuated that mind-set.

In late April 1884 Ferruccio went on a short visit to Trieste, a visit overcast by the death of his faithful friend Luigi Cimoso in a lunatic asylum, which would haunt his dreams for years afterward. Six months before, Cimoso had written his last piece of good, but, as usual, un-heeded, advice to the boy's father:

> I must allow myself to tell you that Ferruccio would have achieved and would in future achieve much more if you had been more friendly to your audiences, to other artists, and to all the people one cannot afford to disregard in such a career. At Trieste they say your concert was delib-erately boycotted by the public and the shareholders of the theater on account of what you said about them. . . . . I heard the same thing about your visits to Vienna, Milan and Arezzo.[30]

Ferdinando had gone alone to Frohnleiten, a resort eighteen miles north of Graz, to nurse his dyspepsia, while his son was in Trieste. Fer-ruccio joined him there in June, and at the suggestion of the Baronin von Todesco, who had had Ferruccio examined in Vienna, underwent an unpleasant cold-water cure, which he maintained did him a lot of good.[31] For part of the summer, the Mayers were also in Frohnleiten, and Ferruccio and Melanie went on long daily walks together, which was regarded as rather a scandal. He sometimes embarrassed her with his exuberant sense of fun, imitating people walking in front of them, or teasing an old peasant woman by pretending not to know what the potatoes were that she had in her basket. But mostly he and Melanie spent the time talking of books. At eighteen Busoni was very familiar with what Somerset Maugham memorably called "the enormous solace of books," and was already widely read, in German and Italian. His tastes ranged from Dickens, Thackeray, Turgenev, and Anatole France to Schopenhauer, but his favorites at the time were the Italian classics, Boccaccio, Manzoni, Dante, and Leopardi in particular. At around this time, he set a poem by the minor German poet Neidhard von Reuen-thal to music, and another by the great medieval poet Walther von der Vogelweide.[32]

It is impossible to assess with any certainty the feelings of Melanie and Ferruccio for one another; there is some evidence that she was in love with him at that time, but that his feelings were only brotherly, al-though their subsequent correspondence tells a slightly more complex story. (Whatever the truth, later, in early 1886, Frau Mayer tried to put a stop to the correspondence, which could have begun to compromise Melanie's reputation at a marriageable age.)

Drawn by half-promises from Hans Richter concerning the performance of his suite, at the beginning of September 1884 Busoni took the train to Vienna alone, going straight from the station to the von Wertheimsteins at Döbling, "where I was received as one of the family and immediately invited to stay."[33] His almost daily letters to his parents give a blow-by-blow account of his continued efforts to get the suite performed, plus details of his other activities, away from the stern parental gaze. (As he knew, one parent would send his letters on to the other parent.) "Last Sunday I went to Kahlenberg with my friend Englmann and another young friend of his, quite respectable, well-mannered, cultured and of irreproachable habits," he wrote in a letter addressed to his mother,[34] who doubtless missed the ironic tone.

It was on October 4 that he had the shattering experience, hidden in the gallery, of hearing an orchestral run-through of his suite—a year after he had first shown it to Richter—and then the next day hearing of its rejection by the orchestra. Richter himself gave him the news, sweetening the pill a little by giving him a detailed account of the orchestra's decision:

[Richter] said furthermore "that they liked the Prelude, the Allegro Fugato and the Gigue very much, and *they all admired and acknowledged my extraordinary talent* and the beauty of the work. That the contrapuntal part, and the instrumentation were perfect, marvelous but that the work as a whole gave an immature and fragmented [*spezzato*] effect.

He then added that he suggested to the orchestra to perform only these three sections, but they would not agree—not even at his request. And he ended by saying that nor would he advise me, in fact he did not want me to have the piano piece heard—this being below the suite in artistic value. [This was probably the Sonata in F Minor for Piano (BV 204), dedicated to Rubinstein.] "Don't let yourself be discouraged, dear Busoni (he said finally) and continue on your way, as I am persuaded that soon you will be able to present me with a work that will content all of us in all respects."[35]

In spite of a valiant attempt at a stiff upper lip, that letter to his father betrayed his deep disappointment:

Although the disappointment was and still is very great, I have still tried to take the matter calmly, not to be discouraged and to continue to nurture faith in my talent and to persevere in going forward. All that was humanly possible, to succeed in my purpose, was done—I have nothing to reproach myself with, I have neglected nothing, omitted nothing. I have worked assiduously, I have walked streets, journeyed, waited in antechambers, worked as copyist and as carrier.

At any rate it was a satisfaction to hear my work, which was read to perfection by the orchestra, and I was most satisfied to reassure myself that I was not deceived in the orchestral effects.[36]

Busoni was going to retrieve the scores that day, he continued, and have a "little talk" with Frau von Wertheimstein, before leaving for Frohnleiten. Then follows perhaps the main reason for the above elaborate self-justification:

The only thing I *beg you* is that you meet me in a good mood and with careless good humor [*indifferente ilarità*]. As soon as I get back I shall set myself to study the piano with new energy, and to finish my variations and fugue on Chopin. Then I want to think of a decision for the future.

In order that you don't believe Richter was to blame for the unfavorable decision I still want to tell you that Krul [Kral?]—days ago—told me that Richter, in making a sketch of the program for the season, had already thought of the position for my Suite and expressed his good intentions about it.[37]

Was there paternal pressure on Ferruccio to concentrate on his piano playing rather than promoting his own compositions, as performing was financially more rewarding? On October 14, still in Vienna, he was writing to Frohnleiten:[38] "I'm happy to be able to send you 90 florins. Frau von Wertheimstein was so kind as to give me another 100 florins, 10 of which I am keeping for my little needs." This was not the first time that autumn that Ferruccio had sent his father money from Vienna donated by his patient patrons. His monthly allowance from the Baronin von Todesco also went straight to Frohnleiten. His mother sent him news of a composing competition organized by the London Philharmonic, and he wrote immediately for information. Nothing came of this. Attempts to renew contact with the impresario Tandler also proved fruitless. A tour of America was mentioned. On October 25

Ferruccio finally went to Frohnleiten, but returned to Vienna on November 4—with his father. (Mopsi, a new canine acquisition, also accompanied him. There was to be a lot about Mopsi in subsequent letters to his mother, although the dog's subsequent fate is unknown.)

Busoni's plans for the future, in spite of his own efforts and those of his friends, were still vague. He nevertheless seemed to have a much shrewder awareness of realities than his parents: on November 27 he wrote to his mother,[39] who had asked his plans and suggested a tour of Germany:

> Without publicity you can't make money, and for publicity you need money too. In Germany I'm not known, and who would come to my concerts? And how can the journey be made, and the long distances separating one city from another? In Leipzig, for example, there are loads of concerts; the hall will be booked for many weeks ahead, one would have to wait. Who would pay for this wait?

It was suggested that he tour Germany together with another musician, one Walter, but his father was against this, as Busoni would as pianist appear in a secondary role.

Ferruccio gave two recitals in Vienna in December, generally badly received—salt rubbed into the wounds of his suite fiasco. (On December 22 he had written to Anna,[40] "I don't speak to Richter any more and avoid meeting him, not trusting myself—something aroused in me.") His self-confidence asserted itself in his writing a further two articles, both on Hans von Bülow, for the Trieste newspaper L'Indipendente.[41] His grandfather, who had read all his articles with great interest, was particularly delighted by the fact that Ferruccio signed these two with his own name.

On January 12, 1885, Anna Busoni celebrated (if that is the right word), her fiftieth birthday in Trieste, her husband and son far away in Vienna. Prematurely aged, relentlessly self-sacrificing, one can only feel pity at the poor hand fate dealt her. Ferruccio and Ferdinando sent a bluff and hearty letter the day after her birthday:[42] "Mia buona Anna," wrote her husband, "At this moment, half past nine in the evening, we have drunk a toast to your health and to your birthday."

On January 25 Ferruccio took part in a concert that included his song setting of Ernst Freiherr von Feuchtersleben's poem "Es ist bestimmt in Gottes Rat" (BV 216), composed the previous year.[43] "Signora Chavanne [Irene Chavanne, 1863–1938, one-time piano pupil of Wilhelm Mayer], who has a most beautiful contralto voice, was able to bring out my works quite well and did them honor."[44] By February 1885, Ferruccio had, in spite of the above reservations, collected money for a German tour from various well-wishers, old and new. (Whatever their shortcomings, those faithful stalwarts, Frau von Wertheimstein and the Baronin von Todesco, both continued to pay him a monthly allowance until he was twenty-one. Frau von Wertheimstein seems to have been the kindlier character: on February 10 Ferruccio wrote that "in the last 'conflict' [presumably on his future] the Wertheimstein proved as always good and reasonable, the Baronin sarcastic and distrustful. One has to appreciate the one and put up with the other.")[45] Grandfather Weiss had also donated two hundred florins for the tour, though his donation was jeopardized by a breakdown in communication between Ferruccio and his mother, both of whom had asked separately for the money. On February 25 Ferruccio left for Leipzig, Ferdinando clinging on limpet-like: he no longer trusted his son not to spend any money obtained on himself and flighty pleasures. There was no evidence that his distrust was justified; no doubt Ferdinando expected Ferruccio to behave the way he himself had behaved as a young man.

Leipzig proved welcoming; the Dutch violinist Henri Petri (1856–1914) and his group played Ferruccio's String Quartet in C (BV 208, date of composition unknown, but probably 1884),[46] and one Fräulein Görlich sang some of his songs at very short notice at a public recital, after Marie Fillunger, the soprano originally billed, had "the happy inspiration of no longer wanting to."[47] Brahms had kindly given Ferruccio a written introduction to Carl Reinecke (1824–1910), the conductor of the Gewandhaus Orchestra and a professor at the Leipzig Conservatory. (Brahms is said to have stated, "I will do for Busoni what Schumann did for me.") Ferruccio also went the rounds of the Leipzig music publishers and managed to sell some of his recent compositions.[48]

On March 26 the two Busonis went on to Berlin, staying at the Grand Hotel on the Alexanderplatz. The pianist and composer Eugen d'Albert, only two years Ferruccio's senior, whom he had met in Vienna, was also in Berlin, and the two young men went off to a piano concert together two days after the Busonis's arrival. Only on April 14,

nearly three weeks after his arrival, did Ferruccio perform his first concert in Berlin: at the Singakademie he played his Variations and Fugue
on Chopin's Prelude in C Minor, which he had premiered in Vienna in
January. He gained a favorable impression of the city. "I am enchanted
by Berlin," he wrote his mother,[49] "which is a city rather more grand,
more modern, more beautiful, more lively than Vienna. The streets are
all well lit, clean, wide, very long and straight." The people were
"rather less Prussian" than he expected. But his assessment of the difficulties of touring proved correct—by mid-May, after two more concerts
in Vienna, father and son were back in Frohnleiten, where they were
to remain almost exclusively until November 1886—eighteen
months—and where Ferruccio spent his twentieth birthday.

Why? At first Ferruccio gave the decision to stay in Frohnleiten a
positive explanation, in a letter to his mother of May 5, 1885,[50] from
Vienna. (This is one of the many occasions when the lack of letters
from Ferruccio's parents is most frustrating for a biographer.)

Your last letters (including the one *Babbo* received yesterday) seem to
me to demonstrate anxiety and suffering for which I cannot fathom the
cause. I see that the substitution of *Babbo*'s letters by mine [i.e., that he
was writing the letters and not his father] has caused your present state
of mind and I understand that [the fact that] the author of my days
has explained to you our affairs, our circumstances, in a rather brusque
manner—inevitably resulted in your bad mood. The devil is not as bad
as he is painted, nor as *Babbo* describes him and even if the *present* leaves
something to be desired, we must enjoy the pleasant memories of the
past (and this refers to my recent successes) and trust in a good future,
to which hope my abilities and my firm resolve give a right. So don't go
distressing yourself, nor running breathlessly around Trieste preparing a
concert that I (between ourselves, now that *Babbo* has gone out) have
no intention of giving. Neither the season, nor the artistic means Trieste
offers, are suitable to these plans, of which I cannot expect a favorable
result. Furthermore it has been suggested to me to *keep quiet* [*tacere*] for
a few years, both in Vienna and Trieste, and thirdly, I hope rather to go
into the country where I look forward to serious and dedicated work.

Meanwhile, waiting for a reply from the Baronin, to which (as I
avoided a face-to-face discussion) la Bettelheim has served as intermediary, who has shown herself recently quite in my favor)—so awaiting a
reply I spend the time here writing and playing and am resting a bit after the strains of the tour.

Meanwhile *Babbo* has returned and has read the above. The fact should calm you down that he too seems to be of my opinion and to give up the idea of Trieste.

Because of the convolutions of the rather rococo prose style Ferruccio used in his letters to his mother, and failing input from the parents, this letter does not really offer us a clear picture. We do not know who made the recommendation to "keep quiet" for a few years, nor the full reasoning behind it, but as Ferruccio then mentions the "Baronin" (von Todesco), from whom he is expecting "a reply," the finger points in the direction of Vienna. And why was "keeping quiet" synonymous with staying in Frohnleiten? Why not with his mother (and, indeed, father) in Trieste? It was strange advice: at this stage in his career, after the impetus—admittedly of limited success, but at least a beginning—of his tour to Leipzig and Berlin, to remove himself from all stimulus to a provincial town. In a postcard to his mother from Frohnleiten of May 15,[51] to announce his arrival there, Ferruccio writes of staying there "the whole summer" only. By mid-June, however, indications are that a longer stay was planned: thanks to the kindness of the Baronin von Todesco, father and son had rented accommodation, in the Villa Audolensky, and had acquired some furniture, but no bedding. In the letter containing this news[52] there is a list of items Anna is requested to send, and the almost grotesquely formal invitation (though possibly containing a hint of sarcasm): "If later you have time and inclination to come and see us, a bed will always be at your disposal." Ferruccio was definitely not happy in Frohnleiten, as his letters to Melanie Mayer, written later that summer, make clear, with their frequent references to boredom and frustration.

The sole companionship of his father also proved detrimental. Tyrannical, lazy, and weak-willed, Ferdinando had now boxed himself into a corner where his own career was concerned, and willy-nilly was blocking what, given Ferruccio's outstanding and generally recognized talent, should have been a relatively smooth upward progression. Ferdinando seemed quite content to have Anna far away in Trieste, sending him money whenever she could, and unable to witness his idle flâneur's life, redeemed if at all by his acting more or less as his son's valet.

To add to his unhappiness, in Frohnleiten Ferruccio became romantically involved with an older (and presumably married) woman, an affair that ended abruptly and painfully and of which only von Kapff was informed—and sworn to secrecy. Although Ferruccio kept occupied practicing—usually four hours a day—he felt imprisoned, and spent hours at the Frohnleiten rail station with an aching heart, watching the trains leaving for the outside world: a habit that was resumed in Zurich when he was in his fifties, in another period of enforced immobility during World War I. Significantly, other than initial sketches for an opera, only four compositions can be dated with any certainty as written in 1885, and the only known composition for the whole of 1886 is a set of five variations for piano, on Siegfried Ochs's Variations on the folk song "Kommt a Vogerl g'flogen" (BV 222).

Indeed, the days of prolific composition were now over: more than two-thirds of Busoni's total known output was written before 1886, although quantity should not, of course, be equated with quality here. Composition was harder for him now, he wrote to his mother[53] in June 1885, "as I write with greater seriousness and care and also less easily than before." "I'm quite content with the very regular life I lead here," he continues (it was still early days),

and the division of my hours which allows me to do everything. To play, to compose, to write, to think, to go for walks. If I said above that I compose with less facility, don't let this worry you. A few days ago, comparing my new works with the old compositions, I noted such progress that I really should not be saddened by this apparent sterility. I look forward to being able to send you in a few months my variations and fugue on the Chopin Prelude and the latter astonished Mayer in every regard and he considers it quite superior to my previous works, including the so-called Fugen-Etude.

At present I am working on a *quartet*, the first movement of which (of which the themes are almost all invented) promises very well. I don't know if I already told you I have composed a male *chorus* for a competition and have already sent it off. A propos competitions, Did you know that the Società del Quartetto di Milano has assigned a prize of 1000 francs for the best string quartet, and I counted on sending my present work in time for the deadline set. But I don't know what this is and I would like to have the circular containing the conditions of the competition. Could you manage to procure it for me in such a way that my name is not revealed. You have to write to the administration or the secretary of the Società del Quartetto di Milano.

Ferruccio had sent his mother a photograph of himself sporting a beard, and she was terrified by the change in him from child to man. His reply,[54] as so often, made him seem by far the more mature of the two:

> Do realize that I'm no longer a child and soon not even a youth and at a manly age, the face also takes on an expression of manliness [virilità], the features become mature and more marked. This is no cause for you to nurture doubts on my behalf; continue to have faith in your son, who loves you and is fully intent on doing his duty by working to provide a peaceful existence for you and a contented old age. And don't put a bad construction on it if I'm forced to be sincere in refusing to go along with your wish regarding religious rites. I don't think I'm under the obligation of justifying my actions to anyone else.

Ouch! There were inevitably tensions with his father too. (*Faute de mieux*, Ferdinando had been practicing the clarinet hard, and in May had given a very successful concert at nearby Leoben, which did little to sweeten his temper, however.)

During that summer, after much persuading, Anna did in fact join them for most of July and August. The reason for her hesitation, she finally confessed, was that she had no money. Ferruccio, appalled, sent seventy florins, and a list of books and other essentials she must bring. (For all the many letters, the lack of meaningful communication between the three is often startling.) There must have been some stormy scenes during the summer, as Ferruccio writes to his mother after her return in late August,[55] "*Babbo* and I are fully reconciled and I have decided to remain here for the two months I had planned." In early September[56] Ferruccio finally lays out their whole financial situation and suggests to his mother how she might help in solving their difficulties.

> You ask me to be frank and I shall be. In the last few days we have calculated the amount of our debts and how much we still have to spend during the two months we count on staying here, and we have come to persuade ourselves that it will be scarcely possible to cover the deficit if you do not come to our aid with the sale of the piano. I understand it's hard for you to take this step, but on the other hand think what a service you are rendering, think that your instrument is reduced to such a

state as to take away any pleasure in owning it and is such that any rented piano would be superior to it. So the loss in itself is not serious and I—this must not be a promise—hope soon to be able to make good the sacrifice with the gift of a new piano.

It is the first time that I have asked you to sacrifice something dear to you and I certainly would not do so if I had other means at my disposal. But the sources are almost exhausted and I would be very happy not to have to count on them from now on. For I have avoided turning to la Wertheimstein in order not to get caught up in unpleasant and too frequent discussions. Having to account for every step I take and having to put up with continuous disapproval is for me a painful and humiliating thing and I have already put up with it too long. So without hastening the sale—as this could damage our interests—do try to rid yourself of that old crock [carcassa] and excuse my frankness and the displeasure that I fear I have given you.

It is not known how the former concert pianist—not to mention wife and mother—received this egoistic and appallingly brutal appeal, nor whether she acted on it. What is known is that her husband and son remained in Frohnleiten, and old Giuseppe Weiss opened his wallet yet again.

In October and in November, despite protestations in the summer that he would not perform there, Ferruccio gave a total of four very successful concerts in Trieste, attended by his proud grandfather (as described with some amusement by Ferruccio in a letter to his father).[57] As his letters also reveal, Ferruccio himself had to arrange the hire of a hall and alert the local press. But after such brief and infrequent forays it was always back to Frohnleiten.

During his eight-week stay in Vienna in autumn 1884 Ferruccio looked into various subjects for an opera; several projects were discussed that came to nothing, but by chance he happened upon a story by Rudolf Baumbach (1840–1905), a popular poet at the time, "Sigune, oder das stille Dorf" (Sigune, or the Silent Village). By December 1885 Ferruccio was working hard at an opera version. Via Otto von Kapff, he had met a young couple while he was in Berlin, Ludwig Soyaux and his wife, Frida Schanz, a poetess, who together wrote the libretto—allegedly: in fact it was the work of Frida Schanz. (Four years later Soyaux had to threaten legal action in order to wrest from Busoni the final 200 marks due for writing the libretto!) Although Busoni worked at the score until May 1889, the work was never completed. The story is no more preposterous than many another opera plot, but it is nonetheless mystifying that Busoni, the great literature enthusiast, should have singled this particular one out.

A young stonemason, Diethart, working on a cathedral, goes walking in the forest one summer's day and sees a vision of a village and a beautiful girl, Sigune, who gives him a golden ring. She and the village vanish. She appears to him in a dream the following night and they plight their troth. The next morning, however, Diethart has forgotten the dream. He marries the girl he was already betrothed to, Lenore, but after the wedding Sigune appears to him and he remembers his vows to her. They die together.

Apart from the near doggerel of the libretto, the opera is further coarsened by too much additional action, which renders the main story line incoherent. But already here, as with his four operas written in maturity, Busoni was drawn to surreal subject matter.

The year 1886 was punctuated by an occasional concert in nearby Graz and by financial vexations: in January, the Baronin von Todesco had forgotten (not for the first time) to send the monthly allowance; Frau von Wertheimstein, having promised money, had not written. Ferruccio was bored and demoralized. (Could Anna send his easel and paints? he wrote in mid-January.)[58] For his twentieth birthday, on April 1, his mother sent Ferruccio Chateaubriand's *Le Génie du christianisme* (1802). The son was scarcely grateful:

> Having nothing to read, the arrival of a book was very appropriate—I don't mean—forgive my usual frankness—that "Le génie du chrétinisme" [cretinism] (sorry! christianisme) is exactly appropriate. It is a book that, as I suppose, other than exalting things and customs that are not to my taste, contains philosophical opinions of other times and that cannot be applied to the situation and the social conditions of today. Nevertheless, I *promise* to read it from beginning to end.[59]

Although not the first critic to condemn a book before he has read it, here Ferruccio more or less hit the nail on the head. He had long distanced himself from Anna's narrow piety, as indeed from organized religion. Separated from husband and son, enduring her father's unpleasant domestic setup, Anna had retreated more and more into her religious faith. Ferruccio at twenty, intensely frustrated as he was, had little understanding of or sympathy for her predicament.

A main confidante was still Melanie Mayer, in conversations—Graz was only eighteen miles away, and Ferruccio visited the Mayers there frequently—or in letters. Even though she was always "*Liebes Fräulein*" and addressed with the polite "*Sie*" form (as his senior she always called him "Ferruccio" and "*Du*"), the letters betray the intimacy of being able to get this and that off his chest (*"über dieses und jenes ausplauschen zu können"*).[60] "Yesterday I read of the death of the composer Ponchielli," he wrote in the same letter, "which made me very sad. In spite of his bad music he was a good soul, simple and without envy. In Milan I enjoyed his personal acquaintance. The days here resemble one another like two drops of water (the drops are mostly frozen)." A week later Ferruccio gives a comic account of missing the train back to Frohnleiten after visiting the Mayers,[61] and at the end of March he alludes coyly to his abortive love affair.[62] But even this outlet was cut off in April by her mother's above-mentioned veto on further letters—in spite of which more letters followed, all with excuses, such as information for the Mayers on house rents in Frohnleiten in summer,[63] or because he was anxious about the publication dates of the essay he had written on Italian music for the *Grazer Tagespost*.[64]

The essay, entitled "Musikzustände in Italien" (The State of Music in Italy), appeared in three installments, on August 31, September 3, and October 20, 1886. It formed a useful corrective to the current dismissive German view of the Italian musical scene, in that it shrewdly and evenhandedly set Italian music—in effect opera—firmly in its Italian historical context. Bilingual by now, and equally at home in both cultures, Busoni—as indeed throughout his life—refused to take sides, certainly in any futile point scoring, which did not mean that he was blind to the defects in either culture.

There was a mild panic that summer when it looked as though Ferruccio might have to return to Italy for military service, but after an interview in Vienna in September with the Italian ambassador, who required an examination by a doctor, and a lot of correspondence with Empoli, the situation was resolved—presumably on health grounds.

Gradually Ferruccio was steeling his resolve to escape from Frohn-leiten and take over his own destiny. Finally, on November 17, 1886, he said goodbye to his father and boarded the train for Vienna. What he did not tell his father on the platform was that he was not coming back. He intended to go to Leipzig, which, his instincts and experience there told him, would be the best place at this time in his life. Not only did it have a very lively musical performance scene, but this in turn at-tracted a lot of young composers—a huge magnet for someone starved of the stimulus of musical intercourse.

Ferruccio wrote a postcard[65] to his father immediately upon his ar-rival in Vienna, and the next day he wrote a long letter to his mother[66] frankly setting out the situation and informing her of his Leipzig plan.

I am in Vienna and this is why. In spite of the quite considerable sums I was able to scrape together in recent times in Graz, almost three hun-dred florins still remained to be paid in Frohnleiten. Now these sums should have covered (such was the intended purpose) these debts and made my journey to Leipzig possible. Having returned to Frohnleiten from Madame R.'s soirée with another hundred florins, Papa gave no sign of helping me move out of there, and having entered into a discus-sion on this subject, he started talking about waiting, of sorting things out, waiting for the right moment, and so on. Now here is the reflection I made, and that he at first did not want to understand. Stopping here in Frohnleiten, "in peace" (as *Babbo* said), I would have no prospects, nor any probability of acquiring anything to cover those debts; *certainty*, on the other hand, of *increasing* them, the more so as the Baronin, this year, will have stopped sending the monthly fifty florins. So that, in another three months, I would find myself in a mess, with considerably greater obligations, there, enchained, and more than ever in difficulties.

Furthermore, as he put it to his mother in the rather stately, formal Italian he often hid behind when telling her uncomfortable truths:

The inertia of that isolated place was no longer appropriate to my years. All Mayer's pupils have been able to gain a position abroad; should not I, who know quite a lot more than they do, succeed? I can't go on like this, living in constant uncertainty regarding tomorrow, in part on the favors of generous patronesses, and in part on the indulgence of creditors! I can-not bear any longer the idea of not relying on myself for my daily bread.

With the little money he had, and what he might collect in Vienna, Ferruccio would go on to Leipzig, with the aim of creating an independent existence. The thought of yet another dismal winter in Frohnleiten was unbearable: "Both of us staying there watching the snow falling—definitely not!" As he knew it would be, the letter was immediately forwarded to his father. He also knew that his father, tied to Frohnleiten by debts, would not be able to extricate himself immediately and follow him.

Since Ferruccio's childhood, other than the sums Anna had sent from Trieste and the odd contribution from Ferdinando, financial support for the family had come through him. One advantage of this was that now he was in control of the situation, and had no intention of having either parent follow him to Leipzig. He had clearly visited the Mayers when he had last been in Graz on what was more or less a begging expedition, as the above letter to his mother indicates, and they were aware of his plan, and obviously approved of it. Now, sitting in the Café Scheidl in Vienna at one in the morning, he wrote excitedly to Melanie:[67] "I write to you in the joy of freedom finally achieved, and in the glorious consciousness of the tasks awaiting me. . . . I can hear your mother exclaiming, 'Isn't that the typical young artist of twenty, who has just found his wings!'" It conjures up a charming picture, but also reveals the rather extraordinary situation, in which he had to recruit mature and level-headed accomplices like the Mayers in order effectively to deceive his parents, and demonstrates yet again the strength of mind and stoicism required to make that begging expedition to Graz and face more of the same in Vienna.

The Baronin von Todesco and Frau von Wertheimstein approved Ferruccio's plans too. "I've just come from the Baronin," he informed his father on November 24,[68] "who is *inclined* to support me, but was still unable to get anything today. For Friday (the day after tomorrow) I have been invited and then I hope to settle the matter." She finally gave him two hundred florins—a large chunk of which was immediately dispatched to his father. Frau von Wertheimstein also contributed. Hans Richter proved unavailable yet again. Eugen d'Albert, now back in Vienna, was friendly and encouraging. The two young men had dined with the agent and publisher Albert Gutmann the day after Ferruccio's arrival in Vienna. Gutmann had published several of Ferruccio's works and seemed keen to help him get some work.

Two days after Ferruccio arrived in the city, Karl Goldmark's opera *Merlin* was premiered at the Hofoper and Ferruccio was given a ticket ("unoriginal and boring," he wrote to Melanie).[69] In the opera house he saw the Milanese music publisher Giovannina Lucca, who had published some of his work years before, and made sure to talk to her. "I seized a favorable moment, namely when she started raving about my beautiful hair,"[70] to secure a commission for "a little piano piece," for which she gave one hundred florins up front to "il mio caro Büsonetto," as Ferruccio comically reported she addressed him.[71] He worked hard, collecting money from any possible source, and preparing the next step, patiently allaying his father's fears—no, he would not go off on tour with one Weiser, an eighteen-year-old violinist; no, he would not team up with d'Albert—always passing on a portion of whatever money he received to Frohnleiten.

Twelve days after arriving in Vienna, he boarded the train for Leipzig.

Notes

1. Melanie Prelinger [née Mayer], "Erinnerungen und Briefe aus Ferruccio Busonis Jugendzeit," *Neue Musikzeitung*, 1927, Heft 1, pp. 6–10, Heft 2, pp. 31–40, Heft 3, pp. 57–61.

2. Wilhelm Kienzl, *Meine Lebenswanderung—Erlebtes und Erschautes*, [Vienna?], 1926.

3. "Nachruf für Dr W. Mayer," reprinted in Busoni, *Wesen und Einheit der Musik* (not in English edition), pp. 191–94.

4. Letter from FB to Otto von Kapff, October 1, 1880, StBB Bus. Nachl. 602.

5. Now in the State Library in Berlin as part of the Busoni Nachlass.

6. Letter from FB to Ferdinando Busoni, June 7, 1881, StBB Bus. Nachl. 998.

7. Pietro Bianchini (1828–1905), composer, violinist, and conductor. From 1878 to 1887 he was an orchestral player and taught counterpoint and composition in Trieste.

8. Letter from FB to Ferdinando Busoni, June 10, 1881, StBB Bus. Nachl. 999.

9. Reproduced, with analysis, by Roberto Gorini Falco in his "Una fuga scolastica di Busoni," in *Musica Università*, Istituzione Universitaria dei Concerti dell'Università di Roma, vol. 4, no. 23 (December 1966), pp. 27–29.

10. In Archivio R. Accademia Filarmonica, Bologna, 1882 file, March 27, 1882.

11. Reproduced in Busoni, *The Essence of Music*, pp. 167–70.

12. See Dent, *Ferruccio Busoni*, p. 43.

13. Letter from FB to Giovannina Lucca, October 24, 1882, in *Ferruccio Busoni: Lettere*, trans. and ed. Sergio Sablich (Milan: Ricordi/Unicopli, 1988), p. 34.

14. Letter from FB to Giovannina Lucca, May 4, 1883, in Sablich, *Lettere*, p. 35.

15. Letter from FB to Antonio Zampieri, July 5, 1883, in Sablich, *Lettere*, p. 35.

16. Postcard from FB to Anna Weiss-Busoni, October 10, 1883, StBB Bus. Nachl. 1008.

17. Letter from FB to Anna Weiss-Busoni, October 14, 1883, StBB Bus. Nachl. 1009.

18. Letter from FB to Anna Weiss-Busoni, October 17, 1883, StBB Bus. Nachl. 1013.

19. Letter from FB to Anna Weiss-Busoni, November [7?], 1883, StBB Bus. Nachl. 1011.

20. Letter from FB to Anna Weiss-Busoni, November 13, 1883, StBB Bus. Nachl. 1012.

21. Letter from FB to Anna Weiss-Busoni, December 6, 1883, StBB Bus. Nachl. 1017.

22. Letter from FB to Anna Weiss-Busoni, December 2, 1883, StBB Bus. Nachl. 1016.

23. Letter from Wilhelm Mayer to FB, December 27, 1883, Dent Papers EJD/2/1, King's College Library, Cambridge.

24. Letter from FB to Anna Weiss-Busoni, January 18, 1884, StBB Bus. Nachl. 1028.

25. Letter from FB to Anna Weiss-Busoni, February 16, 1884, StBB Bus. Nachl. 1031.

26. Letter from FB to Anna Weiss-Busoni, March 31, 1884, StBB Bus. Nachl. 1034.

27. FB to Anna Weiss-Busoni, March 31, 1884.

28. FB to Anna Weiss-Busoni, March 31, 1884.

29. FB to Anna Weiss-Busoni, March 31, 1884.

30. Letter from Luigi Cimoso to Ferdinando Busoni, October 1883, Rowe Music Library, Dent Papers EJD/2/1, King's College Library, Cambridge.

31. Letter from FB to Anna Weiss-Busoni, July 10, 1884, StBB Bus. Nachl. 1041.

32. BV 207. Published by Kistner, Leipzig, 1885. "Unter den Linden" was set again for voice and small orchestra in 1893. It remains unpublished.

33. Postcard from FB to Ferdinando Busoni, September 3, 1884, StBB Bus. Nachl. 1064.

34. Letter from FB to Anna Weiss-Busoni, September 10, 1884, StBB Bus. Nachl. 1051.

35. Letter from FB to Ferdinando Busoni, October 6, 1884, StBB Bus. Nachl. 1095.

36. FB to Ferdinando Busoni, October 6, 1884.

37. FB to Ferdinando Busoni, October 6, 1884.

38. Letter from FB to Ferdinando Busoni, October 14, 1884, StBB Bus. Nachl. 1102.

39. Letter from FB to Anna Weiss-Busoni, November 27, 1884, StBB Bus. Nachl. 1057.

40. Letter from FB to Anna Weiss-Busoni, December 22, 1884, StBB Bus. Nachl. 1061.

41. L'Indipendente, Trieste, December 1884.

42. Letter from Ferruccio and Ferdinando Busoni to Anna Weiss-Busoni, January 13, 1885, StBB Bus. Nachl. 1117.

43. Published, together with his setting of Theodor Fontane's "Es zieht sich eine blut'ge Spur," in Leipzig by Kahnt [or Breitkopf und Härtel?] in 1887. It is not certain which song was performed in addition to the Feuchtersleben setting, as no copies survive of the 1887 edition (see note 46 below).

44. Letter from FB to Anna Weiss-Busoni, January 26, 1885, StBB Bus. Nachl. 1118.

45. Letter from FB to Anna Weiss-Busoni, February 10, 1885, StBB Bus. Nachl. 1120.

46. So much was destroyed in Germany during World War II that, barring the fortuitous discovery of copies, information on much of Busoni's published output remains conjectural.

47. Letter from FB to Anna Weiss-Busoni, March 17, 1885, StBB Bus. Nachl. 1125.

48. Two Old German Songs for Voice and Piano (BV 207); String Quartet in C (BV 208); Second Ballet Scene for Piano (BV 209); Variations and Fugue on the Prelude in C Minor, op. 28, no. 20, by Chopin for Piano (BV 213).

49. Letter from FB to Anna Weiss-Busoni, March 31, 1885, StBB Bus. Nachl. 1127.

50. Letter from FB to Anna Weiss-Busoni, May 5, 1885, StBB Bus. Nachl. 1129.

51. Postcard from FB to Anna Weiss-Busoni, May 14, 1885, StBB Bus. Nachl. 1130.

52. Letter from FB to Anna Weiss-Busoni, June [May?] 16, 1885, StBB Bus. Nachl. 1131.

53. Letter from FB to Anna Weiss-Busoni, June 8, 1885, StBB Bus. Nachl. 1132.

54. FB to Anna Weiss-Busoni, June 8, 1885.

55. Letter from FB to Anna Weiss-Busoni, August 30, 1885, StBB Bus. Nachl. 1140.

56. Letter from FB to Anna Weiss-Busoni, September 4, 1885, StBB Bus. Nachl. 1141.

57. Letter from FB to Ferdinando Busoni, October 18, 1885, StBB Bus. Nachl. 1108.

58. Letter from FB to Anna Weiss-Busoni, January 14, 1886, StBB Bus. Nachl. 1151.

59. Letter from FB to Anna Weiss-Busoni, April 7, 1886, StBB Bus. Nachl. 1156.

60. Letter from FB to Melanie Mayer, January 21, 1886, StBB Bus. Nachl. 372

61. Letter from FB to Melanie Mayer, January 29, 1886, StBB Bus. Nachl. 373.

62. Letter from FB to Melanie Mayer, March 29, 1886, StBB Bus. Nachl. 376.

63. Letter from FB to Melanie Mayer, April 18, 1886, StBB Bus. Nachl. 377.

64. Letter from FB to Melanie Mayer, May 5, 1886, StBB Bus. Nachl. 378.

65. Postcard from FB to Ferdinando Busoni, November 17, 1886, StBB Bus. Nachl. 1167.

66. Letter from FB to Anna Weiss-Busoni, November 18, 1886, StBB Bus. Nachl. 1164.

67. Letter from FB to Melanie Mayer, November 18, 1886, StBB Bus. Nachl. 387.

68. Postcard from FB to Ferdinando Busoni, November 24, 1886, StBB Bus. Nachl. 1173.

69. Letter from FB to Melanie Mayer, November 21, 1886, StBB Bus. Nachl. 388.

70. FB to Melanie Mayer, November 21, 1886.

71. Letter from FB to Ferdinando Busoni, November 21, 1886, StBB Bus. Nachl. 1171.

CHAPTER FOUR

~

Leipzig: December 1886 to September 1888

In Leipzig, Ferruccio immediately sent a postcard[1] to his father to say he had arrived safely, and the next day he followed it up with a letter[2] containing a complete breakdown of where the 200 Austrian florins given him by the Baronin von Todesco had gone—fifty, as Ferdinando well knew, had gone to him; the rest of the Vienna hotel bill came to thirty; tips, eight; journey to Leipzig, forty; leaving Ferruccio with seventy-two. (Meticulous though these calculations are, throughout his life Ferruccio's sums and general accounts of his financial situation often leave a few questions hanging in the mind, such as: Did he really have only 200 florins when he left Vienna?) Ferruccio still had hopes of receiving a regular monthly amount from the baronin, but aspired to pay his own way. By December 5, three days after his arrival, he had found third-floor rooms in the home of a captain's widow, Frau Thekla Spann, at 14 Centralstrasse (now Zentralstrasse—the whole area was almost totally destroyed during the latter stages of World War II). The rooms were very close to the Thomaskirche, revered as the church where J. S. Bach had performed so many of his works when he was resident organist there: a good omen, Ferruccio thought. Board and lodging, all inclusive, came to seventy-five marks a month, payable in advance: cheap, as he told his father, as it was in a good quarter where one could receive anyone. (At this time, one Austrian florin was worth roughly 1.60 German marks, therefore his seventy-five marks monthly rent equaled around forty-seven florins.) Ferruccio described Frau Spann a few days later to Melanie as

> a lady of a certain culture and very intelligent, with whom one can converse sensibly on various matters. But I only see her at mealtimes and then briefly, since the food leaves something to be desired, not only as regards quality, but also quantity. But the price is so reasonable that when a meal is really too insufficient I go straight to a restaurant to follow it with "supplementary volume."[3]

(Soon after, Ferruccio's opinion of Frau Spann apparently sank: "I have made the terrible discovery," he wrote to Melanie at the end of December,[4] "that my landlady—is an authoress; she actually writes under the name Thekla (!) Spann-Weber." Unaware of this horrendous fact, he had actually remarked to the poor woman a few days before that he had an antipathy to women writers. It did not seem to occur to him that this might offend Melanie as well.)

The Sunday after his arrival Ferruccio was to make a "rather advantageous"[5] debut at the hall of the Liszt-Verein, a society to which all the critics belonged. He was to play his own Short Suite for Cello and Piano (BV 215, one of the few works written in 1885), with Alwin Schröder (1855–1928), its dedicatee, a member of the Petri Quartet, who had played Busoni's String Quartet in C (BV 208) in February 1885. The Short Suite was well received and a good start to Ferruccio's stay in Leipzig.

Just before the concert, "when I really didn't have a Pfennig in my pocket," as he rather dramatically and not quite accurately described it to his father,[6] he bumped into Oskar Schwalm, then a young man, and briefly (1886–1888) the owner of the music publishing firm of C. F. Kahnt, and asked him for work. Schwalm offered him 150 marks—fifty marks down, the rest on completion—to write a fantasia for piano on Peter Cornelius's opera Der Barbier von Bagdad, which the firm had just published (some twelve years after the composer's death, and almost thirty after the work was premiered in Weimar). The next day Ferruccio called on the astonished Schwalm with the completed manuscript and was able to collect the whole sum—eighty of which went off immediately to his father. He had worked from 9:00 P.M. until 3:30 A.M., without a piano, and (shades of Mozart) there was not a single correction on the manuscript. A piano arrived only the day after, and Ferruccio knew he would need money to pay the transporters.

On his arrival in Leipzig he had been given a very friendly welcome by Henri Petri, leader of the Petri Quartet. The Petris were settled in Leipzig, and Henri and his wife Kathi and their young son Egon, then aged six, were to become very important in Ferruccio's life from then on. His first Christmas without either parent was made more than bearable thanks mainly to the Petris's friendship and hospitality. (For that matter, as far as can be deduced from letters to his parents, Ferdinando and Anna did not spend Christmas together either: on December 24 Ferruccio sent a letter to his father in Frohnleiten, on January 4 he wrote to his mother in Trieste,[7] telling her about his Christmas, thanking her for her Christmas present—Giorgio Vasari's *The Lives of the Most Eminent Italian Architects, Painters and Sculptors*, which was good for his Italian, "that I am constantly afraid of forgetting"—and saying that if she thought the letter would interest his father, could she please send it on.) His own present to himself was the latest twelve-volume edition of Becker's Universal History, bought with some of the money earned from the fantasia, as he told his mother in the same letter. (In his earlier letter to his father recounting the whole fantasia episode, the money was accounted for rather differently.)

Heavy snowfall in the second half of December had left Leipzig isolated; in places snowdrifts on the railway lines were up to thirteen feet deep. Nevertheless, on December 23 an unknown benefactor sent Ferruccio a hamper of food and drink. The Baronin von Todesco sent eighty marks to get him through January; he could not send any of it to his father, he wrote,[8] as it was needed for rent, laundry, provisions, and (surprising to our eyes, perhaps, for a twenty-year-old) cigars. Other friends were generous: Henri Petri gave him a book on Schiller, Kathi Petri a match holder with cigar-cutter and ashtray. The Mayers sent a parcel of different foods done up in the shape of a doll, plus a very witty letter, both equally appreciated.

In mid-January 1887 Ferruccio gave a concert in Graz, then returned to Leipzig, where he gave another concert almost immediately after at the home of Dr. Max Abraham (1831–1900, from 1863 a partner in the

C. F. Peters music publishing firm and from 1880 sole owner), garnering praise and useful connections: Professor Hermann Scholtz, who had overseen the C. F. Peters's edition of Chopin's works, recommended him to Dresden for concerts. Eugen d'Albert, that other young pianist-composer, whom Ferruccio had met in Vienna, was in Leipzig in January for a concert, and came to call. Ferruccio was still working hard at his opera *Sigune*, begun in 1885, whenever possible, and hopeful of finding a publisher.

On February 28 he played in Dresden at the invitation of the highly influential Tonkünstler Verein (Musicians' Association). Unfortunately, as it was a private occasion, not only did he receive no fee or expenses, but no critics reviewed it. The trip was made possible thanks only to the Baronin von Todesco, who sent him his monthly allowance at the last minute. He nonetheless thought the trip worthwhile, and he was well received. He played Carl Tausig's piano transcription of Bach's Toccata and Fugue in D Minor, some Handel, Domenico Scarlatti, and Chopin.

The going was hard, but at last he felt Ferruccio was moving forward, and more in control of his life than he had ever been before. Not only C. F. Kahnt, but also Breitkopf und Härtel and C. F. Peters, were interested in publishing his work. Dr. Max Abraham was a kindly figure in Ferruccio's life, not only arranging the concert in his own home, but giving Ferruccio free copies of any Peters scores he thought might be of interest (Carl Maria von Weber's *Euryanthe* and *Oberon*, Heinrich August Marschner's *Der Vampyr*, a Bach mass, and "the stupendous score,"[9] as Ferruccio described it, of Adrien Boieldieu's *La Dame blanche*). The next autumn Abraham was to introduce him to Edvard Grieg, whose works were also published by Peters. Grieg, then in his mid-forties, was on one of his by now habitual autumn and winter concert tours and spending some time in Leipzig, as he had done the winter before. Through Grieg Ferruccio met Frederick Delius, his elder by four years, who after two years in the United States had come to Leipzig in August 1886 as a mature student to enroll in the conservatory, considered the best in Europe at the time. He had therefore arrived in Leipzig a few months before Ferruccio: it is frustrating to think they lived a whole year in the same city before meeting. With both Grieg and Delius, Busoni was to form lasting friendships, and throughout his life he promoted their music whenever the opportunity offered.

He also met Gustav Mahler during this time, although a real friendship between the two developed only later. Mahler was six years Busoni's senior, and at twenty-six had made enough of a name for himself as a conductor to have been appointed in July 1886 as second conductor of the Gewandhaus Orchestra, of which Henri Petri was currently the leader. He had already written the piano version of the *Lieder eines fahrenden Gesellen* and preliminary sketches for his First Symphony, among other works. At that time in both their lives, what separated them—age difference, very different backgrounds and temperaments— was more powerful than what they had in common. Mahler had led an independent existence for some eight years, and was also in the throes of an unhappy love affair with a married woman; at almost twenty· one, Busoni was an only child who had just broken away from parental control and therefore had some catching up to do in many areas of his life. (The rapid changes in him over the next two years were to prove an ongoing shock for his mother in particular.) Mahler was nevertheless very friendly and forthcoming. By the autumn of 1887 they were exchanging scores; Mahler had been persuaded by Carl Maria von Weber's grandson to complete Weber's opera *Die drei Pintos*, left uncompleted at the composer's death, and Mahler let Busoni see each of the three volumes as they came back from the printer. Busoni still addressed the older man in the rather florid Italian manner, earning this bluff retort from Mahler:

> Dear friend!
> Why these preliminaries [*Vorreden*]? You know you don't have to announce yourself in advance if you want to visit me.
> So: I am always ready to help you—whether you will find all three Pintos with me is unfortunately a matter of luck, as, because of copying, I seldom have all three volumes together; well, what you don't see one time, you can get a second time. But don't come with empty hands yourself either—please![10]

Leipzig offered abundant opportunities to hear music: there were Thursday evening orchestral concerts at the main hall of the Gewandhaus, then as now the home of the internationally acclaimed orchestra that bears its name, and on Wednesday mornings students were admitted to rehearsals, giving them the chance to see some of the world's greatest soloists at work. On Saturdays there were chamber concerts in the small hall of the Gewandhaus, and in many other venues; and there were the two famous churches, the Thomaskirche and the Niko-laikirche, for organ concerts and choral works. And there was opera at the Neues Stadttheater, built in 1867, which had close links with the Gewandhaus Orchestra, and where, after chief conductor Arthur Nikisch fell ill in January 1887 after *Das Rheingold*, the first installment of Leipzig's first complete *Ring*, Mahler took over for *Die Walküre* and *Siegfried* later that spring. "And all this was to be enjoyed in the company of kindred spirits, young and hopeful and wild with enthusiasm," wrote the English composer Percy Pitt (1869–1932), who at around that time was a student of Reinecke and Jadassohn at the Leipzig Conservatory. "'Kneipen,' it was called—to go and hear the opera, and then on to supper at Helbig's with a dozen fellows who had been there too, to talk and argue and laugh and drink the light German beer."[11]

But Ferruccio's first year in Leipzig contained continued frustrations as well as some of the joys of freedom. The need to earn money for himself and his father curtailed his social life. A lot of the work was drudgery: he took on the compiling of the piano score for Goldmark's *Merlin* for Goldmark's publisher, Friedrich Schuberth. It was a task accepted "for the sole purpose of being able to send you 250 marks," he wrote his father,[12] turning the tables on Ferdinando, who had just written him yet another reproachful letter. Ferruccio earned four hundred marks in all for this work, but unfortunately had borrowed the same sum beforehand from the piano manufacturer Julius Blüthner; then when Schuberth paid him he could no longer settle the whole debt. He still had not written anything for Giovannina Lucca, as promised—and paid for—when he was in Vienna, so he sent her a transcription of Siegfried's Funeral March from *Götterdämmerung* written some time before. Since getting back from Dresden in February, he told Ferdinando in mid-March,[13] he had finished the *Merlin* piano score and corrected the proofs, written a long review of Verdi's *Otello*, acquired a pupil at five marks an hour, and written a humorous novella he had sent to the magazine *Fliegende Blätter* (which was not published). He had continued working on *Sigune* in spite of *Merlin*, often until one or two at night. He was commissioned too by Schuberth to write a concert fantasia on *Merlin*, but when he handed in this twenty-page work it was rejected as being too difficult. The good-hearted Schwalm then listened to it, and, although he would not accept it for publication either, as a kind of pat on the back he paid off the loan Ferruccio had incurred from Blüthner and gave the young man something extra to get through the next month.

The constant demands for money from Frohnleiten weighed Ferruccio down. Often, however, Ferruccio's letters to his father make one really regret that Ferdinando's have not survived: "Your letter made me laugh so heartily," wrote Ferruccio on February 18, 1887, "that I'm making a point of writing back straight away. Bravo Papa, be always like that in your letters . . . and then I shall receive them and reply to them much more willingly."[14]

Oskar Schwalm proposed Ferruccio for membership in the Allgemeiner Deutscher Musikverein, who were to be giving a music festival that summer in Cologne, where Ferruccio hoped to have his ill-fated Symphonic Suite played. Schwalm agreed for C. F. Kahnt to publish the suite, but without payment, as the costs involved were too high. Ferruccio considered it nevertheless worthwhile to agree to this arrangement. C. F. Kahnt was also publishing his Short Suite for Cello and Piano, Two Songs for Low Voice and Piano (BV 216, settings of a poem by Theodor Fontane and of another by Ernst Freiherr von Feuchtersleben, the latter first performed in Vienna in January 1885), dedicated to Melanie Mayer (although without his asking permission— perhaps fearing another parental veto), so there were these proofs to correct too.

On April 29 Ferruccio apologized to his father for not having written for two weeks.[15] One reason was that he had had another of his "usual gastric fevers," not for the first time, nor the last. They were brought on, as always, by nervous and physical exhaustion, which he attempted to allay by recourse to tobacco and alcohol.

Other than the Petris, in that first year he allegedly made few friends at what he considered his own level, partly owing to lack of time, partly owing too, perhaps, to his having no formal contacts with the conservatory. Did he ever join the students at Helbig's after a performance? It is doubtful. Not only did he "never have a childhood," as he famously lamented, but the delights of student life largely eluded him too. Although still only twenty-one, he already had an established name as a concert pianist and, to a lesser degree, as composer, and this would have contributed to set him apart from his student coevals. As he wrote to Melanie Mayer[16] after six months in Leipzig,

> I have no one with whom I can communicate showing myself as I really am. My mother understands very well my attitude to life, but we are staunch opponents in the philosophical, social and above all religious field. My father was able to grasp my importance for art right from my childhood and now he understands my character better and better, but there was a time in which he didn't understand it at all, and from that point to total comprehension the road is long. Here I am incapable of making a single friend at my level, but I have at least two who learn from me and from whom, consequently, I get nothing except for the pleasure of seeing them progress under my guidance. This is the misfortune of precocious maturity.

Arrogant though this sounds, there was some truth in it, and Melanie, he knew, would understand it as such. Nevertheless, there had been a four-month gap between this letter to Melanie and the preceding one, for no apparent reason (the Mayers's parental veto seems to have been lifted now that Ferruccio was far away in Leipzig), which would suggest that he was not quite so lonely as he made out. His character was possibly also to blame. His peculiar life as child prodigy, cosseted by his parents and other adults, kept away from other children, and for that matter anyone who did not buy into the concept of his genius, had helped to make him self-centered and heedless of others' sensitivities, although he was by no means a heartless or selfish nature. (All his life, however, he was never one to suffer fools gladly.) Such an autodidact— which in effect he was in nearly all areas other than music—growing up in isolation from the rough and tumble of the "real" world, might even unconsciously shrink from pitting himself against possible equals.

Ferruccio's acquaintance in that first year was therefore by and large either with ersatz father figures such as Henri Petri or, conversely, with pupils. It is revealing that in that letter to Melanie he brings in his parents, even though he criticizes what he considers their shortcomings too, when bemoaning the fact that there is no one to really understand him. The Petris and the Mayers also provided the kind of unquestioning family love he needed, although his own parents' suffocating concentration on him was still irksome: "Just calm down!" (*Calma, calma e calma!*) he had written at the end of January to his father, who was panicking at threats of war.[17] "No one even mentions war here."

Bismarck was fighting hard to prevent an alliance between France and Russia from turning into a two-pronged attack on Germany, which could have made Leipzig a dangerous place to be; indeed, Leipzig had witnessed massive troop maneuvers in December. Delius was as unperturbed as Busoni: writing to an American friend, Gertrude Rueckert, in December 1886, he blandly observed:

> There are a great many soldiers here. A few weeks ago I saw 25,000 marching to the autumn manoeuvres near Leipzig. They looked very fine marching past. People think there is going to be war with France and Russia. If Germany gets beaten I suppose we shall have 2 or 3 battles around Leipzig, which would scarcely be pleasant, and difficult to study with the bullets flying around one's ears.[18]

In view of the previous war between Germany and France in 1870, necessitating the Busoni family's retreat from Paris, Ferdinando's panic is perhaps understandable. Fortunately, however, the threat of war evaporated.

In the evenings, if he was not working, Ferruccio often ate at the Panorama restaurant and played billiards, as only cold fare was offered at his lodgings. At times, "the publisher of *Merlin*, a first-rate *bon vivant*"[19] (it is not known whether this was Schuberth himself), and one of Ferruccio's pupils, scion of a wealthy aristocratic family, introduced him to some of the adult pleasures of luxury: a *chambre séparée* at the Hotel Prusse, champagne and the society of young ladies of the Leipzig demimonde. "I go there sometimes for the good wine and the excellent cigars on offer." Both this pupil and another, a young Austrian, were studying at the conservatory under Salomon Jadassohn (1831–1902)—as indeed was Delius—but Busoni gave them extra lessons in counterpoint, as they seemed to be making little progress. He was also soon writing for one of the "foremost musical journals (the *Neue Zeitschrift für Musik*), founded in 1834 by Schumann," as he proudly told his parents, mainly reviewing performances. He rashly told them in the same letter[20] that he had gone to two masked balls, "and passed some nights in the company of champagne." To deflect squawks from Trieste, he told his mother he could just as easily have kept quiet about it, so there was no need for her to go on about it in her next letter.

In the summer of 1887 he acquired another dog, Lesko, a black Newfoundland bitch that, like all Busoni's dogs, became an adored—and adoring—companion. His father requested a photograph, which Ferruccio enclosed in a letter:[21] "Here is the photograph you asked for. The dog has come out well, its master and your beloved son has an imbecilic, moonstruck expression and is stiff as a figure in a waxworks show." With this dog Ferruccio explored some of the underside of Leipzig life: according to Edward Dent,[22] in summer 1887 the future music critic August Ferdinand Pfohl once saw Lesko in the street "with a man whom he at first took for a blacksmith, and wondered if she had been stolen." Pfohl then realized that the blacksmith was in fact Busoni. And apparently Kathi Petri once came on Busoni in similar guise haranguing a group of workers on Karl Marx. These were both manifestations of his intense enjoyment of freedom, and of his constantly enquiring mind—also of the fact that he did manage to escape the treadmill quite frequently. (Minus the disguise, taking long walks in all areas of any city he happened to be in became a lifelong habit.) He let his hair grow long and generally behaved in a way normal for his age. His letters to Melanie have more than a dash of the *poète maudit*, the pose undermined somewhat by his seldom-failing capacity for self-mockery.

Ferruccio stayed in Leipzig throughout the summer of 1887, through lack of funds, although at some point he did go to Berlin for three days, as he told his father in the letter in which he sent the photograph of himself and Lesko:[23]

> I was in Berlin for three days, for pleasure (I confess), but I also managed (finally) to make contact with Wolff who, contrary to his usual practice, was quite polite. He wants me to play in the philharmonic concerts in Berlin and he will certainly be able to introduce me there, if he wants. In any case it's always good to have him as a friend—everyone is under him now.

This was Hermann Wolff (1845–1902), the Berlin impresario and agent, who had previously been Anton Rubinstein's secretary; he became Busoni's first agent and did indeed help him.

In late September 1887 Busoni's landlady, Frau Spann, moved, obliging him to find other accommodation. She seems to have sprung this on him at the last moment, and, as he did not have the money to pay a month's advance on new accommodation, he adopted the typically Busonian stratagem of moving into a hotel and sending a telegram to Frau von Wertheimstein, who at the last moment sent 150 florins, to cover the hotel, the move, the new rent, and other debts. On October 2 Busoni moved into his new lodgings, in Arndtstrasse 8, in what was then a suburb south of the town center; they were more spacious (and, at seventy marks, five marks cheaper) than his old ones, with a fine view over the countryside. He had two rooms in a "luxuriously appointed villa," he told Melanie; the food was good and—for him of greater importance—a neighbor was a very intelligent and well-read young Russian, who whetted Busoni's appetite for Russian literature. Busoni's report to Melanie[74] gives a very clear idea of the nature of his friendship with her:

> Names like Dostoevsky, Goncharov, Chernychevsky, Tolstoy are not familiar to us. The latter in particular occupies in Russia a much higher position than Turgenev, and we two will have to read his two novels, "War and Peace" and "Anna Karenina." Do you want to begin? Meanwhile I've read "A Hero of Our Time" by Lermontov, an extraordinary work that I heartily recommend to you.

This Russian diet was perhaps partly responsible for the orating blacksmith.

That autumn Busoni wrote a long essay that appeared in four parts in the *Neue Zeitschrift für Musik*,[25] on Mozart's *Don Giovanni*, which had been premiered one hundred years before. He discusses in a very lively way the influences on Mozart's music, his genius in delineating character in music, how he could change the mood of the opera almost from one bar to another, and much else. It is a very respectable effort from a twenty-one-year-old. The *Neue Zeitschrift für Musik* was not the only musical weekly published at that time in Leipzig; there was also the *Signale für die musikalische Welt*. Both were quite modest by today's magazine-publishing standards, but it is nevertheless astounding, and says much for the incredibly vibrant musical life of this city of well under half a million, that it could support these publications, plus many others with a wider artistic brief.

In late October, thanks to Wolff, Busoni gave three concerts in one week in Hamburg, playing the Tausig transcription of the Bach Toccata and Fugue again, the same composer's transcription of Wagner's "Ride of the Valkyrie," Liszt's transcription of the waltz from Gounod's *Faust*, Liszt's Fantasia on Donizetti's *Lucrezia Borgia*, a Chopin nocturne and polonaise, and some of his own work. These programs scandalized the Hamburg public somewhat, as such treatments of popular opera were considered frivolous. But they were nevertheless a great success, such as Busoni had not experienced since his time as *enfant prodige*, he wrote to his father.[26] His success in Hamburg was the most notable since that of Anton Rubinstein, the newspapers "acclaiming me as one of the greatest artists of the epoch."[27]

Although Busoni earned money from these concerts, expenses were heavy and he ended up just about breaking even. He was hoping for a London concert on November 22, at Covent Garden, through Hans Richter, who had been conducting an annual series of concerts there since 1879. This would have brought great financial rewards, but came to nothing, and Busoni's British debut was postponed. He had also written to Arrigo Boito asking for a post in the 1888 Bologna Musical Exposition, which likewise came to nothing.

Since arriving in Leipzig, Ferruccio had been sending his father part of all the money he received, whether earned or given—the piano manufacturers Julius Blüthner and Theodore Steinway had also been generous. But these sources could not be relied on, and the only regular sums he received—from Frau von Wertheimstein and the Baronin von Todesco—were soon to dry up: April 1, 1887, was his twenty-first birthday. In spring 1887 Ferruccio had tried to get his father a position as a clarinetist/soloist in a Rotterdam orchestra, having seen an advertisement in a music journal, eventually receiving a reply that the post was already filled. It is typical of their relationship that Ferruccio told his father of this attempt only after receiving the reply, and not before applying for the post on his behalf.[28] Ferruccio had just sent him another 640 marks, thanks to the generosity of Blüthner, who had given him 700 marks. In this letter and others Ferruccio desperately and eloquently urged his father to get out of Frohnleiten, where he had no chance to find work and where he could only degenerate "morally and artistically." Three days later he wrote, "Your idea of staying on in that hole is false and mistaken. And except for the material side, just tell me, what contact do you have with those people?"[29] Ferdinando seemed to be living there more or less on the charity of his landlady, Frau Petersheim, whose patience and Christian conscience surely had their limits, his son hinted.

Finally, in November 1887, made desperate by the almost daily letters from his father, and the inefficacy of his own insistence that Ferdinando leave Frohnleiten, Ferruccio took his problems to an older and wiser head: the kindly Max Abraham of C. F. Peters. (He immediately told his father he had taken this step.)[30] He told Abraham the whole story, putting all his cards on the table, which must have hurt his pride, and asked for help. The older man, like the rest of Busoni's well-wishers, was only too willing to help Ferruccio, but was very reluctant to support the flâneur of Frohnleiten; he stipulated that he would only help Ferdinando if he agreed to take a regular post in an orchestra—there was a possibility in Bologna—in which case he would settle Ferdinando's debts and pay his removal costs. Unsurprisingly, this came to nothing, and another year passed before Ferruccio finally dislodged his father from Frohnleiten and the woman he was involved with there (about whom nothing is known except for the odd oblique reference in Ferruccio's letters).

In late November Ferruccio was back in Hamburg, where, because of illness (the usual "gastric fever"), he played only one concert instead of two. Again, this concert was an extraordinary success, with an audience of over a thousand, who called him back six times and demanded two encores. Hamburg's "most important music critic"[31] compared him as a pianist to Hans von Bülow and Carl Tausig, and as a composer to Brahms. In Hamburg Ferruccio was introduced to top society and "fêted like a prince."[32] He went on to play in Halle and by mid-December was able to send another one hundred florins to Frohnleiten, promising a further hundred "in two days."

Ferruccio went back to Trieste for Christmas—as, presumably, did his father: from mid-December to mid-January there are no letters to Ferdinando, although there could be other explanations for this gap, of course, such as the wish to remove all trace of the mystery woman in Frohnleiten. Ferruccio gave a concert in Trieste and another in Graz in January 1888, on his way back to Leipzig (via Frohnleiten), both mammoth performances: Bach, Liszt, Beethoven, Schumann, Mozart, Weber, and his own work. His String Quartet in D Minor (BV 225), composed in June the previous year, was premiered in Leipzig at the Gewandhaus on January 28, 1888, the day after his return, by the Petri Quartet; it had a rather negative reception by the critics. Tchaikovsky was in the audience; in his memoirs he recalled,

> When I heard the quartet, rhythmically and harmonically extraordinarily original, I nevertheless regretted that Mr. Busoni was doing violence to his own nature and was striving at all costs to become a German. I can perceive something similar in yet another Italian of the younger generation, in Giovanni Sgambati. They are both ashamed of being Italian, fear even a hint of melody shining through in their compositions, and want to be "profound" in a wholly German way.[33]

Tchaikovsky nonetheless admired Busoni greatly as a pianist and composer, and was first introduced to him on this occasion, falling under the charm of the young man's personality.

The critic of the *Neue Zeitschrift für Musik,* for whom Busoni himself was now writing, was rather condescending toward his young colleague's composition, and obviously also rather puzzled. After applauding the Petri Quartet for kindly giving their attention to an unpublished work from a "young, aspiring artist," and giving a "truly exemplary performance," the reviewer continued:

> Indeed this composition is worthy of such attention: in it a striving for profundity and thematic meaning emerges, that appears to be inspired partly by "late Beethoven," partly by "Wagner of the Nibelungen." Certainly, in Busoni thought often wrestles with form, and one cannot say that the former emerged everywhere as victor in the quartet and so a certain, not uninteresting conflict entered the whole, which to us seems to indicate more an excess of its own power, than a productive weakness. What it perhaps still needs is that clarity, that certainty of expression, which must be regarded as conditio sine qua non of any fruitful chamber music culture. The quartet was very warmly received.[34]

This proves that then, as now, reviewers can manage to balance on the fence and commit themselves to nothing. The Wagner allusion must have annoyed Busoni, however.

Busoni himself considered the quartet "my most important work so far."[35] The first movement, Allegro energico (a typically Busonian instruction), is full of tripping, syncopated rhythms, with a skillful interweaving of the melodic lines. The work as a whole contains many of the features that remained typical of his work: the driving, slightly sinister staccato rhythms of the Vivace assai, for example; the violin entering and sliding sinuously over the staccato, at times coming close to what a century later is termed "minimalism"; the movement ending with all the instruments united in a frenzy. The final movement, Andantino, which begins in a dignified manner, muted and stately, abruptly slips into an Allegro con brio; spirited and humorous, elaborately chromatic, it ends with a boisterous, joyous climax. Unlike in Busoni's previous string quartets, which, although showing an amazing fluency, were heavily influenced by Haydn, Beethoven, and Brahms, here he confidently parades his own voice. (He continued to think enough of the work to have it included in 1909 in a concert that also contained quartets by Beethoven, Schumann, and Haydn.)

Another work, the Four Bagatelles for Violin and Piano (BV 229), was completed as a seventh birthday present for the Petris's son Egon, who was studying the violin at the time, but was soon to shift to the piano and eventually become Busoni's most famous pupil and himself a great pianist. The Bagatelles were published the same year by C. F. Peters, and the String Quartet in D Minor by Breitkopf und Härtel a year later.

The latter firm was from now on to become Busoni's main publisher. The Hamburg firm of August Cranz, which had also acquired the Viennese firm of C. A. Spina in 1876, had been his first publisher: in 1877, when Busoni was eleven years old, they published his Five Pieces for Piano (BV 71), now also known as his Opus 3, although he had already written some seventy pieces. Cranz was to be his main publisher in the German-speaking world until he went to Leipzig, with the Milanese firm Lucca mainly publishing those of his early works that were premiered in Italy. (Lucca was soon to be swallowed up, in 1888, by its giant rival, Ricordi, which bought up its some 40,000 titles.) Music publishers were commercial undertakings; therefore they must have seen a market for Busoni's youthful works.

Meanwhile, he was still working on *Sigune* and hoping for a performance of his Symphonic Suite on February 23 in Leipzig. The performance was suddenly cancelled, as King Albert of Saxony unexpectedly decided to attend, and the work was considered too difficult for the royal ears. Ferruccio wrote to the king, to no effect, relieving his feelings later in a letter[36] to his father by drawing a comic caricature of King Albert as the King of Spades, himself kneeling before him. He played at Halle, Handel's birthplace, and at Dresden, though again at a private gathering of the Tonkünstler Verein. Although performing more and more frequently, Busoni still had little financial security; many of the concerts brought little financial reward.

Another enormous complication in his life was that sometime that winter he and Kathi Petri conceived a mutual attraction that threatened to get totally out of hand. It later reached the point where they were actually planning to run away together, but Kathi's maternal feelings brought her to her senses: she found it impossible to abandon Egon. It says much for Busoni's powers of attraction as a twenty-one-year-old that he could inspire such strong feelings in a woman some ten years his senior, who was in an otherwise happy marriage. Surprisingly, Ferruccio told his mother, who actually wrote to Kathi and to Ferruccio himself. On March 26, 1888, replying to his mother's letter,[37] he wrote:

> I cannot express what an impression of sorrow and joy at the same time, of remorse and of spur to duty, together with such love—were aroused in me by the words you sent to Mrs. P. . . . By now you will, I believe, have received her letter, from which you can gain knowledge of the heart and mind of this lady. You could not console me more than by addressing her directly; I don't want to add any more, the rest you can easily guess.

He enclosed a photograph of Kathi that he had asked for the day before—"you agree with me, an intelligent and original face."

Lately too there had been a constant barrage of desperate letters from his father. This prompted Ferruccio finally, in early April 1888, to take a desperate step: borrowing 200 marks from Henri Petri, he went to Hamburg to ask for a large sum of money from the piano manufacturer Theodore Steinway. Steinway was at his home in Braunschweig, whence Ferruccio followed him, and obtained the money, ostensibly in order to finish his opera in peace over the summer. Steinway insisted on the young man staying in his splendid mansion for three days before returning to Leipzig. "More like a father than a businessman," Ferruccio described Steinway to his own father, with unconscious irony, in a triumphant letter of April 11,[38] enclosing 1,000 marks. "And all this without contracts, without obligations or receipts or promissory notes, nothing. . . . Here is a sum that will enable you to pay off all your debts." What were Ferdinando's plans? The post of clarinetist in an orchestra would be much less humiliating than the position he had occupied for several years in Frohnleiten, the son pointed out. There was some confusion about the post, so that further reproachful letters arrived in Leipzig before matters were cleared up, marring Ferruccio's joy at the thought of solving his father's problems—an illusory joy, as it inevitably turned out.

Steinway was planning a four-month winter concert tour of America for the young Busoni, for a fee of 25,000 francs, which unfortunately came to nothing, as Steinway fell ill and died a short time afterward— yet another body blow from fate to hamper Busoni's career. Then in late April, through another well-wisher in Leipzig, the musicologist Hugo Riemann (1849–1919), Busoni was offered the post of professor of piano at the Conservatory of Helsingfors (Helsinki), starting on September 15. He accepted at once, seeing it as a secure income at last. Ferruccio immediately relayed to his father the good news of the offer from Helsinki: nine months' teaching a year for an annual salary of 4,000 francs. He had already signed the contract, he wrote. Thinking ahead, he planned to stay only one year and use the post as a stepping stone to a similar position in a "musical center," preferably in Germany. His first thought was to take his mother with him, to provide a congenial home for her at last. From her confused reply to this invitation, he realized she thought he wanted her to look after *him*, and proposed Ferdinando's going instead; it was impossible for her to realize that her son, now twenty-two, was proposing to look after *her*. "*Mia cara ed eccellentissima madre*," he begins a letter[39] of June 24 redolent with barely contained exasperation, going on to explain the true situation through the epistolary equivalent of clenched teeth. "Your letter, although affectionate and very welcome, has the single defect of not rendering it possible for the reader to grasp what you are thinking of doing. I could not understand whether or not you want to come with me, whether you will stay, whether *Babbo* will come, and so on." Her basic premise was wrong, he wrote. It was not because he could not and should not be alone, but because *her* position was so unhappy and worrying, that he had invited her to go with him.

Although Busoni would be renowned throughout his life for his kindness and tolerance, his attitude to his parents, as Edward Dent observed, can only be fully explained in cultural terms: for an Italian, it was unthinkable not to put them first—a fact Ferdinando instinctively capitalized on throughout his life. Anna's attitude was always that of the martyr—in its way quite as much of an incubus as her husband's airy exploitation of their son. Given Busoni's growing reputation at this young age as one of the greatest living pianists, it is shocking to think that he was willing to accept a teaching position in an obscure outpost of Europe—which is what Helsinki definitely was at that time—solely to provide a regular income for his parents (and let us not forget that his father was then only fifty-four). The logical step at this stage in his career would have been to capitalize on his increasing fame, performing more and more frequently in the world's important cities. Another possible reason for his decision to leave Leipzig may have been to escape the temptation of his feelings for Kathi Petri. By now he was mixing with other musicians of the caliber of Mahler, Delius, and Grieg, in what was generally acknowledged to be the musical capital of the time. This was unfortunately not the last time he would make a disastrous decision where his career was concerned.

In late spring Busoni finished the first draft of *Sigune*. He continued to work on it in the summer, then over the autumn and winter in Helsinki and the following summer in Weimar. Nevertheless, the work was never fully finished (the short score is in the State Library, Berlin), and only two years later, Busoni was already cannibalizing music from it, in his *Konzertstück*. The opera doubtless suffered from its long gestation, which spanned a significant period in his artistic development— from nineteen to twenty-three—during which not only his musical style, but also his intellectual concerns, inevitably altered.

Busoni himself (understandably) thought highly of his opera at the time. "It is a very great work," he wrote to his father in early June 1888,[40] "and quite rich and profound, and without doubt is the pinnacle of my artistic development so far. . . . [It] has also a certain I would say reforming importance where style and also form are concerned."

This letter, incidentally, contains many grammar and spelling mistakes—a clear indication of Busoni's growing estrangement from his mother tongue.

In August he was the Steinways's guest in Bayreuth. To the last minute, he was still assuming Anna would be accompanying him to Helsinki, and he was writing instructions on getting to Leipzig, where she would be the guest of the Petris and he would join her, so that they could travel on together. (There was obviously some plan that Ferdinando would go to Tuscany—presumably to Empoli—and in July, Ferruccio had written to his father[41] advising him to remain in Frohnleiten for July and August, to avoid the great heat in Tuscany during those months.

> Forgive me for writing to you in haste, as I still have to write half a dozen letters. If you want my advice: stay in Frohnleiten for July and August, two months during which a stay in Tuscany is not very pleasant. . . . Before September I hope to send you the means to go to Tuscany, although my expenses, for my journey and Mamma's and for the necessary outfit, are very heavy. But I hope to succeed in supporting you both. Within two years, if my calculations are not wrong, we shall be together.

Again, it is extraordinary how passive Ferdinando was in all this, willing to accept his son's advice and instructions at all times.)

At the very end of August Anna announced she would not be going to Helsinki. The party the Petris had planned for her arrival in Leipzig took place without her, and in the first week of September Ferruccio and Lesko set out alone for Helsinki: it was definitely not an advantageous move, but nevertheless it was this city that was to provide him with his greatest good fortune: his future wife.

Notes

1. Postcard from FB to Ferdinando Busoni, December 2, 1886, StBB Bus. Nachl. 1176.

2. Letter from FB to Ferdinando Busoni, December 3, 1886, StBB Bus. Nachl. 1177.

3. Letter from FB to Melanie Mayer, December 15, 1886, StBB Bus. Nachl. 389.

4. Letter from FB to Melanie Mayer, December 31, 1886, StBB Bus. Nachl. 390.

5. Letter from FB to Ferdinando Busoni, December 5, 1886, StBB Bus. Nachl. 1178.

6. Letter from FB to Ferdinando Busoni, December 10, 1886, StBB Bus. Nachl. 1179.

7. Letter from FB to Anna Weiss-Busoni, January 4, 1887, StBB Nachl. 1217.

8. Letter from FB to Ferdinando Busoni, December 24, 1886, StBB Bus. Nachl. 1184.

9. FB to Ferdinando Busoni, December 24, 1886.

10. Letter from Gustav Mahler to FB, autumn 1887, StBB, Mus. ep. Gustav Mahler 64–68 (Bus. Nachl.).

11. Percy Pitt, quoted in J. Daniel Chamier, *Percy Pitt of Covent Garden and the BBC* (London: Edward Arnold, 1938), p. 31.

12. Letter from FB to Ferdinando Busoni, January 22, 1887, StBB Bus. Nachl. 1189.

13. Letter from FB to Ferdinando Busoni, March 13, 1887, StBB Bus. Nachl. 1197.

14. Letter from FB to Ferdinando Busoni, February 18, 1887, StBB Bus. Nachl. 1194.

15. Letter from FB to Ferdinando Busoni, April 29, 1887, StBB Bus. Nachl. 1202.

16. Letter from FB to Melanie Mayer, June 8, 1887, StBB Bus. Nachl. 391.

17. Letter from FB to Ferdinando Busoni, January 28, 1887, StBB Bus. Nachl. 1190.

18. Lionel Carley, *Delius: A Life in Letters; Volume I, 1862–1908* (London: Scolar Press, 1983), p. 9.

19. Letter from FB to Ferdinando Busoni, March 23, 1887, StBB Bus. Nachl. 1198.

20. Letter from FB to Anna/Ferdinando Busoni, February 12, 1887, StBB Bus. Nachl. 1218.

21. Letter from FB to Ferdinando Busoni, n.d. but must be late summer 1887, StBB Bus. Nachl. 1185.

22. Dent, *Ferruccio Busoni*, p. 69.

23. FB to Ferdinando Busoni, February 18, 1887.

24. Letter from FB to Melanie Mayer, October 5, 1887, StBB Bus. Nachl. 392.

25. Ferruccio Busoni, "Zum 'Don Juan' Jubiläum," part I, *Neue Zeitschrift für Musik*, vol. 83, no. 43 (October 26, 1887): 481–83; part II, vol. 83, no. 44 (November 2, 1887): 494–96; part III, vol. 83, no. 45 (November 9, 1887): 505–6; part IV, vol. 83, no. 46 (November 16, 1887): 518–20.

26. Letter from FB to Ferdinando Busoni, October 22, 1887, StBB Bus. Nachl. 1212.

27. Letter from FB to Ferdinando Busoni, October 26, 1887, StBB Bus. Nachl. 1213.

28. Letter from FB to Ferdinando Busoni, April 13, 1887, StBB Bus. Nachl. 1200.

29. Letter from FB to Ferdinando Busoni, April 16, 1887, StBB Bus. Nachl. 1201.

30. Letter from FB to Ferdinando Busoni, November 15, 1887, StBB Bus. Nachl. 1214.

31. Letter from FB to Ferninando Busoni, November 24, 1887, StBB Bus. Nachl. 1215.

32. Letter from FB to Ferdinando Busoni, November 24, 1887

33. P. Tchaikovsky, *Erinnerungen und Musikkritiken*, edited by Richard Petzold and Lothar Fahlbusch (Leipzig, 1974).

34. Review in *Neue Zeitschrift für Musik*, vol. 83, no. 6 (February 8, 1888) 66.

35. Letter from FB to Ferdinando Busoni, June 28, 1887, StBB Bus. Nachl. 1207.

36. Letter from FB to Ferdinando Busoni, February 18, 1888, StBB Bus. Nachl. 1230.

37. Letter from FB to Anna Weiss-Busoni, March 26, 1988, StBB Bus. Nachl. 1241.

38. Letter from FB to Ferdinando Busoni, April 11, 1888, StBB Bus. Nachl. 1232.

39. Letter from FB to Anna Weiss-Busoni, June 24, 1888, StBB Bus. Nachl. 1242.

40. Letter from FB to Ferdinando Busoni, June 1888, StBB, Bus. Nachl. 1235.

41. Letter from FB to Ferdinando Busoni, July 12, 1888, StBB Bus. Nachl. 1236.

~

CHAPTER FIVE

Helsinki, Marriage, and Moscow: September 1888 to August 1891

Ferruccio and Lesko traveled to Helsinki via Lübeck, embarking there on the steamer *Storfursten* to cross the Baltic, a stormy three-day voyage that left the youthful professor hoarse from seasickness. On the ship was one of his future colleagues, also a piano teacher, who, aware that Busoni was going to be on board, came up and made himself known. Unfortunately, Busoni had one of his attacks of intolerance—"our conversation was restricted to the most trivial matters; all my attempts at raising the level came up against a brick wall," he wrote to the Petris.[1] The poor young man received the definitive thumbs-down when he was seen later reading *Die Gartenlaube*, a sentimental magazine much in vogue at the time, and found himself on the receiving end of some scathing remarks, to which he understandably took offence. He became the unfortunate butt of Busoni's enormous sense of apprehension during what was literally a voyage into the unknown.

A young Finnish lecturer in art history, returning home with his wife and child after three years in Italy, met with approval: they had Italy in common. There was also a captain

> from the Pacific Ocean, who spoke a hotchpotch of English and Swedish, that I nevertheless managed to decipher. He asserted that he had traveled in China, India, South America, etc., talked about the climate in these

places, drank a lot of schnapps, smoked stinking cigarettes, was dressed all in gray (including a hat sewn together out of gray check wool) and with his tiny stature and his ruddy, constantly smiling face and continuous hopping on his bow legs, made a very comic impression.

The captain was a new species in Ferruccio's experience, whom he relished encountering.

Seasickness, like breaking one's leg skiing, is one of those misfortunes that inevitably invite mirth, even—with hindsight—in the victim, and Busoni obliged subsequently for the Petris, with a facetious account of the ship as a giant toy in the hands of the Almighty, and himself leaning over the side "feeding the fishes." On the third day, when the weather turned sunny and calm, he recovered from his seasickness and went ashore when they docked briefly in Hangö, a Finnish fishing village about seventy miles west of Helsinki, which was in the process of transforming itself into a seaside resort. They then turned south to Tallinn (then known as Reval) in Estonia; in the evening light, it made a favorable impression on the young traveler.

Finally, with a twelve-hour delay caused by the bad weather, they docked at Helsinki at midnight, where Ferruccio was welcomed by Martin Wegelius (1846–1906), director and founder (in 1882) of the Helsinki Institute of Music (since 1939 the Sibelius Academy), and composer. Wegelius, who had studied in Leipzig under Richter, Jadassohn, and Reinecke, was widely traveled and open-minded, a dedicated teacher and kindly man. He took the young man off for a meal, in spite of the late hour, and saw him to his hotel, where, alone at last, Ferruccio fell prey to an overwhelming sense of loneliness and apprehension, put into words two days later in that first, long letter to the Petris. When the ship had docked at Hangö, he had seen a melancholy sight, the memory of which now released a flood of apprehension, frustration, and loneliness:

> I crept into bed and fell asleep only after very melancholy thoughts. Far from you, from my parents, for the first time among totally strange people who—from my first impressions—will never satisfy me socially, I felt for the first time in my life and precisely at the moment when I am starting on an independent, secure position—abandoned and helpless. I believe—and I'm not ashamed of it—that I cried. Here people will learn

to respect me, as you respect me; but never will they love me as you do and never will they ever understand me even partly, as you, Henri, and you, Kathi, have understood me. I think, as soon as I am certain of remaining ununderstood, I shall completely avoid such an understanding and limit myself to leaving these people to themselves.—O how stupid the world is, how insensitive to the beautiful and the good!—I hate stupidity, and can be hard and ruthless against it.

As we were leaving Hangö, on the lonely, picturesque beach, strewn with rocks, there was a gypsy, a tall man, with a beautiful face, with that special, wild and sad expression typical of his people; his picturesque clothing of southern type contrasted strongly with the nordic character of the landscape. Behind him, around him, the sea, on the unending line of which his figure stood out; to one side, at a certain distance, a group of guests of the bathing resort, who with their repulsive laughter, their noise, their grotesque modern clothing, demonstrated the emptiness of society contrasted with the poetry of the ancient tribe.

It was a case of one stranger in a strange land acknowledging another. But again, Busoni took out his feelings on someone else: "I turned to one of my fellow-travelers [his unfortunate German colleague, one suspects], pointing out to him the figure of the gypsy. 'I only wish,' he said, 'that the fellow were more decently dressed.' 'What,'—I said ironically— 'would you rather he were wearing narrow checked trousers and an immaculate top hat?'—'Of course.'" He finished his first letter from Helsinki, however—addressed, significantly, to the Petris and not to his parents, to whom he had, nevertheless, sent a telegram on his arrival— with an enthusiastic description of the beauties of Helsinki, and the hint that the journey from Lübeck only cost fifty-six marks. (It can only be assumed that at this stage the feelings of Ferruccio and Kathi for each other had not yet been explicitly acknowledged to each other, let alone made known to Henri Petri.)

Helsinki, then still known by the Swedish name Helsingfors, with a population even today of little over half a million, was at that time scarcely more than a picturesque fishing port, with little of the cultural life Busoni was used to. Finland had been a province of Sweden since the twelfth century, and since 1809 a Russian grand duchy. For both these more powerful neighbors it was merely a remote outpost, often too a battleground, its own culture expressly discouraged. Swedish was still spoken by the majority of educated people in Helsinki when Busoni was there, although Finnish had already gained considerable ground. And if politically Helsinki had been a province of neighbors to the east or west, musically it was definitely a province of Germany. (One of Wegelius's pupils at the time, Jean Sibelius, was to do much to inspire Finnish national pride and a sense of national identity.)

A few days after that first letter, Busoni was much less optimistic, especially regarding Wegelius's six-year-old institute. And he announced to his father on September 17[2] that he was determined not to run up any debts there, so that he would be free to leave whenever he wanted, though for the time being he was planning to stay until the end of the contracted year. (Ferdinando was certainly an appropriate recipient of such virtuous resolutions.) Ferruccio had already summed up the sociocultural situation in Helsinki generally and come to his own conclusions—some based more on his own cultural conditioning than on realities: "The relations with women here resemble those of Gomorrah. The life they lead is pretty free—but see hereditary disease in Ibsen's *Ghosts!*" he informed the Petris.[3] He viewed the greater freedom enjoyed by Scandinavian women as evidence of lax morals. He was also shocked by one social restriction: "Jews are restricted by law to a very low, specific number, are only allowed to live in their own quarter, and as soon as the specific number is exceeded by the birth of a child, the family is escorted over the border. Sad, medieval notions!"

Applying the double standards of the time, Busoni himself certainly led a free and easy life in Helsinki. One companion, from the first days, was Jean Sibelius, with whom he struck up what was to be a lasting friendship. As they were nearly the same age (Sibelius the elder, in fact, by four months), the conventional professor-student relationship was ignored. In their many informal conversations on music, Sibelius found the stimulus he needed, which, according to Sibelius's biographer Erik Tawaststjerna, "was of enormous value. . . . Their interchange of ideas in no small measure contributed to [Sibelius's] development and in all probability to his artistic breakthrough in the spring of 1889."[4] It was the first time Sibelius had encountered genius: on studying Busoni's phenomenal piano-playing technique, flawless memory, and enormous repertoire at close quarters, the former was finally convinced he could never be a concert performer. However, even with his inferior keyboard

technique, when he sat down at the piano and developed his own musical ideas, he proved Busoni's equal as a composer. To Busoni's silent
regret, throughout their lives Sibelius never gave Busoni's composing
the same recognition as his piano playing; he himself generously promoted Sibelius's music to the end. (Erik Tawaststjerna pays tribute to
the best in the young Busoni at that time: "In Wegelius [Sibelius]
seemed to arouse a paternal affection, a despotic protective instinct and
an element of irritation, perhaps even jealousy; in Kajanus [founder of
Helsinki's first permanent orchestra], admiration mixed with a trace of
envy. Only in Busoni did Sibelius's genius evoke a pure Apollonian *joie
de vivre.*"[5])

In many ways it was an attraction of opposites, although the contrast
between them possibly owed as much to their very different formative
experiences as to their natures. Sibelius had lost his father when still an
infant, and his family was not rich, but he nevertheless had a stable
bourgeois upbringing, with none of the pressures, artistic and financial,
that Busoni had undergone, and that had made the latter mature in
some ways far beyond his years. They met every day, and in spite of being the same age, even from the beginning Busoni played the role of
wise and sober elder brother to someone who was already acquiring a
rip-roaring reputation.

Nonetheless, at the time they both painted the town red on occasion, together with Sibelius's fellow student at the conservatory, Armas
Järnefelt, and his brother Eero, who were to become Sibelius's brothers-
in-law, and the writer Adolf Paul (1863–1943—real name Georg
Wiedersheim; Paul later became an intimate friend of August Strindberg). The young men formed what Busoni ironically termed "an inspiring cabal," dubbing themselves the Leskovites, after Busoni's dog
Lesko, who accompanied the group whenever feasible. German was the
common language. Music had its place in these gatherings too, mostly
with Busoni playing for his friends. (He dedicated to each Leskovite
one movement of his second orchestral suite, the *Geharnischte Suite*
[BV 242], composed 1894–1895—proof of fond memories.)

Busoni was careful to keep all mention of the Leskovites's activities
out of his letters, even to the Petris, instead painting a melancholy (but
chaste) picture of a lonely young man with only a Newfoundland dog
for company. (Ironically, in his first letter to his mother from Helsinki

he wrote that "here I am as lonely as a dog, or rather worse, since my dog has the *best* company in me and I the *only* company in him."[6]) In a sense, too, he *was* still lonely: in spite of Sibelius and his other friends, he was not bolstered by a congenial wider urban ambiance, such as he had enjoyed in Vienna, Graz, and Leipzig, with their infrastructures of opera houses, theaters, and concert halls, requiring concomitant professional practitioners, all of whom provided a necessary artistic leaven in those cities. And as in Leipzig, he found himself the teacher and leader—a frustrating position for an intelligent twenty-two-year-old eager to learn. He missed both Petris sorely (although, it is to be presumed, Kathi in particular), pouring out his heart to them in frequent long letters.

> One's task here in music is to *give*, but not to *receive*; one can teach, not learn, introduce *new things perhaps* gradually and with great difficulty, not experience new things. In the musical centers it is a rewarding task (where the highest epoch has already been achieved) to continue to build and to add one's own feelings, creativity and thought. *Here* one must be content if one can make up or imitate *one part* of what has been achieved elsewhere.
> There is no opera house here![7]

In another letter, of September 25,[8] Busoni gives us a charming glimpse of the easy friendship he had enjoyed with the Petris in Leipzig: it is gone midnight, but in Leipzig was an hour earlier. He could picture their bedroom, "I can see too the empty dark Kurprinzenstrasse, as it is at the time when I usually closed your front door behind me. Your dear black silhouettes appear once again at the window to salute me; Henri whistles, and I answer—a final wave of my hat, and I turn the corner." In view of his relationship with Kathi at the time, this letter is nevertheless more than a little disingenuous.

Busoni's teaching at the conservatory was a trial to him. Most of his pupils were girls; leaving aside his lifelong prejudice regarding female intelligence, these pupils were, by all accounts, of less than average ability, the few men among them scarcely better. "You know the pictures of a circus clown with performing geese?" he asked Kathi Petri. "Dress your good friend Ferruccio in baggy trousers and paint his face white—you would not have to alter anything in his pupils to have the exact picture! I have fifteen of these waterfowl under my authority: Lesko has been promoted to shepherd dog."[9] There seemed to be no clear teaching program, goal, or considered choice of teaching material. Clementi and Cramer, those stalwarts of the piano primer, were the students' staple fare. Busoni soon applied the shock tactic of Bach's *Well-Tempered Clavier*, which offered equally useful exercises but considerably superior musical content, plus some Beethoven and Chopin, and achieved a certain success. And yet he hoped he could in time obtain some satisfaction from teaching his art, with a gradual development of his own system, his gift for communication, the gaining of an overview of the technical organization of teaching. His only fear was that being surrounded by such low standards might damage his own. But perhaps that very fear, he mused, might spur him to greater things.

An added trial was the experience of giving private piano lessons to the daughters of the *haute bourgeoisie* of Helsinki, who treated him as little better than a servant: a rude shock to a young artist fêted in many of the larger cities of Europe. He needed the extra money, but deeply resented both the humiliation and the time lost from composition. He had, however, told his father in September[10] that he did not intend to take on too many private pupils (although he soon had twelve), as he wanted to continue composing. (True to form, that first letter to his father from Helsinki was mainly taken up with financial matters, with defensive overtones.)

The institute organized musical evenings every two weeks, at which Busoni was expected to perform. He chose an all-Beethoven program for his debut on October 12, playing the *Appassionata* and the Variations and Fugue in E-flat Major, among other works. The concert was an enormous success and Busoni himself considered it his most significant achievement so far as pianist.[11] He threw himself energetically into the musical life of Helsinki, playing a great deal himself in public and promoting other performances. There was scarcely a concert at the institute in which he did not take part. Although the local orchestra, conducted by Robert Kajanus, was far from satisfactory at the time, and had nothing to do with Wegelius's institute, he approached them too, with a view to working together. (In a regrettable small-town manner, Wegelius and Kajanus waged a bitter feud in Helsinki for musical dominance.) Robert Kajanus (1856–1933), who had studied with Carl Reinecke and Hans

Richter in Leipzig, had founded the Helsinki Orchestral Society only in 1882. He remained its chief conductor for the rest of his life, and by the end of the century had brought it up to international standards. He is mainly remembered today for his championship of Finnish music, and of Sibelius in particular.

The enmity between the institute and the orchestra was so great that Sibelius did not get to know Kajanus personally until 1890, when he was studying in Berlin. Busoni was determined to ignore the rivalries between the two bodies during what he now termed his "stay" in Helsinki: by the end of September he had already decided that this was only a transitional situation. Kajanus's orchestral concerts began in mid-October; there were two of these popular concerts a week, seats (at small tables) costing one mark, a price that included refreshments. In Ferruccio's opinion, Kajanus had no conception of how classical music should be performed, but at least it was something.

Ferruccio did not write to his mother until October 26,[12] and spent the first two of the twelve pages on excuses as to why he had not written to her before—there had certainly been plenty of reproaches from Trieste. In his turn he reproached her for refusing to join him in Helsinki, emphasizing his lonely state and hoping she would join him later. It is intriguing and amusing to contrast this picture, and what we glean from other of Busoni's extant letters, with what has since emerged on his Helsinki period via letters and biographies of his contemporaries there, such as Sibelius, through which we learn something of the exploits of the Leskovites, for example. And when Edward Dent wrote his biography of Busoni in 1932, he had to rely heavily on Busoni's widow, who rigorously guarded her husband's reputation and withheld much information she considered detrimental.

As soon as the autumn term ended, in mid-December, Busoni left for Germany, traveling overland via Saint Petersburg. Over the next month, he gave concerts in Hamburg, one in Halle, with the Petri Quartet, and another at the Gewandhaus in Leipzig. He spent Christmas with the Petris, but, in a confused and frustrated frame of mind, he took umbrage at a New Year's Eve party at their house, given in honor of Henri Petri's old teacher, the great violinist Joseph Joachim. Petri had urged Busoni to play his Chopin Variations to Joachim, but Busoni for some reason had taken a dislike to the great man, and flatly refused. There was an embarrassing scene, smoothed over by Petri's good manners and what Busoni perceived as Joachim's patronizing kindness. Immediately after, he wrote an acrimonious letter to Henri Petri that he finally decided not to send, averting a breach. As far as can be gathered, the strength of feeling between Kathi Petri and Busoni, which had begun while he was still living in Leipzig, developed during the Christmas period to the point that the two actually planned to run away together. As related in chapter 4, at the last moment, Kathi came to her senses, and what could only have been a disaster was averted.

In January 1889 came the recital in Hamburg, where Busoni played one of his own piano transcriptions of a Bach organ work, and not one by Tausig. The idea of turning his own hand to transcribing Bach's organ works had apparently been suggested to him some time before by Kathi Petri, after she and Busoni had been to the Thomaskirche one day and heard Bach's Prelude and Fugue.

After the shattering emotional experiences in Leipzig, and his successful concert in Hamburg, Busoni returned even more reluctantly to the cultural backwater of Helsinki. On February 14, he played the Schumann Piano Quintet, op. 44, at a concert in the institute, with Sibelius playing second violin. It was the only time they ever appeared on the concert platform together. By March it seemed that for Busoni things could scarcely get worse: he had quarreled with Max Abraham over publication of his *Finnländische Volksweisen* (BV 227), a work for two pianos based on Finnish folk songs. Oskar Schwalm had now sold C. F. Kahnt, with whom Ferruccio had hoped to publish *Sigune*. And Theodore Steinway, who had held out the promise of an American tour, and a London recital for the coming summer, was dying. These projects died with him shortly after. This was a terrible setback to Busoni's career as a pianist, and, without these projects, it took him much longer to reach an equivalent standing. His letter to his parents dated March 12[13] recounts these sad events and also indicates that he had not written to them for some time. (That he had indeed not written since his letter of January 18, while he was still in Leipzig, which immediately precedes that of March 12 in the collection of the State Library in Berlin, seems unlikely. It is probable that some letters were destroyed, particularly if they referred to Kathi Petri.) Was there anyone he could talk to, or write to, about his personal troubles? It seems unlikely that this would have been a topic for discussion with the Leskovites. He had begun a friendship with Edvard (Edi) Fazer,[14] a pianist a few years his senior, and they apparently spent a lot of time together. But it must have been a wretched time for Busoni.

Then, on March 18, Edvard Fazer offered to take him to see some *tableaux vivants*, organized in aid of charity. He went, and at the supper dance following the performance, Edi brought a young woman to the table, Gerda Sjöstrand, whom Busoni had already noticed and expressed a desire to meet. (Gerda had first had Busoni pointed out to her by the sister of Robert Kajanus at one of the latter's concerts back in November; Gerda had immediately felt strongly attracted to the handsome young man.) Although not a conventional beauty, with her blond curls and lively expression of humor and youthful joie de vivre, Gerda was a very attractive figure. Her own account of what happened at their first meeting cannot be bettered.

Edi[15] took me over to where Busoni was sitting, and introduced me. Busoni quickly rose, greeted me gaily and immediately ordered champagne. I looked at him astonished. His beautiful chestnut hair, golden at the temples, formed a halo round his head. He spoke in a very lively and eager manner and laughed a lot, very heartily, so that you had to join in, whether you wanted to or not.—"So, you are a pianist," he said, "and what are you studying right now?"—"The Erlking," I shot back boldly.—"Oh, oh," he said, "even I can't play that; can you really?"—"I can't play it either," I admitted.—"You are not wearing any rings, Fräulein?"—"No, I don't like them; they get in the way."—"Strange—you are the first girl I have known who doesn't wear rings." My sister came from the dance floor and joined us. "You are a painter, as I have heard. Can you paint?"—"No!"—"Funny, one is a pianist and can't play, the other is a painter and can't paint." We all burst out laughing; the whole room turned round to stare at us.

The evening was very gay, until finally we had to leave. First we took Edi's sister home, then the two young men accompanied us. I was in very high spirits, threw my galoshes in the air, myself into the snow and committed every kind of nonsense. We were helpless with laughter.

That same evening Busoni said to Edi (who told me later): "That's a wife for an artist!"[16]

Two days later, Busoni left tickets at the Sjöstrands' for a concert the following day, as Gerda discovered when she returned from a visit to the dentist. "I was beside myself with joy, jumped on all the chairs and tables and behaved in a totally mad way. At last I was going to hear him," Gerda recalled. At the concert, from where the Sjöstrands sat in the hall, Busoni could see them, and spent every possible moment during the recital staring at Gerda. Afterward Edi came to say that she was to go backstage, and then go to dinner with them. She wisely refused ("The temptation was great, but I heroically resisted," as she ironically wrote to her sister)[17] and went off instead with her father and a family friend, Olga Sjöström, to the latter's house ("Instead—merciful Heaven, what an alternative—we drank small beer and tea at Olga's"). The day after the concert Ferruccio and Gerda met by chance in the street, and Busoni said he wanted to speak to her; he arranged a rendezvous in front of the Catholic Church at four o'clock for the next day. He was already waiting, with Lesko, when she arrived. His approach was utterly direct.

> After he had greeted me, he said at once: "Why did you come, Fräulein?"
> "Oh, I only came to say I'm not coming. But because I had promised, I didn't want to leave you waiting." I wanted to turn back immediately. Then he said: "Wait a moment, Fräulein, we can still talk a bit together!" He talked the whole time; I said nothing.[18]

He urged that they should meet frequently and get to know one another. He talked German, which was to remain their main language of communication, and which at that time Gerda did not speak very fluently, so that when, in his excitement, he spoke quickly, she could scarcely understand. She asked him what he wanted of her.

> "*Only good, Fräulein*," he said, with such a wonderful expression in his eyes, that it went right through me. I didn't respond, just said briefly: "I'm invited to tea, Adieu!" and flew more than walked over the deep snow. I had to give a lesson to a little Russian girl, paid no attention to what she was playing, was given some much too hot tea that I burned my mouth on, and rushed back home again. That was on the Saturday.

On the Sunday the Sjöstrands were invited to the Fazers' (Edi's parents) for lunch, and Gerda and Busoni were seated next to each other. Neither said much. That afternoon, by now in an intensely excited state, Gerda went skating alone, feeling the need for physical exercise as a relief from the tension. She knew that what was happening was very important, and therefore wanted to keep her head and act wisely. On the way home she encountered Busoni and Fazer again, and they invited her out for dinner the next evening. (Not surprisingly, the same Busoni who was so easily shocked at the freedom of Finnish girls energetically overcame Gerda's reservations at dining alone with two men. "But you are an intelligent girl and don't have any stupid prejudices!"[19]) They had a small room to themselves in the restaurant, and after the main meal Edi disappeared on a pretext. Immediately Busoni stood up, came to Gerda, bent over her, and said: "Will you be my wife?" and kissed her. "I said nothing, I was stunned. Edi came back. Ferruccio exclaimed: 'We've just got engaged!' Edi grinned happily and congratulated us; I was as though under a spell, could say neither Yes nor No." This was still only a week after the charity evening.

The next day Ferruccio formally asked Gerda's father for her hand. The Swedish sculptor Carl Aeneas Sjöstrand (1828–1906) had studied in Italy and spoke fluent Italian. He had no trouble accepting this amazing *coup de foudre* between his eldest daughter and an Italian pianist, and immediately gave his assent. Being an artist, he had an instinctive understanding of Busoni's nature, and as a mature, much-traveled man was a good judge of character: when Ferruccio asked him much later why he had immediately agreed to the marriage, Sjöstrand replied: "I only needed to look into your face." He had also spent a long time talking to Busoni (in Italian) on the Wednesday when the latter had brought the tickets for the concert. When the engagement was only a few days old, Ferruccio insisted on putting an announcement in the local paper—which "exploded in the town like a bomb," as Gerda recalled. Extraordinary to relate, it was several months before Ferruccio told his own parents.

Other than a powerful mutual attraction, we can only conjecture on the underlying reasons for the match on Busoni's part: he had just escaped a passionate relationship and the embers must still have been glowing, ready to be fanned into flame again; he was lonely, unhappy, and desperately in need of steady affection. For Gerda, the reasons were possibly more straightforward: here was a handsome, exotic, talented young man who must have stood out a mile from the competition in

Helsinki. Whatever the initial reasons for it, the marriage was to be the sturdy rock on which the rest of Busoni's life was anchored, and a happy and fulfilling union for both of them.

Three years Busoni's senior, Gerda was a lively, independent-minded young woman of twenty-five when she met him. Her mother had died in 1884, and as the elder of two daughters Gerda had now assumed many of the tasks of hostess and housekeeper in the family home. Her father gave her considerable freedom, however—she had recently returned from a period of piano study in Berlin, under Xaver Scharwenka, and before that had studied in Paris—and her strength of character, already manifest, was proved by the tortured events prior to her marriage. She was musical, and played the piano well enough to be giving piano lessons but, according to her own account, gave it up shortly after meeting Busoni.

> Ferruccio very much wanted to hear me play, but I always refused categorically. Once he crept into the room while I was playing Bach, and stood behind me listening for quite a while, without my realizing it. Then he cleared his throat—I jumped up as though possessed—he sat down himself at the piano and imitated me in a most cruel way. I was beside myself and with both fists smashed the glass door to the next room; Ferruccio laughed loudly. Since then I have never touched the keys.[20]

In Gerda's published recollections of her famous husband, in which she is at pains to present him in the very best light, the above is one of the few passages in which she herself reveals his less pleasant side. Perhaps the incident remained a sore point. Nevertheless, she did continue to play, at least until her marriage, as, in one of the letters written to him during their engagement, she tells of "practising for four hours." Another slightly negative anecdote in the recollections relates that for an engagement present to her, instead of the usual gift of jewelry, Busoni gave her the complete Brockhaus Lexikon, which "amused the whole town." "The glorious thing about it was that Ferruccio wanted the Lexikon himself—he knew I did not wear jewelry."

Two happy months followed as the couple got to know each other, a lunch break hastily arranged here, an evening tryst there, marred only by the occasional outbreak of jealousy on Busoni's part. They visited Martin Wegelius and his wife together, at gatherings where there were other young musicians, including Sibelius. It is not known how the other Leskovites took this "Benedictine collapse," as H. G. Wells's Mr. Polly succinctly termed it—although Sibelius had already met his own future wife, and indeed paid court to another young lady.

On April 27, 1889, Busoni gave a mammoth all-Chopin program with himself as soloist. Earlier in April he gave an all-Busoni recital, which included his arrangements of Finnish folk songs (the *Finnländische Volksweisen* for two pianos that had caused the rift with Abraham), which he played together with a colleague at the institute. This was the first time he also appeared on the conductor's podium—yet another valuable experience. In late May a String Quartet in A Minor by Sibelius (the complete score since lost) was premiered in Helsinki, before which the composer had showed it to Busoni. "He sat down at the piano at once," recalled Sibelius, "played through the quartet from beginning to end without having had the chance of even glancing at it beforehand. And *how* he played it!"[21]

Then at the beginning of June, his first academic year in Helsinki over, Ferruccio went to Weimar, intending to remain there, giving an occasional concert in Germany, and to return to Helsinki only on January 15, 1890. This was in accordance with a long-standing plan of spending time in a congenial artistic atmosphere and devoting himself to composition. He traveled with Edi Fazer, who was going to Weimar as assistant to the German pianist Bernhard Stavenhagen (1862–1914); Stavenhagen was engaged to conduct a series of master classes in Weimar that summer.

Ferruccio almost persuaded Gerda to come with him, which she wisely declined. His final attempt was on the ship about to take him to Germany, but she remained steadfast, hard though it was. Although just as much in love as he was, she remained clearheaded; she knew the relationship needed to be tested, but, more importantly, he needed to be left alone to work for a while and to think of his future. One of her many charms was her total honesty. There was no coquettish playing hard to get, or pretending indifference, as her first letter to him after his departure touchingly illustrates, in her rather awkward German.

Ferruccio, that was terrible, to see you going away. I didn't think it would be so difficult. Perhaps I looked quite calm, but I had a feeling as though

I wanted right at the last moment to hop on to the ship and shout loudly in front of everyone: "I *will* come with you." Ferruccio, tell me quite honestly, aren't you glad now that I didn't come with you? How wonderful you looked, when you were looking at me from the ship. I could never forget it. When I could no longer make you out, I ran to the lookout point in the Brunnsparken to watch the ship as long as possible. I looked so fixedly at the ship that I was quite stiff. I felt like a hypnotized person looking at the hand of the hypnotist and following every movement of that hand. I don't know how long I was there, but the ship got smaller and smaller, only like a small black dot, and it seemed as though the sea got bigger and bigger. Finally I didn't even see the black dot any more, there was just mist all around me.

It was a lovely time, these two months, the most wonderful I've had in my life. I thank you for that, Ferruccio, for all the beautiful, wonderful things you have given me, for your company, for your goodness, for your love, for everything, everything.[22]

She continued adding to this letter, as, although a telegram had arrived on the fifth, she was waiting for a first letter from him, which finally arrived on June 9. It had been posted in Berlin[23] but begun on the ship. Did she have the courage and strength to always love him, to follow him, share joys and sorrows with him, he asked, along with many other demands, always to trust in his talents and decisions, to encourage him, always to regard him as great, and spur him on to greater things?

He and Edi Fazer remained in Berlin for a few days, and Edi seriously riled Busoni by constantly remarking "Here Gerda did that, there we did that," recalling the time when the two of them had studied there under Scharwenka, and stirring up already simmering feelings of jealousy. Once in Weimar, Ferruccio began a letter[24] to her that stretched over several days, from June 12 to 17, waiting for a letter from her. Had she met someone else? Finally, he discovered that a letter from her had been lying at Stavenhagen's apartment since the thirteenth! He was so relieved and happy that he drank champagne. A piano had arrived on the sixteenth, but he had been unable to think of work until a letter from her arrived.

On June 14, as Ferruccio told Gerda in the above letter, he had gone with Edi to Leipzig. While there, he went to see Kathi Petri and spent over three hours talking to her, mainly explaining his engagement to Gerda. (He had told Gerda about the whole affair with Kathi before leaving Helsinki.)

I'm pleased, yes, I am happy to be able to tell you that—in the more than three hour long talk I had with her about my engagement—you, my darling, so radiantly triumphed, that I left with a truly relieved heart. In comparison with her you seemed to me like a pure angel. Have no fears, my love, there is no threat of a relapse, and the final danger is past. Oh, if you were only with me!

Poor Kathi, one can't help feeling.

As can be imagined, this letter was a great relief to Gerda, in spite of the jealous outbursts it also contained. "Your letter, your letter," she wrote back exultantly, "this letter I longed for so terribly, is here now. . . . I want to scream, scream—I could stand on my head—I don't know, do something crazy—even drink champagne. . . . How can you write so beautifully? I have read it, kissed it, laughed and cried, all at once. I had to have something to hug, to shake, I threw myself on the floor with Lesko—as though I'd gone mad."[25] (Lesko had remained with Gerda, and at the end of August disgraced herself by giving birth to ten puppies in the Sjöstrands's kitchen.)

Letters flew between Weimar and Helsinki, full of passion, frustration, longing, and at times agony on both sides, but on Ferruccio's side often shot through with jealousy, suspicion, rage, and unreasonable demands; on hers, hurt at his unfairness, but also dignity and reason. They wrote in German, but occasionally, usually toward the end of her letters, Gerda wrote a paragraph or two in Swedish: evidence that in those eight months in Helsinki Busoni must have made quite an effort to learn the language. (It was well into the twentieth century before Finnish became the dominant language in Finland, although even today, most public signposting in the country is in both languages.)

The letters written by the two lovers during this period make agonizing reading, even though they can be read today with the knowledge that the young couple were only suffering the usual angst and agony of young love temporarily frustrated, and that it ended well. Both often made the crucial mistake of writing—and rereading the other's letters—in the wee hours, when few of us see things clearly. Ferruccio even took to marking "significant" passages in her letters with a red line in the margin. Violent outbursts in his letters were followed by telegrams that overflew them and arrived in time to defuse these epistolary bombshells in advance.

Edi Fazer continued to cause Ferruccio unease, and at the beginning of July Adolf Paul arrived from Helsinki to continue studying piano under Busoni. They both stirred things up and, one suspects, rather enjoyed playing Iago to this fiery young Othello, insinuating, for example, that Gerda had led quite a wild life in Berlin. This all triggered off some hysterical letters to Helsinki. (Busoni's main reading matter at the time was Ibsen—one letter to Gerda of July 11[26] is full of *The Wild Duck*, and other plays—*Brand* in particular—are discussed and quoted in some detail; their mention was not calculated to have a calming effect, in the circumstances.) In Berlin, Ferruccio learned, Gerda had acted in student drama productions—a fact that caused quite extraordinary paroxysms of jealousy and suspicion, extraordinary in that his ideas of the moral pitfalls of theatrical life were those of a provincial spinster. He wrote yet another hysterical letter[27] on learning she had apparently shared a room during a visit to Bayreuth with one of the "Flower Maidens" from *Parsifal*. "I know what people say about the 'Flower Maidens' and what is expected of ladies in their company. If *you* don't know it yet, then learn that the famous twenty-four 'Flower Maidens' are the cocottes of Bayreuth! I could weep when I think how you gadded about in Germany; I think you may have landed up in a group of the demimonde, without realizing it!" Instead of being indignant upon receiving this raving nonsense, Gerda calmly replied with a full account of what had actually happened in Bayreuth: she was with perfectly respectable people (whom she named), and nothing at all untoward occurred.

One can only admire Gerda's understanding, tolerance, and patience in dealing with these outbursts. She even acquiesced in no longer posing as a model for her father, as it caused her fiancé such distress. She knew that the man underneath this nonsense was worth it, and over the years she managed to wean him from his narrow moral stance concerning what a respectable woman could and could not do—although she never managed to correct his openly expressed ideas concerning the innate intellectual inferiority of women. At the same time, ironically, she was the recipient throughout the rest of his life of letters containing his innermost thoughts and ideas, to which she was expected to react. (In the letter[28] following the "Flower Maidens" accusation, he writes: "It is right that you consider me as superior to you: for this is the natural relationship between man and woman, which evolves favorably if the woman can acknowledge this.")

At the end of June Ferruccio went to Wiesbaden to take part in a music festival. He was supposed to remain for the whole festival, but precipitately returned to Weimar as he had not had a letter from her for some time. He was under appalling pressures, which certainly explains much of his hysteria where Gerda is concerned. On July 5 he suffered "such a powerful, almost morbid nervous attack that I didn't know what to do. Convulsively laughing and crying all at once, without any apparent special cause."[29] As the passionate passages in his letters make quite clear, he must also have been suffering severe sexual frustration. His financial situation was still dire, and he was trying to negotiate a loan to regularize his finances. Although his father was now in Italy, both parents were still a burden, and now he was contemplating marriage. And at the beginning of July there was another cause for concern: his mother was due to arrive in Weimar at any moment, and he would have to tell her of his engagement. He instinctively knew she would be against it. His father, he also knew, would accept it pragmatically. "My father," he had written to Gerda, "terribly strict in small matters and therefore the terror of my childhood, has a broader view in the larger things of life. He often said to me in his simple way: You must, as you are now becoming a man, live regularly. So either buy yourself a woman or marry one."[30]

It is impressive that Gerda, still only twenty-five, recognized and dealt with Ferruccio's psychological condition as a kind of illness, although it took an awful lot out of her too: in early July a woman friend of the family from Helsinki, who brought him some items from Gerda that he had requested, told him that Gerda looked "pale, haggard and nervous,"[31] which aroused his compunction.

True to form, Anna made difficulties about coming to Weimar, and postponed her arrival twice, which must have cranked up the suspense even more. Finally, on July 16 Ferruccio went to Leipzig to meet her off the train and was pleasantly surprised to find his father had come too. He brought them to his lodgings in Weimar (in the house of Liszt's former cook in the Schröterstrasse) and braced himself. He had not seen them for eighteen months, a period during which he had passed some significant milestones in his life. Their frail appearance was a less than pleasant surprise, as was their mental state: "Both have become petty, anxious, superstitious, bigoted, it's not a happy picture, not a sunny impression that I got: I feel pressured, removed from you in particular through the fact that they (my nearest and dearest), don't know you, my dearest one. I now miss your freshness, your youth twice as much."[32] Both parents were only in their fifties; Anna in particular had aged prematurely, her curly hair now a frizzy white nimbus. The change was obviously more in Ferruccio than in them. He had moved a long distance, while they had stayed still.

They had scarcely arrived at his lodgings when Anna noticed a photograph of Gerda on the desk.

> Mamma went up to the desk and of course the first thing she asked was who the photograph was of. Not to frighten her too soon I said: "It's a girl I like very much." "And who is that in the locket?" "The same girl." Mamma pretended not to have heard the answer. That evening, when we got home after supper, Mamma went to look at your portrait again. "Do you like the girl, Mamma?" "I haven't looked yet, the frame is so beautiful." "But the picture. . . ." "Yes, she's not bad, but she would not be my ideal." "But she's my ideal, and that's enough." "But the frame is beautiful," she repeated, "and now good night."[33]

Amazingly, it was only the next day, and then almost casually, that he finally told them that Gerda was his fiancée.

> At lunch the discussion . . . turned to *women smoking*. "Does that one, in the picture, smoke too," said my father casually. "Yes, if I want; not if I don't want." "So (my father), so there is a relationship between you."— "Yes, *because she is my fiancée*." My parents were not surprised and said they had already talked to one another, that in such a case (that *they* expected) they would never say anything against it, but let me have my own way. I asked for their blessing and telegraphed you.[34]

His father left after a week, to stay with his brothers in Empoli, where he remained for the next six months. Now the real struggle between Ferruccio and his mother began. Her resistance to her son's possible marriage was visceral and relentless, as he had accurately foreseen, although for the moment it was expressed obliquely, for the most part. He also told her the full story about Kathi, and was rather shocked that Anna condemned Kathi and pitied her husband; "Myself, the most guilty one, she let off scot-free."[35]

At the beginning of August his nerves gave out under the unremitting psychological strains of his mother's resistance to his engagement, jealousy at supposed incidents in Gerda's past, and the very natural longing to see Gerda again. Leaving Anna in the care of Adolf Paul, he fled to Helsinki, where the young lovers had a deliriously happy week. He returned via Berlin, where he stayed for a few days to discuss future plans with Hermann Wolff. On his return to Weimar, Anna, though friendly, revealingly remarked that he was wavering between two magnets, his mother and Gerda, and it looked as though the one in Helsinki would win.

From Weimar, his letters to Gerda immediately contained neurotic outbursts again, overtaken by a perfect flurry of remorseful telegrams. One night he even hauled Adolf Paul out of bed to wrest "the truth" from him about Gerda's alleged exploits in Berlin. By now Paul must have been regretting any mischief he might have instigated, and he had also lost patience. "When I left, he said, Don't think about it any more (just like Iago). To promise something like that, I said, is impossible now."[36] There is some evidence that during the week in Helsinki, Gerda and Ferruccio had slept together, unfortunately putting Gerda in the familiar bind of having "allowed" too much, and thereby incurring Ferruccio's suspicion that she had behaved in a similar way before, with someone else. His own behavior was not always above reproach: although he was now in contact with Henri Petri again, who had just moved to Dresden. Ferruccio's interaction with him consisted chiefly of asking for advice on where he could get a loan for 5,000 marks, getting Petri to correct the proofs of his String Quartet in D Minor (BV 225), and asking if he could get free tickets for himself, his mother, and Adolf Paul for a coming four-day *Ring* production in Dresden, among other things. But he was avoiding a meeting with Petri, and one excuse he gave Petri for the postponement of a visit to Dresden was that he had just spent several days in Berlin seeing Wolff, and could not now leave Weimar, as he had far too much work.[37] There was no mention of the Helsinki visit!

As is so often observed in composers, strains in Busoni's personal life apparently had no effect on his creative powers; in that same letter to Gerda of August 15 quoted above, he tells her he is hard at work on his *Konzertstück* for Piano and Orchestra (BV 236), which "had to be finished for Hamburg." (It was completed only in June 1890 and in fact first performed in August that same year in Saint Petersburg.)

Anna continued to apply terrible pressure on him. On August 23, during a walk, it came to a crisis, as he wrote to Gerda.

> Mamma referred to you with careless words and insulted you and me. I didn't say another word, but felt myself go pale and trembling. I was like that for a good half hour—on the street—until my mother said: But Ferruccio, what's the matter with you, I can't see you like that any longer— on which I broke down into convulsive sobbing that lasted a long time. That must have affected my mother a lot; the more so as I remained friendly and respectful to her.[38]

The next morning they talked it over and Anna seemed more accepting. Gerda certainly proved her worth during this period of severe trial, not least in her sympathy and understanding. How many young women of her age would have had the wisdom and strength to act as she did? And in spite of the jealous outbursts, Ferruccio knew her worth, as he often admitted at length in his letters, and was terrified of losing her. He was still only twenty-three, but his life for the last fifteen years had been an almost unremitting strain, the last year possibly the worst, with the initial loneliness of Helsinki; the affair with Kathi, which also almost destroyed his friendship with Henri Petri; and now the prospect of a fulfilled and happy love with Gerda threatened by his mother.

In early September, leaving his mother in Weimar, Busoni toured for a week, playing in Berlin, Dresden, and Leipzig. He decided under pressure from Anna to provide his parents with a secure income, to abandon the idea of staying in Weimar until January, concentrating on composing, and instead to return immediately to Helsinki to resume his teaching at the conservatory, and to take his mother with him. He telegraphed Wegelius accordingly. In mid-September they arrived there, to face the next hurdle: the meeting between Gerda and Anna. Gerda recalled:

> I shall never forget that evening when I went to the station. The impression the mother made on me with her gray hair, her big nose with some moles on it, was that of a witch from *Macbeth*. Yet she was anything but witch-like; she was a good, noble and intelligent woman. She loved her son so much that she was blind to everything else. The thought of now having to lose this son by marriage was simply unbearable for her. She would have been against any girl—I just happened to be the one.[39]

The two women communicated in French, and at first all seemed well. Everyone tried to make Anna welcome in what was for her a very alien environment.

Busoni managed to complete the piano transcription of yet another Bach organ work, the Prelude and Fugue in E-flat Major (BWV 552), which was published by Rahter in Hamburg early in 1890, and in December he set off for recitals in Leipzig. He traveled via Saint Petersburg, where, during a three-and-a-half-hour rail stopover, he ran into Tchaikovsky and Rimsky-Korsakov. Tchaikovsky was particularly kind and initiated plans for future Russian concerts. Busoni hungrily relished the encounter. Tchaikovsky was "like a father" to him. "He asked if next year I could play at the big Moscow concerts, and to come soon to Saint Petersburg to make myself known. With great love and esteem he presented me and recommended me to his colleagues. It was a comfort and satisfaction to find myself in that great [bravissima] society, after the arid months in Helsingfors," he wrote to his mother.[40] In Berlin he had another stimulating stopover, spent with Adolf Paul and Sibelius, who was now studying composition with Albert Becker, and arrived in Leipzig on Christmas Eve. He found all the shops already shut, but managed both to get a room with Frau Spann, his old landlady, and an "excellent Blüthner." He spent Christmas alone in Leipzig, an experience all the more desolate, as the previous weeks in Helsinki had been full of almost unbearable tensions caused by his mother. Anna spent Christmas with the Sjöstrands—which can only have increased her son's agitation.

There were three concerts in Leipzig on January 8, 9, and 11, 1890; in one he played Tchaikovsky's A Minor Trio, in which he was joined by the Russian violinist Adolf Brodsky (1851–1929), a friend from his Leipzig time who was not only to remain a friend, but also often to play Busoni's works (and who had introduced him to Tchaikovsky). In another of the three concerts Busoni took part in a performance of his own Konzert-Fantasie for Piano and Orchestra (BV 230; written 1888–1889 in Helsinki and never published; revised in 1893 as Symphonic Tone Poem for Orchestra, BV 240), conductor Carl Reinecke, which was not very well received. This did not surprise Busoni; in fact, he reported to his mother, it was in too new a style to be understood on first hearing by a public "fed until now on ricotta and polenta, 'caviar for the general' as Hamlet says."[41] It was a bizarre disparagement of the Leipzig public. Busoni's playing, both in Leipzig and later in Saint Petersburg, met with almost universal praise, however.

He stayed in Leipzig until January 19, played in Saint Petersburg on January 29, and at the end of the month he was back in Helsinki. Sometime between then and the end of March he went back to Saint Petersburg, where he gave several more concerts, one of them conducted by the legendary pianist Anton Rubinstein—thus renewing an acquaintance reaching back over ten years to when Rubinstein had written the then twelve-year-old that barbed testimonial. Busoni was invited to settle in Saint Petersburg as a piano teacher, a suggestion he rejected: "I can't even think of burying myself as a piano teacher in that city with its decadent artistic tastes and social prejudices," he wrote soon after to Henri Petri.[42] It was nevertheless an enormous compliment that Rubinstein was paying him. Rubinstein, who had resumed directorship of the Saint Petersburg Conservatory the year before (he had previously been director from 1862 to 1867, when he relinquished it to devote himself to an international career again), had, as part of the celebrations for his sixtieth birthday in 1889, inaugurated the Rubinstein competition for piano playing and composition, and Busoni was invited to compete in August 1890.

In Helsinki Busoni still faced an unbearable situation. His mother continued her insidious campaign against Gerda, and from Empoli, and then Trieste, his father aided and abetted his wife, insisting that the only way to save Ferruccio from a life of immorality—which, he had convinced himself, his son was leading—was to have his mother live with him. One motive behind this "good advice" was that Ferdinando was determined not to live with Anna himself. Ferruccio became more and more determined that his parents *should* live together, clearly seeing too that Anna was almost succeeding in destroying his relationship with Gerda.

Gerda herself, though a strong-minded young woman, almost broke down under the constant attacks from Anna, who told her repeatedly that she should not marry Ferruccio, as he had his parents to support and they should come first. In those early months of 1890, while Ferruccio was back in Saint Petersburg, Gerda decided to break off the engagement, and to meet his train to break the news.

When Ferruccio had notified the time of his arrival, I went halfway to Petersburg to meet him. I only had a short time to wait at a station, until his train from Petersburg (in the direction of Helsingfors) arrived. With my heart banging I got in. Ferruccio, when he caught sight of me, behaved like a madman, whooped just like a Red Indian, threw himself down on his back on the seat and drummed his heels—in short, he was quite demented with joy. So in this mood I was supposed to come out with my decision. When I talked of his mother and that it would be better to part, and in fact now (later it would be only more difficult), he smothered me with a flood of kisses. Never could that happen, he said; his mother should live with his father, who actually needed her a lot, and we must stay together. He spoke a lot and urgently and also very seriously. "If you leave me, I'll lose my strength."[43]

There was no more talk of breaking off the engagement.

In late August he was in Saint Petersburg again for the Rubinstein competition. He entered for both prizes: composition and piano. He played his newly finished Konzertstück for Piano and Orchestra (BV 236), winning first prize in composition. "Herr Busoni," wrote the German-language St. Petersburger Herold, "who is but twenty-four years old, can be counted among those blessed souls who have at their command, apart from talent, stern application matched with intelligence. Take for instance the Konzertstück: fine working-out of themes, brilliant though somewhat noisy scoring, concise and clear form and fairly original piano writing." Max Reger, a more qualified judge and a friend of Busoni, was more straightforwardly enthusiastic in the Allgemeine Musikzeitung following a later performance of the work in 1894: "Here Busoni creates out of fullness and profundity alone, and this, combined with the energetic working-out of the great theme, results in a masterpiece, the like of which is no daily occurrence. . . . The completely polyphonic structure, can without reserve be described as truly great and highly ingenious." It is indeed an ingenious work and, pace Tchaikovsky, full of melody, the final section in fact throbbing with lyrical passion—it was, one should remember, written the year before, during that tumultuous summer in Weimar. Although Busoni soon dropped the work from his repertoire, he revived it thirty years later, adding two more movements, playing the revised version for the last time in 1921. Ronald Stevenson has pointed out a quotation in the original version of a motif from Carl Goldmark's opera Merlin, proving that in spite of the hated drudgery of writing out the piano score for that now almost forgotten opera, some of the music must have lodged in Busoni's memory. He cannibalized from one of his own works in the Allegro molto section: an aria sung by the landlord's daughter Marie in *Sigune*.

Although Busoni had also entered the Rubinstein competition as pianist, he lost the prize in that section to a Russian, one Dubassov: according to the (unwritten) rules of the competition, the same person was not allowed to win both prizes, and a Russian should win at least one. Anton Rubinstein himself was the president of the competition jury; he further assisted Busoni by recommending him for a teaching position at the Moscow Imperial Conservatory, beginning in September that year, which Busoni accepted. (In view of his emphatic rejection of Saint Petersburg earlier that year, the decision to go to Moscow looks very much like desperation.)

After the competition he returned fleetingly to Helsinki and, with some of the 5,000 francs prize money, arranged for his mother to travel from Helsinki to join her husband in Gorizia, a small town about twenty-five miles north of Trieste where Ferdinando had given a concert but—typically—had run into debt and stayed on. Busoni arranged for all his father's debts to be paid, rented an apartment for his parents in Trieste, and settled a monthly income on them. In early September he traveled overland with his mother to Saint Petersburg, put her on a southbound train, and traveled on alone to Moscow.

First impressions were not "exactly favorable," he wrote to Gerda,

> for except for a few points, which are grand, characteristic, strange and fantastic, the whole city is predominantly askew, crooked, old and dirty: *dirty*—I tell you—in a virtuosic evolution [*in einer virtuosen Entwicklung*] of dirt! In furnished rooms I have looked at, half-full chamber pots were on the floor, surrounded by large, wet patches—horrible! *Who* could rent a place like that? . . . Beggars without hands, without feet, without clothes harry passersby. Striking poverty prevails everywhere, side by side with the most tasteless excess of luxury.[44]

No one could accuse him of luring her to Moscow under false pretences. Nevertheless, in his next letter, written three days later, he apologized about his gloomy letter. "The Conservatory here is *excellent*; well organized, and with the best teachers."[45]

Nevertheless, accommodation was found—unfurnished, which meant the expense of buying their own furniture, but furnished rooms were just too squalid. Ferruccio was still under double pressure from his parents, with demands for money from his father, and his mother apparently still unreconciled to his marriage. He even had to justify buying furniture: this cost him 500 rubles, he wrote his father, giving a full breakdown of other expenses. He advised his parents not to get bogged down in Gorizia, then continued tellingly: "Soon I shall be getting married. Although you are against it, I nevertheless consider myself content and my decision a good one."[46] Over four months later, on February 12, 1891, Anna was writing to one Fräulein Sarah Hess, an acquaintance of Ferruccio's who often sent Anna press cuttings of her son's performances, complaining of the marriage. I quote from Edward Dent's rather quirky translation:

> To be sure, when one forms a family everything becomes more difficult and one is obliged to think about securing one's position. And for that reason I consider that Ferruccio should not have dreamed of taking a wife until his reputation had become more widely spread in all the branches of his Art, all the more as he is still too young to bind himself and to take up all the burdens of a family. You will understand without further explanations from me that this decision of his destroyed my most cherished dream of living close to this son of mine, for I love him not only with a mother's affection but with the heart of an artist as well.
>
> This being said (between ourselves) Ferruccio is still the best of sons, but living so far off I can no longer enjoy his companionship which is so dear to me, nor enrapture myself at the touch of his fingers, nor rejoice in the creations of his fervid fantasy![47]

Ferruccio arranged with a German Protestant pastor to marry them in Moscow, as the local Catholic church made difficulties over Gerda's being Protestant, and sent off a telegram to Helsinki to signal that all was ready. On September 27 Gerda arrived with her father and her sister Helmi, Lesko also in tow. Ferruccio met them at the station with the news that they had to hurry immediately to the church, as the pastor was going on holiday that very day. And so they were married, Gerda in the old skirt and red knitted jersey she had traveled in, her wedding dress still in her suitcase. "During the ceremony," wrote Gerda, "my mood was more inclined to laughter than emotion, because the situation was too comic. And the pastor, to make matters worse, was called Dickkopf [fathead]."[48]

The reception accorded to Busoni in Moscow by his fellow musicians was less amusing. By the final decade of the nineteenth century, Russia had found its own musical voice. This had not been easy. Lacking a powerful middle class, that source of so much artistic activity elsewhere, Russia had until recently relied mainly on imported music and performers. Such Russian music as there was (other than folk music) had been written by upper-class "amateurs," most of whom kept their day jobs, as music was not considered a respectable profession for their class. But as in literature, in music too, since midcentury, the reaction of many Russian composers had been to resort to a fierce nationalism, basing their works on Russian themes and often using Russian folk music. Under the leadership of Mily Balakirev (1837–1910), a group that became known as the "mighty handful" (Kuchka), consisting of Balakirev himself, Rimsky-Korsakov, Musorgsky, Borodin, and Cui, strove to bring Russian music up to European standards. And above them all towered Tchaikovsky, the only one to have devoted himself, virtually from childhood, exclusively to music, although his attitude was certainly not narrowly nationalistic.

Since 1889 Vasily Ilyich Safonov had been director of the Moscow Imperial Conservatory. He had studied and then taught at the Saint Petersburg Conservatory, and had had some success as a pianist, touring extensively in Russia and Europe. He was also an enthusiastic teacher, and within a short time he had improved standards considerably at the conservatory in Moscow. He also organized popular concerts and was for two periods principal conductor in Moscow of the Russian Musical Society. He traveled later in the United States, and was conductor of the Philharmonic Society Orchestra in New York from 1906 to 1909. Safonov certainly supported Busoni, and was keenly interested in his career.

Busoni's concert performances of the previous two years, and his winning of the Rubinstein prize, had established him firmly on the international musical map. Given the above-described conditions, and his cosmopolitan background, it was predictable that he would get a frosty reception in this fervently nationalistic atmosphere. Other than

Safonov, in general his Russian colleagues closed ranks and resented him, which left him, always an expansively, friendly, and gregarious man, feeling very lonely, even with Gerda now constantly at his side. And in spite of a generous monthly salary of 200 rubles, living expenses were such that, in view of the constant drain of supporting his parents (who received 100 rubles a month from him), he was in fact little better off than in Helsinki. His work schedule was exhausting: he was obliged to teach for up to thirty-five hours a week, as he took on private pupils to increase his income.

Nevertheless, his first concert in Moscow, at the end of October, was a great success. He knew it was important to make a good first impression and was practicing for six hours or more a day in the week leading up to the concert. He played Beethoven's Piano Concerto no. 5, with his own cadenzas, earning eight curtain calls and two encores. The governor general of Moscow came expressly to hear him. (Unfortunately, the concert was part of his contract at the conservatory and therefore in a sense unpaid, as he had to point out in a letter to his father written a few days later, most of which was, of course, taken up with defensive explanations of his financial state, in reply to a reproachful letter from Ferdinando.)

Over the Christmas period he went on a concert tour in Germany together with Gerda, and the contrast between the musical life in the larger German cities and that in Moscow was made unbearably clear to him. While he was in Berlin, William Steinway (brother of Theodore, and now head of the family firm) contacted him from New York, offering a teaching post at the New England Conservatory of Music in Boston, at a salary three times that he was earning in Moscow. Although he knew that Boston would have some of the drawbacks of Helsinki, he agreed, the more so as his old friend Arthur Nikisch was now living and working there as the conductor of the Boston Symphony Orchestra. He had known Nikisch, ten years his senior, since 1876, when, as a ten-year-old, Ferruccio had played in a chamber music concert with him in Vienna, Nikisch playing the violin. During the period in which Busoni had lived in Leipzig, Nikisch had been the principal conductor of the Leipzig Opera. Their paths were to cross frequently.

Just over a year before, Busoni had refused a post similar to the one offered in Boston, in Cincinnati, clearly seeing the disadvantages: taking travel and other expenses into account, he would end up scarcely better off, and it would interrupt his burgeoning concert career in Europe. (His calculations had all been based on staying in Cincinnati only one year.) But Boston did not sound as remote from the musical scene as Cincinnati. He discussed it with his agent, Hermann Wolff, who encouraged the move to Boston. Whatever the considerations, yet again pressures were building up behind him, pushing him forward on yet another quest for that elusive grail, financial security for the whole family.

By May arrangements for the move to Boston were secure enough for him to be assiduously learning English, and finally to inform his parents of the plan, with the crucial information that he would be earning 18,000 francs for 10 months' work, not counting other occasional earnings. He had the support of William Steinway, he told them. The plan was to stay in Boston for one year, then tour, earning enough to be able subsequently to spend two or three years composing.

> Tell me, dear ones, I beg you—what do you think of this plan. I shall have the first position in the country there; while here in Russia I shall never succeed in beating the Russian celebrities long resident here.
>
> Even if I'm not happy there, well—after a year I'll come back, still with a bit of money in my pocket and the satisfaction of having gone on a fine journey free of charge! The confusions of this plan mean I can't send you the money you need until June. I myself, for the whole of this month, have scarcely 50 rubles.[49]

At the end of the semester, he and Gerda returned to Helsinki; then, at the end of August 1891, the two set sail for Boston. (Lesko was left behind in Moscow with the German pianist Paul Pabst [1854–1897], another piano teacher at the Moscow Conservatory, who became equally fond of her. She died in January 1895, just four weeks before Busoni returned to Moscow on a concert tour.)

Notes

1. Letter from FB to Henri and Katharina Petri, September 12, 1888, MW, p. 16.

2. Letter from FB to Ferdinando Busoni, September 17, 1888, StBB Bus. Nachl. 1240.

3. Letter from FB to Henri and Katharina Petri, mid-September 1888, MW, p. 21.

4. Erik Tawaststjerna, *Sibelius*, Vol. 1, trans. Robert Layton (London: Faber and Faber, 1976), p. 45.

5. Tawaststjerna, *Sibelius*, p. 53.

6. Letter from FB to Anna Weiss-Busoni, October 26, 1888, StBB Bus. Nachl. 1245.

7. Letter from FB to Henri and Katharina Petri, mid-September 1888, MW, p. 20.

8. Letter from FB to Henri and Katharina Petri, mid-September, 1888, MW, p. 24.

9. FB to Henri and Katharina Petri, September 25, 1888, MW, p. 22.

10. FB to Ferdinando Busoni, September 17, 1888.

11. Letter from FB to Henri and Katharina Petri, October 7–17, 1888, MW, p. 28.

12. Letter from FB to Anna Weiss-Busoni, October 26, 1888, StBB Bus. Nachl. 1245.

13. Letter from FB to Ferdinando Busoni and Anna Weiss-Busoni, March 12, 1889, StBB Bus. Nachl. 1248.

14. Edvard Fazer (1861–1943) studied piano in Berlin with Xaver Scharwenka, but became a concert agent. His agency still thrives today, under the name Fazer Artists' Management. He founded the Finnish Opera House in Helsinki, and was its director from 1911 to 1938.

15. Edvard Fazer is described by Gerda as "my good friend," but by Sergio Sablich, in his edition of Busoni's letters (p. 87n), as Gerda's cousin. Also, Dent describes him as a pupil of Busoni, but this seems unlikely, given that Fazer would have been around twenty-eight at this time.

16. Gerda Busoni, *Erinnerungen an Ferruccio Busoni* (Berlin: Afas-Musik-Verlag, 1958), p. 6.

17. Quoted in G. Busoni, *Erinnerungen*, p. 7.

18. G. Busoni, *Erinnerungen*, p. 11.

19. G. Busoni, *Erinnerungen*, p. 12.

20. G. Busoni, *Erinnerungen*, p.14.

21. Tawaststjerna, *Sibelius*, p. 51.

22. Letter from Gerda Sjöstrand to FB, June 2, 1889, StBB, Bus. Nachl. IV, 173.

23. Letter from FB to Gerda Sjöstrand, June 4, 1889, StBB, Bus. Nachl. IV, 204.

24. Letter from FB to Gerda Sjöstrand, June 12–17, 1889, StBB Bus. Nachl. IV, 208.

25. Letter from Gerda Sjöstrand to FB, June 21, 1889, StBB Bus. Nachl. IV 175.

26. Letter from FB to Gerda Sjöstrand, July 11, 1889, StBB Bus. Nachl. IV, 220.

27. Letter from FB to Gerda Sjöstrand, June 23, 1889, StBB Bus. Nachl. IV, 212.
28. Letter from FB to Gerda Sjöstrand, June 24, 1889, StBB Bus. Nachl. IV, 213.
29. Letter from FB to Gerda Sjöstrand, July 7, 1889, StBB Bus. Nachl. IV, 218.
30. Letter from FB to Gerda Sjöstrand, June 23, 1889, StBB Bus. Nachl. IV, 212.
31. Letter from FB to Gerda Sjöstrand, July 7, 1889, StBB Bus. Nachl. IV, 218.
32. Letter from FB to Gerda Sjöstrand, July 16–20, 1889, StBB Bus. Nachl. IV, 221.
33. FB to Gerda Sjöstrand, July 16–20, 1889.
34. FB to Gerda Sjöstrand, July 16–20, 1889.
35. Letter from FB to Gerda Sjöstrand, July 27, 1889, StBB Bus. Nachl. IV, 228.
36. Letter from FB to Gerda Sjöstrand, August 15, 1889, StBB Bus. Nachl. IV, 231.
37. Letter from FB to Henri Petri, August 14, 1889, MW, p. 38.
38. Letter from FB to Gerda Sjöstrand, August 23, 1889, StBB Bus. Nachl. IV, 241.
39. G. Busoni, Erinnerungen, p. 16.
40. Letter from FB to Anna Weiss-Busoni, December 23, 1889, StBB Bus. Nachl. IV, 248.
41. Letter from FB to Anna Weiss-Busoni, January 10, 1890, StBB Bus. Nachl. 1275.
42. Letter from FB to Henri Petri, April 3, 1890, MW, p. 46.
43. G. Busoni, Erinnerungen, p. 17.
44. Letter from FB to Gerda Sjöstrand, September 1–13, 1890 (at this time the Russian calendar was two weeks behind the European calendar), StBB Bus. Nachl. IV, 261.
45. Postcard from FB to Gerda Sjöstrand, September 4–16, 1890, StBB Bus. Nachl. IV, 262.
46. Letter from FB to Ferdinando Busoni, September 14–26, 1890, StBB Bus. Nachl. 1272.
47. Dent, Ferruccio Busoni, pp. 96–97.
48. Dent, Ferruccio Busoni, p. 19.
49. Letter from FB to Ferdinando Busoni and Anna Weiss-Busoni, May 6–18, 1891, StBB Bus. Nachl. 1280.

CHAPTER SIX

Boston and New York: August 1891 to April 1894

At the end of August 1891 the Busonis landed in New York, their arrival duly reported by the *Musical Courier*: "Carlo [*sic*] Busoni, the talented young pianist, composer and winner of the Rubinstein Scholarship in 1890, in St. Petersburg, Russia, arrived in this city last week. He goes to Boston to assume an important professorship at the New England Conservatory."[1] This was followed three weeks later by a short biographical sketch in the same publication,[2] which indicates that Busoni was interviewed. His arrival was also reported in the *New York Times*.[3] He was impressed by New York, with its bustle and vitality, its buses, streetcars, and fourteen-story buildings, particularly when contrasting it with the squalor of "barbarous Moscow," as Ferruccio wrote to his parents.[4]

After only a few days in New York, Ferruccio and Gerda traveled on to Boston, taking up lodgings first at 73 Warren Street, moving later to number 312. First impressions were again favorable, although Busoni was rather shocked by the puritanical attitude to wine in the city, and found it regrettable that only lemonade and ice cream would be served at a reception given in honor of his arrival. The same attitude extended to music making: as he told his mother much later,[5] on Sundays, his students were not allowed to play their instruments or to read anything but the Bible. Such differences in cultural attitudes between Europe and North America, which have evolved as a result of different histories, experiences, and social exigencies, can prove surprisingly difficult to digest, for both sides, as Busoni himself was to learn over the years. But it is a moot point whether "digest" is the correct word here: from first to last, there were many things about the United States that Busoni was not able to stomach.

In the 1890s, the relatively small city of Boston (the population was still under half a million) vied with New York as the intellectual and literary center of North America. Many of the most prominent American writers and poets were either born in the Boston area or had settled there. Emerson, Hawthorne, Thoreau, Whittier, and Longfellow, although dead by the time Busoni arrived, lived on in the intellectual atmosphere they had helped to generate, which was further stoked by the presence of Harvard, America's first university, founded in the seventeenth century, just across the Charles River. The city also attracted the other arts, music in particular, patronized by the wealthy and relatively numerous *haute bourgeoisie* of the town. The Boston Symphony Orchestra had been founded ten years before, in 1881, by the banker and philanthropist Henry Lee Higginson, one of many valiant and public-minded figures who laid the practical foundations for the cultural life of the United States, realizing how crucial a civilizing role the arts could play in the country. Unlike literature, a plant which had been relatively easy to propagate from English cuttings and, as the above names indicate, was already flourishing, music had as yet proved harder to transfer to American soil. One way around this was to import talent from Europe—or, more specifically, from Germany. As Marc-André Roberge has rightly pointed out,[6] "When Busoni arrived in North America in 1891, the German domination of classical music in the United States was still nearly total." The Boston Symphony Orchestra was therefore anxious to attract top players: in addition to Arthur Nikisch, who had become the conductor of the orchestra two years before, a large proportion of the Boston Symphony Orchestra was of German origin, which was also true of the New York Philharmonic and other important American orchestras of the time. Another recent arrival was the cellist Alwin Schröder, former member of the Petri Quartet in Leipzig and dedicatee of Busoni's Short Suite for Cello and

Piano (BV 215), premiered in Leipzig by Schröder and the composer. This all boded well for Busoni.

Situated at that time on Franklin Square, at the corner of Newton and James streets, the New England Conservatory, where Busoni was to teach, had been founded in 1867 by another indefatigable promoter of culture, Eben Tourjée (1834–1891), music educator and founder of more than one music school in the United States, and Robert Goldbeck. (Tourjée, who had died in April that year, had been a lifelong active Methodist, which might explain the lemonade.) The conservatory's director when Busoni arrived was Carl Faelten (1846–1925), a pianist of German extraction who had been teaching in Boston since 1885; he was director from 1890 until 1897.

But the everyday reality of Busoni's life in Boston was a sharp disappointment to him. He was engaged at the conservatory as a professor of piano and composition in the graduate department. However, as a young institution, the New England Conservatory was still not firmly enough established to be too selective about its pupils. And the Boston Brahmin influence was no match for hard-nosed financial calculation of positively Gradgrindian proportions: in their lessons individual piano students were given exactly fifteen minutes' teaching each, and cut off practically in midbar when their time was up. This sausage-machine approach horrified the young idealist. (Just a few years later Sir Henry Wood, having learned of this method of instruction in American institutions, turned down an extremely generous offer to teach singing in the United States.) Also, of Busoni's eighteen piano pupils, sixteen were female! *Pace* Busoni's low opinion of female intelligence, the fact would seem to indicate that piano playing was still principally considered a pursuit for young ladies. Furthermore, not one of his Boston pupils ever had any success then or later on the concert platform, although there must have been such aspirations, whether personal or parental, as some of his students came from as far afield as Kansas, Tennessee, and Iowa. His annual salary was $3,240, divided over four terms, which was generous for the time.

Busoni had made his New York debut three months after his arrival in the United States, on December 7, 1891, in a joint recital at the Fortnightly Club with a singer identified solely as "Miss Hall." (This was only three weeks after Ignacy Paderewski's New York debut; the

great Polish pianist, some six years Busoni's senior, did not enjoy success there initially.) But it was only on January 17, 1892, that Busoni
finally performed one of his own works in New York, the *Konzertstück*
for Piano and Orchestra (BV 236), the piece with which he had won
the Rubinstein Prize. This was at the Music Hall (later to become
Carnegie Hall), at one of the Sunday concerts organized and conducted
by Walter Damrosch (1862–1950). Damrosch, who was also a composer, was born in the German city of Breslau (now Wroclaw, and in
Poland); he had emigrated to the United States with his parents and
elder brother Frank in 1871. The two brothers and their father were incredibly active and influential in the U.S. musical scene throughout
their lives.

On January 31, 1892, Busoni was in New York again, at the Chamber Music Hall, with Adolf Brodsky, another Leipzig friend, now in
New York as leader of the New York Symphony Orchestra. They played
Busoni's Sonata in E Minor for Violin and Piano no. 1 (BV 234), probably composed in Leipzig in 1889. (It was dedicated to Brodsky, who
was still in Leipzig at that time, and published by Rahter in 1891.)
There were few other concerts for Busoni outside Boston that first year.

In the Music Hall in Boston, on February 19, he had the mixed pleasure of hearing excerpts from his ill-fated Symphonic Suite for Orchestra (BV 201), conducted by Nikisch; on April 8 he performed his
Kulsatelle: Ten Short Variations on a Finnish Folk Song for Cello and
Piano (BV 237), together with Alwin Schröder, and four days later, in
the conservatory, he played his Violin Sonata no. 1 again, with
Brodsky.

Busoni held out at the conservatory for only one year, until the
summer of 1892, when he resigned, one reason being that he apparently did not get on well with Carl Faelten, the director. The conflicting demands of performance and composition were bad enough,
but the third demand on his time of teaching was too much, and so it
had to go—even at the expense of a secure income. (He even refused
a much more generous teaching offer from the University of
Chicago.) Four consecutive years spent teaching the piano in three
different music academies had convinced Busoni that he was not cut
out for an academic career; for the rest of his life he would continue
to teach, both piano and composition, but only informally, to hand-

picked pupils. (This attitude was to cause problems later, when he did in fact accept teaching engagements from state institutions in Vienna, Bologna, and Berlin on his own terms, only to find that the bureaucratic system had difficulty digesting this informal approach.) In Boston, as in Moscow, he had composed nothing during his year teaching at the conservatory.

He had decided, as he explained to his parents in May, to make as much money as he could as a pianist, in order to return to Europe.[7] (From first to last Busoni, like many other performing artists, viewed North America primarily as a gold mine, which played its part in his very ambivalent attitude toward the land and its people.) Now he threw himself on the American concert circuit, relying mainly on his American agent, Charles F. Tretbar, but still making every major decision himself—a conditioning from his early years. He found it well nigh impossible later in life to delegate, as his many follow-up letters regarding concert engagements prove. One letter dated June 25, 1892, is typical of this controlling mind-set. It was written to yet another cultural mover and shaker, the great conductor and popularizer Theodore Thomas (1835–1905), another musician of German background (his family had emigrated to the United States when he was ten), who had just taken over the newly created Chicago Symphony Orchestra, and who traveled indefatigably with various orchestras throughout North America. Busoni wrote in German:

> Through Mr. Tretbar you have come to hear—as I believe—of my great desire to come into artistic contact with you.
>
> My participation in one of your world famous symphony concerts in the coming season would be of decisive value for my reputation, and therefore I would ask you to be so kind as to grant me such an opportunity.
>
> Family circumstances do not allow me to present myself personally to you during the summer, something that I would otherwise have done without fail.[8]

The "family circumstances" coyly referred to was the arrival, on May 24, 1892, of a new dependent in the Busoni family: Gerda and Ferruccio's first son, aptly named Benvenuto—partly due to the name's meaning (welcome), partly to perpetuate one of the many names Busoni himself had been given at birth. Benni, as he was soon called, was a great happiness to the young parents. Busoni treated both his sons (a second son, Raffaello—"Lello"—would be born in 1900), as children and as adults, with enormous sympathy, tolerance, and forbearance, never deliberately putting pressure on them; his own childhood— which had been no childhood—was a constant warning. Nevertheless, at age twenty-six Busoni was now supporting four people in addition to himself, which makes his decision to go freelance, announced to his parents just three days before Benni's birth, the more courageous.

A month after the above letter to Thomas, Busoni wrote again,[9] answering enquiries on his repertoire, suggesting Beethoven's Fourth Piano Concerto (but with his own cadenzas), with which he had had great success in Boston, adding that of course he could play the fifth as well, the two Liszt Piano Concertos, and Schumann's, and one of his own. "Would it be advisable for me to introduce myself for the first time as pianist with this work? It won the Rubinstein prize." This would indicate that the work's first American outing, in New York, had been a success.

Since their marriage and until just before Benni's birth, Gerda had always traveled with Ferruccio, but for a while now she was mostly left behind. For him it was a double wrench. She must send a detailed description of the baby, he wrote her in June from New York.[10] Had he grown? She was able to join Ferruccio in Chicago later. In New York again later that summer, where she had joined him, he wrote immediately after she had left with "das Baby-child,"[11] a term in itself endearingly betraying his deep delight in fatherhood.

The Busonis had leased a house in Boston, at 12 Judson Street, Roxbury, for $600, possibly to escape that constant bugbear of professional musicians, complaining neighbors. Nevertheless, in September 1893, Busoni went alone to New York and decided to lease a house there, at 403 West Manhattan Avenue, for $780. He was always most at home in large cosmopolitan cities, and what he perceived as the provincialisms of Boston were beginning to be irksome, in spite of the presence there of old friends such as Nikisch and Schröder, and new friends like the great arts patron Isabella Stewart Gardner (1840–1924), who was to remain another constant in his life. Gerda and Benni joined him in New York in October. His residence in the city was hailed by the *Musical Courier*: "Mr. Busoni, the eminent pianist and composer, has removed from Boston and made this city his place of residence. We welcome most heartily this accomplished and gifted man."[12]

For Busoni's first year as a freelance performer, there had been plenty of engagements in the eastern half of the country: Cincinnati, Saint Louis, Chicago, Milwaukee, Cleveland, Buffalo, Niagara, Albany, and, of course, New York. The second year engagements were fewer. In all, during this first period spent in the United States, Busoni played in public at least seventy-five times, including ten performances in chamber concerts with the Kneisel Quartet (of which Alwin Schröder was a member at this time) and sixteen with the Boston Symphony Orchestra, both in and outside Boston. During the New York period he played often in the city and taught privately. One of his pupils was Augusta Cottlow (1878–1954), whom he taught piano and to whom he was later to dedicate his youthful work, the Etude in D-flat Major (BV 198, also known as "Etude 15, en forme d'adagio d'une Sonate"), written in late 1882 or early 1883 in Italy but never published. This work contains the main theme of the Pezzo serioso of Busoni's Piano Concerto.[13] A more distinguished pupil was Natalie Curtis (1875–1921), whom he taught harmony. Curtis was later to become an ethnomusicologist, and in 1910 introduced Busoni to Native American music, an encounter that produced his *Red Indian Fantasy* for Piano and Orchestra (BV 264) (see p. 275–76).

In spite of his ambivalent feelings toward the country, this period spent in the United States was a time of consolidation and maturity for Busoni. A giveaway phrase from his Moscow year, in the letter to his parents quoted above, was that he would never succeed in "beating" (*vincere*) the local celebrities long resident in Moscow. Frederick Delius remarked that what struck him most about Busoni during their time in Leipzig was his "passionately intense ambition."[14] His competitiveness remained with him for the rest of his life and fed a ruthless, egoistic streak that ran counter to his affable nature. Since early childhood Ferruccio had been almost constantly on the move, driven by his parents' ambitions and needs, which became so absorbed in his own that he could be said never to have been truly his own man. Gerda's humane, undemanding, stabilizing influence, though strong, was nevertheless slow to assert itself: she was, after all, only in her midtwenties when she married. She was sensible and balanced in her outlook, but she was also very much in love, and being married to such a powerful, attractive, and talented personality was an experience that took some time to absorb.

Both marriage and fatherhood gave Busoni a broader, more secure basis on which to assess his career, and the innocent amusements of domestic life were a new, hitherto unknown joy: to surprise him, at Christmas 1893 in New York, at a supper party at his home, Benni was dressed up in brightly colored tail coat and top hat (and apparently not much else), and made his entrance carrying two miniature bottles of champagne. The joyous frivolity of the scene was certainly in sharp contrast to Ferruccio's own childhood.

In New York Bach continued to occupy Ferruccio. Since his first piano transcription, in 1888, of Bach's Prelude and Fugue for Organ (BWV 532), Busoni had completed several more and begun editing some of Bach's piano works. It was the beginning of a lifelong attachment to Bach's work: Busoni's edition of the whole of The Well-Tempered Clavier was completed only in 1920. In fact, for many people even today, Busoni is known primarily as an editor and transcriber of Bach's work, and the same held during his lifetime: legend has it that after a concert in America some years later, an enthusiastic member of the audience rushed up to him and gushed: "Thank you so much, Mr. Bach-Busoni!" to Busoni's wry amusement. Another anecdote has Gerda being introduced by a society matron as "Mrs. Bach-Busoni." The seed casually sown by Kathi Petri in the Thomaskirche in Leipzig, when she suggested he make that first piano transcription, produced a fruitful plant. But Busoni's own debt to Bach goes back much further, as he himself acknowledged: it was through his father that he had been first brought to Bach, and Bach had consequently had an influence on the young Busoni's early compositions. In 1876 the noted Viennese critic Eduard Hanslick commented on this after a concert given by the ten-year-old pianist of his own works: "These reveal the same musical awareness we enjoyed so much in his playing; not a sign of precocious sentimentality or contrived effect, just sheer pleasure in the play of notes, in lively figuration and little combinatorial techniques." Hanslick had given the boy several motifs to improvise on, and had been impressed in particular by his contrapuntal style, which he rightly attributed to a study of Bach. Wilhelm Mayer, Ferruccio's teacher in Graz, had also taught him a great deal of Bach, analyzing the Forty-eight Preludes and Fugues with him and giving him contrapuntal exercises.

Bach remained arguably the strongest influence in Busoni's composition. According to the Australian pianist and composer Larry Sitsky (himself a pupil of two Busoni pupils: first Winifred Burston and then Busoni's most famous pupil, Egon Petri), in his stimulating and invaluable book *Busoni and the Piano*, this influence can be divided into four main categories: transcriptions that are generally faithful to the original; editions intended as a record of Busoni's own interpretations, and/or a pedagogical guide; original compositions based on a piece or fragment of Bach; one major opus by Busoni incorporating all three of the above elements—the *Fantasia Contrappuntistica* on a Bach Chorale Prelude and Fugue, first published in 1910.

Another stimulus was Liszt. In Helsinki, Martin Wegelius had been the first to suggest to Busoni that he study in depth the compositions of a musician he had until then thought of mainly as an executant. While in America, Busoni was given some rare original editions of Liszt's works by a former Boston woman pupil, which prompted him to write to his mother for a catalog of early editions of Liszt such as she might have acquired in her younger years. In time Busoni assembled an important collection of these original editions of Liszt's work (mainly for the piano) and found it particularly revealing and valuable to study the various revisions Liszt made to his own work over the years. This led eventually to Busoni's editorial contribution to Liszt's piano works, published between 1910 and 1912 (see p. 217–18).

The concentration on Bach and Liszt during this period in New York, plus Busoni's growing maturity—he was now in his late twenties—also led to a complete overhaul of his attitude toward piano playing. To put it crudely, up to this point, the main emphasis had been on technical mastery; now he began, in a certain sense almost from scratch, to study the great works of the repertoire for their deeper meaning. As Busoni described it in 1910, in an essay on transcriptions:[15]

> It was at that time of my life when I had become conscious of such deficiencies and faults in my own playing that with energetic determination

I began the study of the piano again from the beginning on quite a new basis. Liszt's works were my guide and through them I acquired an intimate knowledge of his particular method. Out of his "tenets" I constructed my "technique."

Rubinstein, recognized as the king of pianists, was his example, but he was slowly being acknowledged as the crown prince. The composer Luigi Dallapiccola tells a delightful story:

I shall never forget the old piano tuner of the Steinway firm in Hamburg who, when he came to tune my piano some years ago, told me he had gone on four tours in Russia with Paderewsky and I don't know how many with Emil Sauer, and with Moritz Rosenthal and a thousand others. I asked him if by chance he had also worked for Busoni. To which he replied: "But we are talking of pianists, of great pianists. Busoni was a prince."[16]

And when the musicologist H. H. Stuckenschmidt saw Busoni at a concert in 1921 in Berlin he felt,

His very appearance outshone all the pictures one had ever seen of him. As he sat at his instrument, his face was pale and motionless as marble, the almost ethereal features a combination of intelligence and extreme sensitivity. He might have been a *grand seigneur*. With him playing the piano seemed to be merely a means to a more important end: which was to shed maximum light on a work of art.[17]

Given Busoni's constantly curious, avid nature, the only way forward as a pianist, the only way to raise his playing way above any taint of "circus tricks," in a sense to justify to himself intellectually the effort of playing, was to explore ever more profoundly the very essence of any work he was playing. It was this aura of total mastery that was to make his playing truly memorable from now on, although that same exalted mastery, that high intellectual level his playing exuded, meant that he never achieved the broad popularity of a Paderewski or Rachmaninov. For him too, the *quality* of the audience was important: more than once he wrote to Gerda, of a private performance in front of a few friends and colleagues, that he had never played a particular piece so well. And the amazing fact remains that, other than with his father and for a short period in Vienna at the conservatory, when he was a child, Busoni had no formal teaching in piano playing.

In Boston in early 1893 he completed a Symphonic Tone Poem for Orchestra (BV 240), dedicated to Arthur Nikisch, who conducted the Boston Symphony Orchestra at the premiere on April 15 that same year. (Published in 1894, the work has never been recorded.) This was the reworking of his *Konzert-Fantasie* for Piano and Orchestra (BV 230), composed in Helsinki, that had been premiered in Leipzig in January 1890 with Busoni himself as soloist, and not very well received. The initial version has never been published. It was a strange progression for a pianist-composer, one might think: to revise a work by removing altogether the piano part, which is redistributed for harp and other instruments! The piano part of the original *Konzert-Fantasie* was written to blend at times into the orchestral fabric, and the Symphonic Tone Poem in that sense is a progression, achieving the same ends with more effective means. Much of this work is more or less identical in both versions, but the Symphonic Tone Poem has richer scoring and is in three distinct sections. Busoni was already aware of Richard Strauss's tone poems, which he admired. The Symphonic Tone Poem imitates Strauss's literary agenda, with a preface in the published score of quotations from Nikolaus Lenau and Giacomo Leopardi.

The whole experience of this first visit to the United States helped crystallize Busoni's thoughts on how he wanted his life to be structured. In New York, by early 1894, after careful consideration, a further decision was made regarding his future that stemmed solely from him: he would decide on a base that would provide a stimulating environment and be centrally positioned for a concert career mainly confined to Europe. Berlin was the city that in his eyes answered to all these criteria. His view of the city had mellowed over the previous five years, perhaps because distance lent enchantment to the view, or perhaps just due to the contrast Berlin offered to any city in the United States. He had written of "this Jewish city that I hate"[18] to Gerda from Berlin in August 1889, when returning to Weimar from those five days with her in Helsinki (scarcely a context liable to generate a favorable view of anywhere else), "irritating, idle, arrogant, parvenu." In some ways this view of the city remained unchanged, leading him in the first years of the next century seriously to consider moving to London, but he was also pragmatic enough to see the practical advantages of its geographical position, its size, and its extensive musical life, and he desperately needed the stability of a permanent home. He also fully recognized that he desperately needed Europe.

And so on April 3, 1894, after scarcely half a year in New York, the family left for Europe. From March 26 to 31 Ferruccio had played every evening in a different city, which left them with just three days to finish packing and wind up their affairs in the United States. They headed straight for Berlin, which was to remain Busoni's base, except for the tragic parenthesis of World War I, for the rest of his life.

Notes

1. "Musical Items," *Musical Courier* 23, no. 10 (September 2, 1891): 241.

2. "Personals: Something about Busoni," *Musical Courier* 23, no. 13 (September 23, 1891): 327.

3. "Prof. Busoni in Boston," *New York Times*, September 6, 1891, 17.

4. Letter from FB to Ferdinando Busoni and Anna Weiss-Busoni, August 30, 1891, Dent Papers EJD/2/1, King's College Library, Cambridge.

5. Letter from FB to Anna Weiss-Busoni, July 24, 1894, StBB Bus. Nachl. 1287.

6. Marc-André Roberge, "Ferruccio Busoni in the United States," *American Music* 13, no. 3 (Fall 1995): 295–332.

7. Letter from FB to Ferdinando Busoni, March 16, 1892, Dent Papers; letter from FB to Ferdinando Busoni and Anna Weiss-Busoni, May 21, 1892, Dent Papers.

8. Letter from FB to Theodore Thomas, June 25, 1892, in Beaumont, *Letters*, p. 47.

9. Letter from FB to Theodore Thomas, July 29, 1892, in Beaumont, *Letters*, p. 48.

10. Letter from FB to Gerda Busoni, June 27, 1893, StBB Bus. Nachl. 4, 267.

11. Letter from FB to Gerda Busoni, summer 1893, StBB Bus. Nachl. 4, 269.

12. "At Home," *Musical Courier* 27, no. 15 (October 11, 1893): 19.

13. Augusta Cottlow was later to write her reminiscences of her time with Busoni, in Augusta Cottlow, "A Tribute to Busoni," *Musical Courier* 89, no. 8 (August 21, 1924): 7; and "My Years with Busoni," *Musical Observer* 24, no. 6 (June 1925): 11, 28.

14. Dent, *Ferruccio Busoni*, p. 101n1.

15. Originally published in November 1910 in the program of the third Nikisch concert in Berlin; reprinted in Ferruccio Busoni, *The Essence of Music and Other Papers*, trans. Rosamond Ley (London: Rockliff, 1957), p. 86.

16. Luigi Dallapiccola, *Parole e musica* (Milan: Il Saggiatore, 1980), p. 306.

17. H. H. Stuckenschmidt, *Ferruccio Busoni: Chronicle of a European*, trans. Sandra Morris (London: Calder and Boyars, 1970), p. 74.

18. Letter from FB to Gerda Sjöstrand, August 11, 1889, StBB Bus. Nachl. IV, 230.

CHAPTER SEVEN

~

Berlin: April 1894 to 1902

Berlin did indeed make rather a brash, parvenu impression in the 1890s. When the Busonis arrived, the welding of thirty-eight German-speaking states into what became the German Empire lay only twenty-three years in the past. After the intricate and lengthy negotiations leading to unification, Prussia, thanks largely to that arch-Prussian Otto von Bismarck, had ended up holding the reins. Therefore Berlin, the Prussian capital, had become the imperial capital, and the Hohenzollern King Wilhelm I of Prussia had been promoted to kaiser, or emperor, with Bismarck as his chancellor. The throne had since 1888 been occupied by Wilhelm I's grandson, Wilhelm II (who had virtually forced the increasingly autocratic Bismarck into retirement in 1890).

The population of Berlin was still increasing rapidly: from 826,000 in 1871 it was to reach two million by 1905. Fired by the heady mix of nascent nationalism, the desire to turn the new capital into a metropolis to rival London and Paris, and rapidly expanding industrial output, every other sector of activity burgeoned—including music: a determined and ultimately successful effort was being made to wrest musical preeminence from Saxon Leipzig.[1] And there was the purely practical advantage, of importance for musical life too, that by the 1890s twelve different railway lines converged on Berlin.

But underlying this energetic, forward-looking emergent metropolis was still the old Prussia of strict social codes, a stiff-necked notion of honor, and a firm conviction of Prussian superiority, both moral and otherwise, over all others, a conviction reinforced by Prussia's preeminence in the new Germany. (The great writer Theodor Fontane's novel *Effi Briest*, possibly the most telling indictment of those values by— ironically—their greatest chronicler, was appearing in monthly parts as the Busonis arrived.) This rigid and narrow mind-set, which permeated most sectors of Prussian society, engendered a petty and at times vicious intolerance of any deviation from what was considered proper conduct and a contemptuous xenophobia. Busoni's exuberant and colorful personality was to fall foul of this intolerance more than once. It was a mind-set that the confirmed cosmopolitan despised and that led him, some fifteen years later, seriously to consider moving to London.

On their arrival in Berlin on April 12, the Busonis stayed first in the Hotel Kaiserhof; by the end of the month they had found a small ground-floor apartment at Kantstrasse 153, in the middle-class Charlottenburg district, and moved in on May 3. (They moved after one year to a larger apartment in Tauentzienstrasse 10, the eastward continuation of the Kurfürstendamm, near the Zoological Gardens; from 1902 they were living at Augsburger Strasse 55, still in the same area; then in 1908 they moved to a huge, rambling apartment on the Viktoria-Luise-Platz, about half a mile further south. All these buildings have disappeared, mostly destroyed during World War II.)

Since childhood Busoni had been an inveterate collector of books on a wide variety of subjects. Now he had decided on a permanent base, his already considerable library could be put in order, and added to, along with an ever-expanding collection of pictures, antique furniture, and *objets d'art*—one reason why each apartment they moved to in Berlin was larger than the last. In his letters to his wife written when he was away on concert tours there were frequent triumphant accounts of finds in secondhand bookshops in every city he visited—and other, rather mournful accounts of the ones that got away through lack of funds or a spasm of financial prudence. Not only the literature of the main European languages, but archeology, history, aesthetics, philosophy—all were grist to Busoni's intellectual mill. It is a moot point whether this wide-ranging and insatiable curiosity worked for or against his musical creativity. It was part of his Faustian urge to delve into every aspect of human knowledge, an unwillingness to commit himself fully to one thing, whether playing versus composing, being Italian versus being German, or being "merely" a musician versus the charms of being a poly-math. Perhaps his never having had a childhood, as he lamented, left him with a permanent sense of having missed out on something, and his voracious intellectual appetite was a result of this feeling of loss, a quest for the unknown. Or perhaps it was merely a reflection of the roving, essentially undisciplined intellectual habits of the autodidact.

Within days of his arrival in Berlin Busoni had a revelatory experience that certainly did concentrate his mind: Giuseppe Verdi's *Falstaff*, premiered in February 1893 in Milan, had its Berlin premiere on March 6, 1894, at what is now the Berlin State Opera (at that time the *Hofoper*-Court Opera), on Unter den Linden. Busoni saw it there on April 22. "The day before yesterday I heard Verdi's *Falstaff*," he wrote his parents,[2] "which is, of its genre, a little masterpiece. It is really incredible how a man of eighty can still do what he has never done before. Not only that, but various things not even done by others before him. *Falstaff* is—in short—a most original work, fresh, witty and undoubtedly the best Italian comic opera since the *Barbiere*." It led Busoni's thoughts to opera again, a field he had not considered since setting aside *Sigune*. He was also fired to write a letter to Verdi expressing his admiration for his great compatriot, to be accompanied by the score of his just pub-lished Symphonic Tone Poem (BV 240). Neither letter nor score was sent, and the letter now survives only in German translation, from which an English translation was made by Antony Beaumont for his *Se-lected Letters*.[3] The third paragraph contains an interesting self-portrait:

My childhood was occupied with serious study, diligent perseverance and reflection, nourished and supported by the arts and sciences of Ger-many. But scarcely had I developed beyond the theoretical stage, in that period between youth and adulthood—in which I now find myself—than I began to grasp the *spirit* and the *soul* of art, to comprehend and draw closer to it. So it was that I came relatively later—please forgive me—to an admiration of your masterworks, with which I became enrap-tured. Finally *Falstaff* provoked in me such a revolution of spirit and feel-ing that I can with ample justification date the beginning of a new epoch in my artistic life from that time. [Beaumont translation]

What surprised and inspired Busoni on hearing *Falstaff* was not just the work itself, but that Verdi, whom Busoni had tended until then to lump together with all other Italian opera composers and consider definitely inferior to the Germans, was more than capable of holding his own with the best Germany could offer. A naive, not to say disastrously blinkered, conviction, but one dominant in northern Europe at the time, was that opera, other than Wagner, was not worthy of serious attention. The revelation of *Falstaff* turned Busoni's mind not only to opera, but to his native country, and reawakened an ambition to bring about a "renaissance" in Italian music, an ambition first entertained in his late teens, when he was writing his series of articles on Italian music for the *Grazer Tagespost*.

The steady bombardment of reproaches and demands from his parents in Trieste, which had continued unabated while the young Busonis were in America, had immediately switched its target to Berlin, provoking resigned, if exasperated, replies. In the above-quoted letter to his father of April 24, only twelve days after the young family's arrival in the German capital, Busoni was already replying to a telegram urging a visit to Trieste. He pointed out that Gerda's father would also like to see his daughter and grandson, but that neither Helsinki nor Trieste was possible at present. He had neither the time nor the money to visit either city, "But in the autumn I hope not only to see you but also to leave the boy [*il bimbo*] with you for a certain time, even for the duration of the season." (History repeating itself?) Benni, soon to celebrate his second birthday, was given a glowing character reference. It was unlikely that Ferruccio would move from Berlin until his "debut," as he termed it, which this time would be a gala occasion (*coi fiocchi*—literally "with bows on").

On June 1, in response to a letter from his father (the first for over a year: Anna had been the only correspondent from Trieste during this time), Ferruccio's patience gave way.

> Let's see what you have to say to your son (after one whole year), as such and as artist. . . . The last thing I would have expected was that your epistle would contain nothing but the question of money. And this was a double disappointment. Firstly having to realize that my father has nothing to tell me (and that without this subject he probably wouldn't have written to me at all), secondly the raising of a question that I cannot resolve for the moment, if I'm not given time to get my breath back.[4]

With the concert season some way off, there was indeed little money to be earned. However, Busoni practiced the piano for up to five hours a day, and continued with his editing and transcriptions of Bach: that year his edition (BV B25) of both Bach's *Well-Tempered Clavier*, part I, BWV 846–69, and his piano transcription (BV B26) of the Prelude and Fugue in E-Minor for Organ, BWV 533, were published, so there were also proofs to correct. He had also acquired some pupils, including one whom he was coaching for that summer's Rubinstein Competition.

In mid-July Busoni was writing[5] in detail again to his father on the perennial subject of money: Breitkopf und Härtel had recently published his Symphonic Tone Poem for Orchestra, but he had had to pay the eight hundred marks printing costs for the volume of almost one hundred pages—obviously the firm did not yet believe in him enough to risk publishing such a long work all at their own expense. He also personally took on the task (and the cost) of sending the score to forty-five different parties throughout Europe who, he hoped, might be interested in performing it. Nevertheless, he forwarded 150 marks to Trieste. In September too he was defending himself against his mother's charge that he must hate his mother tongue, as his foreword to his edition of Bach's *Well-Tempered Clavier*, part I, was in German: it would have been impossible to find an Italian publisher for such a work, was his blunt riposte.[6] His mother's letter had contained news of the death of Giovannina Lucca, the publisher of some of Busoni's earliest compositions—news he had already gathered from the press. His mother told him of the death of another figure from his early years, however, of which he had been unaware: Josefine von Wertheimstein, his generous Viennese patron.

Busoni's finances, and his attitude toward money, remain a puzzle to some extent. He earned good money in the United States, both at the conservatory in Boston during his first year there, and from his piano playing then and afterward, yet allegedly he was only able to settle his final bills in New York at the last minute, with money earned from that final tour. Before going to the United States, he had explained to his parents that even if he did not stay there beyond a year, he could return to Europe having traveled to interesting places, and with a good sum of money in his pocket. What happened to all the money? In his time, it was expected that a well-known pianist would stay in the best hotels, dress his wife in expensive furs, and live in the best part of town in some style, with domestic staff, all of which Busoni did. But throughout his life he was nearly always in financial straits. I suspect that, like his father, he was simply a bad manager, and also something of a spendthrift. Or, looking at it another way: he believed in enjoying life— once, during that period spent in Frohnleiten with his father, his mother had scraped together to send him a money present, which he spent on a trip to Graz and a meal in an expensive restaurant, a fact he did not feel he had to conceal from her. He had inherited from his father the belief that an artist of some standing (or who aspires to such) must stay in the best hotels and eat at the best restaurants, to give the "right" impression, and he remained true to this belief throughout his life, often in spite of all financial logic.

He definitely relished what money could bring, which is one of the main reasons he endured punishing tours throughout Europe and North America for many more years. The other reason—to meet his family responsibilities—became gradually less urgent, but the tours continued at the same unrelenting rate. He was also generous, and not only to his parents, to support whom he considered it his duty. In other words, he spent money on what he thought worthwhile, whether tangible objects, people in need, or, later, the personal financing of public concerts of music he believed in, all with little regard for tomorrow or bourgeois concepts of cautious thrift. Also, once he was established on the concert circuit, there was the near certainty that tomorrow would bring fresh funds.

He ran up debts throughout his life, not all of which he repaid. One larger unpaid debt from the past caught up with him in the summer of 1895: eight years before, while he was living in Leipzig, Oskar Schwalm, at that time owner of the music publishers C. F. Kahnt, had lent him a large sum. When Schwalm sold the firm shortly after, its debts and credits were passed on to the new owner, who was now demanding five hundred marks from Busoni forthwith! (Busoni ends his account of this to his parents,[7] inevitably used as yet another illustration of his financial difficulties, with *three* exclamation marks, indicating he thought the demand a gross impertinence.) In late 1895 he repaid a debt to Dr. Abraham by offering him six piano pieces (BV 241, published in 1896), some of which he had written some time before. In another defensive letter to

Trieste,[8] giving yet another account of his financial situation, he lists not only this debt to Dr. Abraham, but even thirty marks arrears due to the maidservant, and eighty-five to a music shop—so could he delay their rent payment? (He wrote this letter from the island of Rügen, on the Baltic, where the whole family was on holiday!) Busoni always tended to recount these matters, particularly to his parents, as though they were arbitrary blows dealt by malign fate, rather than the results of his own actions. A month later he borrowed 500 marks from Steinway, in order to be able to send his parents 400.

But in that first summer in Berlin, in 1894, together with his concert agent, Hermann Wolff, Busoni drew up a strenuous schedule for the coming months of his "debut." On October 22, 1894, he played in Hamburg (Gustav Mahler conducting, Busoni playing Weber's *Konzertstück* and the first performance of his own arrangement for piano and orchestra of Liszt's piano solo, *Rhapsodie espagnole*, among other things); on November 3 in Berlin at the Singakademie; shortly after in Leipzig; two more concerts in Berlin; then Liège; and Saint Petersburg, where he took part in a commemoration concert in honor of Anton Rubinstein, who had died on November 20.

With those three Berlin concerts, he caused a sensation. At the very first, on November 3, the superlatives came rolling out from the critics, on a tide of astonishment that this talent was henceforth living in their midst. Otto Lessmann, doyen of the Berlin music critics, reported in the *Allgemeine Musikzeitung*[9] (like Leipzig, Berlin had several weekly music papers):

A highly welcome appearance in the concert hall was the pianist Mr. Ferrucio [sic] Busoni, who introduced himself again as an artist of the very first rank. Mr. Busoni handles the most perfect virtuoso technique almost with indifference, this is, of course, not in that he neglects it, but rather that he possesses such a sovereign mastery of it that for him it scarcely appears to come into consideration as necessary precondition, beside his other artistic attributes. His fingers truly perform wonders, not merely in regard to rapid movement, but even more in the variety of his attack, now strong and robust like bronze, now soft and delicate as swan's down. But Mr. Busoni is more than mere pianist, he is a distinct artistic personality, with qualities perhaps that do not please everyone, but of definite distinctive character that arouses interest.

Busoni played Weber's F-sharp Piano Concerto and his own piano tran-scription of Bach's Chaconne in D Minor for Violin (BV B 24). Of the second concert, on November 13, the *Neue Berliner Musikzeitung*[10] re-ported on this "excellent pianist, who is second to none. One quickly discerns his specialty: it consists of light fluency and in a pianissimo such as one seldom hears." Not that power is lacking, the review goes on, while expressing amazement at his control.

Otto Lessmann wrote of the third concert, on December 1:[11]

> On his extraordinary pianistic capability and musical talent no more doubts could exist among the discerning after the first concerts, but that these qualities also extend into that region that is reserved exclusively for the very greatest among performing artists, was proved above all by the performance of the Beethoven sonata [op. 106]. I pronounce quite simply that I have never heard this work in its totality played by any of our great masters, including Bülow and Rubinstein, with such perfect musical clarity, also with such exhaustive penetration of its poetic content. . . . Mr. Busoni played the work as though he were orchestrat-ing it in his mind. . . . I can only describe this feat as a masterwork of the rarest nature.

The strategy in Berlin of three concerts over a short period had more than paid off. Busoni not only reminded the city of his existence, after an absence of over three years, but brilliantly demonstrated how far he had come in the meantime.

He began 1895 with concerts in Berlin, Moscow, Brussels (at the Théâtre de la Monnaie), and Oslo. These concerts served to reconquer more ground lost during the years away from Europe. Busoni also con-quered new ground—Brussels was one such place, a city he explored with his usual keen interest and described in a letter to his parents[12] containing 400 Belgian francs. ("It is not at all easy for me to send them. Of 800 francs fee, 200 went in travel costs and I have 200 left. But nevertheless I am glad to be able to get them to you in time for the rent.") "Two weeks before," he went on,

> I was in Russia, Moscow, where they gave me the warmest and most en-thusiastic welcome. Really I left and have found again *friends* there. Now I am undecided whether to accept the invitation from Christiania [Oslo]

(Norway), as the journey is tiring and difficult in winter. I feel tired of railways and constant locomotion. . . . Regarding the article on Mascagni, the latter is for me a closed chapter. His music is as wretched as his luck is marvelous. But the former won't last on the basis of the latter.

(Mascagni's *Guglielmo Ratcliff* had been premiered at La Scala on February 16, 1895, therefore the article on Mascagni, apparently enclosed in a letter from his parents, must have been referring to this. Busoni's response is a curiously cavalier dismissal of his fellow countryman, from someone who made little effort to familiarize himself with contemporary Italian music—opera in particular—and, in fact, as his letter to Verdi more or less admits, he viewed it with some disdain.)

Busoni's return to Moscow in January 1895 was triumphant, which possibly shed a rosy light over his recollections of the place. But years later, writing to his friend Isidor Philipp,[13] having just gone through the Twelve Etudes, op. 8 of Scriabin, he recounted,

and the whole atmosphere of Moscow 1890 arose around me, sad, legendary, superficial, wretched, with the desperate flourishes [*les bravades d'octaves*] of the pupils of that time and of that country still in my ears, and everything that is corrupt in my memory. . . . The "professors" came to the Conservatory two hours late, straight from the green [gambling] table where they had passed the night, they themselves pitifully green, but always with a dignified, diplomatic, autocratic air, to which even the eternal cigarette only added pomp. The proud Safonoff tyrannized over everyone and summoned his people to his office like a chief of police.

Vasily Safonov clearly saw the enormous leap forward in Busoni's playing since his time at the Moscow Conservatory: "Your playing is a revelation; I said goodbye to you as a young man, and you come back a great artist."[14]

Busoni's playing met with a mixed reception by the critics in some places: while he was eulogized by some critics, he was accused of sentimentality by others, of eccentricity or again too great a severity. By and large, however, the critics were favorable, and certainly by this point took him very seriously indeed, measuring him against his greatest forerunners. Eduard Hanslick, doyen of the Viennese critics, dubbed him Rubinstein's successor.

According to today's standards, Busoni's treatment of the classics was sometimes idiosyncratic, to say the least; he would often "edit" a piece to suit his own taste—an approach also adopted by other great pianists at the time. As Edward Dent, who heard him often, wrote:

> His recitals, even then [in the 1890s], were only suitable for a public of regular *habitués*; he seemed to assume that his audience knew the classics as thoroughly as he did himself and had no need for them to be explained in the conventional manner. He naturally alienated the sentimental adorers of Chopin, and was charged with eccentricity in his reading of Beethoven. The fact was that whatever he played he threw some entirely new light upon it.[15]

Busoni's aim was to interpret the essence of the work, to translate it into contemporary language, which provoked the accusation that he was "modernizing" works. The Belgian Marcel Rémy, Berlin correspondent of *L'Indépendance*, writing in January 1902,[16] offers not only a vivid impression of Busoni's playing, but of the ambiance and atmosphere in Berlin at his concerts, and something of the conditions of public performance. For example, musicians—*des héros aux doigts ubiquitaires*, as he elegantly termed them—had to pay for their concerts and, in order to be noticed, often had to give away nearly all the seats. This was not the case for Busoni, of course, except in the early years: whenever he was playing, there was a run on the box office. Herds of young girls would come with their music and a pencil and write down every nuance. If for any reason Busoni had to break off the performance, states Rémy dryly, three-quarters of the auditorium would be up to finishing it somehow. Many more women than men were in the audience, and afterward there was an uproar. "Women embrace him, kiss his hands; the fetishism attached to the person of Liszt has been transferred to Busoni."

> He is playing all the Chopin Etudes in a single series. The atmosphere conjured up is miraculous. Each successive item is like a piece that rises in tiers finally to form a gigantic monument. Finally one sees a vibrant, inspired, almost terrible Chopin arising. His song is no longer the plaintive chant perpetuated by legend. It is a vast, human and generous hymn with an at times Beethovenesque accent.

Very old people, "who had heard Chopin cough," were horrified and protested in the name of tradition, "for from artiste to artiste, intimate, complete communication is not established by mere words, by the examinations of ex-priests, but by blinding flashes of insight," opined Rémy.

In response to an earlier, apparently rather niggling review of his playing by Rémy, Busoni wrote:

> The *Pathétique* was an almost revolutionary sonata in its own day, and ought to sound revolutionary. One could never put enough passion into the *Appassionata*, which was the culmination of passionate expression of its epoch. When I play Beethoven, I try to approach the liberty, the nervous energy and the humanity which are the signature of his compositions. . . . Recalling the character of the man Beethoven and what is related of his own playing, I have built up for myself an ideal which has been wrongly called "modern" and is actually no more than "alive."[17]

Busoni claimed that, particularly in piano transcriptions, the music has to be laid out differently in order to achieve the same effect as in the original instrumentation. It is an argument that has no winners; what remains true is that his transcriptions were colored by the taste of the time—an analogy from the previous generation is Liszt's insouciant piano transcription of operatic arias.

What made Busoni such a great pianist—for many, the greatest not only of his time but of all time? There are the obvious answers: Like Liszt, he had been playing since childhood, relentlessly drilled by an ambitious father, so that technical virtuosity became second nature. By his late twenties, the bipolar character of so many areas of his existence—the Italian and the German, the performer and the composer, Bach champion and Liszt champion—had helped to fashion a man with an extraordinarily wide framework of reference. Unlike others who began as child prodigies—Mozart, Mendelssohn, Liszt, Rubinstein, d'Albert—Busoni, as we have seen, from the age of around eight virtually took over as his own promoter, and as head of the family: witness all those businesslike letters to his parents written at an age when most children have no idea where money comes from, let alone how to earn it and manage it. "I never had a childhood." How often does that melancholy knell sound out over his later life! His early life was a grotesque interpretation of Wordsworth's phrase, "The child is father of the man," extended beyond himself to include his own parents. But that forced maturity forged the man and the artist, giving his playing a kind of third-dimensional authority lacking in the mere virtuoso. As intellectual and polymath, he constantly questioned his own creativity, both as performer and as composer.

Contributing to his enormous success as a performer at a more superficial level, there was what in this more cynical age of ruthless promotion would be called "the package": he had stunning good looks— the Anglo-Dutch composer Bernard van Dieren recalled that the two most beautiful men he had ever known were Busoni and the singer Feodor Chaliapin—and a very engaging personality.

He was a musicians' musician. Even today he is spoken of by other pianists in reverential terms: "His piano-playing is the victory of reflection over bravura," says Alfred Brendel. "Busoni made clear the (decisive) significance of subjectivity in interpretation in its whole scope," continues Brendel, "a subjectivity, however, that does not obey blind instinct, but is fed by masterly intellectual refinement."[18]

In August 1895 Busoni was on the jury and also engaged as conductor for the Rubinstein Competition—quite an advance in five years, from competitor to jury member. Experiencing it from the other side, he found it rather hard going listening to competitors for eight hours a day for a whole week.

That summer too he finished his Second Orchestral Suite (Geharnischte Suite) (Armor-clad Suite) (BV 242), an orchestral suite in four movements entitled Vorspiel (Prelude), Kriegstanz (War Dance), Grabdenkmal (Sepulchral Monument), and Ansturm (Assault). It was premiered in Berlin in October 1897, with Busoni conducting (see below), but not published until 1905, in a revised edition of 1903, at which time he decided to dedicate each of the four movements to one of the "Leskovites," his band of friends in Helsinki: Jean Sibelius, Adolf Paul, Armas Järnefelt, and Eero Järnefelt. It has never been commercially recorded—in fact, it has had difficulty in finding performances almost from the outset. "Unfortunately, no one wants to perform it so far," he wrote scornfully to his mother in November 1895, "as it's too difficult to digest for stomachs used to sorbets, lemonade and sugared almonds."[19]

His Six Pieces for Piano (BV 241), published by Peters sometime in 1896, have proved more acceptable, and several recordings have been made. The six titles of the pieces are typical Busoni, in their straddling of German and Italian worlds: "Schwermut" (Melancholy), "Frohsinn" (Lightheartedness), "Scherzino," "Fantasia in modo antico," "Allegro risoluto," "Finnische Ballade," "Exeunt omnes." As stated above, they were not all written in the same period, and not originally intended as a set. And the languages of the titles should not be taken too seriously: "Schwermut," for example, with its dotted rhythm, seems to owe more to Naples than to anywhere in Germany; likewise "Frohsinn" is a waltz.

In December 1895 Busoni finally returned to Italy for a series of concerts. It must have been a disturbing experience. Other than a few, fleeting visits to Trieste, and his family's arrival in Europe via Genoa from the United States, he had not set foot in his native country since 1883, when he was seventeen years old. "This feeling of being known and yet a stranger . . . is quite indescribable," he wrote to Gerda from Milan.[20] "It is strange what a childish pleasure it gives me to speak Italian; to be a foreigner, and yet not." He was saddened by his perception of the musical life of the country. "A thousand thanks for your dear letters," he wrote two days later, still in Milan;[21]

> they are a comfort to me in the dejected mood in which I drag myself round here in spite of my efforts to overcome it.
>
> I sit in the hotel at a miserable upright piano, with a bad cigar in my mouth, in an unheated room. The cool, almost hostile—at least mistrustful—way in which they have received me here, has disappointed me very much. It took the whole strength of my ability and willpower to win the public yesterday evening. I succeeded in the end, and today the papers, with one accord, are full of enthusiasm. . . . The conditions [in Italy] are hopeless at present. Just to raise the country to the level of attainment in knowledge and belief reached long ago by Germany, would be an immense piece of work. And by the time that was achieved the other countries would again be ahead.

It was a harsh view of his native land, and it shows just how little Busoni was aware of current achievements in Italian music. He was missing Gerda terribly, however, and December is certainly not the best month to visit Milan and the Po valley. But further south, the eternal charm of Italy

touched him, and struck chords that reverberated in his next compositions. From Parma ("Parma . . . is genuinely Italian, which Milan is *not*")
he wrote:[22] "We must come to Italy as 'tourists' and enjoy the old things,
the food and the wine. Everything else is worthless." On his way home,
on December 11, he looked in briefly on his parents in Trieste, seeing his
mother for the first time since 1890, just before his marriage, and his father for the first time since the summer of 1889, in Weimar. The short
visit apparently went well. Then it was back to Berlin overnight, via Vienna, where he saw a concert given by his old friend Eugen d'Albert and
bumped into Ludwig von Bösendorfer, who failed to recognize him until
he said his name. It was a happy meeting, as Bösendorfer offered to give
him a brilliant introduction in Vienna, and in fact two days later in Berlin
Busoni received a telegram from him inviting him to play in February with
the Vienna Philharmonic. He joyfully accepted. What should he play? he
asked. Busoni suggested Rubinstein's Fifth Piano Concerto, or something
by Liszt. "I'm afraid (frankly) of introducing myself with Beethoven," he
confessed to the older man, and asked for advice.[23]

By December 17, Busoni was yet again on a train, from Berlin to
Antwerp, for more concerts. There was a break over the Christmas period, then the traveling began again. Gerda went with him in February
1896 for the concert in Vienna, conducted by Hans Richter, no less,
which proved a triumph. "I'm certain it will bring you not a little satisfaction to learn that I managed to get my revenge [*prendermi la rivincita*]
in Vienna," he reported to Trieste,[24] "that I have been preparing and waiting for for years. My success on February 16 was extraordinary. All my old
'friends' were there, Leschetitzky, Brahms, Hanslick, Epstein, Rosenthal,
Gutmann and a thousand others." Hanslick wrote of this performance:

It is well known that the promise of infant prodigies is deceptive, hence we
looked forward to the twenty-nine-year-old artist's performance with a mix-
ture of anticipation and anxiety. He has entirely fulfilled our former hopes.
As a virtuoso namely, for we have heard nothing of his compositions. Busoni is now one of the foremost amongst pianists. I know no other who so
strikingly reminds me of Rubinstein. The same sonorous touch, the same
massive strength, endurance and assurance, the same wholesome supple-
ness of interpretation. In the unbelievably difficult and taxing E-flat Major
Concerto (No. 5) of Rubinstein, Busoni was able to let his technique triumph.[25]

In Vienna Busoni met some old friends again: Otto von Kapff ("still the same and still good and sincere"[26]) and Paula Flamm, now safely married. And so he went back—if only briefly in these years—to Berlin, which was proving congenial. Busoni's old friend Arthur Nikisch, who had returned to Europe in 1893 to become musical director of the Budapest Opera, in 1895 succeeded Hans von Bülow, who had died in February 1894, as chief conductor of the Berlin Philharmonic (and simultaneously of the Leipzig Gewandhaus Orchestra—hyperactive conductors are not a recent phenomenon). Nikisch was another of the many musicians drawn by the magnet of the new imperial capital, and he became part of Busoni's circle. Felix Weingartner, another former pupil of Wilhelm Mayer in Graz, was now Kapellmeister of the Berlin Opera, and in December 17, 1896, conducted Busoni's performance of the Beethoven E-flat Major Piano Concerto in Berlin.

In the preceding three months Busoni had played in Oslo, Göttingen, Vienna (where on December 4 he had played Grieg's Piano Concerto, among other things, in the composer's presence, and Hanslick had compared him favorably to Rubinstein yet again), then Aachen, Krefeld, and by December 19 he was back in Vienna, where he took part in a concert the next day, and afterward went out to dinner with Brahms, Leschetizky, and other worthies. ("It seems I am 'en vogue' here."[27]) During these last three months of 1896 he had also played in Königsberg, Baden Baden, Cologne, Dresden, Darmstadt, and Magdeburg, touching base in Berlin about once a month for a few days.

The next few years were devoted mainly to performing, involving marathon train journeys. Fortunately, the rail network was more or less established all over Europe by this time; very often, Busoni took a sleeper, leaving one city in the evening immediately after a concert, then arriving the next morning in another and going directly from the station to a rehearsal for that evening's performance. It was a punishing pace, and by late 1894, when he had started out on his second European "debut," Gerda was already taking over some of his letter writing—even to his parents (she wrote in French)—to take some of the pressure off him. But he was determined to establish himself permanently this time on the musical map.

In February 1897 Busoni gave two more piano recitals in Vienna, and took Gerda and Benni with him so that they could go on together to Trieste. It was Gerda's first visit, and her first meeting with her father-in-law and the rest of the family. It was all rather a shock for her, but she took it with the unshakeable serenity that never forsook her, and made her so universally admired and loved. She was amazed by Ferdinando's tyranny, not only over his wife (he would call her to hand him a handkerchief lying in front of him on the table) but also over Ferruccio, who was very meek in his father's presence. Nevertheless, the visit went well.

On March 1, back in Berlin, Busoni finished the instrumentation of his Concerto in D Major for Violin and Orchestra (BV 243), having worked on this composition for nearly a year. "He worked on Sunday until one in the morning and all day yesterday until seven, when it was finished," Gerda wrote to Trieste. "Because of that, today he is in a very good humor."[28] He dedicated it to Henri Petri, who was to play it at its premiere at the Singakademie in Berlin on October 8 that same year (see below). The movements flow into one another, beginning with a sensuous Allegro moderato—quasi Andante. Busoni quotes almost explicitly from Brahms and Beethoven, both in the violin and in the orchestra, yet there is a freedom, a self-confidence in the work, particularly in its unabashed *joie de vivre*, that indicates his Italian roots. It was written by a virtuoso of the piano and demands equal virtuosity of a violinist. There are many of the Busoni hallmarks: emphatic tutti passages, with uninhibited use of percussion, and a lot of boisterous humor, particularly in the final Allegro impetuoso. It is a work that has remained in the repertoire for a century now, his only concerto for violin. A premiere of this work had been planned for March 19, in an all-Busoni concert in Berlin, but owing to confusion concerning the date, and conflicting engagements of all concerned, the concert was postponed until the autumn. On March 16, however, Busoni gave a solo recital at the Singakademie of works all new to him (and some new to Berlin), for which he had given himself only six days to prepare. They were: Bach-Busoni, *Chaconne*; Beethoven, "Eroica" Variations; Weber, Sonata no. 1 in C-Major; Meyerbeer-Liszt, *Fantasia on "Le Prophète"*; Mozart-Liszt, *Fantasia on "Don Giovanni"*; Liszt-Busoni, *Fantasia and Fugue on the Chorale "Ad nos, ad salutarem undam" from "Le Prophète"* by Meyerbeer.

Relations between Busoni and the Petris were now fully reestablished, after some stuttering efforts six years before. No letters are extant from Busoni to the Petris from April 1890 to March 3, 1896, although that does not, of course, mean that there were none. Henri Petri was now the leader of the Court Opera Orchestra in Dresden, and in a March 1896 letter,[29] written in the rather ponderously jokey style Busoni often assumed, firstly he thanks the Petris for their recent hospitality in Dresden, then there is a lot of wordplay on orders and being decorated, suggesting that Busoni received some kind of royal recognition in Dresden, which was still the capital of what was left of the kingdom of Saxony. (The reigning king, Albert, was the same monarch who had scuppered the premiere of Busoni's ill-fated suite in Leipzig in 1888.)

In summer 1896, as mentioned above, the young family had gone on holiday to Göhren on the island of Rügen in the Baltic, but the next summer Ferruccio remained alone in Berlin while Gerda and Benni left on July 2 for Thale, in the Harz Mountains, to give him the necessary calm to compose. This became a routine every summer, and Busoni was nearly always successful in keeping those months free (more or less) from performing and the consequent traveling: that spring he had even spent his birthday—April 1—on a train between Saint Petersburg and Vienna. Before Gerda and Benni left in 1897, however, a classic ritual was performed: "I've cut the child's hair, which gives him a rather more mature and in my view more able [*efficace*] and expressive look. Almost at a stroke he has stopped being a baby and now has become a boy."[30]

The only composition of the summer of 1897 was written in one night, however. "I had a remarkable experience last night," Ferruccio wrote Gerda on July 11. "I sat down about twelve o'clock to write an overture and continued writing until morning. *I began and finished it without a break.* Of course nothing is perfect, and the piece will have to be revised. As it is, it is not bad, very flowing, and almost Mozartian in style."[31] This was the *Lustspielouvertüre* (Comedy Overture) *for Orchestra* (BV 245), also premiered in Berlin on October 8. Busoni revised the work in 1904, and it is this revised version that is usually performed today. It is an ebullient work, hinting that the latent Italian in Busoni had been awakened by his visit to Italy, and shaking off some of the German influence. The allusion to Mozart, who, in Busoni's eyes, achieved a kind of synthesis of German and Italian, is another indication of this.

The summer arrangement, as was perhaps to be expected, did not proceed without tensions. In the above-quoted letter to his father Ferruccio announced that he was sending Gerda and Benni out of Berlin "for four to six weeks," which shows that there were doubts about whether it would work. Alone in the country with Benni, Gerda felt rejected, and after just two weeks away she had obviously written a complaining letter, to which Ferruccio replied on July 18: "*Meine liebe Frau,* Your letters are really plaintive and out of sorts. Why do you take the matter so seriously?" She did not have to stay there, and he would come to her whenever she wanted, and she could even come back to Berlin with him afterward. But without Bertha, the maid, who was always away during the summer, it would be difficult. If he came to her, he warned, "I'll only stay a short time, as I am slowly getting back into my work again."[32] On July 22 he wrote that he would be coming the next day, then on July 23 he would be coming "on Sunday"; on July 27 a further delay was announced, as a new rent contract had to be negotiated for their apartment, matters at the bank had to be sorted out, and there were discussions with his agent, Hermann Wolff. Ferruccio finally left at the end of that week. It was a difficult situation for a young couple, resolved slowly although sometimes painfully, thanks to the great love and the close bond that had developed between them, thanks too to the tolerant nature of both. Gerda's situation was the more difficult, not helped over the years by the frequent presence of other people in the apartment in Berlin during the summer months, who apparently did not constitute a disturbance to Ferruccio's creative processes. But there was a price for his leaving Berlin that summer: for the first two weeks of August he was very ill, with what he called a very painful "chill with muscular inflammation."[33] He apparently could not sleep for nine nights, as he could not lie down. Whether there was a psychological basis to this we shall probably never know.

In spite of the summer arrangement, from his family's taking up residence in Berlin in 1894 until the end of the century, Busoni wrote only five works: the Six Pieces for Piano; the Second Orchestral Suite; the Concerto in D-Major for Violin and Orchestra; the Sonata in E-Minor for Violin and Piano, no. 2 (BV 244); and the *Lustspielouvertüre* for Orchestra. The summers "alone" in Berlin were nevertheless important periods of rest and reflection, a time to digest knowledge often accumulated in a haphazard way, almost "on the wing" at times, which was to provide a valuable preparation for his later works, both musical and theoretical.

On October 8, 1897, came the concert in Berlin at the Singakademie, Busoni himself conducting the Berlin Philharmonic in a concert devoted wholly to his own compositions: the Violin Concerto, the Symphonic Tone Poem, the *Lustspielouvertüre* composed that summer, and the *Geharnischte Suite* (see below). This was the first public performance of all these works other than the Symphonic Tone Poem and, as Busoni put it, his "quasi-debut" as a composer in Berlin. The Violin Concerto was such a success with the audience that after returning five times to the stage, Petri was constrained to repeat the finale. It met with a very mixed reception from the press, however, which did not particularly perturb Busoni, even though one writer went so far as to affirm that Busoni had not the faintest idea of symphonic construction. The review began:

> Mr. Ferruccio Busoni, the highly gifted pianist, with a fine individuality bordering on genius, introduced himself to us on Friday in the Singakademie as composer. The cozily cheerful |behaglich heiter| Lustspielouvertüre, which opened the concert, aroused a favorable atmosphere. Reminiscent of Mozart, it is written in a predominantly clear and pleasant way, and contrapuntally interesting.

After then casting aspersions on Busoni's abilities, the reviewer—astonishingly—confessed that he had left before the last item, the *Geharnischte Suite* (Armor-clad Suite), "out of concern that at the end I would really become armored against the composer."[34]

The whole Petri family had come to Berlin for the occasion, which Ferruccio defined as "a milestone in the history of our artistic and human bond: a bond that was first forged between three, now through Gerda's arrival and Egon's growth has become stronger."[35] Was it a milestone, or final nail in the coffin of the affair that had almost cost the Petris their marriage? Either way, much of the old intimacy was gone, which was perhaps natural, as both sides had moved on. Over the coming years the poles shifted too: by 1902 Busoni had begun a deep and lasting friendship with the now twenty-one-year-old Egon, who was to become Busoni's most famous pupil, sporadically his amanuensis, and the recipient of a large number of his letters almost until his death.

At the end of October 1897 Busoni visited London for the first time and stayed until December 11. It was a daunting experience, as yet again he had to conquer a new audience, a campaign demanding six concerts for this initial onslaught. He was well aware of the difficulties. Already with a population of over six million and the capital of a huge empire, London was wealthy, cosmopolitan, and very sophisticated. It had an extremely lively cultural scene: Henry Irving and Ellen Terry still dominated in the theater; George Bernard Shaw was active not only as a playwright, but as a theater and music critic; Oscar Wilde's spectacular fall from grace was only two years in the past—he had left prison, and England, only six months before Busoni arrived; and Ibsen's heavily moralizing plays, a certain antidote to the sardonic wit of the disgraced Irishman, were riding high. Also, the greatest musical performers were all eager for success in London; Paderewski had been there in the spring, presenting the danger of comparison yet again. As Ferruccio explained to his parents,[36] "London is a world apart, and it is very difficult to make one's way here." He was writing to them on a Sunday, a day of *pausa generale*, as he succinctly put it. (He was always exasperated by the Protestant shutdown of most activity on Sundays, wherever he encountered it.) In his volume of memoirs, *My Life of Music*, Sir Henry Wood, the great conductor and founder of the annual Promenade Concerts that now bear his name, mistakenly dates Busoni's London debut as 1900. But his recollections of Busoni, whom he got to know (in some ways) quite well over the years, although written in Wood's rather naive, decent-chap style, are illuminating and often entertaining. One anecdote illustrates the distance between the two men on many levels:

> Busoni fascinated me. Whenever we drove together in one of the old fourwheeled cabs I used to sit with my back to the horse so that I could watch the changes of expression in his face. If we passed the R.A.M. [Royal Academy of Music] he always took hold of the brim of his hat with both hands and raised it reverently, giving the building a solemn bow as we passed. I could never get him to explain why he did this; when I asked him he simply roared with laughter.[37]

Wood guessed, quite shrewdly, that the reason could have been Busoni's "derision of the Macfarren[38] regime" at the academy.

The first London concert, on November 4 at the St. James's Hall,
had gone well, but several were needed to establish Busoni in the public consciousness, as he was practically unknown in London.

Having been an avid admirer of Dickens's works since childhood, Busoni relished seeing the actual settings of the famous novels. But early in
November he also experienced his first London "pea-souper" fog—less
pleasant in reality than in the pages of Dickens. English food was better
than he expected, mainly because there were so many Italian and French
restaurants, he concluded—not quite logically. Drinks were bad and expensive, but he had bought an English pipe, which would need some getting used to. Taste, in clothing, furniture, and many other things, was
much superior to that in any other country he was familiar with, he
opined, so much so that it set the tone today in all of Europe. Everything
was eagerly noted as he explored the city, from the ways of the omnibus
conductors, to the design of the hansom cabs ("the best cabs in the world;
they even surpass the Russian isvostshiks"[39]), and the many bookshops.

Nevertheless, Busoni felt lonely in that enormous, bustling city. He
had arrived on October 30, and late in November Gerda joined him for
a short while, leaving again on December 2. "I felt a pang as I saw the
train leave," he wrote her, "and I have seldom felt so alone as I did
when I woke this morning."[40] Britain was to prove a loyal, steadfast,
and appreciative friend—and subsequently a steady source of revenue.
(Busoni later nicknamed it "Pounds Island.") But he felt depressed, he
had written Gerda after his first concerts, at "always having to begin
afresh, a Sisyphus of débuts. At the age of thirty-one this has not been
necessary for other people."[41] As he recounted in this letter, the reviews
all referred to him as "a young pianist, a new pianist, a pianist simply
called Busoni, as yet unknown—that is how they all begin." In view of
the fact that he was almost completely unknown in London, the trip
there was a courageous gamble: Busoni had to pay for the concerts himself, with some help from Bechstein, and hope that the box office takings would leave him with a profit, which they did. He stayed until December 11, then went on to Vienna, on the Orient Express. The
general consensus was that he had "arrived" in London, and next June,
and the following December, he returned, to even greater success.

On that first visit to London he made many friends, mostly in the musical world, but on subsequent visits his circle of friends was to expand, helping to make London almost a second home for him. Arthur Friedheim (1859–1932), the pianist, conductor, and composer, who had been a pupil of Liszt for the last eight years of the latter's life and had acted as the great man's secretary, was living in London during Busoni's first visit and took to him. On December 4, Busoni played Liszt's *Don Juan* Fantasy to him, "with which he was delighted. 'Liszt himself could not have played it better.' . . . While I was playing he gave me some suggestions that were very stimulating. He heard Liszt play these pieces, revels in recollections, and in spite of that was, apparently, very astounded by my playing. He paid me the highest compliments."[42]

But the London appearances were not yet the financial successes to merit the "Pounds Island" nickname, as Busoni patiently explained to Trieste in May 1898 just before his second London visit, laying out his current financial situation: "Of my takings, 10 percent goes to Wolff [his agent], 5 percent for tax, 20 percent for traveling expenses, 20 percent to you, 25 percent for household and living expenses. Thus 80 percent of my *regular* income is taken care of; of 15,000 marks, 12,000 are hence consumed, without counting any extra expenses. In April I paid out 2,400 marks in cash,"[43] which he then itemizes. His parents were understanding at a certain level, as some of the items on this list do not strike one as being basic necessities: "Furnishings 100, Pictures 180" (not to mention the inevitable "Bookseller 100").

But although the financial situation was to improve as Busoni consolidated his reputation in Britain and elsewhere, these marathon tours outside the summer months, a way of life he had endured almost constantly since early childhood, were starting even now to take their toll on his health and arguably lay the foundations for his later kidney and liver problems (both associated with stress and exhaustion). Those temporary stress relievers, tobacco and alcohol, made their own contribution.

There was an apparent compromise in the summer of 1898: Gerda and Benni went out to Woltersdorf, a village surrounded by many lakes on the outskirts of Berlin, where Ferruccio could easily join them if he felt so inclined and the weather proved tempting; or Gerda could come back into Berlin for a visit. Busoni received other visits that were not so welcome, even though they did afford some amusement: on August 8, at around six in the evening, Ottokar Nováček and a friend turned up, both very drunk and wanting to take Ferruccio out. He got rid of them by promising to meet them at nine, not meaning to go. At eight Vasily Safonov arrived, then the door rang again and, to screams and laughter from the maid Bertha, Nováček and his friend entered again, still drunk. Ferruccio, who always seemed to find drunk people hilarious, recounted all this to Gerda[44] with gusto. (In spite of seeing Gerda often during this summer, he still wrote to her almost daily.)

Busoni's repertoire evolved and altered over the years, some composers remaining, others gradually disappearing—usually a pretty accurate Darwinian reflection of their staying power in musical evolution, but also, of course, a reflection of his own changing musical tastes. In October and November 1898, at the Singakademie in Berlin, he gave a series of four concerts illustrating the history and development of the piano concerto. The programs were divided up as follows: (1) Bach, D Minor; Mozart, A Major; Beethoven, G Major; Hummel, B Minor; (2) Beethoven, E-flat Major; Weber, *Konzertstück*; Schubert-Liszt, *Wandererfantasie*; Chopin, E Minor; (3) Mendelssohn, G Minor; Schumann, A Minor; Henselt, F Minor; (4) Rubinstein, E-flat Major; Brahms, D Minor; Liszt, A Major. There are not many dead dinosaurs there. This list also indicates the Herculean stamina the programs demanded—three to four concertos in a single concert! Busoni's solo recitals were similarly punishing, and his enormous repertoire imposed its own demands on practice and rehearsal hours.

On his third visit to London, in December 1898, Busoni met Frederick Delius again, who was now based in France. Busoni, generous and open as always to fellow musicians, studied Delius's Piano Concerto, composed the previous year, and his setting of Nietzsche's "Mitternachtslied" for baritone, male chorus, and orchestra of 1898. Busoni also met Percy Pitt, whom he had gotten to know in Leipzig, and who suggested he repeat his Berlin series of concerts on the history of the concerto in London. On this visit Busoni ventured beyond London and toured the British provinces, a pattern that continued on subsequent visits to Britain. On December 11 he was in Manchester for a concert, on the sixteenth in London to talk to Henry Wood about the concert series, then back to Manchester, where he stayed with the Brodskys, now based there, for more concerts. Leaving Manchester on December 22, he managed to get to Berlin for Christmas, although by January 9 he was back in London, planning to take the night train to Liverpool, going on to Edinburgh and Manchester, and then back to London. In Manchester in December, another guest of the Brodskys, the American pianist William Dayas (a former pupil of Liszt), had been so inspired by Busoni's playing that he gave a dinner in the latter's honor. "What a pity the Old Man [Liszt] never heard you!" exclaimed Dayas on hearing Busoni play Liszt's Fantasia on *Norma*. "He would have blessed you and died happy." At the dinner, Dayas drank only port. "'This stuff, I don't know, it's like water for me.' And of this water he drank one and a half bottles (for the sake of consistency, out of a water glass) and was finally so totally drunk that he could no longer see, walk or talk."[45] Busoni had intended for Dayas (1863–1903), who took over Busoni's position at the conservatory in Helsinki, to be the dedicatee of his Piano Concerto, but Dayas died before its completion.

In June that year, in London yet again, Busoni met Hans Richter in the street, who professed regret that he had missed Busoni's recent Vienna concert. Richter tried to gossip about Mahler, who had conducted in that concert, but had needed a lot of preparation—according to Richter, any self-respecting conductor should be able to conduct at sight. All this and more was amusingly reported to Gerda,[46] Ferruccio quoting Richter's words in a phonetic rendering of his thick Viennese accent. (Mahler, appointed Kapellmeister of the Court Opera in Vienna in 1897, although enjoying some success with his performances there, nevertheless proved controversial, particularly in his Philharmonic Concerts, which he took over from Richter in 1898. There was inevitably rivalry between Richter and Mahler, a rivalry fanned by the gossip-loving Viennese. Busoni saw the funny side of all this and considered himself well out of it.)

In the same letter, Ferruccio reported on another hazard of the virtuoso's life: society hostesses. Clarita, wife of the London merchant Theodor Matesdorf, landed him, "like a commonplace flounder," for a Sunday afternoon at home, "to which I look forward with as much pleasure as a child to a hiding." Nevertheless, he appreciated the Matesdorfs's kindness and hospitality, and generally stayed with them for the next few years whenever he was in London. Another friendship cemented at this time was with the Belgian violinist and composer EugèneYsaÿe (1858–1931). Busoni and Ysaÿe both took part in a concert that also included the great Australian soprano Dame Nellie Melba, then aged thirty-eight and at the height of her fame. "Without boasting, I had the greatest success yesterday in spite of [Ysaÿe] and Melba," he nevertheless did boast to Gerda.[47] Ysaÿe was an enthusiastic supporter of new music, particularly French and Belgian, and organized a series of concerts in Brussels throughout the 1890s to this end. This provided a further bond between him and Busoni.

In November Busoni was back in Britain yet again. "My recital yesterday went brilliantly," he wrote on November 23 from Manchester, regarding a London concert a few days before.

> I played as well as I can play. Nothing went wrong, and the enthusiastic success and the reviews that have appeared already today show a big step in the process of taking root in London. As you see, for the first time, there is no censure, and the *Daily Telegraph* is very detailed. There will always be a coolness in the tone of the newspaper reviews, for this belongs to a certain kind of distinction in journalism in this country. I see that, not only in my own reviews, but in those of the other artists who have been well known in England for a long time.[48]

He went on to Nottingham, back to London, then in the first week of December he was in Glasgow on the fifth, in Manchester again on the sixth, and by the eighth back in London, playing different programs in each concert.

> Now the worst is over. Until yesterday I was working like a dog. I was obliged to prepare the last program (106 Beethoven [the "Hammerklavier"], 4 Chopin Ballades, Chopin A-flat Polonaise and "Robert" [transcriptions of Lieder by Robert Schumann] by Liszt) in a day and a half, but it went well, really excellently. And after this great effort came the evening soirée at the Matesdorfs. Among the interesting people there, I found I was most sympathetically and quickly in touch with [John Singer] Sargent. . . . He was pleased with my love for painting and general outlook on it, and he enjoyed my playing very much. Perhaps he will paint me, which would give me absurd pleasure (and you, too, I am sure).[49]

Unfortunately, this idea came to nothing.

By mid-December Busoni was back in Berlin, leaving only on January 12, 1900, for a concert the next day in Essen, followed by one on the sixteenth in Cologne; in early February in Strasbourg, by the twentieth in Zurich, the twenty-fifth in Basle, and so on. For some time now, his letters to Gerda were not only a way of sharing with her what he saw and experienced, but gradually too his thoughts on more profound matters. But he seemed to wrest some enjoyment from almost anything: while in Essen in January 1900, looking through a French dictionary, he discovered that in French *buson* was a kind of bird, but also slang for "a stupid man." In passing on these gems to Gerda, he drew a picture of a bird with his own head, dancing on a Steinway piano keyboard.[50] (The same letter also contains a drawing of him asleep at a table.) Three days later, in Cologne, he sent Gerda an account of some marionettes in a variety theater performance he had seen there the day before. He was fascinated by the perfection of the marionettes' movements:

> For instance, the first number was given by a trapeze artist. The movements, the bending of the body, etc. were absolutely right. At the end, when he sprang down from the trapeze, he made another little spring as he touched the floor, which is what the law of elasticity demands. That is fine. Then came two so-called music clowns. They had bells on their hands and feet that were made to ring through the shaking of their limbs. There were 8 bells. They were tuned so that a melody could be shaken (not played) on them.[51]

The whole of the marionettes' act is described in meticulous and appreciative detail, recalling that marionette performance he saw as a child with his mother in Trieste, on the night his father returned. His fascination with marionettes was to be a strong and productive thread throughout his life.

This same letter from Cologne contains a vivid description of what happened when he came out of the theater into the real, human world:

> When I came out of the theater there was snow on the ground, hard, dry snow. This, combined with the cold, affected the people on the streets like champagne. First, some boys in a side street began to slide on the slippery ground. Soon a gallery of onlookers formed. Some of them with-

drew from it and started to slide in the main road themselves. The shop girls on their way home from work were infected. Then it spread even more. Everyone, even men in spectacles, were sliding or trying to slide. They ran into one another, crashed into the one in front, or fell down. If anyone fell the bystanders laughed. Before long the whole street was laughing. There was a sliding, running, pushing, falling and laughing, as if everyone were intoxicated. I have seldom seen such a comical and lively picture.

There are shades of Christmas in Dingley Dell, in *Pickwick Papers*, which Busoni was familiar with, and which the scene may well have recalled. The passage shows the influence of his voracious reading, but it also shows his unwaning zest for all types of human experience.

In June that year Busoni was back in London, and again in October, after a concert in Frankfurt. "The twenty-four hours' journey which followed the concert was hard work after an incomplete night's rest," he reported on October 19. "I was obliged to cancel my rehearsal today, I am too done up! But London is always pleasant and it is a pity I must leave again tomorrow evening." Three days later he was in Aachen, then Brussels, where he dined with Ysaÿe, "who has a beautiful home, beautiful wife, and beautiful children. The composer Fauré, from Paris, was there; he played his own variations to us. . . . The fiftieth performance of Saint-Saëns's *Samson and Delila* will be given tonight. He is here himself, and I shall make his acquaintance." He did, and from then on championed Saint-Saëns's music too.

When Busoni and Gerda were apart, letters passed between them almost daily; on rare occasions, she joined him. By 1900 Benni was eight years old and at school, needing her presence in Berlin during schooltime. And on February 1 that year their second child, Raffaello (Lello) was born, restricting her mobility even more. Our gain is their correspondence—or at least, Ferruccio's letters. They communicated in German, which by now Ferruccio spoke flawlessly; not so Gerda. To the end of her long life she was ashamed of her faulty German, which led her to have most of her letters destroyed. This was doubtless not the only reason: she was always modest and guarded her privacy. Whereas Ferruccio's letters dealt primarily with his professional life, and what he saw on the world's stage in the widest sense, hers (as is proved by the few remaining) were mainly filled with personal detail, which makes their loss the greater. In spite of a few eyewitness accounts, no sharply focused picture remains for us of this woman who was Ferruccio's rock and strength, and attracted fervent admiration often bordering on adoration from nearly all who got to know her.

In addition to Lello's birth, 1900 saw another important change in the Busonis's lives: the Grand-Duke Karl Alexander of Saxe-Weimar, a generous and enthusiastic patron of the arts, invited Busoni to conduct master classes in piano playing in Weimar from July to September. The classes were a great success and repeated the next year. They were held in the Tempelherrenhaus, an old hothouse in what is now known as the Goethe Park, which was converted into a teahouse in 1786 and used for small parties and receptions. The building was converted again in the fashionable neo-Gothic style in 1811 and decorated with four statues of Templars (hence its name) by Martin Klauer. The great Goethe himself, Weimar's most famous resident, designed a tower. In the last months of World War II, the building received a direct hit; now only the entrance and Goethe's tower remain, as romantic, ivy-clad ruins.

Lessons were held in a large rectangular room with huge windows offering views of the park. The Busonis rented a house for the three months in Weimar, which became an unofficial home to many of Ferruccio's students, the eternally equable Gerda making everyone welcome. The students were handpicked and from many different countries. Busoni, now thirty-four, emerged here as inspiring teacher and guide, giving unorthodox lessons bound by neither time nor place, in a spirit of Socratic dialogue, at the piano, over wine, or during long walks in and around Weimar. His teaching, although anchored on piano playing, ranged over aesthetics, art, and philosophy, all aimed at emancipating his students to a wider outlook on the way they lived their lives and their art. They remained devoted to him; the same held for subsequent pupils elsewhere, in piano playing and later—and more importantly—in composition. By now his reputation as a pianist was so great that to call oneself a pupil of Busoni was to wear a badge of very high quality indeed.

Nevertheless, some lesser talents slipped in. One was that intriguing figure, Maud Allan (1873–1956), who attended the 1901 master classes. She was living in Berlin at the time, and had been to many of Busoni's recitals there, and finally managed to meet him. According to her, it was in the Busonis's home the winter before that she first danced, wearing one of Gerda's shawls around her shoulders. In her decidedly unreliable memoirs,[52] she gives a rather gushing account of the Weimar master classes.

But these two summers robbed Busoni of his usual time spent alone in Berlin composing. Meanwhile, for the rest of the year, the marathon tours continued. He was earning large sums of money by now; nevertheless, Busoni was always under pressure to earn more, not only from his parents, but perhaps Gerda too: there are frequent pleas for understanding in his letters to her. "Please, dear Gerda, write that you agree and are not angry," he begs in a letter[53] from Berlin in July 1903, in which he tells her he has decided not to go to London that month for two concerts, but concentrate on his Piano Concerto instead (perhaps the most significant decision of his life: for once, composing took precedence over earning money). "I feel so free and am so happy otherwise. . . . Perhaps a little telegram, just to oblige? Would be very hurrah-ed." At other times he apologizes for canceling concerts owing to exhaustion.

The marriage was manifestly a happy one, as is also shown time and time again in Ferruccio's letters, which are full of endearments, longing, gratitude, and humor. And on the strength of the letters as a whole, and of eyewitness accounts of Gerda and their marriage, it is difficult to imagine Gerda heartlessly pushing him. Was his early conditioning and sense of responsibility so great that in effect he was writing to himself in these letters? Or was he transferring to Gerda the powerful urge not only to make money but to appear before the public and excel, the urge that took him from composing? The ambition Delius noted in him certainly played a part. The strain on him did occasionally put a strain on the marriage too, as apologies for his behavior in some letters reveal.

A large proportion of Busoni's performances were of one or two items in a concert, and he often played together with other soloists, some of whom became friends, although the pressures of performance often caused problems, including conflict with fellow musicians. One such was Eugène Ysaÿe, with whom Busoni played at the concert with Nellie Melba in June 1899. He was glad, he wrote to Gerda at the time, that he had got to know Ysaÿe better. "He is a *great* artist and an amusing man."[54] But the man had his shortcomings: in London again in February 1902, he pushed Busoni's patience too far:

Yesterday Ysaÿe was so rude to me that I lost patience with him. It was about a rehearsal for the Saint-Saëns (that I didn't know at all, had neither seen nor heard and had to play on the same evening). Y. made me wait for three hours at Bechstein's [piano showrooms where he often practiced] and to three messages I sent, the answer was always that he was sleeping or lying down. It was 1 o'clock (the train left at 2 [for Birmingham, where they were to play]), I had eaten nothing. I went to him and said I couldn't play the piece under these conditions. He made a frightful scene, so that finally Newman,[55] who was there, had to tell him he was being rude, was in the wrong and should shut up. It made me (nervous as I already was) very upset and by the evening I was finished. We rehearsed the sonata (that is, sight-read it through) one hour before the concert in a store. I was almost ill, we played like a couple of cobblers, as was inevitable.[56]

Not everyone came up to his high standards of conscientiousness, he was learning, nor to his high levels of knowledge and general curiosity. He was often scathing about what he perceived as the shallow mentality of many of his fellow musicians.

One whose company he always relished was his old friend Jean Sibelius. Henry Wood gives us a pleasant picture of the two friends in London:

I could generally manage Busoni when I had him to myself, but my heart was always in my mouth if he met Sibelius. I never knew where they would get to. They would forget the time of the concert at which they were to appear; they hardly knew the day of the week. One year I was directing the Birmingham Festival and had to commission a friend never to let these two out of his sight. He had quite an exciting time for two or three days following them about from restaurant to restaurant. He told me he never knew what time they went to bed or got up in the morning. They were like a couple of irresponsible schoolboys.[57]

The spirit of the Leskovites apparently lived on.

Busoni also enjoyed the touring much more if Gerda could be with him, as she was in Italy for most of March in 1902. London, where she also often joined him, was a favorite city, and it was in Britain that the tours became the most lucrative, although in general he hated the provinces, associated in his mind with narrow-mindedness—a serious defect. But where Busoni himself was concerned, the old adage that travel broadens the mind was certainly proved true. He was exposed not only to very different cultures and opinions on a broad variety of subjects, which appealed to his endlessly eclectic mind, but also to a broad variety of music, particularly new music, and by the beginning of the new century he had decided to share some of his discoveries with his chosen home, which, he was to discover, could also be narrow-minded where music was concerned.

Notes

1. See Celia Applegate and Pamela Potter, eds., *Music and German National Identity* (Chicago: University of Chicago Press, 2002), for an excellent overview of the perceived role of music in Germany, particularly as it emerged in the nineteenth century.

2. Letter from FB to Ferdinando Busoni, April 24, 1894, StBB Bus. Nachl. 1296.

3. Ferruccio Busoni, "Brief an Giuseppe Verdi," translated into German and published by Friedrich Schnapp in *Zeitschrift für Musik* 99, no. 12 (December 1932): 1057. English translation by Antony Beaumont, *Ferruccio Busoni: Selected Letters* (London: Faber and Faber, 1987), p. 53.

4. Letter from FB to Ferdinando Busoni, June 1, 1894, StBB Bus. Nachl. 1293.

5. Letter from FB to Ferdinando Busoni, July 16, 1894, StBB Bus. Nachl. 1295.

6. Letter from FB to Anna Weiss-Busoni, September 20, 1894, StBB Bus. Nachl. 1288.

7. Letter from FB to Anna Weiss-Busoni, August 1, 1895, StBB Bus. Nachl. 1313.

8. Letter from FB to Ferdinando Busoni and Anna Weiss-Busoni, August 9, 1896, StBB Bus. Nachl. 1315.

9. Otto Lessmann, review of concert at Singakademie on November 3, 1894, *Allgemeine Musikzeitung*, no. 45 (November 9, 1894): 589.

10. Review of concert at Singakademie on November 13, 1994, *Neue Berliner Musikzeitung*, November 15, 1894, 502.

11. Otto Lessmann, review of concert at Singakademie on December 1, 1894, *Allgemeine Musikzeitung*, no. 49 (December 7, 1894): 649–50.

12. Letter from FB to Anna Weiss-Busoni, February 20, 1895, StBB Bus. Nachl. 1308.

13. Letter from FB to Isidor Philipp, June 24, 1922, StBB Bus. Nachl. 352a.

14. As reported in letter from FB to Anna Weiss-Busoni, May 25, 1895, StBB Bus. Nachl. 1310.

15. Dent, *Ferruccio Busoni*, p. 109.

16. Marcel Rémy, in *L'Indépendance*, January 31, 1902.

17. Letter from FB to Marcel Rémy, dating from 1902, translated into German and edited by Friedrich Schnapp and published as "Brief an Marcel Rémy, Musikkritiker und Korrespondent des Brüsseler *Courrier musical* in Berlin," *Zeitschrift für Musik* 99, no. 12 (December 1932): 1058.

18. Alfred Brendel, *Nachdenken über Musik* (Munich: Piper, 1977), p. 154.

19. Letter from FB to Anna Weiss-Busoni, November 12, 1895, StBB Bus. Nachl. 1314.

20. Letter from FB to Gerda Busoni, December 5, 1895, StBB Bus. Nachl. IV, 278.

21. Letter from FB to Gerda Busoni, December 7, 1895, StBB Bus. Nachl. IV, 279.

22. Letter from FB to Gerda Busoni, December 9, 1895, StBB Bus. Nachl. IV, 280.

23. Letter from FB to Ludwig von Bösendorfer, December 14, 1895, StBB Bus. Nachl. 1130.

24. Letter from FB to Ferdinando Busoni and Anna Weiss-Busoni, February 27, 1896, StBB Bus. Nachl. 1320.

25. Review by Eduard Hanslick in the *Neue Freie Presse*, February 23, 1896; English translation in Beaumont, *Selected Letters*, p. 55. Busoni was so pleased with this review that he "quoted" it from memory in a letter to his parents of February 27, 1896, StBB Bus. Nachl. 1320. Hermann Wolff had the review printed as a publicity handout.

26. Letter from FB to Ferdinando Busoni, April 2, 1896, StBB Bus. Nachl. 1321.

27. Postcard from FB to Gerda Busoni, December 20, 1896, StBB Bus. Nachl. IV, 291.

28. Letter from Gerda Busoni to Ferdinando Busoni and Anna Weiss-Busoni, March 2, 1897, StBB Bus. Nachl. BII, 1163.

29. Letter from FB to Henri Petri, March 3, 1896, MW, p. 47.

30. Letter from FB to Ferdinando Busoni, June 22, 1897, StBB Bus. Nachl. 1326.

31. Letter from FB to Gerda Busoni, July 11, 1897, StBB Bus. Nachl. IV, 298.

32. Letter from FB to Gerda Busoni, July 18, 1897, StBB Bus. Nachl. IV, 301.

33. Letter from FB to Anna Weiss-Busoni, August 31, 1897, StBB Bus. Nachl. 1329.

34. Review of concert at Singakademie of October 8, 1897, *Vossische Zeitung*, October 9, 1897.

35. Letter from FB to Henri Petri, October 13, 1897, MW, p. 53.

36. Letter from FB to Anna Weiss-Busoni, November 7, 1897, StBB Bus. Nachl. 1331.

37. Henry Wood, *My Life of Music* (London: Gollancz, 1946), p. 141.

38. Walter Macfarren (1826–1905) was a pianist and composer who from 1846 to 1903 was professor of piano at the Royal Academy of Music. Grove refers to him guardedly as "a sound performer of the older school," which offers a hint for Busoni's hilarity. Henry Wood was one of his pupils.

39. Letter from FB to Gerda Busoni, October 31, 1897, StBB Bus. Nachl. IV, 308.

40. Letter from FB to Gerda Busoni, December 3, 1897, StBB Bus. Nachl. IV, 311.

41. Letter from FB to Gerda Busoni, November 5, 1897, StBB Bus. Nachl. IV, 310.

42. Letter from FB to Gerda Busoni, December 4, 1897, StBB Bus. Nachl. IV, 312.

43. Letter from FB to Anna Weiss-Busoni, May 7, 1898, StBB Bus. Nachl. 1333.

44. Letter from FB to Gerda Busoni, August 5, 1898, StBB Bus. Nachl. IV, 330.

45. Letter from FB to Gerda Busoni, December 16, 1998, StBB Bus. Nachl. IV, 343.

46. Letter from FB to Gerda Busoni, June 22, 1899, StBB Bus. Nachl. IV, 348.

47. Letter from FB to Gerda Busoni, June 23, 1899, StBB Bus. Nachl. IV, 349.

48. Letter from FB to Gerda Busoni, November 23, 1899, StBB Bus. Nachl. IV, 351.

49. Letter from FB to Gerda Busoni, December 8, 1899, StBB Bus. Nachl. IV, 357.

50. Letter from FB to Gerda Busoni, January 13, 1900, StBB, Bus. Nachl. IV, 358a.

51. Letter from FB to Gerda Busoni, January 16, 1900, StBB, Bus. Nachl. IV, 359.

52. Maud Allan, My Life and Dancing (London: Everett, 1908), pp. 67ff.

53. Letter from FB to Gerda Busoni, July 16, 1903, StBB, Bus. Nachl. IV, 437.

54. Letter from FB to Gerda Busoni, June 23, 1899, StBB, Bus. Nachl. IV, 349.

55. Robert Newman was the impresario who founded the Promenade Concerts (the "Proms") in the Queen's Hall in London in 1895; they were to become known as the Henry Wood Promenade Concerts, and now take place in the Royal Albert Hall (the Queen's Hall was destroyed by bombing during World War II).

56. Letter from FB to Gerda Busoni, February 4, 1902, StBB, Bus. Nachl. IV, 405.

57. Wood, My Life of Music, pp. 141–42.

CHAPTER EIGHT

Berlin, Return to the United States, Touring, Piano Concerto: 1902 to 1906

On November 8, 1902, Berlin saw the first of a series of twelve concerts, spread over several years, at the Beethovensaal that Busoni or
ganized, together with his agency, Hermann Wolff. (Hermann Wolff
himself had died in February that year; his wife Louise took over the
agency and continued to represent Busoni.) The programs were all of
new music, a large proportion of it non-German, plus other rarely performed pieces, that initially at least encountered some vociferous
opposition.

The astounding achievements of German and Austrian composers
from Bach and Handel in the early eighteenth century; through to
Mozart, Haydn, Beethoven, Mendelssohn, Schumann, Brahms, and
Wagner in the nineteenth; continuing with Mahler, Bruckner, Richard
Strauss, and others well into the twentieth, had brought German music to the front rank in Europe, but unfortunately helped feed a growing chauvinism, and the belief that only German music was worth taking seriously. ("There is no French music," Hans Richter is said to have
stated loftily, although he did concede the existence of British music.)
Mozart's and Wagner's operas were included in this exalted pantheon,
but otherwise opera was widely considered frivolous and inferior. This
blinkered attitude had its adherents beyond Germany's borders, too,

but Busoni, through birth, upbringing, and cosmopolitan life experiences, plus his receptive, constantly curious, and open-minded nature (it was no accident that he acquired languages easily), was reaching his own conclusions. That said, even he had been once under the influence of this attitude to a certain degree: witness his attitude to Verdi until he saw *Falstaff*.

By the early years of the twentieth century Busoni had acquired a reputation in Berlin as a maverick in the musical world. This series of concerts consolidated that reputation, but also gained him converts to a more catholic outlook. The first of his Beethovensaal concerts, on November 8, 1902, began with the Prelude and Angel's Farewell from Elgar's *The Dream of Gerontius* (composed 1899–1900), and continued with works by the French composer Joseph Guy Ropartz; the Overture to *Les Barbares* by Saint-Saëns and a "Rondo Infinito" by the Norwegian Christian Sinding, another friend from Busoni's Leipzig days; Tartini and Corelli represented former generations.

The Berlin critics satisfied expectations: Elgar's work was described as "the most barren piece of senseless music-fabrication heard for a long time,"[1] and the other contemporary works fared scarcely better. In the next concert, a week later, Busoni continued the onslaught with works by Sibelius (the first German performance of *En saga*); Théophile Ysaÿe (1865–1918, brother of Eugène), soloist in his own Piano Concerto; and Delius (the nocturne "Paris," which was compared by one critic[2] with a lively imagination to the "morning-after" feelings following a riotous night out—not that Busoni himself was very enthusiastic about "Paris": "What are you trying to do with this poor score," he wrote to Delius's friend, the artist Ida Gerhardi, who was always promoting Delius's work. "What are you up to, peddling it around like this?").[3] The *Berliner Neueste Nachrichten* sniffily remarked that "after the complete fiasco of the second concert, the announcement that these orchestral concerts would be continued in the autumn of 1903 sounded little short of blasphemous."[4]

In several of these concerts, the composers themselves either conducted their own work or played the solo part. Not all the living composers featured have become household names: Joseph Guy Ropartz, Christian Sinding, Théophile Ysaÿe, Eugène Ysaÿe, Heinrich Schenker, Ottokar Nováček, Albéric Magnard, Otto Singer, Eduard Behm, Louis

Delune, Hermann Behr, Johan Wagenaar, Hugo Kaun, and Paul Ertel are very much also-rans today. But Busoni's list also included Elgar, Saint-Saëns, Sibelius, Delius, Debussy, Franck, Nielsen, Pfitzner, Rimsky-Korsakov, D'Indy, Fauré, and (in the last concert, in January 1909) Bartók, who conducted the Scherzo from his Suite for Orchestra, no. 2: all composers whose surname suffices today, and most of whom were represented more than once in the concert series. Busoni himself conducted several of the works; it was an activity he was turning to more and more.

For the first three months of 1904 Busoni returned to the United States, after a gap of ten years, for what was to be a triumphal tour of the northeast of the country. Gerda and the children were with him for part of the time, but at the beginning of March they embarked again for Europe from New York, and for the rest of that month Ferruccio traveled alone, writing to Gerda sometimes more than once a day and missing her terribly. The first letter was written on the train from New York to Boston, after having seen Gerda and their sons onto the ship: "Parting from you was harder for me than I showed and I shall never forget the feeling which came over me as I waded through the ugliness of Hoboken to reach that eternal ferry. It was like a relapse in an illness one thought had been overcome; because on the *Moltke* I almost felt 'European' and my spirits started to rise again."[5] They had been assisted in New York by Oliver H. Clark, who had been a voice student at the conservatory in Boston when Busoni was teaching there, and had somehow entered Busoni's circle at the time. In the same letter to Gerda, Ferruccio reported: "I begged Clark to write at once and tell me what time the boat left. We had barely time to pack and have some breakfast; with both of which Mr. Clark 'helped' me with equal pleasure and taciturnity. (Only once he broke out into a short but enthusiastic hymn to you: 'if he married it would have to be a woman like you' (but there is no second you)." Ferruccio also apologized for his recent behavior: "I must ask you to forgive me for having given you some unhappy moments here, but I was unable to prevent it and it was with difficulty that I suppressed half my bitter mood; you were always so good and I thank you." He was obviously dreading the strains of this final month of touring.

"Dear Gerda," he ends a letter from Boston two days later, "I am writing to you for the *third time* today; but I am so accustomed to telling you about everything I see and experience that it has become a necessity.

(Today I'm off to Chicago—oh!)"[6] After fourteen years of marriage, they had their own language, sometimes literally: he had his special names for her ("Derdi" and "Derdi-Frau" were the most frequent), and nearly always signed himself off "Dein Ferromann," and once, in March on that tour, from Cincinnati, "Just think I have only 5 more days here!!!!! May our next meeting be as soon and as happy as possible. . . . Tschi-pu-li-ki!! (which in Japanese means: Your very loving), Ferromann."

In Boston Busoni stayed with Isabella Stewart Gardner, the rich hostess and patron of the arts whom he had first met when he was teaching there, who proved a congenial and generous friend (she was another who lent him sums of money, including $1,000 that was apparently never repaid), and whose house was full of original works by Titian, Velasquez, Cellini, and others. But Busoni hated America; in his eyes it had material progress and practical conveniences, but was almost entirely lacking in everything he valued most. So why did he make the lengthy sea crossing several times? The tours eventually earned him considerable sums of money, but the adulation must have been attractive too.

He certainly had recognition and success during this tour: on January 29 he even played at the White House before Theodore Roosevelt. His reception nearly everywhere was wildly enthusiastic, the reviews often mere gasps of amazement rather than any form of criticism. As the *Detroit Tribune* gushed:

> Busoni left very little to criticize after he had completed his piano recital at the Church of Our Father last evening. . . . When one writes about such mastery of the art, and of one who can sit for nearly two hours on a stool in front of the piano and reel off hour after hour of the wonderful and difficult music of the great masters without an error, one is inclined to drop his pen and silently wonder at the retentive memory of the man.[7]

Following a concert on March 9 in the Music Hall in Chicago, reviews also commented on his incredible memory, but mentioned his technique too: "The programme, which was long and varied, offered almost unsurmountable difficulties for any artist, however great he might be. But Busoni overcame them all. His technique is that which conceals Technique. One does not notice the intricacies of a passage, so readily does be master them."[8] The reviewer ("F. H. G.") in the *Record-Herald* for the same concert gave a much more informed account of the recital:

Ferruccio Busoni, at his recital in the Fine Arts Building last evening, gave new evidence of the varied character of his remarkable abilities. He opened his programme with one of his own arrangements of Bach's works. These arrangements have been undertaken largely with the object of increasing popular interest in Bach, and for his labors in this direction Mr. Busoni has earned the gratitude of all musicians who have the best interests of their art at heart. His work on the "well-tempered clavichord" is in itself a monument to his industry and abilities.

For the second number he gave Beethoven's sonata, opus 109, not often heard, which was read with reverence and great beauty of tone.

This was followed by a reading of the twelve Chopin etudes, opus 25, which left an indelible impression on all who heard them. In these etudes he displayed his tremendous technique and versatility to great advantage. At one moment he dealt in the heroics of piano playing, at another his touch was wonderfully light and swift. The study in thirds deserves mention as an example of smooth, rapid legato playing which it would be almost impossible to surpass. In some of the numbers he took liberties, such as indulging in repetitions where none was indicated, but it was all done with an artistic object. In the closing etude, in C Minor, the ear caught some smashing chords where only two notes are indicated in the score.

Whether he plays a thing exactly as it is written or not, Busoni is always interesting. He has the gift of concentration which enables him to give supreme attention to detail. His touch and pedalling are worthy of the closest study. He occasionally operates the pedals so rapidly that he almost seems to be trilling with his feet. The result is a remarkable clearness and unusual carrying power in the tone.[9]

"E. K. W." in the *Chicago Journal* gives us a particularly vivid account of this concert and of Busoni's effect on audiences (plus a flattering photograph), that is worth quoting in full:

Busoni Captures All Music Lovers
"I never heard anyone just like him."
"He's the best yet!"
"I could listen to him forever."
"He has a head like John the Baptist's."
"'Rah! 'Rah! Do it some more!"
"Is he married?"

The above were some of the remarks fluttering around among the big crowd that listened to and went crazy over Busoni last night at Music Hall.

There is no question about it. The man is sui generis. He belongs to no established creed. The way he knocks down honorable and gray-haired precedents is astonishing. He bows allegiance to no predecessor. He is Busoni.

* * *

The cream of Chicago's musical intelligence sat in Music Hall last night and expressed its sentiments long after the tired pianist had played his last number. It expressed them so long and so loud and so determinedly, in fact, that the poor man, perspiring and limp, was forced to return and play the encore which had been withheld during the rendition of the programme. Apparently Busoni doesn't care about giving encores.

* * *

The programme was a remarkable one—the three Bs: Bach, Beethoven, and Brahms, with twelve of Chopin's Etudes.

It has been said that Busoni is the greatest Bach player known to the musical world today. With reference to piano playing, this is probably so. At any rate, no pianist has visited this city who has infused so much fervor, dignity, power, and love of the Master into his work as Busoni has done. His arrangement of the toccata, adagio, prelude, and fugue, given last night, demands respect by itself. Even to the adagio he loaned some beauty, though this is among the least happy of Bach's writings. The short prelude was made into chords which created a wonder that any mortal hands were capable of executing them upon a piano. The fugue voices stood out as clear as stars on a bright night. It was a wonderful performance.

The Beethoven op. 109 is among the least beautiful of the sonatas. It is not written in the usual order, and if anybody but Beethoven had given to the world the last variation of the andante it would be called a monstrosity of garbled sound. But where there was beauty, Busoni found it and held his hearers in rapt attention.

And with what verve did he play Brahms! Busoni does not make the mistake of bowing down in unmitigated awe to Brahms, leaving us breathless with respect, but lacking in enjoyment. Last night Brahms was a rollicking, very tuneful human being. He was given a new nature, a likeable nature, warmed by an Italian temperament into a sparkling and vivid living. May we have more Brahms as Busoni plays it.

The Chopin Etudes—it is impossible to say how well he played them. The sixth—that famous one in thirds so often attempted and so seldom achieved—was a marvel in liquid smoothness, warmth, and tone shading— but he wouldn't repeat it. The popular ninth, also, he would not repeat, in spite of demands. The tenth was taken at a tempo that made one gasp— and perfectly played. The eleventh, with which he finished, was painted on so great and grand a scale, that the great audience sat stunned for a moment after the final scale—the original of which he doubled—was run.

Busoni is a "big" player. His technique is so perfect that he has ceased to care about it. It is as natural as thinking with him. He cares nothing for the means in creating an effect. If he wishes to acquire an organ richness and volume of tone, he keeps his foot down on the loud pedal as long as he thinks it necessary, whether carping critics and music masters think it is the proper thing or not. He is fond of unacorde effects. His pianissimos are like distant singing voices. His fortissimos are like the roll of thunder, the crashing of great seas, the rush of the wind through a forest—big, big. He is a painter on great canvases. He uses the flat of the brush, but with such nicety that the result is perfect in effect.[10]

This is hyperbolic perhaps, and written the same evening clearly under the influence of Busoni the man and Busoni the artist, but a good example of the reception wherever Busoni played in North America.

But his relief was enormous on March 24 when he too finally embarked for Europe again, on the *Blücher*, having played a total of at least twenty-six concerts.[11] On the ship, among other books he read Robert Louis Stevenson's novel *The Strange Case of Dr. Jekyll and Mr. Hyde* with great admiration, and amused himself writing a "critical analysis" of it. There was a Steinway grand on board but he did not dare to touch it, dreading the ensuing attention. On his birthday, April 1, he staged a hoax that went slightly wrong: the Captain announced the night before that Busoni would be giving a concert next morning at eleven; most of the passengers consequently got up "early," but Busoni stayed in bed, giving the excuse that he was ill—which unfortunately was true. In spite of resting during the voyage, he arrived in Europe feeling ill. "I was unwell yesterday evening and early this morning and the condition of exhaustion, which is familiar to me now, was not far off," he wrote[12] just before the ship reached Cuxhaven, its final destination. Ominous words.

188 ~ Chapter Eight

At that time, even an artist of Busoni's stature was not automatically given the care and attention expected today. Three months later, in early July 1904, for example, arriving in London after an exhausting overnight journey ("I made a pillow of frock coat, trousers and overcoat; but it wasn't high enough, not even when I put a fresh handkerchief on top"), he wrote: "In the station I ran into [Hermann] Draber and he wanted to take me off to his apartment. He and Egon [Petri] are living in their own apartment in St. John's Wood. I refused, went to Langham's Hotel, but as they had no rooms free, I decided to join the new generation, so I'm living in Queen's Terrace."[13]

Hermann Draber (1878–1942) was a flautist who had nevertheless studied piano in Busoni's master classes in Weimar in 1901; he later worked for a while as Busoni's secretary. Egon Petri, who as a child had first known Busoni when the latter's friendship with Kathi and Henri Petri began in Leipzig in the late 1880s, had first studied violin, and from 1898 to 1901 had played in the Dresden Court Opera Orchestra, of which his father Henri was the leader, and as second violin in the Petri Quartet. A few years before, however, he had already contemplated switching to the piano, which he studied in Berlin with Busoni, among others, and he made his piano debut in 1902 in Dresden. His importance in any biography of Busoni lies in the close relationship between them, which began as that of master and pupil; went through a very rocky patch as Egon struggled to break free, not only from the role of pupil, but also from the role of ever-available amanuensis whose personal life was expected to take second place; and finally settled into a friendship of equals. Petri was the only one of Busoni's pupils to achieve this degree of intimacy, and was called on constantly to assist Busoni in editing his work, writing out scores, and countless other tasks, as well as acting as discussion partner. Busoni's letters to him, of which 314 survive, dating from 1902 to 1923, complement those to Gerda in offering a rounded picture of Busoni's character and concerns.

Busoni also acted at times as arbitrator between Egon and his father, who had a rather bourgeois attitude and disapproved of his son when he went through the inevitable bohemian period—Egon joined an artists' colony that had been founded in the 1880s in the village of Worpswede in northern Germany by a group of painters, sculptors, and writers (including the poet Rainer Maria Rilke for a time). Hermann Draber also spent periods in Worpswede.

A surprising element of the Beethovensaal concerts in Berlin had been the lack of works by Busoni himself in the first three concerts. But the fourth, on November 10, 1904, contained the world premiere of Busoni's Concerto for Piano, Orchestra and Male Chorus (BV 247), with the composer as piano soloist, Karl Muck conducting. The concerto had taken him three years to compose. It is a vast work, lasting some seventy-five minutes, and requiring not only a large orchestra, but a forty-eight-strong male chorus. Its five parts—Prologo e Introito, Pezzo Giocoso, Pezzo Serioso, All'italiana, and Cantico—are further indications of its individuality. Busoni gave the work a long Italian title, although it was published in 1906 in Leipzig by Breitkopf und Härtel: "Concerto— per un pianoforte principale e diversi strumenti ad arco, a fiato e a percussione—aggiuntovi un coro finale per voci d'uomini a sei parti—le parole allemanni del poeta Oehlenschlaeger, danese, la musica di Ferruccio Busoni da Empoli." This was a statement at many levels.

Only an intellectual magpie like Busoni could have chanced on Oehlenschläger for the words to the final chorus of his concerto. Adam Gottlob Oehlenschläger (1779–1850), a leading figure in Danish literature of the Romantic period, had much in common with Busoni, not least his eclecticism. After travel in Germany (where he met Goethe, among others), France, and Italy, Oehlenschläger finally settled back in Copenhagen and became a professor of aesthetics. Busoni uses an excerpt from Oehlenschläger's own German translation from the Danish of what is considered his greatest work, the poetic drama Aladdin, written in 1804–1805, and with which, at the age of twenty-six, he established his reputation in Denmark. Based on the tale from A Thousand and One Nights, the play has a broad canvas in which pantheism, heavily dosed with mysticism (Aladdin's lamp symbolizes intuitive poetic genius) and didactic idealism, all play their part. Strongly influenced by Goethe's Faust, it nevertheless seeks to prove that happiness on earth can be achieved without diabolic aid. Aladdin is an innocent, having much in common with Parsifal or Tamino (he has to undergo trials). It is a massive work, intended to be performed over two evenings. It has fallen into obscurity today, even in the poet's native Denmark.

Busoni's initial intention was to create an opera from this play— an intention not abandoned even after the completion of the Piano

Concerto—but by February 1902 his intention had changed for the time being, as he informed Gerda from London, during yet another tour:

> I have thought it out and decided not to use Oehlenschläger's Aladdin for an opera, but to write a composition in which drama, music, dancing and magic are combined—cut down for one evening's performance if possible. It is my old idea of a play with music *where it is necessary*, without hampering the dialogue. As a spectacle and as a deep symbolic work it might be rather similar to the *Magic Flute*; at the same time it would have a better meaning and an indestructible subject. Besides this, I have planned 6 works for the summer, the principal being the pianoforte concerto. How wonderful![14]

(The beginning of this letter offers insight into some of the difficulties under which the concerto was written: "Don't be angry with me for having cancelled the concert in Aberdeen. I *really* needed to. Ysaÿe, Pitt and singers [?] as travel companions were too much for me." Having given himself three days off in this way proved beneficial: "As soon as I feel free, ideas come and that is the true and only joy in life.")

This second scheme was also soon abandoned, the only piece actually written being a musical setting of the "Hymn to Allah" with which Oehlenschläger's *Aladdin* ends, and which Busoni used for the concluding Cantico of his Piano Concerto. While never careering off into the downright wacky, like the work of his Russian near-contemporary Aleksandr Scriabin (1872–1915), Busoni's scheme bears more than a little resemblance to the former's ambitions for his ultimately unwritten *Mysterium*, in its striving to nail down an all-purpose meaning to the complexity of human existence.

This was very much a sign of the times. H. G. Wells and George Bernard Shaw, among many others, strove at copious length to bring order and coherence, in practical and/or ideological ways, into a world that was now changing at a frighteningly accelerated rate. (The eminently pragmatic and practical Victorians, with a belief in human progress based more on the results of technical advances and a rapidly expanding British Empire than on religion or philosophical theory, led the field here.) The more leisurely speculations of former times were often abandoned in favor of the diktat. Wells in particular, whom Busoni read and admired, was an energetic and loquacious creator of what, in the preface to his *The World Set Free* (1914), he grandly termed "fan-tasias of possibility," espousing with gusto eugenic theories on "improv-ing" the human race and creating a World State, among other things. Unlike Wells, who died in 1946, Busoni did not live long enough to see the horrors of a social theory brutally applied, and therefore in a sense retained his innocence. However, Busoni's voracious and wide-ranging reading throughout his life was a crucial component of his own creative work; his letters, particularly those to Gerda, often offer a running com-mentary on his current reading matter.

In Berlin in the summer of 1902 he had begun work in earnest on the Piano Concerto, and wrote to Gerda:

> The enclosed drawing is crude and clumsy, but not ridiculous. I have a
> little weakness for it. It is the idea of my piano concerto in one picture
> and it is represented by architecture, landscape and symbolism. The
> three buildings are the first, third and fifth movements. In between come
> the two "lively" ones; Scherzo and Tarantella; the first represented by a
> miraculous flower and birds, freaks of nature; the second by Vesuvius and
> cypress trees. The sun rises over the *entrance*; a seal is fastened to the
> door of the end building. The winged being right at the end is taken
> from Oehlenschläger's chorus and represents mysticism in nature.

Busoni's sketch was used as the basis for the *Jugendstil* drawing by Hein-rich Vogeler, a leading graphic artist, that appeared on the frontispiece of the published score. Vogeler was a founder-member of the Worp-swede artists' colony and had been introduced to Busoni by Egon Petri.

Busoni worked hard on the concerto that summer, breaking off only in October for yet another concert tour. It is not known exactly how much he composed during the summer in Berlin, but from letters to Gerda, who was in Sweden, it appears that most of the work was mapped out and the Tarantella completed. While touring that winter and in spring 1903 he certainly continued work on it, and finished the pencil sketch in Berlin on July 15, 1903. It was the next day that he made the decision to cancel the two London concerts that month and concentrate on writing the full score, as he explained to Gerda:

> What I was most concerned about was the interruption while I'm writ-ing down the concerto. I felt it would never be completed if once I were
> interrupted; (nobody would be able to understand the pencil sketch) and

I thought, too, that the distraction would make me forget all the important details not yet written down. . . . Finally, I decided I really ran the
risk of not finishing the concerto if I didn't work at the sketch anymore
until the end of July.[15]

The scoring nevertheless took him another year: the word "finis" on
the full score is dated August 3, 1904.

If the programs for the orchestral concerts Busoni organized at the
Beethovensaal were generally regarded as a provocation, his Piano Concerto, premiered as the final item[16] in the fourth concert, constituted his
own personal challenge. The work departed from the German norm not
only in its Italian title, five movements, and male chorus, but also in its
eclectic choice of musical and philosophical themes, and supranational
allusions. The first movement, Prologo e introito, has a long orchestral
introduction, slow, stately, lyrical, and distinctly Brahmsian, rising to a
rousing tutti storm, which ebbs and flows; the piano enters on the crest
of the final wave, at first alone, in pounding runs, soon merging into the
opening theme, supported first by woodwind, then horns; then, after urgent piano cadenzas, the strings enter, are chased away again by the piano, return. The strings in this movement play a soothing role, contrasted often with the turbulence and vast energy of the piano, bringing
sporadic calm. The piano itself calms down to lyrical trills, and even the
wind section is soothed; the piano still gives hints of turbulence, echoed
by the brass, but the movement ends peacefully.

The second movement, Pezzo giocoso, makes up for the calm, not
with storms, however, but with trills on the piano, ending in a wild
dance taken over by the orchestra to intoxicating rhythms, passed from
strings to trumpets, slowing to a short oboe passage, the strings pulsating behind. The piano makes itself heard again, briefly, to a more
stately dance rhythm; this swells to triple trills on the piano, taken up
by the trumpet, and turning into a wild, delirious bacchanal, based on
a Neapolitan folk song ("Fenestra che lucivi"), unabashed, virile, with
ghostly string tutti sections flitting across, offering sudden respite. The
piano turns the tune into a sensuous dance, accentuating the basic
rhythm of the folk song (there are even tambourines). This is explicitly
autobiographical in its italianità, the piano part reminiscent of a Liszt
tone poem. The movement ends abruptly and quietly.

The third movement, Pezzo serioso, is in four sections. The introduction opens with a slow figure on cellos, double basses, and lower
wind, soon answered by a more dramatic theme for oboes and *cor
anglais*, tremolo strings in the background. The piano enters quietly, introducing a theme taken up by the brass, which in turn introduce the
theme for the next section, Prima pars, a chorale now taken over by the
piano, underlined by strings. This theme is taken from Busoni's youthful opera *Sigune*, where Ulrich, the master builder, looks up at the great
cathedral in the twilight. The theme is fittingly solemn and majestic,
and the full resonance of the piano is used to elaborate variations on it.
The orchestra quietly resumes the theme, creating a calm evening
scene. This ends with a sudden short piano crescendo backed by horns.
In the third section, Altera pars, in a long, melodic, passionate phrase,
former themes return, building up to an uninhibited climax, with a relentless two-tone rhythm, with wild rushes on the piano and horns,
tutti passages, the piano pounding on; after thunderous percussion,
there is sudden calm, the piano gently wandering, joined by a single
trombone, and rushes of earlier themes, ending in a resumption of the
"cathedral" theme. The final section, Ultra pars, rises feverishly
through a resumption of former themes, plus one new theme, leading
to a masterly resolution of this long and complex movement.

The fourth movement, rather superfluously entitled "All'italiana,"
was described by Busoni in a letter to his wife as "like coming out of the
Forum onto a crowded Roman street."[17] He also referred to it as the
"Tarantella" ("The Tarantella will be like Naples itself," he wrote, "only
cleaner"),[18] which anchors it, like the second movement, a little further
south. This movement is indeed Italian, full of exuberant life. It begins
feverishly, with hints of the Neapolitan folk song heard in the second
movement, tossed exuberantly from piano to orchestra, various instruments taking it up, snatching a few notes before being caught up in a
general joyous whole. In this movement all those years out of Italy fall
away, and Busoni stands revealed: as Italian as Rossini in his uninhibited *joie de vivre*, with boisterous use of glockenspiel; a second folk song
theme enters (the "Canzone del Serpentino"), brash, loud, taken up by
dissonant trumpets, a frenzied dance, the piano boiling, the rest of the
orchestra caught up in the fever, leading to what Busoni himself described as a "Vesuvius eruption," the second theme riding over strident

brass. The movement ends with pyrotechnic cadenzas on the piano; the full orchestra then punches out the Tarantella rhythm with full-blooded force, ending in three muted chords—an exhausted panting. No wonder Wilhelmine Berlin was shocked rigid. This was the movement that gave Busoni most trouble in its composition. ("The Tarantella will still give me many a nut to 'crack,'" he wrote to Gerda in July 1903,[19] later reporting that it had been "successfully 'cracked.'"[20] The fact that he had already worked on this particular "nut" for a year is proof of his prediction.) The challenge was to bring this wild explosion into disciplined shape, keep up the momentum (most of it in 6/8) without flagging or becoming repetitive. The cadenza in particular caused problems: Busoni later wrote a second version, and it is this that is usually played today: it ties in more closely and effectively with the rest of the work.

In the fifth and final movement, Cantico, the work moves from the pulsating exuberance of Neapolitan street life to the rarefied reaches of one of the masterpieces of Oriental literature: the Thousand and One Nights, as seen through the eyes of the Danish poet Oehlenschläger and, specifically, the setting of the "Hymn to Allah" with which Oehlenschläger's play Aladdin ends:

Lift up your hearts to the Power Eternal,
Draw ye to Allah nigh, witness his work.
Earth has its share of rejoicing and sorrow.
Firm the foundations that hold up the world.
Thousands and thousands of years march relentlessly,
Show forth in silence his glory, his might,
Flashing immaculate, splendid and fast they stand,
Time cannot shake them, yea time without end.
Hearts flamed in ecstasy, hearts turned to dust again,
Playfully life and death stakes each his claim,
Yet in mute readiness patiently tarrying,
Splendid and mighty both, for evermore.
Lift up your hearts to the Power Eternal,
Draw ye to Allah nigh, witness his work.
Fully regenerate now is the world of yore,
Praising its Maker e'en unto the end.[21]

Horns herald a slow opening, with languid woodwind, rising scales in thirds, the piano entering almost imperceptibly; themes, including the Aladdin theme, float past, with flashes of glockenspiel triads. The chorus begins and immediately dominates (although Busoni specified the singers should remain invisible throughout), the orchestra apparent only in brief pauses in the singing at first, later more emphatically underlining the words. Only after the strident end does the piano return, to lead an orchestral crescendo into the final Allegro con fuoco, with which the work rather abruptly ends. (Realizing that this final movement with male chorus reduced the work's chances of performance, Busoni subsequently wrote an alternative ending [BV 247a, Coda supplementaria], consisting of a passage linking the end of the cadenza of All'italiana with the end of the Cantico. Larry Sitsky is—I think rightly of the opinion that "artistically such a cut is inexplicable. It ruins the overall archsymmetry of the Concerto, ends conventionally with the fast fourth movement and destroys the sense of mystical tranquility which Busoni claimed was the essence of the work. . . . The Concerto should be played as it stands, with no compromises.")[22]

The German critics were almost unanimously horrified, one of them betraying the general attitude by condemning the fact that the work's premiere was held in "a hall sacred to the name of Beethoven."[23] The concerto's division into five movements and its length were criticized, but the main thrust of criticism was of course aimed at its content. The sly wit of Busoni's writing, particularly for the piano part, either passed the critics by or incensed them: they interpreted it as impertinence. They were also baffled that the piano part, although requiring awesome ability, was nevertheless an integral part of the whole composition and never a vehicle for virtuoso display. The breadth of the work's intellectual canvas also antagonized: from its Brahmsian beginning, to its Italian exuberance and its mystic final chorus of a hymn to Allah.

"Noise, more noise, eccentricity and licentiousness provoked yet more noise and had the same effect on us," fumed the *Tägliche Rundschau*, revealing a vivid, not to say eyebrow-raising, imagination: "For five movements we were submerged in a flood of cacophony; a *pezzo giocoso* painted the joys of barbarians lusting after war, and a tarantella the orgies of absinthe drinkers and common prostitutes. At the end a *Cantico* demonstrated to our extreme horror that a composer can take seriously the absurdities of a male choral society. It was frightful!"[24] One of Berlin's leading critics, Max Marschalk, wrote in the *Vossische*

Zeitung: "One must have an unshakeable faith in one's own greatness to write music of this kind."[25] There was more cutting down to size in the *Signale*: "The composer would have done better to stay within more modest boundaries."[26] The *Deutsche Zeitung* conceded that there was "a certain strain of greatness in the work which repeatedly called our attention."[27] Leo Kestenberg, at the time one of Busoni's youthful pupils, wrote an inevitably favorable review in the *Neues Montagsblatt*.[28]

Busoni already had quite a large body of supporters in Berlin, however, who managed to hold the balance. Posterity has been generally favorable—although Alfred Brendel considers the concerto "monstrously overwritten."[29] Busoni passed his own judgment on it in 1912:

> I endeavored with this work to gather together the results of my first period of manhood and it represents the actual conclusion of that period.
>
> It does not indicate the future at all, but represents the present of its moment of birth. The proportions and contrasts are carefully distributed and, because the plan was definitively established before the execution began, there is nothing accidental in it.
>
> The old does not yield to the new, but to the better. We have the advantage over the academics in that we hope for the new, while honoring the old; in that we can suffer and enjoy at the same time; in that we willingly bow down, without remaining inactive.[30]

This somewhat gnomic statement is typical of a lot of Busoni's writings on music, art, and other matters, much of which began in letters to Gerda. A considerable body of these writings was collected into a volume first published during Busoni's lifetime, in 1922, entitled *Wesen und Einheit der Musik* (Essence and Oneness of Music), an English translation of which, by Rosamond Ley, was published in the same year. (The above quotation was also included in the book, in the section entitled "Self-Criticism.") Both editions were reissued with many additions in 1956. We shall be returning to these writings later. They are mentioned here merely as an indication that by his late thirties, Busoni was emerging as an authority, a voice respectfully listened to—an extension of his function as a teacher.

A longer essay he began writing around this time, the *Entwurf einer neuen Ästhetik der Tonkunst* (Sketch of a New Aesthetic of Music), which he described in the work's opening sentence as "the result of long and slowly matured convictions," appeared much earlier in book form. He finished it in November 1906, and it was published early in 1907 by his Trieste friend Carlo Schmidl, and printed in Berlin in the Berliner Musikaliendruckerei. The slim volume of 119 pages also contained two of Busoni's opera libretti, *Der mächtige Zauberer* and *Die Brautwahl*. Later in 1907 Schmidl republished the *Entwurf*, minus the libretti. The *Entwurf* achieved only modest success at the time, much of that due to energetic self-promotion on the author's part, and it was not until it was republished, considerably revised, in 1916 as one of the familiar Insel-Bücherei series that it caused a sensation in the German musical world (see chapter 10).

It seems a strange proceeding to publish an opera libretto before the music is written, and in the case of the above two, ultimately only one—*Die Brautwahl*—was ever set to music. *Der mächtige Zauberer* (The Mighty Magician) was based on "L'illustre magicien" a tale in the *Nouvelles asiatiques* (1876) by another admirer of *A Thousand and One Nights*, the French diplomat and amateur ethnologist Joseph Gobineau (1816–1882). With titles such as *The Inequality of Human Races* (a four-volume work published 1853–1855), asserting the "superiority" of the white races over all others, Gobineau's work meets generally with opprobrium today. It would, however, be foolhardy to conclude that Busoni's thinking ran along similar lines; there is little in any of his letters or other writing to suggest this. As recounted elsewhere, in common with many Europeans in the early years of the twentieth century, he was drawn to social theories, the search for some moral and social utopia, often with mystical overtones, and *Der mächtige Zauberer* is not the only libretto he wrote in these years reflecting such themes—themes he also dealt with in his other writings.

Busoni's most probable route to "L'illustre magicien" was via his exploration of *A Thousand and One Nights* and Persian literature. The story, which Busoni follows, tells of a mysterious dervish who renounces material things and is not even daunted by death in his striving to achieve spiritual perfection; there is also a young man who wishes to emulate the dervish but ultimately, owing to his overwhelming love for his wife, remains bound to earthly things and lives.

Der mächtige Zauberer was not the only libretto by Busoni never set to music. Fragments are extant of such texts dating from his childhood, his youth, and later, in addition to four completed but unpublished texts. *Der Ring des Niebelungen*, translated into Finnish and dating from his time in Helsinki, is a grotesque parody of the myth, dedicated to Martin Wegelius on the latter's birthday. Its humor is elephantine: the Rhine maidens have mutated into men, Fafner and Fasolt receive a box of cigars with the brand name "Freia," "Molly Brunhilde" is a fighter for the emancipation of women, and one of the Valkyries has a horse called Richard. *Frau Potiphar* (1909) is another parody—this time of operetta—that Busoni himself described as "very indecent,"[31] which is probably why he abandoned any intention of setting it to music; *Der Tanz vom Leben und vom Tode* (Dance of Life and Death) was written in 1914, and *Der Arlecchineïde Fortsetzung und Ende* is a quite unsettlingly cynical and bitter text written in 1918 (see chapter 9, p. 297). There are also four published libretti—*Der mächtige Zauberer, Das Geheimnis* (The Secret), *Die Götterbraut* (The Bride of the Gods), and *Das Wandbild* (The Wall Painting)—in addition to the libretti of Busoni's four completed operas.[32]

Ferruccio attempted his first libretto, *Don Cchischiotte* [sic] when he was about nine years old. It deals with two episodes in Cervantes's masterpiece: the Countess Trifaldi episode and the Altisidora episode, both in part II, but the libretto did not proceed beyond a sketch of its intended structure. A few years later, around 1878, Ferruccio attempted a libretto on another episode from *Don Quixote*, which he called *Der Blödsinnige* (The Idiot), *Comedy in One Act*, and which was also abandoned. The works can be dated only on the basis of his signatures: on the first he calls himself "Ferruccio Weiss-Busoni," a name he no longer used after 1878, and in the second "Ferruccio Benvenuto Busoni," which he used subsequently, but only for a short period. The *Don Cchischiotte* is the first and only time he wrote a theater text in Italian; the fact that he wrote *Der Blödsinnige* in German would suggest it was written toward the end of the "Ferruccio Benvenuto Busoni" period—1878 or 1879—when his German was fluent enough. What is interesting in both these fragments, particularly the second, is that he already had a well-developed appetite for the grotesque and bizarre. In adulthood, this appetite became an element in his concept of what opera "should" be. Here he did manifest a Wellsian weakness for the diktat that rivaled Wagner's, and in some aspects anticipated Bertolt Brecht's "Alienation

Effect." (For a full discussion of Busoni's ideas on opera, see chapter 9, p. 219–20.)

Busoni tried while still in his teens to interest librettists to write for him, such as in the case of *La Figlia del Re Renato*, based on the play *King René's Daughter* by the Danish writer Henrik Hertz, for which he had (vainly) approached the poet and journalist Michele Buono (see chapter 3, p. 53). Busoni was successful in obtaining a libretto for his uncompleted opera *Sigune*, but henceforth he wrote all his own libretti—and, typically, soon formulated his own theories on the superiority of this proceeding, which will be discussed in chapter 9. One wonders if anyone ever had the courage to challenge him on this: surely merely citing the name Lorenzo da Ponte, without whom three of Mozart's greatest operas would probably never have seen the light of day, would have reduced Busoni to silence, or at least reflection. His inability—or willful refusal—to understand and appreciate the aesthetic of nineteenth-century Italian opera is also regrettable.

Critically mauled though his Piano Concerto might have been, by late 1904 Busoni was firmly established in the Berlin musical scene. His series of concerts at the Beethovensaal was an invaluable service to new European music, initially bankrolled by Busoni himself—an extraordinary act of generosity and a typical example of his total commitment to his art. In the winter of 1904–1905 he also gave a series of recitals in Berlin devoted entirely to Liszt, which gave the Berlin public and critics yet more opportunity to be shocked, but gradually persuaded many to a more respectful view of Liszt's work, until then widely regarded as virtuoso display with little substance.

Busoni was now one of the most famous living musicians in the western world, and at the height of his powers. The Austrian writer Jakob Wassermann (1873–1934), later to become a friend and dedicatee of the first edition (1922) of Busoni's *Wesen und Einheit der Musik*, left this impression: "When I first met Ferruccio Busoni he was thirty-eight, a man of astonishing beauty, very well-groomed, very spoiled, elevated by the world's applause, illuminated by the love of his pupils, admirers and hangers-on, but still the complete virtuoso, if a typical virtuoso with all the characteristics of hard-won mastery."[33]

There were others too who, although they were drawn to him, did not subscribe wholeheartedly to the often sycophantic adoration of his pupils and the other (mostly young) people Busoni gathered around him. In 1903 the twenty-one-year-old Percy Grainger was introduced to Busoni in London by Clarita Matesdorf (wife of Theodore Matesdorf, the rich patron of the arts with whom Busoni often stayed on Mount Street when he was in London). Grainger's accounts are always a little suspect, but the main facts of their meeting are true: the young pianist and composer was asked to play to Busoni; he played his own harmonizations of two Scottish folk songs (thinking this less dangerous than anything Busoni might know), "An Irish Tune from Country Derry," then, emboldened by Busoni's approval, the Toccata from Debussy's suite "Pour le piano," which Busoni was very taken with; he offered to give Grainger lessons in Berlin. These two men, so different in so many ways, could never really have got on together, so that when Grainger took up the offer in June that same year in Berlin, strains soon became apparent. Grainger noticed immediately that Busoni insisted on ruling the roost and (an exaggeration) liked to people his house with "the poor, and the maimed, and the halt, and the blind," an extraordinary statement probably based on the fact that Rita Boetticher, Busoni's longtime secretary, was hunch-backed, and that summer there was a very sick young student, Marga Dehner, whom Emilio Anzoletti, a young Italian friend of Busoni's (see p. 205), used to carry up and down the stairs to the Busonis's apartment.

Grainger and Busoni found common ground in Bach; Busoni would often demonstrate his skill with Bach:

> None of his pupils or other admirers could have admired Busoni as a pianist more than I did, for I admired him without reservations of any kind and revelled in everything he did pianistically. He was not a "normal" player as Paderewski was and even de Pachmann was, unfolding the composer's music straightly and faithfully. Busoni was a twisted genius making the music sound unlike itself, but grander than itself, more superhuman. I cannot recall ever hearing or seeing Busoni play a wrong note. He did not seem to "feel" his way about the keyboard by touching adjacent notes—as most of us do—he smacked the keys right in the middle.[34]

Like many, Grainger was not nearly so impressed with Busoni's compositions, and was unable to hide it:

> As a composer he never interested me for one moment. I never heard a single musical phrase of his that had the least charm or pith of meaning.

1. Ferdinando Busoni, ca. 1866.

2. Anna Weiss-Busoni in Trieste, ca. 1864.

3. *Busoni age 10 in Gmunden, 1876.*

5. *Busoni age 11 in Vienna, early 1878.*

4. *Busoni with Nanni, September 1877.*

6. Busoni age 15 in Milan, 1881.

7. Busoni age 18 in Vienna, 1884. With dedication to "My dear, old, intelligent friend, Otto von Kapff."

8. Melanie Mayer, ca. 1886.

9. Busoni with Lesko in Leipzig, 1888.

10. Henri Petri, ca. 1890.

11. Busoni in New York, 1892.

12. Busoni with Ottokar Nováček in New York, 1892.

13. Busoni with Benvenuto Busoni ("Benni") in Trieste, 1898.

14. Busoni in Berlin, 1898.

15. Caricature of Busoni and Gustav Mahler, 1899.

16. Busoni in London, 1901.

17. Busoni's first Weimar master class, 1900. Busoni seated fourth from left. Gerda seated second from right.

18. Busoni in Weimar, August 1900.

19. Percy Grainger in London, ca. 1903.

20. Raffaello, Gerda, and Benvenuto Busoni in Berlin, 1902

21. *Busoni and Benni in London, 1904.*

22. *Busoni with Eugène Ysaÿe in Berlin, 1905.*

23. *Drawing by Busoni enclosed in a letter to his wife dated March 12, 1904. "Map of the West of the United States showing the long and dolorous Tour, the anti-sentim[ent]al journey of F.B., 1904, Chicago."*

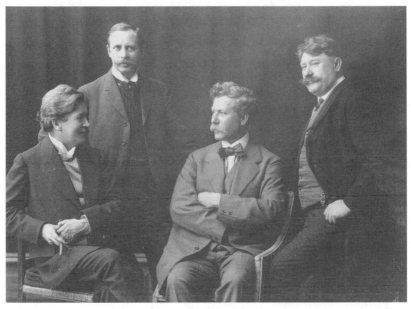

24. In Dortmund, August 1911, on the occasion of the first performance of Frederick Stock's orchestration of Busoni's Fantasia Contrappuntistica. Left to right: Ferruccio Busoni, Frederick Stock, Wilhelm Middelschulte, and Georg Hüttner.

25. Busoni at the piano with Gerda in Berlin, ca. 1912.

26. Busoni in Milan, 1912.

27. Busoni with Umberto Boccioni in San Remigio, 1916.

28. Busoni in Zurich, 1916.

29. Stage set by Albert Isler for the premiere of Arlecchino in Zurich, 1917.

30. *August Richter, who sang Kalaf in the premiere of* Turandot, *in Zurich, 1917.*

31. *Busoni with Giotto in Zurich, 1918.*

32. Busoni in Maud Allan's apartment in West
Wing, Regent's Park, in London, autumn 1919.

33. Portrait of Busoni in
Zurich by Max Oppen-
heimer, 1920.

34. The music room in the Busoni's apartment on Viktoria-Luise-Platz in Berlin.

35. Viktoria-Luise-Platz in Berlin, ca. 1904.

Perhaps he sensed my unfriendliness to his own compositions, and perhaps it was that that changed his initial kindliness towards me into scorn and hostility. On the whole Busoni was nice to me up to the end of the Berlin period. He gave me a lovely photo of himself and wrote on it: "To my dear Percy Grainger (as dear as he surely will be great). Very affectionately Ferruccio Busoni." He also gave me a full score of a choral setting by Liszt of one of the psalms. He worshipped Liszt.[35]

But Grainger was most caustic concerning Busoni's craving for adoration. In the evenings that summer in Berlin, Busoni would often take some of his pupils to Bartolini's, his favorite Italian restaurant where an Italian tenor sang and played the guitar; "then Busoni would play very much the Italian as well as the great man, condescending to the folk level. I suppose it was only natural that Busoni, the Italian part of whose nature was still very well preserved, should want to relax in some Italianish way, but to my ears the singing and the common-place chords on the guitar were boring in the extreme."[36]

Like everyone, Grainger had nothing but praise for Gerda:

In Berlin, [Busoni's] Swedish-Finnish wife seemed to take a great fancy to me and her wide smiling face was like the sun shining and she certainly affected Busoni that way. When she was out of the house he would get sour & spiteful, but when the door opened and she appeared he rose with an exclamation of violent relief and greeted her with charming Italian manners. . . . The presence of his wife transformed him utterly.[37]

Although Busoni could be spiteful and jealous, Grainger was not alone in testifying to his generosity where the compositions of others were concerned. They met in London in 1907 and discussed Grainger's *Hill-Song Number 2*, and Busoni played one part of the two-piano arrangement from sight. Afterward, according to Grainger, Busoni said in a rather sad and unwilling voice, "That is a fine piece, I must admit it. That is a fine piece."[38]

The French composer Edgard Varèse (1883–1965), a finer, more balanced mind than Grainger, offers a view of Busoni that, while registering Busoni's foibles and character flaws, fully acknowledges his genius and his strengths. Varèse and his first wife, Suzanne, went to Berlin around the end of 1907, and it remained his base for the next seven years, expressly so that he could study composition with Busoni. Busoni not only generously encouraged the young man, but also accepted his revolutionary music on its own terms. Varèse was already experimenting with new materials for producing "organized sound," as he preferred to call music, and forms not dependent on accepted ideas of harmonic progression. As Louise Varèse, Varèse's second wife, wrote in her biography of her husband, "One cannot overassess the importance of Busoni's influence on Varèse in his twenties. Varèse was not only stimulated as never before by Busoni's brilliant personality and caustic intelligence but in Busoni Varèse found the first musician whose ideas on the future of music were, as Varèse has said, like an echo of his own thoughts."[39] They constantly discussed new directions music might take, and Busoni was so open-minded that Varèse was surprised at the comparatively orthodox style of Busoni's own music—yet another of the countless dichotomies in Busoni's nature. Varèse's own recollections are particularly revealing of Busoni:

> To musicians who have known Busoni only as a pianist, or through his scores, this ambivalence will come as a surprise. It was as though his heart, loyal to the past, refused to follow his adventurous mind into so strange a future. In any case I owe a most tremendous debt of gratitude to this extraordinary man—almost a figure out of the Renaissance—not only one of the greatest pianists of all time, but a man of wide culture, a scholar, thinker, writer, composer, conductor, teacher and *animateur*—a man who stimulated others to think and do things. Personally, I know that he crystallized my half-formed ideas, stimulated my imagination, and determined, I believe, the future development of my music.[40]

One anecdote is both revealing and endearing:

> From the beginning Busoni took an interest in my work and let me bring my scores for criticism. But one day—by then I had known him for three years or more—I brought him my latest score—whether *Les Cycles du Nord* for orchestra, or an opera based on Hugo von Hofmannsthal's *Oedipus und die Sphinx*, I cannot remember. In any case he seemed surprised and expressed pleasure at the way I had developed. He went over the score with special attentiveness and asked many questions. At certain places he suggested modifications which I found contrary to my conception. He asked me if I didn't agree with him, and I said emphatically, "No, Maestro," and gave him my reasons. "So," he said, "you will not

make these changes." "No, Maestro," I repeated, somewhat belligerently. He looked at me for a moment and I thought he resented my rejection of his recommendations as youthful conceit. But then he smiled and, putting his hand on my shoulder, said, "From now on it is no longer *Maestro* but *Ferruccio* and *Tu.*" We spoke either Italian or French when we were alone together.

Together we used to discuss what directions the music of the future would, or rather should take and could not take as long as the straitjacket of the tempered system ("the diplomatic two semitone system," as he called it) continued to keep it unmovable. He deplored that his own keyboard instrument had conditioned our ears to accept only an infinitesimal part of the infinite gradation of sounds in nature. However, when I said that I was through with tonality, his quick response was: *"Tu te prives d'une bien belle chose* [You are depriving yourself of something really beautiful]." He was very much interested in the electrical instruments we began to hear about and I remember particularly one he had read of in an American magazine, called the Dynamophone, invented by a Dr. Thaddeus Cahill [see chapter 11, p. 305], which I later saw demonstrated in New York and was disappointed. All through his writings one finds over and over again predictions about the music of the future which have since come true. In fact, there is hardly a development that he did not foresee, as for instance this extraordinary prophecy: "I almost think that in the new great music, machines will be necessary and will be assigned a share in it. Perhaps industry, too, will bring forth her share in the artistic ascent."[41]

Varèse's memory fails him in one point: he states elsewhere in the above reminiscences that he had read Busoni's *New Aesthetic of Music* in its first, 1907 edition *before* he went to Berlin, which was impossible; he spoke no German at the time, and an Italian edition was published only in 1911, and a French edition, although planned for 1957, was ultimately never published.

The year 1905 began with yet more tours, including two weeks in Madrid in May with Gerda that offered a rare pleasure: Busoni took part in the celebrations for the tricentenary of the first edition of Cervantes's *Don Quixote*. The book had been a favorite with Busoni since early childhood, and he eventually had a collection of forty-seven different editions, in six languages. It was obviously an enthusiasm he shared with Egon Petri, as he sent him the catalogue of the exhibition mounted as part of the celebrations in Madrid, soon after his return to Berlin. Egon Petri was supposed to have taken part in the Rubinstein Competition that summer, for which Busoni was again on the jury, but pulled out at a late stage. Winners that year were the pianist Wilhelm Backhaus (1884–1969) and Béla Bartók.

That summer, Gerda and the children went to stay in Godinne, in Belgium, near the Ysaÿes, who welcomed them when they visited, but did not ask them to stay, as the Busonis had apparently expected. In Berlin, Busoni turned his attention to the stage again and, as he wrote to his mother, specifically to the Italian stage: "*Babbo* [Daddy] will perhaps be happy to know that I have recently attempted a first step towards the theater, but in an unusual direction; not with an *opera*, but with descriptive music for a play . . . an old tragicomic theatrical tale by our Carlo Gozzi."⁴² The play was *Turandot*. Friedrich Schiller had provided a somewhat free German translation of the play at the end of the eighteenth century and it is to this version that Carl Maria von Weber had written his incidental music. (Busoni was of the opinion that between them they had ruined a masterpiece of Italian literature.)

Busoni's *Turandot Suite for Orchestra* (BV 248), as its name suggests, was first conceived as a concert piece, some of its various sections having German and some Italian titles. It is scored for orchestra and women's chorus. In this initial form it was premiered on October 21, 1905, at one of Busoni's Beethovensaal concerts, in a program that included the first German performance of the complete *Nuits d'été* by Berlioz. The *Turandot Suite* remained in this form until 1911, when Busoni added two more sections, *Verzweiflung und Ergebung* (Despair and Resignation) (BV 248a). The reason for the addition was that the Austrian theater director Max Reinhardt (1873–1943), arguably the greatest European director of his era and a lasting influence on the theater, invited Busoni to revise the music to accompany a new German adaptation of Gozzi's play by Karl Vollmoeller at the Deutsches Theater in Berlin (still today one of Europe's foremost theaters). It was to be some years before Busoni applied himself to a full-scale opera version of *Turandot*.

In early February 1906 Gerda was summoned to Stockholm, where her father lay dying. Ferruccio had an important series of concerts in Berlin on January 24 and February 3 and 14, playing works by Liszt and

Schubert. Carl Sjöstrand died on the day of the last concert, and Gerda, thoughtful and protective as ever, made sure the news was kept from her husband until after the concert. Carl Sjöstrand was someone Busoni had always deeply admired as well as loved, but after yet another recital with the violinist Bernhard Dessau in the Singakademie in Berlin, Ferruccio had to embark immediately on a concert tour of Germany and Switzerland and Austria (where Gerda managed briefly to join him in Vienna), and was therefore forced to do his grieving "in harness." The tour continued to Trieste, where he stayed in a hotel: "It was three hours before I could resolve to drag myself to the 'Schmiedegasse' [Smith Street, i.e., Via dei Fabbri, where his parents lived]."[43] The situation there was as depressing as ever. "There is nothing worse than looking back," he wrote two days later, "or than places, people, and facts that lead one to do so. I seldom do it and should like never to do it, but here I cannot help it. Therefore I feel uncomfortable and as if in the night I had been shunted off my track on the main line to a side-station."[44] The contrast between his parents and Carl Sjöstrand was striking—"The description of Pappus' beauty in death moves me so much every time I read it," he had written Gerda earlier in the tour, from Basle. "How relieved I am to know you will have no painful impression to remember."[45]

Busoni spent several weeks in Italy that spring. It remains unclear whether he returned to Berlin after Trieste, although, given the circumstances, it is highly probable. In late March he was in Paris with Gerda, after which he returned to Italy. Back in Berlin on May 10 he wrote to his friend Emilio Anzoletti to thank him for "pleasant days."[46] Anzoletti (1874–1950) was an Italian engineer and amateur cellist who had met Busoni while he was studying engineering in Berlin in the late 1890s and early 1900s. A lasting friendship developed between them—no doubt initially prompted in Berlin by the common Italian bond. Anzoletti had been a frequent visitor during Busoni's summers "alone" in Berlin, in the summer of 1902 seeing him on a daily basis. The friendship later expanded to include Anzoletti's brother Augusto, subsequently the translator of the libretto of Busoni's opera Die Brautwahl into Italian.

On April 29 Busoni had played his Piano Concerto and the Turandot Suite in Bologna (for which Emilio Anzoletti had written the program notes), and been fired by further thoughts of reviving Italian music.

"Every seed contains a germ and my stay in Italy has sown some ideas in me," he wrote to Anzoletti in the same letter.

> One of them, which sprung up yesterday evening during one of those walks which one can undertake in Berlin better than elsewhere, especially in the "wonderful month of May," as Heine says, I want to tell you— Almost all the cities in Italy lack systematically organized orchestral concerts. And of all of them none would satisfy me enough to choose that one alone. Therefore the plan came to me of an Italian orchestra that would supply all the main cities, regularly, following a well-planned system.

He then sketches out the rest of this wildly optimistic plan. His subsequent brush with reality was to cause him much anguish.

In early July 1906 Gerda and the children went to stay at Schloss Habrovan as the guests of Karoline von Gomperz, one of Ferruccio's old benefactors from Vienna; she and her husband, it will be remembered, had offered to adopt Ferruccio as a child. It is to be presumed that the Busonis had revived the friendship when they were in Vienna together in February.

Given Busoni's long-standing attraction to the darkly surreal and subversive world of E. T. A. Hoffmann, it was not surprising that he had turned to one of Hoffmann's tales for his next opera project, *Die Brautwahl* (literally "The Bride-Choice"). Like his *Turandot*, Busoni's *Die Brautwahl* was only slowly to mutate from embryonic instrumental form to full opera. Busoni had begun work on the opera that spring, and continued writing the libretto in June during a British tour. In Berlin, by early July he had finished the libretto plus the music to most of act 1, before going off alone on July 18 to northern Italy, taking the *Brautwahl* libretto and manuscript paper with him.

Perversely, he felt lonely in Italy, for which he shifted the blame to Gerda, complaining to Egon Petri that he could not even work owing to the lack of stimulus: "And why am I here? Gerda said I needed it . . . and I gave in."[47] She had indeed suggested the trip, in her first letter from Schloss Habrovan, and he had joyfully agreed. "This is my traveling plan," he had written to her on July 17 from Berlin, "one night through to Munich, then on to Innsbruck, and if I don't like it enough there I shall go on to Bolzano and Trento."[48] The rest of the letter is buoyant and he was clearly looking forward to the trip. (At this point, their

marriage seemed to be an excellent one. Ferruccio wrote: "The relationship between us has reached a beautiful maturity and should never
alter. Thank you for the recent paradisiacal weeks."[49] He took her letter suggesting the trip with him to Italy. It seems a rather extraordinary
situation: she had made the suggestion scarcely a week after she had left
him for Schloss Habrovan. Again, if we only had her letter, we might
know what had prompted it all.)

He wasted little time on the journey, spending a couple of days in
Munich, which he ironically summed up as "joyfully masculine,"[50] and
deciding to go straight on to Trento ("I have had enough of green
clothes, goats' beards and bare knees"). After five days he was complaining to Gerda too of the loneliness and lack of stimulus, slightly be-
lied by a long description of a visit to a Capuchin monastery, and another of a walk in the hills above Trento. But he found everyone sad and
bored and irritable—more a case of projection than the actual truth, one
imagines. Nevertheless, the Italian landscape slowly released its effects
into his mind over the coming months, reminding him yet again that he
was Italian. Old memories were stirred too by Trento: "I was here when
I was 13, when we left Vienna and wandered from place to place as
though on a fairground wagon."[51] He remembered playing in a room in
the Palazzo Salvotti and that it was freezing. "Also, I believe I experienced my first male arousal there; in the hotel a chambermaid with very
red hair and very black eyes let me kiss her once, whereupon my mother
said 'non è bello' which brought me to my senses."

But alone in Trento that summer, although he had arranged for a piano in his room, he was restless, traveling to various other centers on day
trips, and usually wishing he had not. "Yesterday I . . . traveled one and a
half hours on a branch line to Levico, a spa in the mountains. . . . I
stepped into a little inn: on an old piano lay Sinding's Frühlingsrauschen
[Rustle of Spring] and Puccini's Bohème."[52] This was the trigger for yet another irritable tirade, this time on the low standard of popular taste. (To
compound its shortcomings, Trento had no secondhand bookshops!) Busoni had just bought the score of Verdi's Un Ballo in Maschera—"a strong
work, brutal, but it has great power. . . . Some moments in it belong to
Verdi's best. . . . But the libretto! And the lyrics!"[53] On August 3 there
were further thoughts on libretto writing: "The only solution for an
opera composer is to write the text himself and I enormously regret not

being able to write it *now* in Italian. It is wonderful how, during composition, one can remove, add and alter, according to musical requirements."[54] Did he really not know how close the collaboration can be
between opera composer and librettist?

The next day Busoni suddenly decided to go back to Berlin. He sent
a telegram to Gerda that he was leaving immediately for Innsbruck,
and also wrote her a letter: the heat in Trento had become even worse
and he could neither eat nor sleep.[55] The following day he was in Innsbruck, which he found rather rustic after Trento, and charmless.

By August 8 he was back in Berlin, with his books, and in contact
with the outside world—back in harness, where he felt more comfort-
able. He immediately entered into planning concerts for the coming
season. He was reading *Don Juan Tenorio* by the great Spanish dramatist
Tirso de Molina (1584–1648) and thinking of suggesting a production
to the great theater director Max Reinhardt, for which he would write
the music. In October he played in Amsterdam, in late November in
Trieste, where he conducted his *Turandot Suite*, among other things. Immediately following this concert he had intended to go to the station to
board the train for Calais, on his way to London to take part in what
cynics might term Adelina Patti's first farewell concert, on December 1
in the Royal Albert Hall, but the Trieste audience would not let him go,
so that he arrived at the station to see the end lights of the train disappearing into the distance. He boarded a later direct train to Calais:

> I could stay in the same Trieste wagon, had a thorough rest, slept ex-
> cellently for two nights and spent Friday reading and thinking and
> eating . . . but this damned sea-crossing caused upset yet again, so that
> I arrived in Dover in a very feverish state. . . . Between the Adriatic
> coast and the Channel, what a distance! I have never observed such
> an enormous difference before. Here, fog, storm, cold—fog, storm,
> cold—all the wintry devils together, and only the day before yesterday
> that summer sunset in Trieste![56]

He was dreading another sea crossing to Ireland at the end of the two-
week British tour (a crossing that, in Liverpool, he finally got out of by
putting his foot down with the agent Schulz-Curtius after reading that
ships to the United States were being delayed owing to extremely
stormy weather).

Busoni was always attracted to the bustling cosmopolitan atmosphere of great cities like London and Paris. In London he could also largely have control over his social life, not so on tour to the hated provinces. Manchester at least had become more attractive: since 1905 Egon Petri had been teaching at the Royal Manchester College of Music, now the Royal Northern College of Music. Petri was now married, and in early November 1906 a daughter, Karin-Ulla, was born. When in Manchester, Busoni often stayed with Petri and his wife Mitta. On this December 1906 tour, Busoni's tour partner, not for the only time, was the Spanish violinist Pablo de Sarasate, twenty-two years his senior and, according to Busoni, lacking in brains and temperament, and also in interest in and understanding of new work and new ideas—which, for the voracious polymath Busoni, made him a boring and contemptible traveling companion: "He has some of [Adolf] Brodsky's Olympian obstinacy and also some of my father's way of dismissing things without any reflection: that is the Latin in him."[57] Busoni spent much of his spare time on this tour, in trains and hotel rooms, working on the libretto of *Aladdin*, for an opera based on Oehlenschlager's play—the work already plundered for the final movement of his Piano Concerto. This was a project that had still to run into the sand.

At forty, Busoni was realizing yet again that he must make a greater effort to focus his life and marshal his energies more efficiently—in other words, he needed a more settled existence, but one that would provide enough funds and time for him to devote himself more fully to composition. He must have realized too that his energies were already failing: he was constantly fending off exhaustion and subsequent nausea. And he needed Gerda, and his children, in a normal family setting: "My mind is always active," he wrote to her in December from Manchester.[58] "But my body demands a little repose, for latterly everything has gone at a gallop. I have such a longing for your letters, dear, dear Gerda; perhaps never before have I felt so happy and so together with you as now. . . . I am very much in favor of the Vienna idea now; it might give me a *kind of* freedom for three years." The "Vienna idea," however, proved unable to provide any kind of freedom. After twelve years in Berlin of at least as settled an existence as he could hope for, he was about to make another disastrous decision.

Notes

1. Quoted in Dent, *Ferruccio Busoni*, p. 131.
2. Quoted in Dent, *Ferruccio Busoni*, p. 131.
3. Quoted in Lionel Carley (ed.), *Frederick Delius: Music, Art, and Literature* (Aldershot, England: Ashgate, 1998), p. 176.
4. Review in *Berliner Neueste Nachrichten*, November [16?], 1902.
5. Letter from FB to Gerda Busoni, March 3, 1904, StBB Bus. Nachl. IV, 458.
6. Letter from FB to Gerda Busoni, March 5, 1904, StBB Bus. Nachl. IV, 460.
7. Review in *Detroit Tribune*, March 9, 1904.
8. Review in *Evening Post* (Chicago), March 10, 1904.
9. "F.H.G.," review in *Record-Herald* (Chicago), March 10, 1904.
10. Review in *Chicago Journal*, March 10, 1904.
11. It has not been established whether Busoni played in Canada on this tour. On later tours he played many more concerts, but still far fewer than other artists. To confine ourselves to pianists: Sigismund Thalberg gave 330 concerts in the two concert seasons of 1871 and 1872; Anton Rubinstein 215 in 1872–1873; but the clear winner was Ignacy Paderewski, who gave 107 concerts in 117 days in 1891, in addition to attending eighty-six dinner parties! And later, between 1915 and 1918, according to Adam Zamoyski, Paderewski "gave some 340 speeches and almost as many concerts" (Zamoyski, *Paderewski* [New York: Atheneum, 1982], 52).
12. "Daybook," dated April 2, 1904, contained in Ferruccio Busoni, *Letters to his Wife*, trans. Rosamond Ley (New York: Da Capo Press, 1975; first published London, 1938), p. 83.
13. Letter from FB to Gerda Busoni, July 7, 1904, StBB Bus. Nachl. IV, 478.
14. Letter from FB to Gerda Busoni, February 10, 1902, StBB Bus. Nachl. IV, 408.
15. Letter from FB to Gerda Busoni, July 16, 1903, StBB Bus. Nachl. IV, 437.
16. It was preceded by the overture to Mozart's *Die Entführung aus dem Serail* and Ottokar Nováčeks *Hymnus* from his String Quartet, op. 13. Nováček, who had died in 1900, had been a member of the Brodsky Quartet in Leipzig, and later played viola in the Boston Symphony Orchestra under Nikisch in 1891 and then in the Damrosch Orchestra in New York. Busoni had known him since his Leipzig days and renewed the friendship in Boston and New York.
17. Letter from FB to Gerda Busoni, July 11, 1902, StBB Bus. Nachl. IV, 414.
18. Letter from FB to Gerda Busoni, August 1, 1902, StBB Bus. Nachl. IV, 422.
19. Letter from FB to Gerda Busoni, July 29, 1903, StBB Bus. Nachl. IV, 441.
20. Letter from FB to Gerda Busoni, August 6, 1903, StBB Bus. Nachl. IV, 443.
21. Translation by Walter M. Clement published in a concert program for a performance of the Piano Concerto given by Egon Petri at the Queen's Hall, London, on February 21, 1934.

22. Larry Sitsky, *Busoni and the Piano* (New York: Greenwood Press, 1986), pp. 116–17.

23. Review in *Tägliche Rundschau*, November 11, 1904.

24. Review in *Tägliche Rundschau*, November 11, 1904.

25. Max Marschalk, review in *Vossische Zeitung*, November 11, 1904.

26. Review in *Signale*, November 11, 1904.

27. Review in *Deutsche Zeitung*, November 11, 1904.

28. Leo Kestenberg, review in *Neues Montagsblatt*, November 11, 1904.

29. Alfred Brendel, *Nachdenken über Musik* (Munich: Piper, 1977), p. 162.

30. Ferruccio Busoni, *Wesen und Einheit der Musik*, new ed. (Berlin-Halensee: Max Hesses Verlag, 1956); first published in the journal *Pan*, February 1912.

31. Letter from FB to Egon Petri, July 19, 1909, MW, p. 107.

32. The original manuscripts of all these works are now in the collection of the State Library in Berlin, Bus. Nachl. CI; where published titles are concerned, copies of these are also in the collection.

33. From Jakob Wassermann, *Selbstbetrachtungen*, quoted in the foreword to the 1956 edition of *Wesen und Einheit der Musik* (not in English edition).

34. In "Grainger's Anecdotes," a handwritten collection of autobiographical jottings variously dated between 1949 and 1954, now in the Grainger Archives, White Plains, N.Y. Quoted in John Bird, *Percy Grainger* (London: Paul Elek, 1976), p. 79.

35. Bird, *Percy Grainger*, p. 79.

36. Bird, *Percy Grainger*, p. 79.

37. Bird, *Percy Grainger*, p. 80.

38. Bird, *Percy Grainger*, p. 81.

39. Louise Varèse, *Varèse: A Looking-Glass Diary* (New York: Norton, 1972), p. 48.

40. Edgard Varèse, quoted in L. Varèse, *Varèse*, p. 50.

41. E. Varèse, quoted in L. Varèse, *Varèse*, pp. 49–50.

42. Letter from FB to Anna Weiss-Busoni, August 18, 1905, StBB Bus. Nachl. 1342.

43. Postcard from FB to Gerda Busoni, March 2, 1906, StBB Bus. Nachl. IV, 529.

44. Letter from FB to Gerda Busoni, March 4, 1906, StBB Bus. Nachl. IV, 530.

45. Letter from FB to Gerda Busoni, February 25, 1906, StBB Bus. Nachl. IV, 528.

46. Letter from FB to Emilio Anzoletti, May 10, 1906, in Sablich, *Lettere*, p. 129.

47. Letter from FB to Egon Petri, July 30, 1906, MW, p. 82.

48. Letter from FB to Gerda Busoni, July 17, 1906, StBB Bus. Nachl. IV, 537.

49. Letter from FB to Gerda Busoni, July 13, 1906, StBB Bus. Nachl. IV, 534.

50. Letter from FB to Gerda Busoni, July 20, 1906, StBB Bus. Nachl. IV, 539.

51. FB to Gerda Busoni, July 20, 1906.

52. Letter from FB to Gerda Busoni, July 30, StBB Bus. Nachl. IV, 547.

53. Letter from FB to Gerda Busoni, July 28, 1906, StBB Bus. Nachl. IV, 545.

54. Letter from FB to Gerda Busoni, August 3, 1906, StBB Bus. Nachl. IV, 551.

55. Letter from FB to Gerda Busoni, August 4, 1906, StBB Bus. Nachl. IV, 552.

56. Letter from FB to Gerda Busoni, December 2, 1906, StBB Bus. Nachl. IV, 562.

57. Letter from FB to Gerda Busoni, December 13, 1906, StBB Bus. Nachl. IV, 570.

58. Letter from FB to Gerda Busoni, December 4, 1906, StBB Bus. Nachl. IV, 563.

CHAPTER NINE

Vienna, *Die Brautwahl*: 1906 to 1913

In late 1906, just before his third British tour of that year, Busoni was approached unofficially by the board of the Vienna *Gesellschaft der Musikfreunde* (Society of Friends of Music), which included the conservatory where the nine-year-old Ferruccio had briefly studied piano, to take over master classes in piano. On December 22 he wrote to Ludwig von Bösendorfer,[1] the member of the board he trusted most, setting out his ideas on how he would conduct the classes. (Ludwig Bösendorfer [1835–1919], whose father, Ignaz, had founded the famous piano-manufacturing firm in Vienna in 1828, had been a generous friend to Busoni since the latter first went to Vienna as a child. In 1899 he had sent Busoni one of the firm's concert grands, though this could be described as enlightened self-interest.) As Busoni had not yet received an official offer from the conservatory, he felt he could write openly on the matter to Bösendorfer, who, Busoni said, was free to do as he wished with the information.

> Since I left the Boston Conservatory—about fourteen years ago—I have come to enjoy and love almost unlimited freedom and independence. In this sense too, even "favorable conditions" would never quite allay a feeling in me that I had sacrificed my freedom of action—I say this, once again, only to make it clear to those concerned that I would be losing

just as much as I would be gaining. On the other hand, I am fully aware of the honor such trust means for me: I also appreciate the artistic possibilities offered by such a position.

He might find himself at odds with the musical life of Vienna, Busoni explained frankly. "If I find myself alienated from musical Vienna, I would either have to make a great effort at rapprochement or—remain an outsider." Nevertheless, he had decided in principle to take on the post, but wanted to make his intentions clear.

> The class would meet *as a group* and no pupil would have the right to a specified period of tuition for himself alone. The time would be self-regulating and proportionate to the talent and diligence of the pupil.— Intrinsic to *group* tuition, furthermore, is mutual competitiveness and criticism, and each pupil would have the benefit of the instruction given to his classmates. . . . I would schedule this class tuition for two afternoons a week.

The agreement would depend on the number of pupils. "I consider *artistic* tuition impossible if the number of students exceeds a certain limit." However, Busoni suggested that for an admission fee, some nonparticipating students could be admitted as listeners. "In past years I have made a reputation for myself abroad, and it is to be expected that a large number of students would be foreigners. When I held a summer school in Weimar, eight young pupils attended it the first year, in the second over forty. Who sets the limit here, and what relation would it have to my fee?" Given the fact that he was now at the height of his career as a pianist, it would be impossible for him to interrupt it; therefore he would have to be free to take a leave of absence at any time and without complicated formalities. He also considered an initial contract for one year to be advisable, and suggested an annual salary of 12,000, or 15,000 Austrian crowns, which would be increased if the number of students increased.

To give some idea of the purchasing power of this amount: around this time, the monthly rent for the Busonis's apartment in a smart district of Berlin was 300 marks. In other words, just over a quarter of his Vienna fee for two afternoons' tuition a week could pay the rent. (Another example: in summer 1907 Busoni bought a new raincoat in

KaDeWe, still today Berlin's top department store, for thirty-two marks.) Other expenditure being proportionate, if the whole family transferred to Vienna, they could live quite well on this fee alone, leaving Busoni free to compose, and would have a secure and more tranquil lifestyle. But as Busoni pointed out in the above letter to Bösendorfer, he was at the peak of his international career as a pianist, and there were future engagements already programmed—including another American tour. He was walking yet again into the trap—or vicious circle—of being given a prestigious teaching post on the strength of his reputation as a pianist, when the demands of his performing career would inevitably severely disrupt his teaching program. By April 1907 an agreement was reached with Vienna for a trial year. Knowing Vienna as he did, however, he was cautious, and did not for the time being contemplate moving there lock, stock, and barrel with his family—in this way already violating one of the main purposes of taking on the job.

The first half of 1907 was spent touring—in March to Marseilles, Freiburg, Munich, returning to Berlin at the beginning of April. From Freiburg Busoni complained, "Once more I have come to the end of an almost unbearable week and I regard these days (March 8–15) as thrown entirely to the winds."[2] He was scathing about the public in Marseilles, and had spent an inordinate number of hours in trains. In Freiburg he made some more piano rolls, this time of Liszt, at the Welte-Mignon company (*Réminiscences de Don Juan, Réminiscences de Norma, Polonaise, Fantasy on Beethoven's The Ruins of Athens,* among others; now available on CD). In November 1905 he had recorded for Welte-Mignon for the first time, using this method. He hated the restrictions it imposed on his playing, and the nerve-racking pressures of playing with total accuracy, but knew these records of his playing were important.

In mid-April Busoni was in Italy again, in Florence, where he was being honored with two orchestral concerts in the Pergola theater—the first contained his *Lustspielouvertüre* and the second his *Turandot Suite*—then back to Berlin, where he continued working on his opera *Die Brautwahl.* Early in the year his *Entwurf einer neuen Ästhetik der Tonkunst* had appeared. As already stated in chapter 8, in this first edition it failed to create much of an impression outside Busoni's own circle, although there were those outside his circle who had certainly noticed it. The English musicologist Ernest Newman reviewed it in the

Birmingham Post[3] in August, and a year later Paul Bekker reviewed it in the *Allgemeine Musikzeitung*.[4] And a more personal reaction: in July he was proud to report to Gerda: "A young student accosted me on the street, in a voice shaking with excitement, in order to tell me of the great impression my little book had made on him. It was very gratifying to see this devoted and uncritical receptivity among the better young people."[5] Busoni himself had sent copies to sixteen "important" people, mostly journalists, but also directors of concert halls and opera houses and some influential friends.

In 1907 his summer months in Berlin were interrupted by a concert[6] on August 1 on Norderney, one of the East Friesian Islands just off the coast of Lower Saxony, and at the time a fashionable resort. It must have been an extremely well-paid engagement; otherwise, it is difficult to understand what induced him to make this rather arduous journey. "It gives me a strange feeling being obliged to play in public again, after an interval of three months. I feel 'shame' in doing it, more than ever," he wrote Gerda,[7] who was in Drottningholm in Sweden, staying with her sister Helmi. The shame he had felt as a child in Vienna, when his father brought home strangers and ordered Ferruccio to "let him hear"—*fagli sentire*—remained in him like a virus, ever ready to flair up again, particularly as he wanted to concentrate on *Die Braut-wahl*. The shame was aggravated on Norderney by a request from two of the kaiser's sisters, present during a rehearsal, to play more. He refused. "I hope for a letter from you here. Your last, the golden one," he continued, "I have kept in my pocket-book."[8] One's natural curiosity alone makes one regret the loss of Gerda's letters, golden or otherwise. There had been a suggestion that Egon Petri join him on Norderney for a few days, but the weather had turned stormy and Egon arrived two days late. When Ferruccio himself had arrived, the atmosphere was like *The Flying Dutchman*, he felt, and when he went to rehearse, the first thing he heard was the overture to Wagner's opera. After the concerts on Norderney, he and Egon left together, Egon to go to the artists' colony in Worpswede, which he still often visited, although he left almost immediately for Airolo in Switzerland, and Ferruccio to go to Weimar, via Berlin. There seemed to have been some disagreement between the two men, and Egon had apparently gone off to Airolo in a huff, in order to put a greater distance between them than Worpswede to Weimar. Probably Busoni was putting too much pressure on him. He had already persuaded Egon to undertake the piano score of the Piano Concerto. Whatever the truth, Busoni certainly did not hold a grudge now when Egon resisted the pressures, and his letters continued to be affable and unruffled, for the most part, though there was an occasional reproachful dig if Egon failed to write for a time. Egon had mentioned on Norderney that he had met George Bernard Shaw, which fired Busoni with the idea (which he suggested to Egon in the first letter[9] after their Norderney meeting) of asking Shaw to write a libretto for him, using Egon as the initial go-between. The idea came to nothing, and it was over ten years before Busoni and Shaw finally met.

Busoni was in Weimar for a prolonged session with the Liszt Foundation, which was preparing the publication of the complete works of Liszt, and had asked Busoni to join the editorial panel. Since the early 1890s he had been collecting Liszt editions, and Liszt had formed an ever-increasing proportion of his repertoire. He had already published several transcriptions and other versions of Liszt's works. Later that summer he told Egon in some triumph that the Berlin music publisher Robert Lienau had given him four apparently lost works by Liszt, printed but never published; they were the first versions of the piano pieces *Venezia* and *Napoli* (op. 159). Such was Busoni's reputation by now as a Liszt expert, that Lienau had apparently asked Busoni to confirm that the works were indeed by Liszt—which, after carefully studying the scores and playing them several times, he was able to do.

Busoni arrived in Weimar on August 4 and immediately went to the Liszt Foundation, where he worked for over five hours with Oskar von Hase and Aloys Obrist, leading members of the editorial panel. "Yesterday we went through *every single Liszt volume*, not to mention sketches, manuscripts and every possible fragment, some very interesting ones among them. They were both rather surprised at my professional knowledge of it all," he proudly informed Gerda.[10] The work of editing and publishing Liszt's complete works was a daunting one, as Liszt often wrote several different versions of particular works; he himself issued many of his works in different editions. Between 1901 and 1936 the Liszt Foundation published thirty-four volumes, of which Busoni edited three: those numbered II.1, II.2, and II.3; he also wrote an introduction for the first and explanatory notes for all three. His work on these volumes stretched over several years. The volumes contained: *Etude en douze exercices, Douze grandes études, Mazeppa for Piano; Etudes d'exécution transcendante, Grande fantaisie de bravoure sur "La Clochette" de Paganini for Piano; Etudes d'exécution transcendante d'après Paganini, Grandes études de Paganini, Morceau de salon, Ab Irato, Trois études de concert, Gnomenreigen, Waldesrauschen for Piano.* Almost to the end of his life, Busoni continued to publish versions and transcriptions of Liszt. There was much to unite them; not only that they were both great pianists and both composed, but also that they shared what Larry Sitsky terms an "almost necromantic quality."[11] As Sitsky explains:

> One of the aspects that fascinate us about Liszt is his dualism, the presence in his music of the divine and the satanic, side by side. Busoni's dualism of the same basic kind, although extended and rarified. Liszt's more obvious religioso moods, sometimes verging on ecstasy, have been replaced by a more elusive, more personal mysticism. Liszt's devil is the fully fledged romantic variety, breathing sulphur and swishing his tail. . . . Busoni's dark forces are more subtle, more fleeting, more grotesque, often more frightening by their very insubstantiality.[12]

After a few days in Weimar it was back to Berlin and work on *Die Brautwahl.* In September Busoni was first in Vienna, selecting pupils for the master classes, then in Britain yet again, playing in London, Cardiff, and Manchester, where he visited Egon Petri. By mid-October he was in Vienna to begin the classes.

He was—perversely but perhaps unsurprisingly—disappointed by the standard of his pupils in Vienna, even though he had helped select them in September. He and Gerda had been planning to move to a larger flat in Berlin, and he wrote[13] to her laconically that she could certainly continue looking. (The next year they moved to their final home in Berlin, a large, two-story apartment at Viktoria-Luise-Platz 11, just south of the previous one on the Augsburger Strasse.) As he had done with his students in Weimar, Busoni tried several ways of making the classes work—taking some of the students out to supper, trying to interest them in wider issues, demanding a possibly unrealistic intellectual standard: "There is scarcely one with whom I can converse about a picture, a book, or any human question. If one draws a comparison from psychology, aesthetics, or from nature, it meets with incomprehension. All I can teach here is fingering, pedaling, piano and forte and rhythm."[14] Busoni's increasing disinclination to play the piano in pub-lic was spilling over into teaching it as well. Eventually he found a few students who did respond, and many of the rest were won over to some degree by the force of his personality and became fiercely loyal. His at-titude toward them therefore changed over the year—at least toward the male students: the women students were more or less ignored, as far as their piano playing was concerned, and certainly not respected. "A pity you are not here," he wrote to Egon Petri in June 1908. "The group of students—the men anyway—is really delightful, they all have good brains. They are very able. One of them[15] recently played the Liszt [B Minor] sonata so well that I had to struggle not to cry. They are not en-vious of one another and all noble chaps."[16]

With Gerda and the children left behind in Berlin, his evenings were spent either in the café or the opera house: "Yesterday evening (in order to know!) I decided I would hear *Madame Butterfly*. It began at seven o'clock. The ticket cost fourteen Kronen; at twenty minutes past seven exactly I was out again. I went for a walk, had something to eat and went back again for the last act. *It was indecent*."[17] Like Sarasate, Busoni too had his willfully blind spots. Puccini had come to Vienna to direct this, the first Viennese production of *Butterfly*, a fact Busoni must have known, but he made no attempt to meet his fellow countryman. (Mahler, as director of the Court Opera in Vienna, had been responsi-ble for securing the Austrian premiere of the work. In December Mahler was to leave Vienna for New York. It is not known whether he and Busoni renewed their acquaintance, begun nearly twenty years be-fore in Leipzig.) Busoni's reaction to the work sounds very much like jealousy at Puccini's enormous success.

Although Busoni's sense of humor could be Rabelaisian, he had a very prudish side to his nature, and this probably fed into his opposition to love scenes onstage, indeed to any public expression of strong emotion. It is one reason why he was drawn to the grotesque stylization of com-media dell'arte, which places reality at one remove, and to the surreal grotesquerie of E. T. A. Hoffmann. There were other reasons. In his es-say "The Oneness of Music and the Possibilities of Opera," written in 1921 and contained in the volume of essays *The Essence of Music and Other Papers*, Busoni lays out his credo on the relationship between

debut, he wrote, as it was the first time most of his pupils had heard him in public, but a success. Soon after, he left for concert engagements in Switzerland, Berlin, Paris, and London. In spite of Busoni's letter to Bösendorfer prior to accepting the teaching post, the conservatory took a very dim view of this long absence, and in February peremptorily dismissed him. From London he replied, defending his position at some length, and insisted on continuing the course until the summer, as agreed in his contract. Where the conservatory board had put themselves completely in the wrong was in announcing to the press what they were going to do before notifying Busoni himself, even announcing his successor. He proposed a solution, for the sake of his pupils, and "the preservation of my honor": to be allowed to continue the course to the end. He would be back in Vienna on March 14, for a week, then again on tour, but from April 21 would remain in Vienna and "devote myself without interruption to my office." He sent a copy of this letter to Gerda,[24] asking her to send copies to Bösendorfer and to the *Neue Freie Presse*, one of Vienna's main newspapers. The press took up the quarrel in Vienna and Berlin. Both sides acted in a long-winded and rather pompously high-minded way. Busoni's twenty-eight pupils entered the fray, the American Georgine Nelson organizing a meeting in which they decided that if Busoni were not reinstated, they would all follow him to Berlin—a rather weak card to play. With true American insouciance, she went to the director with a petition to this effect, sending Busoni in London a comic account of the meeting on March 2.

Busoni returned to Vienna in mid-March, as promised, but soon left again, for Munich and Berlin; he was back briefly in mid-April, then off to Berlin, Rome, Milan, and Paris, returning to Vienna on April 27, where he did in fact remain until the course ended, except for a very short trip to Leipzig for a recording session with Phonola. (Vienna did offer delights for the bibliophile: he had found a music bookshop that still had a lot of old editions of Liszt works and two copies of the first printing of Schubert's "Ständchen," both of which he bought: one for him, one for Egon, who was turning into as eager a bibliophile as Ferruccio.) "*Everyone knows I am here*," he told Gerda,[25] who had taken the whole affair very badly. "The story, even if an unpleasant one, is of no importance. Don't take everything so hard, dear Gerda, the world *is* like this." Lessons were now given—unofficially—at the Hotel Bristol, at Busoni's expense, and from April 27 he was staying in private accommodations at Wallfischgasse 1 (previously he had stayed in accommodations provided by the conservatory). He maintained that he was contracted to teach 280 hours over the academic year, and was honorbound to do so, whether paid or not. On July 13 these classes came to an end. He devoted some of the teaching time to performances, at which he played three times. Béla Bartók was persuaded to perform his own 14 Bagatelles, op. 6, prompting the remark from Busoni, "At last something really new." The Portuguese composer and pianist José Vianna da Motta (1868–1948), who became a close friend and collaborator—particularly on the editing of Liszt's works—also played one of his own works.

In recognition of Ludwig von Bösendorfer's constant kindness and decency, after the last day of his master classes Busoni sent him a final report,[26] explaining the structure of the classes, held regularly, with twenty-five students and about a dozen observers. He then lists the students he considered to have distinguished themselves: Leo Sirota (1885–1965, from Kiev), Louis T. Gruenberg (1884–1964, from New York), Louis Closson (from Belgium), Josef Turczynski (1884–1953, from the Ukraine), and Ignacy Friedman (1882–1948, from Poland).[27] He thanked Bösendorfer for the support given to him and his students with his "stupendous instruments."

Busoni's faithful, if somewhat mournful, old friend Otto von Kapff, of Graz days, who was living in Vienna, surfaced again during this period, and in late June his self-pity and general gloom exhausted even Busoni's patience:

> The day before yesterday . . . at the end of a strenuous class, Kapff came and detained me for another two hours, with the most pessimistic bankrupt kind of conversation. I can't help it, but I can't have anything to do with people who have finished with life. . . . Felt neither friendship nor sympathy for Kapff. I should have liked to make him a present of a revolver. It is the first time I have felt so hard. Is that bad?[28]

As soon as the classes were finished, Busoni returned to Berlin. Yet another master plan for a more ordered, financially secure life hit the wastepaper basket. The fact was that he needed freedom, and the adrenaline of public performance; even the traveling had become a kind of drug, but a drug that was sapping more and more of his strength. Nevertheless, in spite of all, he had managed to continue working on *Die Brautwahl*, adding another eighty pages to the piano score, so that everything but the final scene was finished by the time he left Vienna.

It would appear that Gerda and the children stayed with Ferruccio that summer in Berlin. Two of his Vienna pupils, Closson and Gruenberg, followed him to Berlin, and Egon visited in August. Ferruccio was delighted to be able to show him the *Brautwahl* score, and the version of the Piano Concerto without chorus, with which Egon made his Berlin debut on October 3 that year, Busoni conducting. Before that, in early September, Ferruccio was back in Italy, giving concerts in Verona and Milan, agonizing yet again over what he perceived as the drawbacks of the country, and infused once more with messianic zeal. In the first[29] of three letters written to Gerda on September 9 in Verona, in a Garibaldiesque fit of fervor, he (mis)quoted—he is not the only one—from the seventeenth-century poet Vincenzo da Filicaia's breast-beating sonnet: "Italia, Italia, o tu, cui feo la sorte; Dono infelice di bellezza . . . / Deh, fossi tu men bella, o almen più forte" (Italy, Italy, to whom fate gave the unhappy gift of beauty. . . / Ah, if only you were less beautiful, or at least more strong). "Dear Gerda," Busoni ended the third letter[30] that day, "a great idea dawned on me this morning. I should like to give this Italy a national opera, as Wagner gave one to Germany. . . . I feel I can do it, and that it will be my life's work." (It did not seem to occur to him that in Giuseppe Verdi Italy already had its own national opera composer, albeit one certainly not composing according to Busoni's rules.) Back in May, in Vienna, he had seen Verdi's *Rigoletto* for the first time since he was nine years old (he was astonished at how much he remembered of it). This had also prompted the idea of an Italian opera:

> For two days I have been pursued by an idea, stronger than any previous ones; that, as the natural outcome of some fifteen years' development, I *must* write an Italian opera! It seems to me now to be the right thing to do, and if it were possible, I would gladly give up all the Meyrin[c]ks,[31] Shaws and Gobineaus for it. I feel that my style will unfold and come into full bloom there, for the first time, and I shall reach the place where I ought to be. The question of a libretto is a difficult one. I thought of

Boito, and of Italian tales, witty ones, but it is safer to take a ready-made stage figure (like Falstaff). Goldoni is no good. Gozzi, hardly, but perhaps—there is very much to think about here too. Perhaps you will write about it.[32]

He had just read a biography of Leonardo da Vinci, a polymath figure with whom he empathized strongly, and whom he saw as a figurehead for Italian greatness. This flooded his mind with ideas for an opera, in Faustian mode, on the painter's life. "The historical background of the *Sforzas* is great and one could make Leonardo the central figure of the action, like Hans Sachs in the "Meistersinger." The episodes, when he arranged the festivities at the court of the Sforzas . . . are quite reminiscent of the role of Faust in the puppet play by the Duke of Mantua that Goethe also used in the second part of Faust." (Parts of this concept were eventually to be translated into Busoni's final opera, *Doktor Faust*.) In January 1909, in Trieste, Busoni discovered that "two unknown Italian gentlemen" had published a drama, *Leonardo da Vinci*, and this temporarily killed the idea of an opera on the subject. "It is true it is a miserable concoction; but my idea is deflowered and profaned."[33] Before then, in early November, he had crossed the Channel yet again, playing first in London, then touring to Newcastle, Leeds, Liverpool, and Manchester.

He had gone hastily to Trieste in January on learning that both his parents, now in their mid-seventies, were seriously ill of some unspecified disease. His mother was over the worst, but Ferdinando was still in danger and acting true to type. "Papa is like a child of three and if for two minutes there is nobody standing by his bed, he starts screaming."[34] Ferdinando revived in early March, when Busoni was touring in Rome, Bologna, and Milan; Ferruccio went again to Trieste on March 10, on his way from Milan to Fiume, glad to find his mother up and about. In Milan he visited the composer Arrigo Boito again and was pleased to find their views on drama and Wagner coincided. It had been suggested that *Die Brautwahl* be translated into Italian and performed there, and Busoni wanted the older man's advice. Boito, now sixty-seven, was absorbed in finishing his own opera, *Nerone*, a project that had been dragging on for decades. Nevertheless, the two men discussed the idea of an Italian version of *Die Brautwahl*; Boito thought the translation might cause difficulties.

From Rome, in early March, Busoni had written to Emilio Anzoletti[35] on a preface to the Italian version of the *Entwurf einer neuen
Ästhetik der Tonkunst*, and also on some of his ideas on music in Italy.

The development of the art of music in our country wavers between the
recent influences of a Wagner and even more recent ones of the French
school on the one hand—and as a counterbalance the famous words of
a great man [Verdi]: *"Torniamo all'antico"* [Let us return to the past] in-
sinuate themselves into the present time, but only skimming the surface.

While willingly acknowledging the great uproar Wagner has caused in
Italy, it does not seem to me that it can similarly be acknowledged that
his music has "got under our skin," and our composers have profited from
it only apparently. Closer—through similarity of race—the French have
succeeded more in dominating us, and proof of this is the most celebrated of our living composers [Busoni is most probably alluding to Puccini here]. It is a certain lack of confidence in ourselves, faced with the
technical marvels of foreigners that pushes us to appropriate those qualities. While the Italian character in fact rebels at a form of expression
which is characteristic of another race, of a contrary race.

In this way we are afraid of being Italian without succeeding in being
German; and however much we gain from the French, its value is only
that of imitation, always a negative value; in fact this influence makes us
less genuine and less strong and substitutes an artificial perfume for the
wholesome smell of the earth.

The other trend in the direction of Verdi's call has not yet—I think—
acquired meaning other than a purely theoretical one. It is the war-cry
of the peaceful. And what would be the meaning of that call: *torniamo
all'antico*. Cherubini in his book on counterpoint talks of the rules "of
the ancients." And now he himself has become an ancient. To what
point in antiquity must we turn? To Palestrina? Cimarosa? Donizetti?

Those who like old music are free to reread, rehear and readmire the
works of past times and the first step should therefore be to revive the
scores of a Monteverdi or a Caccini, and stage them again.

Such an experiment would certainly be worthwhile: we shall not return to the "antico" but at the old sources we could draw on a new art,
while remaining Italian. The call we need should be, now and forever:
"Let us progress and remain Italian."

This is not only the articulation of Busoni's gradually developing concept for his own music, but also a shrewd summary of what was hap-

pening to Italian music: overawed by musical advances north of the Alps, in a misguided attempt to imitate those advances, much of Italian music was indeed to detach itself from its roots and its intimate bond (mainly through opera) with the Italian people, and wither. Ironically, the same process arguably hamstrung Busoni's own music too, to a large extent.

On May 12 Ferdinando Busoni died, shortly before his seventy-fifth birthday, when Ferruccio was in London. On May 18, back in Berlin, Ferruccio wrote[36] to his cousin Carolina ("Carla")—who, with her sister Ersilia, had carried most of the burden of his parents—expressing sententious and rather trite sentiments, and asking her for a list of expenses and information on what was to happen with his mother. From the rather defensive tone of the letter, it would appear that there had been reproaches from Trieste—not least, one would imagine, that Ferruccio did not go there for the funeral. Not until June 1 did he write to his mother.[37] It was obviously a letter he dreaded writing. Some of the sentiments are those of the letter to Carla, but infused with more sincerity:

> *Mia cara, buona e santa Mamma,* Finally I've succeeded in steeling myself to write to you—I couldn't collect myself to do it before—a great and *unique* event takes away the breath and the words. I say to myself: how astounded we are face to face with those mysterious and brutal forces. And the first feeling is: the inexplicability of the fact and the incredulity of the limited mind in dealing with it. And this time the limited and incredulous mind is that of a son. And it is to the mother herself that he has to turn. An immense task for which we are always surprised to find ourselves not at all prepared. Thinking that it is to him that I owe my joys and my sufferings, all my life—and that he is no longer—I feel I am an atrocious debtor. And this blessed spring that unfolds all its enchantments over a grave—it too is cruel and sometimes I am ashamed of being able to enjoy it.

He would like to be with her, but hints that he has to take care of his own health. By the end of June he is writing[38] that he is sending two hundred florins so that she can go away for the summer, and she is to let him know if it is not enough. He also tells her he has written something in memory of his father; this is—appropriately— the Fantasy after Johann Sebastian Bach for Piano (BV 253). Against the weight of all Ferdinando's shortcomings can be placed that one great gift of Bach to his son. All who have heard the piece have been moved to tears, Busoni told his mother, even without knowing its personal history. It is indeed a melancholy piece, skillfully merging the music of three Bach chorales and original contributions by Busoni himself. It was premiered at the Bechstein Hall (now the Wigmore Hall) in London on October 16, 1909, Busoni as pianist, and published by Breitkopf und Härtel the same year. It has often been recorded, most notably by Egon Petri and John Ogdon.

That summer in Berlin Busoni was very busy: he wrote a Berceuse for Piano (BV 252) in early June, and, over the next two months, *An die Jugend* (To Youth): *A Series of Piano Pieces* (BV 254), an optimistic counterpoint to the piece he had written in memory of his father. Like the elegies, each of these pieces was dedicated to one of his students. In early August he went to Italy again, alone, for a ten-day holiday; in Florence, he contemplated buying a villa not far from the nearby village of Fiesole—although his impressions of the people were as negative as ever. He was in a state of exhaustion, and realized when he came out of Italy, to Basle, that the trip had been an inadequate remedy:

> one must be strong in order to feel that strength is pleasant. The temperature and abundance of everything in Italy were too strong for me in the condition I was in when I came away. It is no use going to Italy in the summer in order to make a recovery; it is only good as a place to rest in after recovery! . . . Yet today, I feel—as a kind of reaction—a good effect from being in Italy.[39]

The feeling that time was pressing, intensified by the death of his father, prompted a rush of creativity. Did the frequent visits to Italy not also play their part in this increased creativity?

Busoni did not go to Trieste, nor did he write to his mother again until August 21,[40] when he was back in Berlin, and she was in Cividale di Friuli, a small town about fifty miles north of Trieste. (He addressed the letter to her hotel in Cividale, probably having learned of the address on his return to Berlin. He was glad that Ersilia was with her on holiday, he wrote, and he was sending 250 crowns—that inadequate assuager of guilt. "In your inexhaustible goodness and patience you will be able to forgive my long silence. I think it useless to list my reasons to you—it suffices as justification to state that they exist." On October 3, Anna Weiss-Busoni died, not unexpectedly; she had been fading since her husband's death in May. The laconic record in her son's diary,[41] which he had begun on January 1 that year, reads: "Madre †." The telegram from Trieste arrived only the following day, however, so the above diary entry was written a day late. The entry for October 4 reads: "*Telegramm aus Triest*" then, in English, "Our Lady of Sighs," a reference to a character in Thomas de Quincey's collection of essays, *Suspiria de Profundis*, which Busoni was reading at the time: the Mater Suspiriorum, not only the comforter of the outcast, but the visitor of every woman "sitting in darkness, without love to shelter her head, or hope to illumine her solitude." Anna had sighed her way through life (provoking many a sigh from her son—and, no doubt, her husband), humbly bearing her fate, at the same time exerting that subtle tyranny of the doggedly self-sacrificing. Poor Anna, forced all her life into molds of others' choosing, so that finally, like Byron's Prisoner of Chillon, she "learned to love despair." And suppress it, or at least control it, as he might, Busoni's grief, inevitably tinged with guilt (particularly as he had been in Italy that summer and had not visited her), was profound. As he wrote years later to his friend, the violinist Arrigo Serato (1877–1948),[42] whose father had just died, he never overcame the sense of loss, possibly colored forever by that serendipity of sometimes questionable benefit that leads us to be reading a particular book at a turning point in our lives. (It is strange that Busoni harks back here to his own mother's death, and not his father's, although it was Serato's father who had died.)

By mid-October Busoni was on tour again in England, a tour that lasted until early November and included, as stated above, the first performance of the Fantasy after Johann Sebastian Bach for Piano (BV 253) in memory of his father, on October 16. He went on to the Festival of Newcastle, where Egon Petri played his Piano Concerto (the complete version, with male chorus), Busoni conducting the London Symphony Orchestra; then Busoni went on to Manchester. During this strenuous tour he nevertheless continued composing, and on October 27 finished a *Berceuse élégiaque for Orchestra: Des Mannes Wiegenlied am Sarge seiner Mutter* (The Man's Cradle Song at His Mother's Coffin) (BV 252a), for chamber ensemble, in Anna's memory. This was in fact an extension of the Berceuse for Piano (BV 252) written in June, the latter to become the seventh in his Elegies for Piano (BV 249). In addition to de Quincey, Busoni's literary inspiration here was the Danish poet Oehlenschläger's *Aladdin*, which he was still considering turning into an opera. The poet's own mother had died while the play was being written. A berceuse would seem a strange choice for a memorial piece to his mother, but his reading matter, and perhaps his loneliness on this long tour, led his grief back to that first piano version, so that in the intervals between the concerts, "I was compelled to write the score, frequently working until deep into the night, in order to free my mind of it."[43]

It is an intensely moving piece, starting with the same right-hand motif, of a rising minor third, of the piano version, but the orchestration provides more subtle coloring, with different instruments taking up the slow, rocking rhythm. Busoni himself felt the work contained such innovatory elements that he wanted to delay publication until he had actually heard it. He wrote out the orchestral parts himself (a task he usually managed to bestow on a current amanuensis) within days of finishing the work, and on November 1 Henry Wood allowed him an hour with the Queen's Hall Orchestra in London to try it out. It provoked puzzlement, as it was unlike anything people had come to expect of Busoni, a reaction repeated when Oskar Fried gave the work a playthrough with the Berlin Philharmonic the next year. As the musicologist Hugo Leichtentritt recorded: "Its polytonality, its collisions of major and minor triads, its strange enervated harmony, its symphony of sighs appeared altogether novel in 1910."[44] According to Antony Beaumont, the work is "one of the unique compositions of our century and . . . Busoni's undisputed masterpiece."[45] The *berceuse* was published in 1910 but received its first public performance only on February 21, 1911, in New York, in a concert mainly of Italian music, conducted by Gustav Mahler (see page 240).

After his strenuous British tour, Busoni traveled on to Cologne, Basle, and Belfort. In his still exalted mood, he was particularly receptive to an almost mystical experience during the sea crossing:

The sky was clear when we started, and then I enjoyed the most remarkable picture I have seen in the whole of my life, perhaps. The splendor of the stars was magnificent and I was absorbed in looking at it. And—listen!—instead of the sky looking as it usually does, like a concave hemisphere, with little holes for light in the ceiling—all at once I saw endless space above, and the planets floating in it, some higher or lower, nearer or further away, in groups, cascades of varying intensity in light, color and size. It quite moved me, and then, as if man were not allowed to glance into such a mystery, suddenly a wall of fog arose on all sides and—my shadow fell on it![46]

In Cologne, on November 8, Busoni received the Italian translation of the first act of *Die Brautwahl* from Augusto Anzoletti. He was very pleased with it. Egon Petri had offered to see to the piano score, which pleased him even more.

In late December 1909 Ferruccio, Gerda, and the children crossed the Atlantic again, after a gap of five years, spending Christmas at sea. It was a bad crossing from which they all suffered. Nevertheless, on Christmas Eve Ferruccio went to the children's cabin and read them Andersen's "The Christmas Tree," which cannot have cheered them up much, it being one of the gloomy Dane's gloomiest efforts. On January 6 in New York Ferruccio played Liszt's arrangement for piano and orchestra of Schubert's *Wandererfantasie*, Gustav Mahler conducting, evoking this response from the *New York Post*: "The Philharmonic audience at Carnegie Hall last night enjoyed the equivalent of what in the opera house is called an all-star cast. One of the greatest living pianists played with a conductor who has no superior anywhere."[47] Mahler, who was conductor of the New York Philharmonic from 1909 until forced by illness to retire in 1911, attempted in that short time to do for new music in New York what Busoni was attempting in Berlin, introducing works by Debussy, Elgar, Enesco, Rachmaninov, Richard Strauss and, of course, Busoni.

After New York, a strenuous tour began, crisscrossing North America, as far north as Montreal, as far west as Denver, and as far south as New Orleans—further than Busoni had ever been before—and occasionally returning to New York. Gerda did not accompany him everywhere, often remaining in New York, and she and the children returned to Berlin at the end of February 1910. Busoni's tour continued until the end of April, with over forty performances. He missed Gerda terribly ("You leave a gap here and a most golden memory")[48] and each

232   Chapter Nine

of her letters was treasured. He filled in the longueurs between performances with work: the first plans emerged for his *Fantasia Contrappuntistica*, on "Bach's last and greatest work" (the Chorale Prelude
"Allein Gott in der Höh' sei Ehr"), as he termed it,[49] which was to assume many forms. During the Atlantic crossing to the United States,
in spite of storms and seasickness, he had continued working on a critical edition of Bach's *The Art of Fugue* as part of a projected complete
edition of Bach's keyboard compositions.

On January 1, still at sea, Busoni jotted down in a notebook an initial idea: "Out of the preceding 14 forms one could make up a *set of variations*, append the 'completed' *Fuga a 3 Soggetti* as a (concertante) finale and perhaps create a prelude out of the dubious Chorale." In order
to understand Bach's unfinished final fugue more thoroughly, he started
copying it out, jotting down notes as he went. In mid-January, in
Chicago, he ran into Bernhard Ziehn (1845–1912), composer and musicologist, whom he had first met in Leipzig, and also one of Ziehn's
pupils, the organist Wilhelm Middelschulte (1863–1943), both German by birth, but now settled in the United States. Busoni found Ziehn
particularly stimulating; he said of him later, "He is a theoretician who
points to the possibilities of undiscovered lands and trains Columbuses.
A prophet through logical conclusions. In particular as a master of harmony he stands alone."[50] Ziehn wrote several books on harmony and
other aspects of musical composition. In conversations with the two
men, not only did Busoni's ideas on what he called the "new
polyphony" begin to crystallize, but the concept of these two musical
theorists working in the shadow of Chicago's skyscrapers prompted him
to write an article for the German musical journal *Signale*, "The 'Gothics' of Chicago" (reprinted in the original German edition of *Wesen und
Einheit der Musik*, but not in the English edition). Ziehn and Middelschulte are these "Gothics," in Busoni's eyes upholders of the torch
of art and enlightenment in the barren canyons of cities dedicated to
the worship of Mammon, while "Americanization penetrates ever more
urgently into our ancient historic regions, while in Italy strange men,
without baring their heads, set up cinemas in churches, childish 'sport'
and ephemeral politics." The article is a gloriously full-blooded attack
on what Busoni perceived as shallow modern artistic values, comparing
the pure "Gothic" style with Victorian Gothic (now more often than

not employed when building railway stations), and by analogy Bach with Mendelssohn, works by medieval authors with nineteenth-century historical novels, "and—let's be honest—the whole Old Germanic business [*das ganze Altgermanentum*] of Wagner."[51] But can the highest art forms of a former time be brought to life again? Here Busoni narrows his focus to Bach, and the possibility of a resolution of some of Bach's ideas. Ziehn in particular helped Busoni, and both men stimulated him to turn his mind toward what was to become the *Fantasia Contrappuntistica* (BV 256). (Middelschulte in fact wrote an organ transcription of the work.) They inspired Busoni to write other articles for *Signale* and also led him to examine counterpoint again, and to experiment on the fourth subject of that quadruple fugue with which Bach had planned to complete *The Art of Fugue*. In one week Busoni managed to write eighteen "essays" on the first three of Bach's subjects in the final fugue, and then realized he could use these, plus other studies, for the *Fantasia*. By March 1, in New Orleans, he had finished what he called "this monster fugue,"[52] "the most important of my piano works."[53] "Yesterday and today toiled for a good nine hours on the Fugue," he noted in his diary on March 2. One hundred copies of this initial version, *Grosse Fuge: Contrapuntal Fantasy on the Last and Unfinished Fugue from the "Art of Fugue," BWV 1080, by Johann Sebastian Bach, for Piano* (BV 255), were printed privately in New York by Schirmer in time for Busoni's birthday on April 1 (which he spent in Colorado Springs). *Fantasia Contrappuntistica for Piano (edizione definitiva): Chorale Prelude "Allein Gott in der Höh' sei Ehr" and Fugue with Four Obbligato Subjects on a Fragment by Bach* (BV 256) was finished later that same year, in Leipzig, and both works were dedicated—with every justification—to Wilhelm Middelschulte. The first public performance of the latter, with Busoni at the piano, was on September 30, 1910, in Basle.[54]

Busoni also worked on a "little analysis"[55] of his *Turandot Suite* for Mahler, who was to conduct it in New York in March. With his usual generosity and unquestioning acceptance, Busoni saw through the difficult man Gustav Mahler and found the artist, and greatly prized what he found. Busoni was in New York for the concert. "What a pity you did not hear *Turandot* under Mahler," he wrote Gerda.[56] "With what love and unerring instinct this man rehearsed! Artistically, and humanly, it was both gratifying and warming." Alma Mahler came to Busoni's box afterward to persuade him to take a bow. "'Do go, give Gustav the pleasure.' And I went on the platform as shy and 'unused to it' as if I had never stood in front of an audience before."[57] The piece was not a critical success in New York, but that fact was brushed urbanely aside by its composer: "The papers did not wish to take it quite seriously, but the world is full of errors and misunderstandings." Arthur Farwell (1872–1952), however, writing for *Musical America*, took some trouble to understand the work:

> The whole work is distinctly spicy. Being primarily theatrical music, the separate movements scarcely give the impression of lucid, well-outlined and self-supporting musical form. One feels the theater back of the suite at almost every point. The composer has been happy in his choice of motives, and has worked them out with much elaboration, displaying extraordinary ingenuity in the orchestration. The latter is often as piquant as Ravel, and there are moments when one can almost imagine Busoni also to be an exponent of *pointillisme*.[58]

Busoni's attention had been alerted to the native North Americans by Natalie Curtis (1875–1921), who had studied harmony with him in New York years before, and who had spent some time living in close proximity to the Hopi tribe in particular, studying their culture. Curtis was one of a handful at the time of what we would today call ethnomusicologists, performing a valuable service in changing white attitudes toward the native peoples of North America, who, only a century ago, had been forbidden to perform their own music and ceremonies. Their plight, and their very different values—in particular compared to what Busoni perceived as the extreme materialism of white Americans—appealed strongly to the romantic in him. Natalie Curtis defied legal restrictions and collected their songs and legends, which she published, illustrated by photographs and designs, in a 550-page volume (*The Indians' Book*), a copy of which she had given Busoni after the concert in New York in 1910 when Mahler had conducted the *Turandot Suite*. Curtis's book was to be the main inspiration for Busoni's three works on "Red Indian" themes (see chapter 10), and led to a lengthy correspondence with Busoni, mainly on Native American music. While in Columbus, Ohio, Busoni went out of his way to contact some Native Americans himself:

I spoke to a Red Indian woman. She told me how her brother (a talented violinist) came to New York to try to make his way. "But he could not associate his ideas with the question of daily bread." How much good it does one to hear of such a sentiment in the United States!

Then she said that her tribe ought to have an instrument something like this: A hole should be dug in the earth and strings stretched all round the edges of it. I said (in the spirit of the Red Indians): An instrument like that ought to be called "the voice of the earth." She was quite enthusiastic about this.[59]

By the end of March Busoni was exhausted. From Des Moines he wrote:[60]

From the standpoint of a touring artist, the concert yesterday was very satisfactory—full house, a feeling of excitement and enthusiastic reviews. The heat had reached the highest point for the year. I was dead tired. But a beautiful piano, good acoustics, and the feeling of great expectation in the hall hypnotized me for the two hours I was on the platform.

From the standpoint of a thinking artist, no longer young, it was an unforgivable waste of strength, time and thought, which can never be recovered, in order to make a momentary impression on a small number of insignificant people.

In Chicago, with Middelschulte and Ziehn, Busoni had ascended the rarefied heights of a study of Bach's finest work; the contrast down in the lowlands of provincial performance was unbearable. His only therapy was in his thoughts and ideas, mostly contained in his flood of letters to Gerda, but there was the frustration of receiving no post from her, while she was on the voyage back to Europe. As he virtually always played familiar repertoire, he scarcely needed to practice, but there was the occasional revelation, demonstrating his scrupulous attitude: "I have also learned, at last, how to attack the first movement of the Waldstein Sonata that never went quite as I wished. And I have played it for almost thirty years!! These last two sentences ought to be written out and hung up in Conservatories."[61] Busoni often traveled with other star musicians in North America, few of whom came anywhere near his intellectual level, and most of whom he despised, for what he saw as their lack of intellectual vigor and their vanity—particularly female

opera singers: "Good God, the method they have here of turning people into celebrities makes one's heart sink into one's boots. Is it possible that such a small, ordinary person as Melba can really be a great
artist? Even from an 'opera singer's standpoint'? I cannot believe it, and
I have never heard of her being extraordinarily good in any of her
roles."[62] Even the great Polish pianist Ignacy Paderewski, who was also
a moderately successful composer in his time (Busoni had in fact included some of Paderewski's compositions in his repertoire), drew Busoni's scorn, or rather the excessive public adulation accorded him did.
The whole silly circus of the star system—then as now a fact of life for
those performing in public—humiliated him (even though it did mas-
sage his vanity). One impresario in the United States even tried to persuade him to stage a car accident to generate extra publicity. The "musical Ishmael," as Bernard van Dieren[63] quite shrewdly dubbed Busoni,
was tiring more and more of his wanderings.

The star system induced in Busoni a very negative outlook on the
hand that was feeding him—from a material point of view, at least. He
was appalled by the lack of information—and the lack of curiosity—in
the United States concerning the outside world, and tried to explain to
Hochmann, his piano tuner, some of the differences between the
United States and Europe:

> I tried to explain that in the old culture industrial inventions were the
> *result* of growing necessities. While in America an invention is made and
> a use for it is thought out afterward, so that the public can be made to
> feel that it is a necessity. How in Europe the railway arose from the de-
> sire among towns and nations to communicate with one another,
> whereas here the railways are made first and then the towns are built.[64]

There was a lot more criticism, much of it springing more from Busoni's dissatisfaction with his own life than from any dispassionate assessment of the country and its society. (And he was scarcely to know
that he was in many respects describing the future of the Western
world.) He was completely exhausted well before the end of the tour. By
March 17 he was ready to throw in the towel, "but Hanson [the agent]
will not let me off the Brooklyn Recital, April 28. There are six whole
weeks until then, which would be enough time for a big tour really. I
shall close my letter for today, for I am overtired and quite exhausted."[65]

But the letter was reopened: "I have opened the closed envelope again because your *extraordinarily* dear letter from Berlin has just come and been received with equal love by me. . . . Your dear words and feelings have given me the strength to go on further, when it was threatening to fail me." There were compensations in America, however. In Boston on April 12 there was a pleasant interlude when he visited Arnold Dolmetsch in nearby Cambridge. "He builds pianos, clavecins and clavichords. The clavecin (the English harpsichord) is magnificent. I made capital out of it at once and, first of all, brought the instrument into the *Brautwahl* (when Albertine accompanies herself on it) and, secondly, begged for one to be sent to Berlin."[66] And in Denver a few days later, Busoni was fascinated by the pioneering activity:

> to get here one has to travel across the steppes, past tents and young men on horseback, who are beginning a completely new life. With horses, pistols, tents and a couple of ploughs, they make a new way through difficult country. And these courageous, primitive instruments of civilization are badly nourished and have only the meanest pleasures of life to cheer them.[67]

And in a second long letter written the same day he suddenly observes: "A cowboy has just galloped past my window. I love having the desk at the window, one is alone and yet in contact with the outside world."[68] Even when exhausted, he never lost his lively interest in the world around him. And he always read voraciously; Strindberg was his rather cheerless reading matter for much of this tour.

Finally, on May 1, Busoni boarded the ship for Europe and home. The North American tour had been a triumph: in April the *Musical Courier* enthused that his playing had brought a new tone to concert life (and this in a country in which Paderewski had made concert tours on an almost annual basis since 1890). In the January issue the reviewer fell into the kind of hysterical gushing that affected not only Busoni's paying audiences but very many critics:

> It is practically impossible to speak of Busoni's stupendous pianism in the measured and limited terms of ordinary musical phraseology, and yet the very essence of his art is so musical that to drift into superlative comparisons outside of the strict realm of tone were to give the reader a

wrong impression of this astonishing man and the marvelous things he does. . . . The audience fairly hurled its applause at Busoni after each number and the "Don Juan" ended in a riot of cheers, hand clapping and foot stomping so clamorous that the hall appeared to shake with the cyclopean tumult.

(One should be cautious in evaluating the judgments of the *Musical Courier*: its offices and those of Martin H. Hanson, Busoni's American manager, were both at 437 Fifth Avenue in New York, and the European intermediary between Hanson and Busoni was Arthur M. Abell, the magazine's representative in Germany. As Marc-André Roberge has pointed out: "The magazine was noted at this time for praising individuals who advertised in its pages and condemning those who failed to do so."[69] Nevertheless, other reviews of Busoni's playing were also overwhelmingly positive.)

Where repertoire was concerned, Busoni was shrewd enough to accept that American audiences, particularly outside New York, Boston, and Chicago, wanted the familiar, staple fare—which meant few performances of his own work outside the three cities mentioned. He acted strategically to ensure some performances of his works in the United States, mainly through friendships with particular prominent musicians, during periods when he was touring there. Nevertheless, there were only eighteen concerts in the United States featuring Busoni's orchestral music between 1905 and 1924—a strong indication that, as popular and acclaimed as he was as a pianist, he was certainly not recognized as a composer, neither by the public nor by the critics. The latter, apart from being generally negative toward "modern" music, were often condescending. Louis Elson, for example, reviewing Karl Muck's performance of the *Geharnischte Suite* in Boston in 1906 for the *Boston Daily Advertiser*,[70] reveals his own prejudices:

Mr. Ferruccio Busoni has proved himself such a great student of Bach that we may assume that if he adopts the ultra-modern vein in his compositions he does it from choice and not from any inability to work in the accepted shapes. . . . While we emphatically do not like the school, we demand for Busoni the same respect that is accorded to other modern dissonancists. The more we get of this rambling, difficult, "impressionist" school, the better, for the fever will have sooner run its course.

It would have been interesting to know exactly how Elson defined a "dissonancist."

Back in Berlin, Busoni fell into an apathetic state, rousing himself in June for another highly successful visit to London. July and August were spent with his family in Berlin, and he worked hard at *Die Braut-wahl*. Egon Petri's piano score was more or less ready and was being fed to Breitkopf und Härtel. Busoni was urging Petri to come to Berlin, to travel with him to Leipzig to discuss printing the score, and to tour more, but Petri was now the father of two small children and preferred to spend most of his time in Manchester—a fact that drew considerable scorn from Busoni.

From September 1 Ferruccio gave master classes coupled with recitals at the Musikhochschule in Basle for one month (the year before, through his intercession, Egon Petri had taken the classes); on September 30 he gave the first performance there of his Sonatina for Piano, no. 1 (BV 257), which he had written a month before, and on October 4 Egon Petri played his Piano Concerto at the same venue, Busoni conducting. Busoni then toured to Strasbourg, Hamburg, and Vienna, with short stays in Berlin between. On December 20, 1910, he was on board the *Oceanic*, bound yet again for New York. ("Dreading the thought of America," he had written in his diary on November 6.) Again, Gerda accompanied him for the first few weeks. The mighty dollar was an irresistible attraction: on the trip earlier that year, he had received $700 to $1,000 gross per concert, and on this trip the fees were even higher.

(The children did not accompany them this time; Benni was now eighteen and Lello ten, and they were presumably being looked after by a housekeeper. There are occasional mentions of the children in Busoni's short diary entries: "Paris with B[enni]" on April 23, 1909, for example, but Benni and Lello in their childhood years remain shadowy figures. From their letters written as adults, many now in the State Library in Berlin, we find confirmation of their characters occasionally hinted at in the little extant evidence on their childhood. Busoni was an indulgent father in the sense of allowing the boys to follow their own inclinations, but his strong views and overpowering personality, his very existence, heavily influenced the development of Benni in particular, an oversensitive character full of resentment and ready to rebel.

In Rome in March 1909, replying to a letter from Gerda on Benni, Busoni gives a long list of what he thinks Benni should be reading: *Don Quixote*, Shakespeare, Dickens, among others, but not "these black, pessimistic, suicidal authors; no Lenau, Schopenhauer, Werther, Leopardi—the 'Suicide Club' of literature." The boy had early shown talent for drawing, and was now at the academy in Berlin. It was decided, on Egon Petri's recommendation, to send him to Worpswede for a few weeks in the summer of 1909, to study under the painter and graphic artist Heinrich Vogeler, who had provided the title page for Busoni's Piano Concerto. From 1909 on, Busoni sometimes took Benni with him on his travels. Lello was always a more sunny, balanced character, and caused his parents little anxiety.)

In Boston in February 1911, after Gerda had left again for Europe, Busoni heard Richard Strauss's *Don Quixote*:

> It is a work which has great qualities; commonplace in the lyrical places, unusually exciting in the grotesque parts, naive in a boorish way and yet on the other hand too cultivated: badly assembled as regards form, but the daring texture of the sound is excellent. On the whole, one of the most interesting works of our time and the richest in invention; perhaps the composer's best work. . . . I admit willingly that beside this work, *Turandot* . . . is less brilliant, and fortunately I have developed enough to be able to recognize this myself.[71]

In New York on February 21 Mahler conducted the world premiere of Busoni's *Berceuse élégiaque*, written in memory of his mother, at Carnegie Hall, in the first of two concerts of mainly Italian music. After two recalls for Mahler, Busoni was obliged to bow twice from his box. "The audience doesn't like the piece, but they like me,"[72] he remarked. According to Mahler's wife Alma it was Mahler's last appearance in public. At the second "Italian" concert, a repetition of the first, on February 24, Mahler was too ill to conduct and at two hours' notice Busoni was asked to step in to conduct the *Berceuse*. (The violinist Theodore Spiering, leader of the New York Philharmonic, conducted the rest of the concert, and stood in for Mahler until the end of the season.)

The legendary Italian conductor Arturo Toscanini (1867–1957) had been at the February 21 concert, and a few days later Busoni was his guest.

Last Sunday (the 26th) I was at Toscanini's. He lives in a private suite
in a big hotel and keeps his own Italian cook. It was the most pleasant
evening I have spent, since you left. The food was excellent and the conversation animated and interesting, right up to midnight.

Consolo[73] was there. I played them the Sonatina, the Mephisto Waltz,
the St. Francis legends. I was brought still more into the right atmosphere by a Steinway which thunders and *sustains the tone* (it is so long
since I've had that pleasure!). Toscanini is the most intelligent musician
I have met up until now (with perhaps the exception of Strauss).
Tremendously lively, quick, farsighted, and artistic.

He repeated whole pages out of my Aesthetic. I mean, he spoke my
thoughts and did not say one word I could not corroborate wholeheartedly. He seemed to have a particular sympathy for me, for (according to
Consolo) it is seldom he is so communicative.[74]

Toscanini had been artistic director of the Metropolitan Opera since
1908—he was to remain in the post until 1915—bringing that theater
to one of the high points in its history, imposing his discipline and high
artistic standards. In Italy, where he had become artistic director at La
Scala Milan in 1898, at the age of thirty-one, and worked with other
orchestras on often adventurous programs of opera and orchestral music, he had put his phenomenal energies into raising musical standards
in his country, as he was to continue to do all his life, whenever circumstances permitted.

Busoni was feeling ill at the end of February, but still had five weeks'
touring to endure, including this time his first visit to the West Coast—
"I played yesterday, four hours after my arrival from a twenty-hour journey [from Los Angeles]," he wrote[75] from San Francisco. "I have to
travel another thirty-two hours from here to Seattle! . . . Chickering [his
agent], without any scruple, wished to send me to Honolulu. . . . 'It is a
very interesting trip,' he said. . . . I feel as if I were being posted like a
parcel." In spite of his exhaustion, he was reading as avidly as ever (H. G.
Wells's newly published *The New Machiavelli*, among other things), cor-
responding with Natalie Curtis about using "Red Indian" motifs in a
composition, and writing down some thoughts on "Melody belongs to
the future," which he enclosed in a letter to Gerda from Los Angeles.[76]
These thoughts, and other ideas jotted down in letters to Gerda, were
subsequently turned into an essay with the same title, included in both

the German and the English versions of *The Essence of Music*. Busoni viewed the remote provincialism of the West Coast, and the (to him) exasperating and equally remote nationalism of the German and Italian colonies there with a very sardonic eye.

In New York on April 8 he boarded the ship for Europe. Alma and Gustav Mahler were on board, and the logorrheic Austrian writer Stefan Zweig (1881–1942), who was to write extensively on Busoni in his various volumes of memoirs. Mahler was very ill and kept mostly to his cabin. In 1907 a heart condition had been diagnosed, but now he was suffering from a bacterial infection of the throat and lungs that was to kill him just over a month after they landed in Europe. Alma Mahler's not always reliable memoirs give us a glimpse of Busoni at his most attractive:

> Busoni was on board. He sent Mahler crazy specimens of counterpoint to amuse him, and also bottles of wine. Busoni had a really good heart. He and I walked on deck together one day while Mahler was sleeping. He loved him and talked of him all the time. "The Germans," he said, "are a funny lot. Even now they have not absolutely put the stamp on Mahler's genius. They blow hot and cold. They don't really know anything about him. But if he—if he were taken from them, ah, then—!"[77]

After Mahler's death, Alma Mahler chose Busoni as one of the trustees for a fund organized in Mahler's name for young musicians. Richard Strauss and Bruno Walter were the other trustees.

"Berlin!!!" was the eloquent opening entry to Busoni's diary in May. "Sundays in the city. Daily 4–5 pages of score." "Joy of creation," he notes in June, "thoughts stream out, work flows." He was to give no more concerts until mid-October. He was alone in Berlin for July, working on *Die Brautwahl* and reading—Balzac's letters and a book on Buddhism, which prompted the following:

> I have reached the point now of regarding teaching, philosophies and religions as works of art, and I side with the art that has the best preacher. I hardly think that the individual will be happier or wiser for any of them, among the masses. I've found that the shoemaker in the Bible, in the Thousand and One Nights, or in ancient Rome, is always the same shoemaker. And the artists, the priests and the whores are the same.

When a soldier with a Bible in his left hand strikes out in anger; or a
Saracen cuts off heads while talking about Mahomet; it is exactly the
same thing.[78]

Not exactly original thinking, this little outburst also betrays a pessimistic contempt for humanity at large. And a subsequent letter reveals how Busoni was influenced by the many ideas that were rolling
around the decks of Europe at this time like so many loose cannons, before some of them were caught and held by the chains of Fascism. This
is not to suggest that Busoni would have subscribed to Fascism: his aristocratic disdain held him from that, if nothing else. And he was no
gullible fool, as his reactions in the early 1920s to the growing menace
were to prove. Hindsight is a wonderful thing, but we should be wary
of condemning those in the early decades of the twentieth century
whose attention was engaged, often only fleetingly, by ideas that ultimately led to horror. Such as the following:

> Now, in this era, I see a real supremacy of its "three powers":
> Money,
> Industry,
> Sport.
> After that, Jewish activity threatens to be supreme; the wish to pull
> individuals out of the masses and to stamp the individual into the
> masses. Money and Socialism are trying to eat each other up, like
> Siegfried and Fafner; Fafner and Siegfried.
> Industry, with its noble aims of cheapness, quickness and mass pro-
> duction, is quixotic.[79]

It would be pointless to ignore what today would be described as anti-
Semitic in the above, and it was not the only time that Busoni came out
with anti-Jewish sentiments—and anti–African American, for that
matter: in his letters from North America, there are disparaging references to "niggers" that strike us today as extremely offensive (although
he also sent to Egon Petri a shocking newspaper account of the lynch-
ing of some African Americans, as a warning as to the worst side of
American society). The indefensible cannot, logically, be defended, and
many of Busoni's views are indefensible—including, for that matter, his
firmly held view throughout his life that "an intellectual woman" was a

contradiction in terms: a view held in spite of the fact that most of his ideas were shared first and foremost with his wife. Another regrettable strand in his nature was lack of sympathy for the underdog. Sometimes he was lucky enough to have the disastrous end results of some lines of thought made clear to him: in April 1912 he was reading *L'Ève future* by Villiers de l'Isle-Adam (1838–1889), a novel published in 1886. Its author took a very skeptical view of the current belief in human and technological progress, in this novel of an artificial woman allegedly superior in every way to a real woman. Busoni was aghast to realize that in the novel many of his own ideas were shown to be "so discouraging as to make one want to give up completely. The tragical aspect for me is that in this diabolical work I find my own views carried through to the final—unsuspected—consequence and I myself am horrified by it."[80] Goethe's poem "The Sorcerer's Apprentice" and Mary Shelley's *Frankenstein* had, of course, already warned of the dangers of "playing God," but *L'Ève future* was explicitly referring, in what is essentially a three-hundred-page monologue, to modern scientific advances.

At the end of July Gerda returned to Berlin from a month's holiday in Göhren, on the Baltic, and on August 9 Busoni's cousin Ersilia came from Trieste on a visit. At the end of the month Busoni was in Basle with Gerda and both boys, then went on to Milan with Benni, leaving him then with the Anzolettis in Bergamo, where the nineteen-year-old stayed until the end of October. Busoni himself only stayed until mid-September and, as usual when he was not working and supposed to be resting, he became querulous and slept badly. But he did not lose his sense of humor completely.

> There is a new entertainment building. . . . Among the attractions are—roller skating. . . . They irritated me so much there, with their stupid, vain faces and the lifeless carriage of their bodies, that with my whole soul I wished one of them might tumble and do himself some injury. Five minutes later, the "Master" fell and tore his left trouser leg completely in two at the knee. Was it my fault? "They will say you have the evil eye," said Anzoletti.[81]

In Berlin in October, Busoni finished the *Brautwahl* full score, but was cast down by the news from Hamburg that the premiere had been put off until February 1912 (in fact it finally took place on April 13). Then he was off touring: Wiesbaden, Strasbourg, Basle, Heidelberg.

On October 27 came the premiere of Karl Vollmoeller's adaptation of Carlo Gozzi's *Turandot*, at the Deutsches Theater, directed by Max Reinhardt, with Busoni's *Turandot Suite*, rearranged, plus the two new pieces, *Verzweiflung und Ergebung* (BV 248a) specially written for this production. This was the second stage of the work that was finally to become the opera *Turandot* in 1917. As Busoni wrote in the *Blätter des Deutschen Theaters*, the theater's house magazine, he used only Gozzi's original Italian text as reference, and based the music solely on oriental motifs. The convention of masks current in Venetian theater builds a bridge leading to this imagined Orient, reinforcing the stylization and what a later generation in Berlin would call the *Verfremdungseffekt* (alienation effect). All of this, in Busoni's opinion, is totally absent in Schiller's version.

Reviews were mixed, and one of Berlin's leading theater critics, Siegfried Jacobsohn, was particularly damning in his judgment of Busoni's contribution: "It could have been so wonderful!" Jacobsohn begins his review, then goes on to say what is *right* about the production, praising Vollmoeller's translation as far superior to Schiller's, with one or two carping exceptions.

> But neither because of this nor in general is Vollmoeller to blame for the slowly languishing effect of this artistically ambitious evening. Rather Busoni. Certainly, Gozzi himself prescribed music. Busoni provides too much and, perhaps, for this light play, too heavy music. (I judge it here as theater critic, not as musician.) It does not prime [*untermalt*] but paints over [*überpinselt*]. It is not always in the service of "Turandot," but at times in the service of itself. Beethoven does that too in "Egmont" and Mendelssohn in "A Midsummer Night's Dream." But it is precisely this memory that is most dangerous for Busoni. Ultimately his instrumentation—the sixty-strong orchestra terrified me from the outset—is almost throughout too loud.[82]

The criticism is undeniably justified. (Reinhardt also came in for criticism for overloading the stage with visual delights.)

In mid-March 1912 Busoni was yet again in London, his mood fluctuating: "Now Sunday has come; reflection of the English nation; amputation of life. . . . Everything repeats itself; London and Sunday; exhaustion and books. Just as it was ten years ago."[83] But two days before, he had found a first edition of *Gulliver's Travels*: "It cost seventy marks, but it is worth it and may increase in value,"[84] he rationalized the outlay. And on March 18 he went to an exhibition of the Italian futurist painters. "Boccioni seems to me to be the strongest of them; he has a picture called 'The Rising City' which is truly great."[85] Umberto Boccioni (1882–1916) was soon to become a friend, and later painted Busoni's portrait (see chapter 11, pp. 293ff.). Busoni, after much wavering, bought "The Rising City" (now in the Museum of Modern Art in New York) when the exhibition reached Berlin later in the year. The futurists were a lively group of young Italian artists and writers, led by the writer Filippo Marinetti (1876–1944), who had published a futurist literary manifesto in *Le Figaro* in Paris on February 20, 1909. It was a hotheaded incitement to reject traditionalism, destroy all institutions that preserve the past, and glorify the present, in particular speed, power, violence, and war (in 1915 Marinetti wrote a pamphlet urging Italian intervention in the war, and in 1924, in *Futurismo e fascismo*, earned the support of the nascent Fascist Party in Italy). In February 1910 the painters and sculptors in the group published in Milan their own "Manifesto of the Futurist Painters." The ever open-minded Busoni was attracted by their zest and enthusiasm, but viewed their wilder excesses with more than a little skepticism. His tenuous connection with the futurists, and his open-minded attitude toward them, was to cause him some difficulties in the coming years. But Busoni's main preoccupation at this time was the imminent premiere of *Die Brautwahl* in Hamburg.

Busoni had begun work on his opera *Die Brautwahl* (The Bride Choice) in 1905, by writing an initial version of the libretto, published in 1907 with the first version of *Entwurf einer neuen Ästhetik der Tonkunst* (see p. 196), beginning the music the next year. This was written in snatches, very often during long concert tours, with long lapses between: "Those old friends Thusmann and Leonhard [characters in the opera] are coming out of hibernation. They stretch, yawn and turn round before actually getting up," he wrote to Gerda[86] in April 1908 from Vienna. And in June the same year: "I sweat over my little love duet—today it is beginning to 'dawn.'"[87] "The trouble was in the text," he writes two days later.[88] "The 'sitting for the portrait' had to go, it would have torn the threads. Now the duet is finished! Everything is running smoothly now." (The epilogue was finished in 1908 in England; the last page of the short score is signed "1.2.3 December, Hull-York-Doncaster.")

The story is taken from E. T. A. Hoffmann's *Die Serapionsbrüder* (The Serapiontic Brotherhood), a collection of twenty-eight tales published in 1819–1820, chronicles of the meetings of a fictional group of friends who call themselves *Serapionsbrüder* (based in part on a group of Hoffmann's friends who actually called themselves by this name), who tell fantastic tales and discuss them—the best-known internationally being "Nutcracker and Mouse King," thanks largely to Tchaikovsky's ballet. The book was written in the heyday in Germany of societies, associations, and circles: with a press censored almost to the point of creating an informational vacuum, and with other restrictive laws aimed at stifling political activity, these groupings were—consciously or unconsciously—a refuge where like-minded people could express their ideas, in the case of the fictional Serapiontic Brotherhood, via their chronicles, a device used in other great collections of stories such as the *Thousand and One Nights*, Boccaccio's *Decamerone*, and Chaucer's *Canterbury Tales*. (Hoffmann was not the only writer to take refuge in the fantastic during this period in Germany; Goethe, and most of the German Romantics, did so too.)

Serapion, according to Hoffmann in the first of the tales, is a man originally from a bourgeois German family who, for very complicated reasons, has become a hermit, identifying with a second-century namesake (in fact, more than one Serapion features in early Christian history), and claiming to have met Ariosto, Dante, and Petrarch. "Time is a concept just as relative as number," he asserts (a century before Albert Einstein). This is the "serapiontic principle" that runs through all the tales: to reach beyond human limitations, all one needs is imagination. And here we already see why Hoffmann's tales appealed to Busoni, the eternal investigator into new possibilities. Following this principle, Hoffmann translates ancient myths into his own time; many of the tales—*Die Brautwahl* is one—are even set in Hoffmann's Berlin.

Of all the fantastic tales in *Die Serapionsbrüder*, "Die Brautwahl," is certainly not the one best adapted to dramatic treatment, nor an obvious choice for Busoni, who altered it considerably when writing the libretto, and switched the sequence of some of the action, to clarify an extremely confusing plot, albeit with limited success. To follow Busoni's version: in an open-air restaurant in the Tiergarten, a huge park in Berlin, the young painter Edmund Lehsen contrives an introduction to *Kommissionsrat* (Commissioner counsellor) Voswinkel in order to be presented to Voswinkel's daughter Albertine. The two fall instantly in love. Leonhard, Edmund's patron, appears and decides to further this development.

It is night; *Geheimer Kanzlei-Sekretär* (Privy Chancellery-Secretary) Thusman is hurrying home past the town hall. He notices Leonhard banging on the door of the clock tower. A figure appears at an upper window: Albertine. Leonhard explains to Thusman that this is a vision that only appears at the autumn equinox and it means that by the next spring that girl will be the happiest bride in Berlin. He leads Thusman off.

In a wine cellar an old Jew, Manasse, is alone. Leonhard and Thusman enter and the latter announces he is going to get married. Manasse says he is too old and ugly, but Thusman says he has a secret weapon: Thomasius's *Brief Outline of Political Expediency*, in particular chapter 6 (chapter 7 in Hoffmann—why the alteration?), dealing with marriage and how to approach it, from which he quotes at length, provoking Manasse to curse him. Leonhard tells the story of Lippold the Jewish coiner, who was executed in 1572 for forging gold coins (a historical event). Thusman suddenly realizes he knows the girl at the window and says he is going to woo her. Leonhard pretends to be angry and warns him off, his face meanwhile changing into that of a fox. Manasse takes a huge radish out of his pocket and cuts it into slices that turn into gold ducats. Leonhard picks them up and they vanish. The two men terrify Thusman more and more with their tricks until he rushes off.

Act 2 begins in Voswinkel's house, where he is admiring his own portrait, painted by Lehsen. Thusman enters and gives an account of the previous night. Voswinkel dismisses the story as drunken ravings. Manasse enters and announces that his nephew, who has recently been granted a noble title, is pressing for Albertine's hand. After he has left, Voswinkel tells Thusman he forgives him his drunken evening and asks him to marry his daughter.

In another room, Albertine is with Lehsen, allegedly sitting for her portrait. As they embrace, Thusman enters. Lehsen paints a green

stripe over Thusman's face. Voswinkel enters and there is pandemo-
nium. Leonhard arrives and threatens that unless Thusman withdraws
his suit he will never remove the green stain. Manasse returns with his
nephew, Baron Bensch, who makes crude advances to Albertine. Leonhard catches the fainting girl, and claps his hands three times, which
makes the others dance till they are exhausted.

Thusman, still with a green face, joins the frogs in a pond in the Tiergarten; he throws the Thomasius book into the pond, and attempts suicide by drowning. Leonhard appears and stops him, then turns his face
back to its normal color, but only on the condition that Thusman gives
up any idea of marrying Albertine, otherwise he will be turned permanently into a frog. There follows a three-caskets scene à la *The Merchant
of Venice*, in which Thusman, Baron Bensch, and Edmund Lehsen have
to make their choice in order to win Albertine's hand (this is the "bride-
choice" of the title). Lehsen, inevitably, wins, but then in the opera's final moments sets off alone for Rome and a great future as an artist.

The end of Busoni's opera is some way before Hoffmann's end, in
which Lehsen and Albertine both cool off during his year in Rome and
it is indicated that she has found another young admirer. Much of Hoffmann's at times admittedly rather heavy-handed lampooning of social
foibles is also sacrificed, but the essential mood is preserved. This is not
surprising: Busoni's large library contained not only rare first editions of
Hoffmann's work, but also a large body of secondary literature. He himself eventually became an acknowledged authority on Hoffmann and,
according to Egon Petri, almost came to believe he was a reincarnation
of the earlier poet and composer. There were similarities in their characters, not least in their fascination with the grotesque. Like Busoni,
Hoffmann at times sought refuge in the bottle, that bottomless source
of fantasy, and in the anonymity of the tavern. No wonder Busoni identified with him from an early age; his first musical composition drawn
from Hoffmann dates from his midteens: "Klein Zaches" (from Hoffmann's novella of the same name), one of three "Character Pieces for
Piano" with the title *Racconti fantastici* (BV 100).

And Hoffmann, like Busoni, was also a polymath who wrote copi-
ously on the future of opera and the spiritual significance of music. "Is
not music the mysterious language of a distant realm of the spirit, whose
wonderful accents echo within us and awaken a higher, intensive life?"

Hoffmann wrote in his essay "The Poet and the Composer"—sentiments that found favor with Busoni. In fact the last act of Busoni's *Die Brautwahl* ends with a kind of apotheosis of art: "Deus et ars et natura / Vera sunt trinitas," sings an invisible chorus; art and nature are the true trinity, and Leonhard (Hoffmann, Busoni), the teacher and guide, sends the young artist off to Rome.

In his libretto to *Die Brautwahl*, Busoni unfortunately presupposes a knowledge of Hoffmann's original text equal to his own, as he refers to events and facts in Hoffmann's tale omitted in his opera; this at times makes the opera's meaning impenetrable to the average audience. The abridgement is clumsy in other ways: Busoni leaves in the constant repetitions of pretentious titles—a German predilection heavily satirized by Hoffmann, and certainly still prevalent in Busoni's day. This can be amusing on the page, but dramatic demands are different. And the opera contains too many longueurs, when dramatic tension slackens disastrously; this is particularly true for the interlude after the first scene between Thusmann and Leonhard at the clock tower, for example, as they are on their way to the tavern. It could have been inserted to allow time for a scene change, but it slows down the tempo.

It had been difficult enough to pin down an opera house to premiere the work. Before it was finished, Busoni had touted it unsuccessfully in Italy: even though his friend Augusto Anzoletti had translated the libretto into Italian, Ricordi declined it. There had been negotiations with Angelo Neumann at the New German Theatre in Prague in 1909, with Otto Klemperer willing to conduct, which led to nothing. Busoni had offered it to Hans Richter in London, to be told, "One doesn't perform that kind of thing!" Busoni alleged that Toscanini was interested in a New York production, but that also came to nothing. Finally, in 1910 the Stadt-Theater in Hamburg had agreed to stage the premiere.

However, the Hamburg premiere was also bedeviled: a contract had been signed with the Harmonie Verlag to publish full score, vocal score, and libretto. Given the unexpected length of the full score (over seven hundred pages), Harmonie decided to postpone publication, but Busoni continued to send sections to the engravers, which landed him in debt to the tune of some 10,000 marks; a protracted legal battle began, which Busoni eventually lost. (The piano score was published in 1912, but the full score only in 1914.)

Another complication was the music: the six years over which it was written was a period in which Busoni's style underwent significant changes, not always reconciled in the work. Half of it was written before the Elegies; the rest before the *Berceuse élégiaque*: both significant milestones in his development as a composer. Furthermore, the music is eclectic in a literal sense, in that music from other composers and sources is quoted directly: the band in the park in the opening scene, for example, plays excerpts from Rossini's *Moses in Egypt* (to underline the Jewish Voswinkel's travails with his cigar) and Mozart's German Dances, and interspersed here is a—for today's audiences—rather offensive parody of American black slave music when Voswinkel is singing in praise of cigars ("*Ja, wir sind recht musikalisch,/ob der Ton auch kannibalisch*"). Innovative and witty though the music is, and with lushly melodic passages that rival those of Richard Strauss, the opera as a whole is spiked with perhaps too many subtle musical allusions, evidence of a somewhat lugubrious humor, possibly too erudite for its own good. In act 1, part 2, which begins with the old Jew Manasse sitting in the wine cellar, the music is all based on old Jewish melodies, and when the caskets are brought in at the end of the opera, Busoni quotes a motif from Giacomo Carissimi's oratorio *Jephte*, in which a daughter is betrayed and sold by her father. How many would have caught these allusions? And, more pertinently, how relevant are they to the work's accessibility, not to mention dramatic impulse? Usually an audience can meditate on a new work's deeper meanings afterward, possibly with the aid of a weighty (in every sense) program; Busoni expected his audience to come to the opera house already fully primed.[89]

His total lack of practical experience in the opera house (he was now forty-six, and this was his first completed and performed opera), where the sheer mechanics of writing for this particular form are consciously and unconsciously absorbed, certainly militated against the work's success, both intrinsically and with the public. The most interesting music is going on in the orchestra: the voice is definitely not of paramount importance. When the fussy bureaucrat Thusman is hurrying past the clock tower, his orchestral accompaniment of rapid, staccato wind instruments is witty and accurate, but Thusmann's vocal line less so. And giving a different musical character to each figure is too subtly done— at least on first hearing—if we compare it to Mozart's *Don Giovanni*, where, to take just one example, there is no doubt when Don Giovanni is singing, and when Leporello is (a fact which—ironically—Busoni specifically drew attention to in his essay on *Don Giovanni* published in the *Neue Zeitschrift für Musik* in 1887).

Busoni's approach to the text was almost exclusively literary, with little regard for what is dramatically effective. Even his knowledge of his beloved commedia dell'arte was mostly derived from books. *Die Brautwahl* smells of the lamp, and it is this, more than its lack of dramatic thrust, or its subject matter, that makes directors shy away from it even today. "Imagine," he had written to Gerda[90] from Berlin back in the summer of 1907,

today I found a sort of "History of Berlin" that actually contains a picture, after an old engraving, of the "Execution of the notorious Court- and Mint-Jew [*Hof- und Münzjuden*] Leuppoldt," as well as a portrait of a "Leonhardt Thurneisser," goldsmith from Thurn, in his forty-fifth year (a beautiful face). The Jew's portrait, too, is inserted in the picture of the execution; it shows a very clever head, sharp features, and almost Arabic character. They tortured him dreadfully and, unfortunately, after he had borne so many cruelties there could be no doubt about his death.[91] As artists I love both these figures very much and, while I am working, I am constantly adding little characteristic traits. I feel almost certain now that the *Brautwahl* will be effective. I am quite impatient, for example, to show you "the privy chancellery secretary Thusman's improbable report," now it is finished.

Endearing though his enthusiasm is, the insatiable polymath was led up side alleys a little too often for the good of his opera. (He not only was reading Villiers de l'Isle-Adam's *L'Ève future* [see p. 244] a week before the premiere of *Die Brautwahl*, but devoted several paragraphs to it in two letters[92] to Egon Petri of April 5 and 6!)

By late March 1912 Busoni was in Hamburg to attend rehearsals of his opera, with which he was in general satisfied, though with inevitable fluctuations of mood. "Frl. 'Albertine' would like to accompany herself on the piano; but I hope to prevent this!" he observed caustically on March 25.[93] ("Albertine" was sung by Elisabeth Schumann [1888–1952], at that time, aged twenty-four, still at the beginning of what was to be an illustrious career.) Busoni had little idea of the practicalities of opera production, and consequently little patience with any of those involved who did not reach his standards. "I am extremely glad you are coming tomorrow," he wrote to Gerda[94] a week before the premiere, in the last of a series of daily letters from Hamburg. "The more work that is put into everything for the opera, the more insecure it all becomes. The singing was fine when they were alone; with the orchestra—not so good; on stage—even worse. Each one adds his own little inaccuracies and in the end there is a whole mass of them. The last two days I have been quite crushed."

Busoni was not satisfied at all with the production, as he wrote to his friend Robert Freund, who had been at the premiere and sent his impressions to Busoni. After criticisms of the singers he states. "The style of the production was wrong from the outset. It should have been more subtle, *less realistic*, more with the character of an illustrated book, of a puppet play. The technical means of the old theatre in Hamburg were inadequate to realize the magic scene."[95]

The opera was a critical success at its first performance in Hamburg on April 13, 1912, conducted by Gustav Brecher, but it ran for only four performances. An abridged version was staged a year later in Mannheim, conducted by Artur Bodanzky (again without much success), and then not again in any form until 1926 in Berlin, two years after Busoni's death. Since then the opera has had relatively few stagings, the most recent being at the Staatsoper in Berlin in 1992, a production by Nicolas Brieger, conducted by Daniel Barenboim, revived in December 1999. (Its lampooning of Jewish characters causes some squeamishness today, although nearly everyone in the opera is ruthlessly lampooned.)

After the premiere the Busonis returned to Berlin, and on April 22 all four left for Italy. They visited the Anzolettis in Bergamo, then went on to Milan, Florence, Bologna, and Rome, as part of a concert tour. In Bologna they saw a performance by masked actors of an old *commedia dell'arte* play of 1692, *L'inutile precauzione*. The play contained a Harlequin (Arlecchino), triggering off an idea in Busoni's mind for another opera, which finally emerged as *Arlecchino*. "The Arlecchino was a very effective figure; it was played by an actor [Emilio Picello] who conferred on him an almost monumental character. None of the low comedy of the German (into which—for example—my Thusman also fell)."[96]

The Faust legend was simmering away in the background too, fed by Busoni's reading of Marlowe's play *The Tragical History of Doctor Faustus* (sent to him by Edward Dent), but as yet nothing concrete had emerged. By mid-May Busoni was back in Berlin, where he stayed until August. In July Gerda had gone to Ringenberg, near Interlaken in Switzerland, and Ferruccio used his time in Berlin well, finishing a *Brautwahl* Suite for Orchestra (BV 261), the Sonatina Seconda for Piano (BV 259), and a minor edition of the *Fantasia Contrappuntistica* (BV 256a); he also finished the editing and revision of Franz Liszt's Fantasia on Two Themes from Mozart's *Le Nozze di Figaro* (BV B 66).

Frank Wedekind (1864–1918), the controversial German playwright, best known in the opera world as the author of the original two plays on which Alban Berg was to base his opera *Lulu*, had approached Busoni via Karl Vollmoeller at around this time to write twelve numbers as incidental music for a new play, *Franziska*, a Faust parody. After protracted negotiations, during which by all accounts Busoni acted somewhat deviously, the project was abandoned. The rebellious Wedekind, whose life included a spell in prison for writing satirical poems about Kaiser Wilhelm II and sexual adventures that rivaled those in his plays, would have been a somewhat incongruous artistic collaborator for the bookish Busoni.

Vollmoeller also featured in preliminary negotiations between Busoni and the Italian poet Gabriele D'Annunzio on an opera collaboration. D'Annunzio and Busoni first met in Paris in August that year. Almost at the opposite end of the spectrum from the earthy Wedekind, the languid superaesthete D'Annunzio would nevertheless have been an equally unlikely collaborator for Busoni. Ultimately, Busoni wrote all his own opera libretti, which was their weakness and their strength. Their artistic cohesion contributed to their power, but the input from another artistic source might have made them more accessible.

Busoni had given himself a week's semiholiday in Paris in order to meet D'Annunzio, and he had had the idea of moving to Paris, and was looking for a house to buy. The latter plan came to nothing, as the house in question would, he found, need as much spent on it again as the purchase price in order to be habitable. A collaboration with D'Annunzio was still in the cards.

That autumn the touring continued: in early October to Britain, where Busoni played his Second Violin Sonata (BV 244) in Liverpool with the great violinist Fritz Kreisler; Busoni also played in London, Bedford, Eastbourne, Glasgow, and Edinburgh. Then he went on to Saint Petersburg, Moscow, and Riga (Gerda was with him in Russia for part of the time), and in January 1913 to London yet again, where Vollmoeller's version of *Turandot* was performed at the Saint James's Theatre, in the Max Reinhardt production and using Busoni's music. Typically, Busoni apparently fled after two acts. He stayed, as often, with his former Weimar piano pupil Maud Allan (1873–1956), now a well-known dancer in the Isadora Duncan mode living in some splendor in an apartment at West Wing, part of Holford House, a huge villa overlooking Regent's Park. A few years before, Maud Allan's career had taken a sensational upward turn in London, and for several years she earned vast sums of money and also entered high society. Around 1909 she persuaded Margot Asquith, the independently wealthy wife of Herbert Asquith, the Liberal prime minister, to pay the lease on West Wing, an arrangement that continued for some twenty years. (There is some evidence that Busoni had an affair with Maud Allan. She was not the only one, but after Busoni's death, Edward Dent, his first biographer, and Gerda between them destroyed virtually all incriminating evidence, in order to present a very sanitized version of Busoni's life.) Busoni was back in England in March, again staying with Maud Allan, for whom he sketched out a scenario for her to dance to, then in Italy for April and May.

In Milan he gave a series of eight piano recitals (which he dubbed his "Octomerone") at the Verdi Conservatory, covering the entire repertoire; the last recital, on May 12, was devoted to his own works, including the first performance of his Sonatina Seconda (BV 259), which created an uproar. What were perceived as the futurist overtones of the Sonatina Seconda were objected to. Filippo Marinetti, founder of the literary wing of the futurist movement, came to blows with protesters, but apparently it all ended well, with a dinner afterward at which Toscanini, Marco Enrico Bossi, Filippo Marinetti, Umberto Boccioni, and the composer Leone Sinigaglia (1868–1944) were also present.

Busoni then went on to Mannheim, where the premiere of the shortened version of *Die Brautwahl* took place on May 24, conducted by Artur Bodanzky. There was a perceptive review (if in well-nigh impenetrable prose) in the *Kölnische Zeitung*:

> The opera possesses "artistic attraction." In the final scenes it overindulges in artistic language and in its opposite, kitsch: what cannot be defined is considered artistic. . . . Leaving aside the adjective "artistic," let us say that *Die Brautwahl* demonstrates a personality of great fascination which, however, applies itself above all to the intellect and culture of the listener, not to his feelings, and in fact is based on Busoni's surprising mastery in manipulating the elements of art: if one will, then, on a great artistic ability. . . . To the question of whether this opera is endowed with vitality one must answer in the negative, even after this performance: because it disregards the audience's desire for beauty and warmth, in favor of an interesting ugliness. But it constitutes a valuable contribution to the enrichment of modern means of expression, and can be fearlessly considered a manual worthy of being used for this purpose.[97]

In Paris again in June, Busoni visited D'Annunzio. They had further discussions, this time on collaborating on an opera on Leonardo. D'Annunzio was uninterested, thinking Leonardo too passionless a figure for the stage ("a brain, borne by a skeleton, like a burning light in a lantern"),[98] until Busoni described Leonardo as "an Italian Faust." "There I had him where I wanted him to be."[99]

Busoni went to the Châtelet theater to see D'Annunzio's latest play, *La Pisanelle*, with music by Ildebrando Pizzetti. Yet again, Busoni left before the end—a rather startling move for someone intending to collaborate with D'Annunzio. He described it all derisively in a long letter to Gerda:

> I was so tired and so irritated that I went out in the rain. . . . The rue de Rivoli, with its long row of lamps (one in every arch) looked almost gruesome. . . . The whole play seemed old-fashioned, declamatory, pathetic and motley; full of excitable gestures, long tirades, inexplicable stabbings, deaths, and screams. . . . On the other hand, it may be a masterpiece, and I may be revealing myself as unappreciative.[100]

His hard training in life always made him look at D'Annunzio's posing with a sardonic eye. Telling Gerda of a conversation in which D'Annunzio told him how unhappy he was, he ended: "D'Annunzio looked quite blissful as he added, 'For how could I create if I were not unhappy!'"[101]

Busoni vacillated for a few more days regarding a collaboration with D'Annunzio: he found the man ludicrous, but admired the artist. He realized that the intimacy of a close artistic collaboration was scarcely feasible—"to me his feeling for the mystical and his practical ideas are incongruous"[102] was one objection—and D'Annunzio seemed to be getting cold feet too: "All the same, he is quite right when he says, 'Why should we plague ourselves for three or four years, when we can do nothing with the work when it is finished?'"[103] It does not sound as though either of them had much faith in the project. Busoni escaped back to Berlin, and no more was heard of it.

But the idea of reviving Italian music continued, although soon political events were to overturn everyone's plans.

Notes

1. Letter from FB to Ludwig von Bösendorfer, December 22, 1906, StBB Bus. Nachl. BI, 282a.

2. Letter from FB to Gerda Busoni, March 15, 1907, StBB Bus. Nachl. IV 573.

3. Ernest Newman, review of *Entwurf einer neuen Ästhetik der Tonkunst*, *Birmingham Post*, August 24, 1907.

4. Paul Bekker, review of *Entwurf einer neuen Ästhetik der Tonkunst*, *Allgemeine Musik-Zeitung*, July 1908.

5. Letter from FB to Gerda Busoni, July 7, 1907, StBB Bus. Nachl. IV, 575.

6. Busoni played the Beethoven C Minor Piano Concerto, Liszt's "Héroïde élégiaque," and a piano version of the "Rákóczy March."

7. Letter from FB to Gerda Busoni, August 1, 1907, StBB Bus. Nachl. IV, 588.

8. Letter from FB to Gerda Busoni, August 1, 1907, StBB Bus. Nachl. IV, 588.

9. Letter from FB to Egon Petri, August 9, 1907, MW, p. 88.

10. Letter from FB to Gerda Busoni, August 5, 1907, StBB Bus. Nachl. IV, 590.

11. Sitsky, *Busoni and the Piano*, p. 213.

12. Sitsky, *Busoni and the Piano*, p. 211. For an exhaustive study of Busoni's relationship with Liszt's music, chapter 12, "Busoni and Liszt," cannot be recommended too highly.

13. Letter from FB to Gerda Busoni, October 19, 1907, StBB Bus. Nachl. IV, 604.

14. Letter from FB to Gerda Busoni, October 16, 1907, StBB Bus. Nachl. IV, 601.

15. Probably the Russian-born (but American citizen) Louis Theodor Gruenberg.

16. Letter from FB to Egon Petri, June 3, 1908, MW, p. 94.

17. Letter from FB to Gerda Busoni, December 16, 1907, StBB Bus. Nachl. IV, 615.

18. Ferruccio Busoni, *The Essence of Music and Other Papers*, trans. Rosamond Ley (London: Rockliff, 1957), p. 7.

19. Busoni, *Essence of Music*, p. 10.

20. Busoni, *Essence of Music*, p. 11.

21. Letter from FB to Gerda Busoni, December 3, 1907, StBB Bus. Nachl. IV, 613.

22. Sitsky, *Busoni and the Piano*, p. 62.

23. FB to Gerda Busoni, December 3, 1907.

24. Letter from FB to Gerda Busoni, March 3, 1908, StBB Bus. Nachl. IV, 622.

25. Letter from FB to Gerda Busoni, April 27, 1908, StBB Bus. Nachl. IV, 625.

26. Letter from FB to Ludwig von Bösendorfer, July 13, 1908. StBB Bus. Nachl. BI, 286a.

27. The complete list of Busoni's Vienna pupils is in the Dent Papers, EJD/2/1, King's College Library, Cambridge.

28. Letter from FB to Gerda Busoni, June 27, 1908, StBB Bus. Nachl. IV, 646.

29. Letter from FB to Gerda Busoni, September 9, 1908, StBB Bus. Nachl. IV, 648.

30. Letter from FB to Gerda Busoni, September 9, 1908, StBB Bus. Nachl. IV, 650.

31. Gustav Meyrinck (1868–1932), an Austrian writer whom (like Shaw) Busoni had considered approaching for a libretto.

32. Letter from FB to Gerda Busoni, May 19, 1908, StBB Bus. Nachl. IV, 636.

33. Letter from FB to Gerda Busoni, January 12, 1909, StBB Bus. Nachl. IV, 668.

34. Letter from FB to Gerda Busoni, January 14, 1909, StBB Bus. Nachl. IV, 670.

35. Letter from FB to Emilio Anzoletti, March 1, 1909 (date of postmark), in Sablich, *Lettere*, p. 149.

36. Letter from FB to Carla Colognatti, May 18, 1909, in Sablich, *Lettere*, p. 150.

37. Letter from FB to Anna Weiss-Busoni, June 1, 1909, StBB Bus. Nachl. 1353.

38. Letter from FB to Anna Weiss-Busoni, June 28, 1909, StBB Bus. Nachl. 1354.

39. Letter from FB to Gerda Busoni, August 12, 1909, StBB Bus. Nachl. IV, 700.

40. Letter from FB to Anna Weiss-Busoni, August 21, 1909, StBB Bus. Nachl. 1355.

41. A typewritten copy of this diary, which runs from January 1, 1909, to December 31, 1914, is in the Staatsbibliothek in Berlin, as Busoni-Nachlass CI 162.

42. Letter from FB to Arrigo Serato, February 2, 1920, in Sablich, *Lettere*, p. 418. (This letter is not included in Beaumont, *Selected Letters*.)

43. From the program note by Busoni for the premiere of the *Berceuse élégiaque*, New York, February 21, 1911.

44. Hugo Leichtentritt, "Ferruccio Busoni," *Music Review*, November 1945, 205–9.

45. Antony Beaumont, *Busoni the Composer* (London: Faber and Faber, 1985), p. 147.

46. Letter from FB to Gerda Busoni, November 8, 1909, StBB Bus. Nachl. IV, 703.

47. Review in *New York Post*, January 7, 1910.

48. Letter from FB to Gerda Busoni, February 22, 1910, StBB Bus. Nachl. IV, 713.

49. Letter from FB to Gerda Busoni, February 19, 1910, StBB Bus. Nachl. IV, 711.

50. Busoni, "Die Gotiker von Chicago," in *Wesen und Einheit der Musik*, p. 198 (not in English edition).

51. "Die 'Gotiker' von Chicago," in Busoni, *Wesen und Einheit der Musik*, pp. 195–96.

52. Letter from FB to Gerda Busoni, March 1, 1910, StBB Bus. Nachl. IV, 715.

53. Letter from FB to Gerda Busoni, March 3, 1910, StBB Bus. Nachl. IV, 716.

54. For masterly accounts of these works, and their evolution, the reader is referred to Antony Beaumont's *Busoni the Composer*, Larry Sitsky's *Busoni and the Piano*, and Marc-André Roberge's "Ferruccio Busoni, His Chicago Friends, and Frederick Stock's Transcription for Large Orchestra and Organ of the *Fantasia contrappuntistica*," *Musical Quarterly*, summer 1996.

55. Letter from FB to Gerda Busoni, February 27, 1910, StBB Bus. Nachl. IV, 714.

56. Letter from FB to Gerda Busoni, March 12, 1910, StBB Bus. Nachl. IV, 719.

57. Letter from FB to Gerda Busoni, March 15, 1910, StBB Bus. Nachl. IV, 721.

58. Arthur Farwell, "Reveals Busoni as a Composer," *Musical America* 11, no. 19 (March 19, 1910): 18.

59. Letter from FB to Gerda Busoni, March 22, 1910, StBB Bus. Nachl. IV, 727.

60. Letter from FB to Gerda Busoni, March 29, 1910, StBB Bus. Nachl. IV, 731.

61. FB to Gerda Busoni, March 29, 1910.

62. Letter from FB to Gerda Busoni, April 25, 1910, StBB Bus. Nachl. IV, 731.

63. Bernard van Dieren, *Down among the Dead Men* (London: Humphrey Milford/Oxford University Press, 1935), p. 44.

64. Letter from FB to Gerda Busoni, March 6, 1910, StBB Bus. Nachl. IV, 717.

65. Letter from FB to Gerda Busoni, March 17, 1910, StBB Bus. Nachl. IV, 723.

66. Letter from FB to Gerda Busoni, April 12, 1910, StBB Bus. Nachl. IV, 736.

67. Letter from FB to Gerda Busoni, April 18, 1910, StBB Bus. Nachl. IV, 740.

68. Letter from FB to Gerda Busoni, April 18, 1910, StBB Bus. Nachl. IV, 741.

69. Marc-André Roberge, "Ferruccio Busoni in the United States," *American Music* 13, no. 5 (Fall 1995). I am indebted to Professor Roberge for much of the information in this chapter.

70. Louis Elson, "Musical Matters: The Symphony Concert," *Boston Daily Advertiser*, April 2, 1906, 5.

71. Letter from FB to Gerda Busoni, February 18, 1911, StBB Bus. Nachl. IV, 753.

72. Letter from FB to Gerda Busoni, February 22, 1911, StBB Bus. Nachl. IV, 757.

73. Ernesto Consolo (1864–1931), Italian pianist.

74. Letter from FB to Gerda Busoni, February 28, 1911, StBB Bus. Nachl. IV, 761.

75. Letter from FB to Gerda Busoni, March 20, 1911, StBB Bus. Nachl. IV, 773.

76. "Die Melodie der Zukunft," enclosed in letter from FB to Gerda Busoni, March 15, 1911, StBB Bus. Nachl. IV, 770.

77. Alma Mahler, *Gustav Mahler: Memories and Letters*, 3rd ed., ed. Donald Mitchell, trans. Basil Creighton (London: John Murray, 1971; first published 1946), pp. 194–95.

78. Letter from FB to Gerda Busoni, July 17, 1911, StBB Bus. Nachl. IV, 788.

79. Letter from FB to Gerda Busoni, July 18, 1911, StBB Bus. Nachl. IV, 789.

80. Busoni, quoted in MW, p. 176.

81. Letter from FB to Gerda Busoni, September 5, 1911, StBB Bus. Nachl. IV, 795.

82. Siegfried Jacobsohn, "Turandot," *Schaubühne*, October 27, 1911.

83. Postcard from FB to Gerda Busoni, March 17, 1912, StBB Bus. Nachl. IV, 805.

84. Letter from FB to Gerda Busoni, March 15, 1912, StBB Bus. Nachl. IV, 804.

85. Letter from FB to Gerda Busoni, March 18, 1912, StBB Bus. Nachl. IV, 807.

86. Letter from FB to Gerda Busoni, April 30, 1908, StBB Bus. Nachl. IV, 626.

87. Letter from FB to Gerda Busoni, June 16, 1908, StBB Bus. Nachl. IV, 640.

88. Letter from FB to Gerda Busoni, June 18, 1908, StBB Bus. Nachl. IV, 641.

89. For insight into the composition of *Die Brautwahl*, in particular the final two years before the premiere, see MW, pp. 121ff.

90. Letter from FB to Gerda Busoni, July 30, 1907, StBB Bus. Nachl. IV, 131.

91. In 1572 Lippold, a Jewish coiner, was accused of witchcraft and burned in Berlin.

92. MW, pp. 175–76.

93. Letter from FB to Gerda Busoni, March 25, 1912, StBB Bus. Nachl. IV, 811.

94. Letter from FB to Gerda Busoni, April 6, 1912, StBB Bus. Nachl. IV, 817.

95. Letter from FB to Robert Freund, April 22, 1912, in Sablich, *Lettere*, p. 215.

96. Letter from FB to Egon Petri, May 3, 1912, in MW, p. 177.

97. Review of *Die Brautwahl, Kölnische Zeitung*, May 31, 1913.

98. Letter from FB to Gerda Busoni, June 23, 1913, StBB Bus. Nachl. IV, 860.

99. FB to Gerda Busoni, June 23, 1913.

100. FB to Gerda Busoni, June 23, 1913.

101. Letter from FB to Gerda Busoni, June 26, 1913, StBB Bus. Nachl. IV, 864.

102. Letter from FB to Gerda Busoni, June 27, 1913, StBB Bus. Nachl. IV, 865.

103. FB to Gerda Busoni, June 27, 1913.

CHAPTER TEN

~

Bologna, Berlin, United States: 1913 to 1915

Before the birth of opera in Europe—"officially," with the first performance of *Dafne* by Jacopo Peri (1561–1633) in Florence in 1598,
which was essentially a musical accompaniment (now lost) to a pas-
toral by Ottavio Rinuccini—music in Italy was largely confined to folk
music, church music, or instrumental and vocal music as entertainment
for the ruling class. From that first effort by Peri and other efforts soon
after, most notably those of Claudio Monteverdi (1567–1643), opera
caught on and rapidly developed into a form we can still recognize today. But it was the opening of the world's first purpose-built opera house
in Venice in 1637, in front of a paying public, that triggered opera's extraordinary success and popularity (soon beyond Italy's borders) and
was responsible for the phenomenal output of opera over the next two
and a half centuries. The rise of a moderately wealthy bourgeoisie
stoked the demand—but the concurrent relative decline of the ruling
class, many of whom had been, musically speaking, highly literate and
sophisticated, often expert musicians themselves, and who had patronized composers since the early Renaissance—brought with it a gradual
decline in the general standard of music in Italy.

By the nineteenth century, Italian music was dominated by opera,
which was in its turn dictated to in large part by facile but voracious

264 ~ Chapter Ten

audience expectation, creating a vicious circle that militated against development. The output of operas in Italy, which reached floodlike proportions in the eighteenth century, many individual composers producing a total of seventy or more operas, was still high in the nineteenth. Rossini (1792–1868) wrote some thirty-nine operas before he retired at the age of thirty-five, Saverio Mercadante (1795–1870) around sixty, Gaetano Donizetti (1797–1848) sixty-six, just to name three of the better-known composers. Every town of any size had an opera house, and each audience demanded new work every season. These were expected to be entertainments conforming to formulaic demands: plenty of arias to show off the singers' vocal accomplishments, a dramatic, sentimental story line, and all in a very accessible musical style. It was, essentially, disposable entertainment. The rise of the great music publishers, Ricordi in particular, helped establish the idea of a more lasting fate for particular operas, and released composers from this treadmill to an extent.

There were, of course, Italian composers of note writing nonoperatic work, many of whom had studied abroad. The following are a few of these who were active in the second half of the nineteenth century and well into the twentieth: Ottorini Respighi (1879–1936); Alfredo Casella (1883–1947) who, on his return to Italy from France, even founded the short-lived (1917–1919) Società Italiana di Musica Moderna; Ildebrando Pizzetti (1880–1968); Gian Francesco Malipiero (1882–1973); that enigmatic and tragic figure Lorenzo Perosi (1872–1956); another Italo-German, Ermanno Wolf-Ferrari (1876–1948); and Giovanni Sgambati (1841–1914)—known as "the father of the modern musical movement in Italy," protégé of Liszt and promoter of the latter's music in Italy, and of the music of Wagner and other modern composers. Sgambati, another pianist-composer (he first performed in public at the age of six), was admired by Busoni, who indeed played his music from a young age. Sgambati did sterling work in Rome throughout his life to improve and broaden musical life in his country. He was cofounder in 1877 of the Liceo Musicale di Santa Cecilia, linked to the older Accademia, having previously organized the Liceo on an informal basis as a free school for poor piano students, the lessons given in Sgambati's own home. But the music of Sgambati, and that of most of the other above-named composers of nonoperatic music, cannot claim to have entered the European mainstream.

The reasons for this are many and complex. Generally speaking, however, the basis was lacking in Italy itself for sustained development of non-operatic music: consistently good teaching and—equally important—a broad-based, musically educated public for whom concertgoing was an essential component of their cultural life. And in the opera house, the blast of the newer styles emanating from beyond the Alps merely served to weaken an exhausted art form still further. By 1910, the phenomenal flood of Italian opera, stretching over nearly three centuries, had become a trickle.

In northern Europe, the likes of Mahler, Bruckner, Richard Strauss, Grieg, Elgar, Sibelius, Debussy, and Saint-Saens had been nurtured in the richer soil prepared by their great forebears, in an atmosphere of high expectation and constant cross-fertilization, and with very keen audiences. Hindemith, Schoenberg, Varèse, Weill, and Bartók simply continued this development—most of the latter helped, ironically, by Busoni, who, having made that decision as a very young man to go to Leipzig, had in effect nailed his colors to the German mast. Hence his knowledge of the realities of Italian music remained essentially that of an outsider. He had never been an organic component of the movement to which his Italian contemporaries belonged, and his dialogue with them had been minimal.

As the composer and conductor Guido Guerrini, who studied under him in Bologna and remained a friend, argues in his study of Busoni (published in 1944), Busoni had an impressively thorough knowledge of Italian history and culture, and had access to the key figures in Italian musical life wherever he traveled in Italy. But a huge library and stimulating talks with colleagues when one is passing through are not enough; Busoni's attitude to Italy, writes Guerrini, was one of "suffering and bitterness almost like that of a betrayed lover."[1]

Busoni's attitude to Italy was very complex: at a visceral level he identified with his native country, but could not forgive it for not coming up to his expectations. Living so long in the sober, austere, and earnest German environment had inevitably influenced his perception of Italy and Italians—in effect, whether he realized it or not, he wanted them to be more German. Perhaps too he was transferring his dissatisfaction with his own life. This transferring—if such it was—in the form of harsh criticism was frequently aimed at any country he happened to be in, and none escaped his scorn: America was materialistic, naive, and without culture; the French were sophisticated but superficial; although as a cosmopolitan he loved London, and the palpable energy emanating from the hub of a huge empire—it was around this time he seriously considered moving there—the British were prudish and hidebound; and Germans were all bourgeois provincials. He would periodically go off into such rants in letters to Gerda and Egon Petri in particular. It was all rather immature and self-deluding (albeit many of his criticisms hit the mark).

Where Italy was concerned, however, Busoni did see through to what he believed to be one important truth: Italian music had to progress on the basis of its own tradition. It was wrong for Italian composers to write "secondhand" German music. Like Verdi, he believed that progress could be achieved by reconnecting with the past, with the great Italian composers of former times, epitomized by Monteverdi.

Busoni therefore regarded it as a chance to put some of his ideas on the revitalizing of Italy's musical life into practice when, on May 1, 1913, during the Italian concert tour that spring, he signed an agreement in Bologna with the mayor, the town clerk, and the local member of parliament to assume directorship of the Liceo Rossini (now the Conservatorio di Musica G. B. Martini) at Bologna, beginning that autumn. This music academy, with roots reaching back to the mid-sixteenth century, had already had two directors over the preceding two years, since the early retirement from the post in 1911 of Marco Enrico Bossi (1861–1925), another musician and composer who looked north of the Alps for inspiration, and promoted new music—up to a point: he drew the line at what he considered the more radical departures of younger composers. After Bossi came the pianist and composer Bruno Mugellini (1871–1912), who died shortly after taking up the appointment, then Luigi Torchi (1858–1920), who held the post for one year as a stopgap, pending the appointment of a new director. Busoni's directorship was to be similarly brief.

The terms of his contract could scarcely have been more generous: the appointment was "for life," but—at Busoni's insistence—with an initial trial year, and the right to resign at any time after that first year. Administrative duties were to be kept to a minimum, and he was to be allowed generous leave for concert tours. The day after signing the contract he received fourteen telegrams from individuals in Bologna, high and low, "expressing wild enthusiasm at my acceptance." "One cannot entirely disregard such a demonstration of solidarity," he wrote[2] rather pompously to Egon Petri, continuing with positively Micawberesque hyperbole:

> nor underestimate the unanimous wish of an entire city. But the rest of Italy too is resounding with a welcoming fanfare that is for the moment perfectly in tune. Bologna is the intellectual center of the country, its Institute the oldest and most respected. Even *Mozart* studied here and I shall be working in the same building in which that young prodigy went to school. . . . Others will see to all practical and administrative affairs and I am not even asked to teach.

It was the institution too that had conferred on Busoni its diploma for composition and piano playing when he was a mere fifteen—only Mozart had been younger when he received the same honor. Busoni's salary was to be higher than that given to any previous director, although it would be much lower than that paid for a similar position in Germany.

Bologna was certainly the most forward-looking Italian city, musically speaking: a *Società Wagneriana* was founded in the city in 1887 (using the Liceo as its base), which gave annual concerts devoted to Wagner's music, and the first Italian performances of many new foreign works had been given there. Also, unlike the rest of the country, there was a relatively open-minded, keen audience on hand. Nevertheless, caution—and the absence of wholehearted conviction—stopped Busoni yet again from burning his bridges in Berlin: the family had only three years before moved into what was to be their final home there together with his now vast collection of books, paintings, antique furniture, and *objets d'art*.

There was much else he would be leaving behind. On June 17, 1913—six weeks after he had signed that agreement in Bologna— there had been a private performance in the Busonis's apartment of Arnold Schoenberg's *Pierrot Lunaire*. The work had been premiered publicly the previous October in Berlin, when Busoni was touring in England, and he had arranged this performance now in order to hear it for himself. The select audience included the pianist and composer Artur Schnabel

(1882–1951), Edgard Varèse, and the violinist Arrigo Serato (1877–1948), another Italian who had migrated to Germany (although he was to return to Italy at the outbreak of World War I), and was one of Busoni's wide circle in the German capital.

There was a certain air of grand patronage in Busoni's manner, and Percy Grainger was not the only one of his protégés to observe it with a sardonic eye. The Hungarian-born viola player Egon Kenton (1891–1987), studying in Berlin at the time, left an account of that memorable private performance, to which he had been taken by Varèse:

> When we arrived the salon was crowded. Varèse made his way to the end of the room where Schoenberg was standing near the players. He introduced me and we stood there, Varèse, Schoenberg, and the violinist Arrigo Serato, during the performance. Afterward, when the applause had subsided, Schoenberg, timid and a little awkward, started toward the players, but Busoni, handsome and imposing, was already there, congratulating them. Then Schoenberg, screwing up his clever monkey face in a wry smile, turned to Varèse and said: "And now he's distributing the decorations."[3]

The relationship between Busoni and Schoenberg was now ten years old: in 1903 Schoenberg had sent Busoni a copy of his symphonic poem *Pelleas und Melisande*, hoping for a performance at one of Busoni's concerts at the Beethovensaal. (In the event, the work received its first performance on January 26, 1905, in Vienna.) Although Busoni did not accept it for performance, the contact was made, and from then on Busoni showed a friendly interest in Schoenberg's work. In 1909 Schoenberg again submitted work to Busoni—the Piano Pieces, op. 11, nos. 1 and 2. Again he was unsuccessful, as the last of the Beethovensaal concerts had been given on January 2 that year. Nevertheless, after looking through the Piano Pieces, Busoni was very encouraging in a letter of July 26, 1909:[4]

> I have received your pieces and the accompanying letter. Both point to the thinking and feeling person I had already believed to have discovered in you. . . . Your instrumentation of Schenker's dances (which I performed in Berlin) bore witness to your astounding orchestral virtuosity.

From these established points of reference, your piano pieces came as no surprise to me—that is: I happened to know what I could expect. It was therefore self-evident that I should find a subjective, individual art based on emotion—and that I would encounter refined artistic entities. . . . It is now five days since I received your pieces, and I have occupied myself with them every day. I believe I have grasped your intentions and feel confident, after some preparation, to produce sonorities and atmospheres according to your expectations. But the task is hindered by their excessive *conciseness* (that is the word).

A lively correspondence followed, at first on the Piano Pieces (on which Busoni wrote a paraphrase, received by Schoenberg with mixed feelings), but soon moving on to other subjects. Busoni, generous as ever to other composers, recommended Schoenberg to his own publishers, Breitkopf und Härtel; at the same time Schoenberg received an offer from Universal Edition, and signed a ten-year contract with the latter. The two men did not actually meet until the autumn of 1910, when Schoenberg moved to Berlin, but before and after their meeting, the letters continued. The relationship was definitely on the basis that Busoni gave, Schoenberg took, which the former accepted with a certain wry amusement. Schoenberg was a nervous and demanding correspondent. Several times, when he did not receive an immediate reply, he assumed he had somehow offended Busoni, yet often delayed his own answers if he was immersed in composition: it never seemed to occur to him to assume the same explanation for Busoni's silence. Throughout, Busoni showed great restraint and tolerance toward Schoenberg's often outrageous behavior. In spite of their overwhelming emphasis on Schoenberg, the letters are an invaluable record of the creative processes of both men, and of their characters. They are also a testament to Busoni at his best: very soon, he got the measure of Schoenberg and, as with Mahler and several others, simply overlooked the flaws in the younger man's character and saw through to his genius. Here were two articulate equals talking a common language—a rare situation Busoni always reveled in. Strangely enough, Busoni never performed any of Schoenberg's work in public.

It was people like Schoenberg and Varèse, and the whole vibrant and daringly creative environment of Berlin that constantly attracted such people—Busoni himself included—in the first place, that Busoni would also be leaving behind by moving to Bologna. In a letter to Egon Petri he tried to rationalize the situation, asserting that the time usually spent touring—that is, away from Berlin—would be taken up by the academic year in Bologna. In other words, Berlin would remain his base; which speaks volumes for the depth of his commitment to Bologna and a renaissance of Italian music.

Between September 1912 and July 1913 he had written a *Nocturne Symphonique* for Orchestra (BV 262), premiered nearly a year later, on March 12, 1914, at the Beethovensaal in Berlin, Busoni himself conducting. (After a rehearsal a few days before he wrote in his diary: "achieved, what Schoenberg has striven for in his best moments.") He had begun composing the work on September 5, 1912, just after finishing his *Sonatina seconda* for piano. Busoni began the *Nocturne* as a third sonatina, but within days he had decided to turn it into an orchestral piece. As he wrote to Egon Petri from London in October, where he was continuing work on it between engagements, "The third sonatina seems to be a sort of butterfly (hoping for the best)—anyway, it is metamorphosing, at the moment it resembles the caterpillar, is feeding on smuggled half-hours and is crawling up the trunk of the orchestral tree."[5] He continued composing the next month, in Russia, where he met Scriabin and had stimulating discussions with him, which possibly influenced his attitude to the *Nocturne*. For whatever reason, the work was then temporarily abandoned in favor of the *Red Indian Fantasy* for Piano and Orchestra (BV 264, the first of his treatments of Native American themes), and eventually finished on July 6, 1913.

Ferruccio spent the summer of 1913, as usual, in Berlin (Gerda went to Alt-Aussee again for the second half of July), working on the *Red Indian Fantasy*, which was only finished in February 1914. In mid-September he set off for Bologna, in some trepidation, leaving Gerda and Lello behind. ("This morning I had a similar feeling to the one I had when I first went to Leipzig," he wrote Gerda from Heidelberg on September 17.)[6] He was making a holiday of the slow journey southward, and from Heidelberg went on a side trip to see the Austrian conductor Artur Bodanzky, who was engaged at the theater in Mannheim and had conducted the shortened version of *Die Brautwahl* there in

May. Bodanzky was a keen supporter of new music, and suggested various commissions for Busoni, such as writing music for Ibsen's *Peer Gynt*,
as he did not like Grieg's. This contributed to Busoni's very confused
state of mind: "I came back to Heidelberg at one in the morning and
slept for ten hours. This afternoon I shall travel further. . . . This inertia which seems to have got inside me makes it difficult for me to continue the journey."[7] He went on to Basle, but in his peevish, restless
state disliked everything he saw, and took the next train out. Geneva
pleased him no better, although Benni was there, studying art. On the
journey, Busoni was reading the nineteenth-century poet Giosuè Carducci, "to practice my Italian," "an excellent little book by Schopenhauer 'on writing and style,'"[8] and Goethe's *Urfaust*.

"Tomorrow I shall go on," he wrote[9] from Geneva a day later, "I
don't know where yet (theoretically I like to imagine I have unbounded
freedom), probably I shall stop once more before Bergamo." On September 24 he arrived in Milan; "I shall go to Bergamo this afternoon,"
he wrote on the twenty-fifth, "and, probably (after another two days)
to Bologna. If only I had *one* person there with whom I could talk freely,
and who 'knows' me, it would be much easier for me."[10]

In Bergamo he stayed with his friend Augusto Anzoletti. His unwillingness to reach Bologna seeps out of his daily letters to Gerda. The
day before he left Bergamo he wrote ominously:

> During the last few days I have come to the terrible conviction that the
> Italians (now) are not a people with a feeling for art. They read, hear,
> and see badly; what they build is ugly; they have no taste in their homes,
> in all these respects they are ignorant and either badly influenced or not
> influenced at all. They draw a thick line between what belongs, histori-
> cally, to the past and what belongs to the present.[11]

He had already rejected them.

Both Augusto and his brother Emilio Anzoletti traveled with Busoni
to Bologna. Busoni was met at the Liceo by the wife of the concierge:
"fat, good-natured, white-haired, mustached," who greeted him with
uplifted arms, and her husband exclaimed, "I knew you as a boy and
now you have become so famous!"[12] It was a manifestation of a side of
the Italian character that Busoni loved. At the Liceo he was immediately plunged into administrative plans—and day-to-day experience of

what for him was palpably now an alien culture: "The people are coming back to the town gradually from the country [after their summer break, the *villeggiatura*]. . . . I see from the calendar that tomorrow and the day after are public holidays. Here, instead of the date one says the name of the saint. Tomorrow is not the 4 October but 'San Petronio.'"[13] On that day he told[14] Gerda, who had gone to Weimar for a few days: "Your letters are refreshing, real and vivid, like your whole nature. . . . Your card from Weimar has just arrived. . . . Here I miss those warm autumn landscapes . . . *if it is not too late to transplant myself back again* [author's italics]?"

He had thought at first of taking up quarters in the academy itself, but soon realized he was not up to it, as it would have meant walking through the whole deserted building at night, carrying a candle, to reach his quarters.

> The walls are hung with portraits of old gentlemen and the appearance of some of them does not invite intimate acquaintance. There is a dwarf in particular who, to me, is odious. I imagined he came into the room with Rossini's wig on and presented me with his roll of music to play through. [Rossini's wig was in a glass case in a room that also contained Rossini's huge bed, and was adjacent to Busoni's apartment.] And close by is the library, wrapped in silence and clinging to its old, useless and boring books, all classified. There is a spinet in the library—suppose it were to begin to tinkle?[15]

(Even today, it must be confessed, the library conveys that impression.)

On October 9 Busoni saw a large house, the Villa Marsigli, outside the Porta Maggiore; he thought it might be a suitable home for them. His plan was, he wrote Gerda, "to pass the spring and autumn here, to travel in the winter and to be in Berlin for a short time (at Christmas and in January). It is impossible to be here during July and August. . . . Therefore I should very much like to keep to my summer work in Berlin."[16]

Frustrations were already accumulating by mid-October: "Although so much is left in my hands it is very difficult to get anything done. (It is as though someone made me a present of an island and took away the ship in which to get there.)"[17] Included in his responsibilities as director of the Liceo were the organization of concerts, collaborating on a new musical journal, and being a board member of the opera house, deciding on opera performances—"the last is the most hopeless of all, for everyone trembles before Ricordi and he is in command."[18] Although Busoni had been assured he would have few administrative duties, this assurance soon proved hollow, as nearly all final decisions were passed on to him.

There were visitors, some more welcome than others: Baronin Jella Oppenheimer arrived from Vienna on October 7 and they did some sightseeing together. The American dancer Isadora Duncan (1878–1927), whom he had met in Paris, arrived on October 22. Six months before, both her children (one by the English theater director and stage designer Edward Gordon Craig and the other by the millionaire Paris Singer) had been drowned when the car the children were traveling in went into a river. In spite of his obvious sympathy for her over the tragedy, Ferruccio's sardonic side was uppermost when reporting the meeting to Gerda: "When she told me that now she was only spirit, and how a month before the catastrophe she constantly saw three black birds fluttering in the room, and that these birds in olden times were thought to be harbingers of death—when she said all that and other things, it reminded me of D'Annunzio."[19]

More stimulating was an invitation to the home of the tenor Giuseppe Borgatti and his wife Renata. Borgatti, one of the few Italian tenors to make a name for himself singing Wagner, sang two scenes from *Parsifal*, accompanied by his wife. Also present was Ottorino Respighi, the Bologna-born composer who had studied at the Liceo, and in Russia under Rimsky-Korsakov, and 1908–1909 in Berlin. It was in Berlin that he had first met Busoni, who always much appreciated the younger man's wit. Respighi was about to move to Rome as a professor of composition at the Liceo Musicale di Santa Cecilia.

Then there was a week of examinations at the Liceo. Busoni was impressed by the standard of the singers and string players, but as usual severe on the pianists, and shocked at the leniency of the other examiners. In October he wrote in his diary: "Liceo: like Faust in Parma wasting time." Then in English: "The man who could work miracles" (the title of a short story by H. G. Wells—here obviously an ironic allusion to the enormity of the task facing him in Bologna). At the beginning of November, after scarcely a month in Bologna, he left for a two-week concert tour of Russia. "Please, do agree to come to Russia with me, or else I shall feel quite lost," he wrote[20] to Gerda. "This is not an order, of course, but I think it is what you wish too." Of course she complied, and met him in Saint Petersburg, where he arrived with influenza but was nevertheless persuaded to play by the conductor Sergey Koussevitzky (1874–1951), who already had a reputation as an energetic promoter of new music. (Busoni played his own Piano Concerto, among other things.) As in the year before, the concerts there were an enormous success. Busoni went on to Warsaw, Gerda returning to Berlin, where he finally joined her at Christmas, and was pleased to be asked to write the foreword to a volume of E. T. A. Hoffmann's *Phantastische Geschichten* (Fantastic Tales).[21] By early January 1914 Busoni was back in Bologna, but after just a few days at the Liceo, he was off again for Strasbourg, Paris, Nantes, and Bordeaux.

March was spent in Berlin, where he gave four concerts of his own works at the Beethovensaal. The second concert, on March 12, in addition to the *Brautwahl Suite* (BV 261), a solo piano version of the *Fantasia Contrappuntistica* (BV 256a), and the *Berceuse élégiaque*, contained the first performances of the *Nocturne Symphonique* and the *Red Indian Fantasy*, all but the last conducted or performed by Busoni. They were a great public success, although the critics were not convinced by the two new works, one referring to the *Nocturne Symphonique* as "Chaos, disintegrated music, protoplasma."[22] Max Marschalk was more discerning:

> Such music is to be greeted not only as a valuable human and artistic statement, but also as an experiment which extends the expressive possibilities of music and passes on new technical aids to a coming generation. . . . We would like to think that Busoni is now occupied with forging the sword which he can later wield, so that he can prove to us with a large, serious work that he is truly one of the elect.[23]

It is a short (some eight minutes), elegiac piece, for full orchestra, bringing particular instruments into very sharp focus for a few bars, then moving to others, at times with extraordinary lyricism and polyphonic harmony. It is in three sections: Sostenutissimo, Adagio, and Allegretto tranquillo. The themes unite in the final section. The overall impression is of a tone poem, and Antony Beaumont believes its literary inspiration to come from Dmitri Mereshkovsky's fictionalized biography of Leonardo da Vinci, the episode when Leonardo devises a system of musical crystal spheres for a court entertainment.[24] The musicologist Hugo Leichtentritt, in the program notes to the last concert, explained the language of the *Nocturne Symphonique* as follows: "Voice is not countered by voice, nor instrumental groups countered by one another, but note by note, each separate instrument against every other. Different chords are often superimposed, major and minor sound simultaneously, unexpected chords frequently collide."

The *Red Indian Fantasy* for Piano and Orchestra, which Busoni had gratefully dedicated to the ethnomusicologist Natalie Curtis, got off more lightly with most critics, who were rather nonplussed by the unfamiliar musical language and subject matter. Busoni had to wrestle hard to turn the music, generally pentatonic, into European musical language: "The Indian melodies are not very pliable or productive. I shall have to graft in quite a lot of my own."[25] Nevertheless, his constantly enquiring mind was intrigued by these motifs, which, he found, were perfect examples of absolute melody:

Absolute Melody: A row of repeated ascending and descending intervals, which are organized and move rhythmically. It contains in itself a latent harmony, reflects a mood of feeling. It can exist independent of words for expression and without accompanying voices. When performed, the choice of pitch or instrument makes no alteration of the nature of its being.[26]

Busoni wrestled hard almost to the end: in January 1914, a few weeks before its Berlin premiere, he wrote to Petri from Paris: "Five times I have come to the end of the slow movement of the Red Indians, four times I have had to scalp it, but I hope I've found the solutions today."[27] The work is in three parts: Fantasia, Canzone, and Finale, and lasts some twenty-two minutes.

At first Busoni had thought of using the material for some form of theatrical performance, but quickly turned to the idea of a large piece for piano and orchestra, even giving it the provisional title of "Concerto secondo." This slowly changed into its final form. In his guidelines written to Hugo Leichtentritt[28] to help the latter compose the program notes, Busoni explained:

Consists of three sections without a break: a *Fantasy* . . . a *Canzone* formed out of two songs; and a *Finale* based on three genuine motifs and one original one. . . . The most frequently used scale in the *Fantasy* is the pentatonic, which corresponds to the black keys of the piano, but the Hungarian gypsy scale also appears. Scotch snap. No program. But poetic simulations, such as the melancholy of the race; a glimpse of the Mississippi caught in passing; a hint of warlike proceedings; exotic coloring.

A performance a few days later of the *Red Indian Fantasy* in Munich was badly received by the critics, one of whom found the work "very exotic . . . but rather tedious, a collection of curiosities with no apparent meaning or purpose, lacking in shape and order."[29] Its American premiere, in Philadelphia on February 19, 1915, with Busoni as soloist and Leopold Stokowski conducting, was a great success. Natalie Curtis was in the audience and attended the morning rehearsal:

> just a handful of friends, Madame Busoni on one side of me and on the other Percy Grainger. . . . With the first bars of the orchestral introduction . . . the walls melted away, and I was in the West, filled again with that awing sense of vastness, of solitude, of immensity. . . . The spirit of the real America (a spirit of primeval, latent power) Busoni had felt while traveling across the continent, and had tried to reproduce.[30]

Our musical palates today have perhaps been corrupted by the soundtracks to too many Hollywood Westerns to be able to savor the work as Busoni's contemporaries did.[31]

Busoni returned to Bologna in early April, soon to be saddened by bad news: Henri Petri had died on April 7, at the relatively young age of fifty-eight. In late April and early May Busoni gave a series of three concerts in Bologna, with a newly constituted orchestra, made up of prizewinners from the Liceo (Italy at this time had only one permanent symphony orchestra, resident in Rome). The programs were an eclectic mix of Weber (overtures to *Der Freischütz* and *Oberon*), Saint-Saëns (Fifth Piano Concerto), Beethoven, Brahms, Bach, and Busoni's own *Brautwahl* Suite. He conducted a great deal himself in these concerts, and in one of them he hit the third finger of his left hand on a metal music stand, which was to have consequences, and he ever after associated the injury with Bologna, referring to it as his "Bologna finger."

The previous autumn he had seen a church, the Santa Lucia, that had been turned into a gymnasium but now, at his instigation, was being converted into a concert hall. The project foundered, however, owing to the usual bureaucratic bungling and obstructive maneuvers that were so typical of Italian life at the time, and that caused him (and others) so much frustration. Busoni's other practical plan—again started in the autumn—was to modernize the sanitary arrangements in the Liceo. Here at least something was achieved: by April the work was well in hand, and it was in fact later completed. The fact that this provision of decent toilets in the Liceo was his sole completed enterprise during his tenure was subsequently to cause him much wry amusement.

Gerda had finally arrived in Bologna in April, a few days after Ferruccio. As the Villa Marsigli would not be available until the autumn, they rented rooms in a huge villa, in which they had to pass through several vast and empty rooms to reach their own quarters. Until Gerda returned to Berlin in June, Ferruccio found this bearable, but once alone, the ordeal of passing through those gloomy, empty rooms, often on returning late at night, just as he had had to do to reach his apartment in the Liceo, proved beyond him, and he went back to the Hotel Baglioni. One advantage of living in the hotel, in his eyes, was that he felt hidden; it is revealing that he regarded invisibility as an advantage. Another perceived advantage, equally revealing of his attitude to Bologna, was that "staying in the hotel has given me a feeling of being on my way home."[32]

A phrase in his very last letter to Gerda from Bologna, dated June 21, 1914, spoke volumes on his continuing sense of alienation in Bologna. He had briefly met the Berlin playwright Karl Vollmoeller while the latter was waiting for a train connection: "I was another person during that half-hour. One could talk about things *without first explaining what the things were* [author's italics]."[33]

Busoni's own creativity was faltering. In May he had written in his diary: "Planning a violin piece for [Arrigo] Serato, but what?" Serato, who throughout his career as a violinist often played Busoni's compositions, was to wait in vain for this violin piece: Busoni wrote nothing more for the instrument, except for three cadenzas to Beethoven's Violin Concerto, which he finished in August that same year.

When he left Bologna on June 22, 1914, Busoni was expecting to return in the autumn, although reluctantly. Many things contributed to this state of mind, but the main cause was his own lofty and unrealistic attitude: "I feel as though I've married the maid," he once commented, referring to being bound to Italy by his obligations to the Liceo. Instead of seeking out the many other Italians already making valiant efforts to promote and enliven the musical scene, he marched grandly ahead and expected the rest to follow. When they did not, he lost interest. Generous as he was to young composers of talent, he was far too impatient and egoistic to be an effective reformer. Was it all connected to his own relative lack of success as a composer? Did he subconsciously relate to Italy's fallen musical status, or hope for the heroic status in Italy as composer and musical reformer that was denied him in Germany? Whatever the truth, it had been an extraordinary move to contemplate throwing his energies into the school in Bologna, which would have been the only way to achieve anything, and which he signally failed to do.

His last letters to Gerda from Bologna had been full of his latest reading: "Miracle," from the *Nouveaux Contes Cruels* by Villiers de L'Isle-Adam, the Faustian overtones of whose *L'Ève future* had fascinated him the year before. Busoni also wrote to Gerda of his "state of happy expectation" at leaving, and there was yet more criticism of the Italians. ("They remain too much in their own country.")[34]

Just over a year before, when he had signed the agreement with the Liceo, he had written[35] from Bologna to the flautist and musicologist Hermann Draber, who was still part of the Busoni circle in Berlin: "What I have always dreamed of, a position of great authority in Italy, has just been offered me. In a stroke I could make Bologna a city of music, focal point of the country, and perhaps even raise it to occupy a higher position in Europe. . . . Yet I am agonizingly undecided. . . . And my wonderful wide world," he continues significantly, "that I feel really at home in, would grow distant and become a foreign country. . . . But the Italians have fully recognized me as their compatriot, finally—while Berlin will always consider me a foreigner and rail against my way of playing Beethoven." But now, after nine months of sporadic residence in Bologna, rather bruised and battered by the political realities of running a public institution, his perceptions were altered and his enthusiasm largely evaporated.

He was home in Berlin by June 25, and on June 28, six days after he had left Bologna, on the other side of the Adriatic to Italy, in Sarajevo, the student Gavrilo Princip shot dead the Archduke Franz Ferdinand of Austria, heir to the Habsburg throne, altering the map of Europe and millions of lives, including Busoni's, forever. In spite of all his railing against the Italians, Italy remained one of the two poles of Busoni's existence. The other was, of course, Germany, and the tension between those two poles, which had until now been largely creative, and over which he had some measure of personal control, was over the next four years effectively to destroy him.

In July Busoni stayed in Berlin as usual and worked: that summer he sent off the scores of yet more Bach transcriptions and editions for piano to Breitkopf und Härtel in Leipzig. His output in these transcriptions was prodigious over the next three years: Eighteen Short Preludes and Fugues and a Fughetta; Four Duets for Piano; Capriccio in B-flat Major on the Departure of His Beloved Brother; Air with Thirty Variations (Goldberg Variations); Prelude, Fugue, and Allegro in E-flat Major; Fantasy, Adagio, and Fugue; Chromatic Fantasy and Fugue; Three Toccatas in E Minor, G Minor, and G Major; Canonic Variations and Fugue from the "Musical Offering"; Fantasy and Fugue in A Minor; and Fantasy, Fugue, Andante, and Scherzo. He was also already working on his new opera, *Arlecchino*.

"Drunk on new idea," he wrote enigmatically in his diary on July 29. Then, on August 1: "Mobilization!" With astonishing rapidity, the political structure of Europe collapsed: on July 28 Austria-Hungary declared war against Serbia; Russia went to Serbia's defense, provoking Austria-Hungary to declare war on Russia on July 30. France refused to obey Germany's demand that it remain neutral, so that on August 3 Germany declared war against France and Russia, and invaded Belgium. As the ally of France and Russia, Britain declared war against Germany on August 4, and against Austria-Hungary on August 12. On August 3, Italy declared its neutrality. The extreme rapidity of the domino effect, ostensibly initiated with the declaration of a localized war between Austria-Hungary and Serbia, meant that most of Europe was not only caught unawares, but refused to take the situation seriously. Busoni too at first brushed it aside; the diary entry for August 2 reads: "Started on Goldberg Variations." The entry for August 4: "It will never again be as it was—daily exercises in counterpoint and Goldbergs" betrays a dawning uncertainty. As Italy was to remain neutral until May 23, 1915, the Busonis's continued residence in Berlin posed no problems as yet.

On September 10, Busoni began a special diary that he called "Notes from momentous times,"[36] in which he gave vent to his contempt for the nationalistic saber rattling by now heard all around him. A first salvo was aimed at one Dr. Ferdinand Scherber, Viennese editor of *Signale für die musikalische Welt*, who had written an article entitled "War and Art," published in the September 9, 1914, issue. Scherber's article was a crude attempt to prove the superiority of the German race in things musical; the race, he maintained, would acquire further strength and purpose through victory on the battlefield, a statement that drew from Busoni the ironic comment, "an outcome, incidentally, which he visualizes only for the Germans and Austrians." The racist overtones of the article, in which even the Austrian (but Jewish) Arnold Schoenberg is rejected ("with as much force as if he were Japanese at least"), drew Busoni's particular scorn.

In mid-September Busoni fell ill, the illness so long-lasting he had to postpone an October 5 Bach recital to October 10. His "Bologna finger" continued to give him trouble that autumn too: "Bologna finger hurts even when I'm asleep," was a diary entry for October 5. It was not only his Bologna finger that was disturbing his sleep, however, but Bologna itself, in the light of a war that, it was becoming obvious by then, would not be over by Christmas. In his diary on October 30 Busoni recorded that he had written to Bologna to ask for two years' leave, although in letters to friends, for example to Emilio Anzoletti[37] on September 17—therefore six weeks before—he had written, "I have asked for *one year's leave*." In September he was still wavering regarding a trip to America planned for January 1915. In the same letter to Anzoletti he also wrote, "For me this war is a real tragedy. . . . If Italy is spared, it will have a great cultural responsibility on its shoulders: to fulfill everything which the other countries will have to neglect—during the coming ten years." The egocentricity betrayed in the first sentence here was partly the fault of what Bernard van Dieren, an admirer but also a shrewd man of the world, called "the idiotic solemnities of Busoni's peripatetic clique of Byzantine courtiers," who, according to van Dieren, frightened off "many potential admirers."[38] Most of this clique lived in Berlin.

But the statement reflected not just egocentricity, or the parochial-ism of the arts practitioner; for Busoni the arts, philosophy, everything that led the questing human mind "onward and upward," was being threatened by the frenzied belligerence and readiness with which so-called civilized peoples lapsed into "primitive bestiality," as he called it, and for which he had nothing but contempt. His sardonic humor was in evidence as always. "Today *Antwerp* 'fell,'" he wrote in his diary on October 10. "What do they actually intend to do with Belgium? Hand it back a little damaged?" His personal history certainly militated against any kind of nationalistic fervor in his own makeup, but he was aghast at how many friends and colleagues in Germany and beyond had succumbed to the prevalent frenzy. As a practical step in the direction of the inevitable, on October 28 a carpenter came to take measure-ments for a new, much more solid door to his library. "Strange, ghastly Faust-feeling, when new library door is closed," was a diary entry for November 21.

Busoni had been particularly hit by the death of the French com-poser Albéric Magnard, whose Symphony no. 3 had featured in one of his Beethovensaal concerts of new music on January 12, 1905, and whom Busoni knew personally. Busoni had heard that the Germans had executed Magnard as a sniper; the truth was slightly more complex. Alone in the house, Magnard had been surprised by a party of German cavalry outside, and fired on them from a window, killing two; their re-turn fire set the house ablaze and Magnard died in the flames.

There was a burst of creativity in late December: Busoni wrote the last two scenes to the libretto of his *Doktor Faust*: "It came to me unin-terruptedly and unhesitatingly, like a revelation."[39] On January 2, 1915, he had still not fully decided whether or not to go to America, as had been planned the previous autumn, but two days later he shut up his Berlin apartment and in effect fled, taking his whole family with him. It was to be nearly six years before he entered it again.

They traveled via Zurich and Genoa, and sailed from Naples on the SS *Rotterdam*. They were held up in the Mediterranean for two hours while a torpedo boat removed two passengers from their ship, then went out into the Atlantic. The Busonis finally reached New York on January 23. Busoni had plenty of books to read: his beloved H. G. Wells (again in utopian mode: the author's 1902 lecture "The Discovery of the Future"), Graham Balfour's biography of Robert Louis Stevenson (on which Busoni was scathing), and a heavily annotated edition of Goethe's *Faust*.

For all the Busoni family, it was exciting to see the New York waterfront again, though they were all nervous. They took an apartment on Riverside Drive, which served as a base. Busoni soon began criticizing yet again what he perceived as America's shortcomings, descending into the downright petty in his vituperations: an English friend, the conductor Walter Henry Rothwell (1872–1927), had been relieved of his post in St. Paul, Minnesota. The orchestra was financed by a railway company

> which made use of it to inform the cities on its line that Saint Paul was a cultural center worth visiting. But evidently Saint Francis found a readier audience among the birds than Saint Paul among the cities of Minnesota, for the orchestra, being deemed an unprofitable undertaking, has been disbanded. To the great joy of the neighboring, rival city of Minneapolis, which is now proclaiming its orchestra as the cultural figurehead of the entire state and sending it out and about. Their conductor is a German who (when he wears a hat) has a head of long, thick hair, but is bald when he takes his hat off, wears gold-rimmed glasses and likes to be photographed in tails.[40]

On January 31, Busoni gave his first concert in New York, playing the Liszt E-flat Concerto, at Carnegie Hall. People were kind, and old friends were there, including Percy Grainger. "The ice is thawing," Busoni ended the above quoted letter to Petri, "but not in my heart. Even *with* a war, Europe is preferable." A change in this attitude was scarcely encouraged by a New York journalist who said to him, "There are three great organizations in world history: the Catholic church, the German army and the American Oil-Trust Company."[41] Busoni toured in March, with a particularly depressing experience in Kansas City, when he met one of his old Vienna pupils, Georgine Nelson, who had been so lively in support of him only seven years before, in 1908:

> Three days ago I was in Kansas City, where our old friend Georgine N[elson] is living . . . as a prostitute. Poor G! She came to my concert, the manager having extracted a promise from her that she would remain

sober. She was an outrageous sight! With peroxided blond hair and bloated, coarse features, coated with make-up—and I fear this is not yet the end of the story.[42]

By April Busoni was back in New York, loathing everything about America, his jaundiced view exacerbated by his misery and frustration at events in Europe. Although nationwide prohibition on alcohol was not to arrive until 1919, it was already in force in many states, and provided yet another target for scorn. In New York there was little prospect of further work: owing to the war, New York was awash with famous musicians. "There are about twenty famous and distinguished pianists at present in New York," he had written to Petri in March from Chicago, going on to list eighteen of them. "The American reaction: nobody wants to hear them. As soon as anything becomes easily available here, its value drops."[43] Busoni's forty-ninth birthday brought congratulations from a group of friends in Berlin—including a heartfelt message from Arnold Schoenberg—and an increase in his depression.

He desperately wanted to return to Europe, but wavered. On May 23 Italy declared war on Austria-Hungary, which at first made Busoni feel the way back to Europe was blocked. "Yes, I have to remain here indefinitely," he wrote in early June in English to Harriet Lanier, a friend and founder of the Philadelphia Society of Friends of Music, "on account of the awakened heroism of my sympathetic countrymen. The way leading back to my home is cut off."[44] As he wrote to Edith Andreae, a Berlin friend,

I cannot overcome a feeling of missing something which is irretrievable. And your description of the glories of Berlin makes my detested exile intolerable to me. . . . When one is no longer *master of one's own freedom of movement*, life has no further value. Now I am seriously considering coming to Switzerland via Italy. (I would give 100 United States for one corner of old Europe.)[45]

Turning to what he found to be a more congenial side of North America, that summer Busoni wrote a further work based on Native American music, the *Red Indian Diary, Book One* (BV 267), four studies for piano. Much of the music is a reworking of the *Red Indian Fantasy*.

Artur Bodansky was coming to the Metropolitan Opera House in the autumn, Busoni learned. Elisabeth Schumann, who had sung "Albertine" in the Hamburg production, had been and was coming back. Saint-Saëns was in New York, and when he and Busoni were seen together at the Met, the news was cabled to the *Vossische Zeitung* in Berlin, which made much of it to accuse Busoni of disloyalty to Germany. (Busoni wrote a long and rather devious exculpatory letter to the newspaper.) The Italians were accusing him of disloyalty too, for canceling a concert in Rome. These reactions provoked his scorn, but they also increased his distress.

He wavered between Switzerland and Italy as a European base: although as yet Italy had only declared war on Austria-Hungary, he felt he could not return to Berlin. He knew it was only a matter of time before hostilities extended to Germany (in fact, Italy was to declare war on Germany on August 28, 1916). Owing to his own vacillations, and several changes in the municipal administration in Bologna, his return to the Liceo was no longer an option. Alfredo Casella offered him what he considered a rather minor post as piano teacher in Rome, which he indignantly rejected. His fees for concerts in the United States were between $600 and $1,200 per concert; therefore after his spring tour he had no immediate money worries. Nevertheless, with few prospects of further work, owing to the stiff competition, there was little to keep him in New York. By early August he had decided to leave, and at the end of the month he, Gerda, and Lello sailed for Naples, with Zurich their ultimate goal. (Benni, now twenty-three years old, having been born in Boston and consequently entitled to U.S. citizenship, remained behind. He had become a tortured, complex young man, subject to deep depressions, mood swings, and disastrous love affairs. His diaries and notebooks, beginning in Boston in 1916, make distressing reading. "Benni remains a lonely man and a foreigner to life," wrote[46] his father to Sybil Matesdorf, daughter of his London friends, from New York, in English, that July. "He is super-critical and spoils many beautiful things by this unhappy tendency. But he is a thinker and a gentleman in his soul, sometimes with violent outbursts. Now he stays—quite alone—at a country place, and I know very little of his doings.")

Busoni claimed later that he had sworn not to live in a country at war, hence the choice of Switzerland. As many others who fled there were to appreciate, it was the only place where one could, for practical purposes at least, avoid taking sides. After the war, in July 1919, Busoni told Frederick Delius that he had chosen Switzerland as he "didn't want to have to swallow my convictions, didn't want to give any nation the semblance of preference, as I thought the same of all of them."

The three Busonis arrived in Naples in mid-September after an anxious voyage, and went straight on to Milan, where Busoni lay ill for nearly two weeks. After initial difficulties regarding visas, by early October the family was in Zurich, where they soon found an apartment at Scheuchzerstrasse 36, on a hill above the old town, which remained their base until 1920. (In 1926 a plaque was unveiled on the wall of the house commemorating Busoni's residence there.) For the next four years, the "musical Ishmael" was more or less grounded.

Notes

1. Guido Guerrini, *Ferruccio Busoni: La vita, la figura, l'opera* (Florence: Monsalvato, 1944), p. 191.

2. Letter from FB to Egon Petri, May 3, 1913, MW, pp. 207–8.

3. Quoted in L. Varèse, *Varèse*, pp. 98–99.

4. Letter from FB to Arnold Schoenberg, in *Ferruccio Busoni: Selected Letters*, trans. and ed. Antony Beaumont (London: Faber and Faber, 1987), Appendix: The Schoenberg-Busoni Correspondence, 1903–1919, p. 384. I have used Beaumont's translation. The original correspondence, in German, first appeared in print in *Beiträge zur Musikwissenschaft* 19, no. 3 (1977), ed. Jutta Theurich; it also appears as an appendix in Sablich, *Lettere*.

5. Letter from FB to Egon Petri, October 8, 1912, MW, p. 194.

6. Letter from FB to Gerda Busoni, September 17, 1913, StBB Bus. Nachl. IV, 871.

7. Letter from FB to Gerda Busoni, September 19, 1913, StBB Bus. Nachl. IV, 873.

8. Letter from FB to Gerda Busoni, September 21, 1913, StBB Bus. Nachl. IV, 874.

9. Letter from FB to Gerda Busoni, September 22, 1913, StBB Bus. Nachl. IV, 875.

10. Letter from FB to Gerda Busoni, September 25, 1913, StBB Bus. Nachl. IV, 877.

11. Letter from FB to Gerda Busoni, September 28, 1913, StBB Bus. Nachl. IV, 880.

12. Letter from FB to Gerda Busoni, October 2, 1913, StBB Bus. Nachl. IV, 883.
13. Letter from FB to Gerda Busoni, October 2, 1913, StBB Bus. Nachl. IV, 883.
14. Letter from FB to Gerda Busoni, October 4, 1913, StBB Bus. Nachl. IV, 885.
15. Letter from FB to Gerda Busoni, October 5, 1913, StBB Bus. Nachl. IV, 886.
16. Letter from FB to Gerda Busoni, October 10, 1913, StBB Bus. Nachl. IV, 888.
17. Letter from FB to Gerda Busoni, October 15, 1913, StBB Bus. Nachl. IV, 891.
18. Letter from FB to Gerda Busoni, October 10, 1913, StBB Bus. Nachl. IV, 888.
19. Letter from FB to Gerda Busoni, October 23, 1913, StBB Bus. Nachl. IV, 896.
20. Letter from FB to Gerda Busoni, October 28, 1913, StBB Bus. Nachl. IV, 898.
21. This essay is contained in Ley's English translation of *Wesen und Einheit, The Essence of Music*, p. 186, but not in the 1956 German edition.
22. Walter Dahms, in the *Neue Preussische Zeitung*, March 14, 1914.
23. Max Marschalk, in the *Vossische Zeitung*, March 14, 1914.
24. Beaumont, *Busoni*, p. 185.
25. Letter from FB to Gerda Busoni, July 18, 1913, StBB Bus. Nachl. IV, 867.
26. Letter from FB to Gerda Busoni, June 22, 1913, StBB Bus. Nachl. IV, 869.
27. Letter from FB to Egon Petri, January 18, 1914, MW, p. 223.
28. Letter from FB to Hugo Leichtentritt, February 25, 1914, in Beaumont, *Letters*, pp. 176–77.
29. Review in *Münchener Neueste Nachrichten*, March 18, 1914.
30. Natalie Curtis, "Busoni's Indian Fantasy," *Southern Workman*, October 1915.
31. For an excellent account of the genesis and a musical analysis of the piece, see Beaumont, *Busoni*, pp. 190–203.
32. Letter from FB to Gerda Busoni, June 15, 1914, StBB Bus. Nachl. IV, 914.
33. Letter from FB to Gerda Busoni, June 21, 1914, StBB Bus. Nachl. IV, 916.
34. FB to Gerda Busoni, June 21, 1914.
35. Letter from FB to Hermann Draber, April 18, 1913, in Sablich, *Lettere*, p. 239.
36. These diaries are inserted, in chronological order, in both Beaumont, *Letters*, and Sablich, *Lettere*.

37. Letter from FB to Emilio Anzoletti, September 17, 1914, in Sablich, *Lettere*, p. 266.

38. Dieren, *Down among the Dead Men*, pp. 92–93.

39. Diary entry for January 2, 1915, in Beaumont, *Letters*, p. 189.

40. Letter from FB to Egon Petri, January 31, 1915, MW, pp. 233–34.

41. Letter from FB to Egon Petri, March 29, 1915, MW, p. 235.

42. FB to Egon Petri, March 29, 1915.

43. FB to Egon Petri, March 29, 1915.

44. Letter from FB to Harriet Lanier, June 6, 1915, in Beaumont, *Letters*, p. 199.

45. Letter from FB to Edith Andreae, June 23, 1915, in Beaumont, *Letters*, pp. 202–3.

46. Letter from FB to Sybil Matesdorf, July 28, 1915, StBB Bus. Nachl. BI, 683.

CHAPTER ELEVEN

~

Zurich: 1915 to 1920

Zurich was the city of choice for the majority of people flooding into neutral Switzerland from all directions, victims of the political turmoil. The influx included a great many artists—James Joyce and family had arrived in June from Trieste, and for a while shared an apartment with Philipp Jarnach, who became a pupil and then amanuensis of Busoni. Joyce and Busoni were to meet, but had little in common. The Irish writer's flippant attitude was firmly disapproved of. There were several German writers and composers, and another Italo-German composer, Ermanno Wolf-Ferrari, among others, from Italy. Spies, black marketeers, speculators, and revolutionaries—including Lenin—also trod the city's narrow streets.

One witness to life among all these artistic refugees was the endlessly verbose Austrian writer Stefan Zweig, who had already met Busoni in 1911 on the ship from New York that was carrying the dying Mahler. Zweig, at the time living in Vienna, managed to get to Zurich in 1917 on what could be called a cultural propaganda ticket: a play of his, *Jeremias*, had been offered a first performance by the Stadttheater in Zurich. Bizarrely—the play was very antiwar and stood little chance of a production in Vienna—the Austrian authorities saw the propaganda value of "open-mindedness" and allowed him to travel. Although Zweig's accounts are often gushingly romantic, and wrenched into a form that suited his own personality, they provide some valuable insights. "The more Europeanly a man has lived his life in Europe, the harder he is chastised by the fist that shattered Europe," he wrote in *Die Welt von Gestern* (The World of Yesterday—one of his many volumes of memoirs).[1] And specifically of Busoni: "'Where do I belong?' he asked me once. 'If I dream at night and wake up, I know I was speaking Italian in the dream. And then when I write, I think in German words.' His pupils were scattered all over the world—'one is perhaps now shooting at the other.'"[2]

During the first few months back in Europe, Busoni wrote his third work based on American Indian themes, the short *Gesang vom Reigen der Geister* (Song of the Spirit Dance) (BV 269), a Study for Small Orchestra, also known as the *Indian Diary, second book*. As Antony Beaumont[3] writes, "In this work . . . he finally achieved a true integration of his own creative personality and the chosen material. Had Busoni been endowed with a talent for publicity, the work could have become well-known." And as Beaumont eloquently remarks at the end of the chapter "The Indians' Book,"[4] "In the Red Indian works we find an expression of his growing concern to establish 'the Oneness of Music'—a unity that knows no frontiers between men, whatever their race or culture, no matter how widely scattered they may be on the face of the earth." But this was not a time when the brotherhood of man was high on the agenda.

In Zurich Busoni was eventually to resume the habit of his young years in Frohnleiten, and spend hours at a café table in the railway station, either with Gerda or—mostly—alone. Again we have Zweig's (perhaps romanticized) account: "And once I met him late at night in the main hall of the station restaurant, he had drunk two bottles of wine alone. As I went past, he called out to me. 'Anaesthetic,' he said, indicating the bottles. 'Don't drink! But sometimes one has to anaesthetize oneself, otherwise one couldn't bear it.'"[5]

By early 1916 Busoni had acquired another dog, a young Saint Bernard he called Giotto. The dog became his constant companion, and the two were soon well-known figures in the town. The writer Elias Canetti, then a child, was living on the Scheuchzerstrasse, the same street on which the Busonis had their apartment, and, like the other local children, found Busoni a figure of fun—until his music-loving mother indignantly explained who the "white-haired old gentleman" was (Busoni was in his early fifties) who absentmindedly wandered the streets, calling out "Dschoddo komm zum Papa!" whenever the dog ran off. The children called him "Dschoddo komm zum Papa" behind his back.[6] It is unlikely that the dog obeyed this order, as he apparently had a mind of his own, to Busoni's secret delight: one hot summer day Giotto decided to take a bath in a public fountain; when a policeman informed his master that this was not allowed, Busoni suggested he inform the dog himself. On another occasion, in a restaurant, an officer in uniform at the next table took off his sword and leaned it against the wall, where Giotto soon knocked it down with his tail. Busoni excused him by saying "he's antimilitarist."

It had been largely through the efforts of Volkmar Andreae (1879–1962), director of the Zurich Conservatory and chief conductor of the Tonhalle-Gesellschaft, that the Busonis had been granted asylum in Switzerland. As Andreae related at the unveiling of the memorial plaque on Busoni's house in Zurich in 1926, "Previously I had known Busoni only as artist and intellectual. Now he was a human being harried by the confusion of war, seeking help with tears in his eyes. I have seldom been so moved and at the same time so delighted; moved by the embarrassment of this great man, delighted by the fact that I could now call Busoni one of us." Andreae immediately offered Busoni four piano concerts for the winter season, and early in 1916, when he was called up, he handed over the direction of the Tonhalle subscription concerts to Busoni. These were either orchestral concerts or piano recitals and were all immensely popular. At the last piano recital of the series, in April, Busoni played to an audience of around 2,000, as he wrote to Egon Petri[7] with some satisfaction. He also gave four concerts in Basle over the winter months, and played in other Swiss cities: fifteen concerts in all between mid-January and the beginning of April. The Swiss banker Albert Biolley and his wife Elisabeth, an amateur flautist, had helped the Busonis financially on their arrival in Zurich, and remained friends throughout their stay.

That year the distinguished musicologist Hugo Leichtentritt published a first biographical study of Busoni,[8] with the subject's collaboration. Although the book is short (101 pages), and half of it concentrates on analyses of Busoni's works, it was a significant acknowledgment, in the year of Busoni's fiftieth birthday, of his importance. The author had submitted some draft passages to Busoni, whose corrections and explanations are illuminating:

> I cannot agree with your concept of "wrong" notes: have you not realized the painstaking measurements with which a Schoenberg writes down an interval? (My efforts are, at least, no slighter.) Any other note would grieve him. It is just as impossible for sounds to be "wrong" in music as it is for stones, plants or formations in a forest. We just have to learn to discern harmony away from the textbook.[9]

And later, replying to a letter from Leichtentritt:

> I was surprised at the news you sent me of the microtones which have been produced in physics laboratories, because I have struggled in vain for years to render thirds of tones audible. But I did succeed in New York, where an old Italian organ builder . . . fashioned reeds for me which were retuned accordingly, and which I have with me in my workbox. I beg to protest at your confusing third-tones with *quarter*-tones, and would like to claim for myself the sole right of having worked out the theory of a system of thirds of tones in two rows, separated from each other by a semitone.[10]

As this proves, in spite of the situation, Busoni's mind and energies were still strongly focused on his main musical concerns. It also illustrates how difficult it was even for an expert like Leichtentritt, though he admired Busoni, to throw off the shackles of traditional conceptions of what music "should" be, and follow him in making that daring leap into the unknown.

Busoni's editing of Bach was nearing its end, and in January 1916 it was definitely palling for him, and he suggested to Egon Petri that they share the editing of the remaining few items. For the first year in Zurich Busoni still enjoyed some freedom of movement beyond Swiss borders—at least in a southerly direction. In early March 1916 he was in Rome, as pianist and conductor, for four concerts at the Santa Cecilia and at the Augusteo, where he conducted the premiere of his *Rondò arlecchinesco*, composed the previous spring in America. (The *Rondò* received a very negative review in *La Tribuna*, and Busoni's conducting of Beethoven's "Eroica" Symphony was also sharply criticized—a view shared by Toscanini, who was in the audience. Toscanini had conducted Busoni's *Berceuse élégiaque* in January at the Augusteo.) In Rome Busoni saw a marionette performance of Rossini's short opera *L'occasione fa il ladro*, which had a seminal influence on how he conceived his next two operas. Back in Zurich by March 7, a week later he was in Milan, where he gave two concerts.

In late May 1916 Ferruccio and Gerda were invited by a new friend, the Marchese Silvio della Valle di Casanova, whom they had met in Zurich, to stay at his villa, San Remigio, near Pallanza on Lago Maggiore. The Marchese, like Busoni, spoke German and Italian equally well, and was a man of wide-ranging culture, having studied piano with Liszt and written several volumes of verse in German. One attraction of San Remigio for Busoni was the presence of a large collection of Liszt manuscripts in the library; the other was the futurist painter Umberto Boccioni, who had also been invited to the villa, to paint Busoni's portrait. (The portrait now hangs in the Galleria d'Arte Moderna in Rome. Another portrait of Busoni, also dating from 1916, by Max Oppenheimer, is now in the Nationalgalerie, Berlin.)

One of the Liszt manuscripts at the villa was of the first, 1849 edition of Liszt's *Totentanz for Piano and Orchestra*, and Busoni spent some of his time there preparing a new edition of it, which he eventually finished in November 1918 (BV B 72). He also reworked his variations on the Bach Chorale "Wie wohl ist mir, O Freund der Seele" into an Improvisation for Two Pianos (BV 271). Boccioni was on a month's leave from the front, and spent most of this period at the villa. He insisted on painting Busoni's portrait outdoors, which meant being dependent on the weather; this dragged out the sittings, but the men got to know each other well. Boccioni also painted a portrait of Gerda—presumably on the rainy days. On June 23, after five weeks at the villa, Ferruccio and Gerda returned to Zurich, taking the now completed portrait with them, and Boccioni returned to the front. On August 16, while out on a cavalry exercise near Verona, he fell from his horse, suffering severe injuries. The next day he died. Busoni was distraught at the news, and directed all his frustrated anger at this waste of a promising young life (Boccioni was thirty-four) into a general indictment of war, which he published in a front-page article in the *Neue Zürcher Zeitung* on August 31, 1916, as "Der Kriegsfall Boccioni" (The war case of Boccioni).[11]

What particularly incensed Busoni was that in war the old cliché is true that truth is the first casualty: Boccioni's death was used in the Italian press for a patriotic encomium to war, intimating that Boccioni had died in battle in a glorious cause. Busoni knew only too well, both from their period together at the villa and subsequently from Boccioni's letters to him written in the few months remaining before the young man's death, how much he had loathed and resented military life. Nevertheless, there was something typically egoistic about Busoni's protest: "Three weeks living together with me seemed to have stimulated him very much, to such a degree that, when we parted, Boccioni, filled with new ideals, felt himself facing a decisive period of work." He quoted from a letter Boccioni sent a few days before the latter's death: "This whole period of my life is under your influence, and I have only you to thank for the strength to bear this terrible life. . . . There is no longer any question of art. The strains are enormous and my brain is no longer functioning." It was as though Busoni took Boccioni's death as a personal affront.

(Busoni's reaction earlier in May that year to news of the death of the Spanish composer Enrique Granados, who had drowned when the ship in which he was returning from the United States was torpedoed, had been chillingly different: "A composer called Granados, who had been invited to New York last season with a great flourish, *sank* in the English Channel on his return," he wrote to Egon Petri.[12] "Fate often acts so prudently." Perhaps an obscure guilt prompted this callous bravado—Harriet Lanier had tried to interest him in Granados's music while he was still in New York the previous year, and he had dismissed it: "'Goyescas' is the work of a distinguished amateur.")

In Vienna, Arnold Schoenberg heard of the Boccioni article in the *Neue Zürcher Zeitung* and asked Busoni (apparently in vain) for a copy. Nevertheless, on the basis of a secondhand account of it, and U.S. president Woodrow Wilson's note to all the warring countries in December 1916 outlining his suggestions for ending hostilities, Schoenberg wrote his own wildly utopian fifteen-point plan for world peace[13] in January 1917 and sent a copy to Busoni, asking him[14] if he could help to get it published, preferably in a Swiss newspaper. It was to remain unpublished until printed in a German edition of the Schoenberg-Busoni correspondence in 1977.[15] Schoenberg, now aged forty-two, had nevertheless been called up and spent ten months in the Austrian Army, but was eventually exempted as unfit. The experience did little to engender enthusiasm for war.

In Zurich in the summer of 1916, Busoni was hard at work completing his one-act opera *Arlecchino*, and by early August he could write triumphantly to Petri:[16] "I am taking three days' holiday—or perhaps more! On the 8th I finished the score of 'Arlecchino'." He had hoped for a production by Max Reinhardt in Berlin, a hope dashed when on August 28, 1916, Italy declared war on Germany, completing his separation from the two main German-speaking territories. The Zurich Stadttheater was interested in the opera, but demanded a second work to fill up the evening, prompting Busoni to return to the *Turandot* theme. He completed the one-act opera *Turandot* in three months, and the two works were premiered on May 11, 1917, Busoni himself conducting.

The libretto of *Arlecchino* had been completed by the end of 1914; as so often with Busoni, the music was written in snatches, and the world had a kind of preview of the piece before the actual opera music was completed. As related above, the *Rondò arlecchinesco* for Orchestra, composed in America in the spring of 1915, was premiered in Rome in March 1916. Busoni had felt so alienated and depressed in America that, as he gnomically wrote to Edith Andreae from New York:[17] "I didn't dare set to work on the opera . . . for fear that a false start would destroy my last moral foothold." Here he is referring to his *Faust* opera, which was also simmering in the background, as well as *Arlecchino*. He therefore rewrote the music planned for *Arlecchino* up to that point as an orchestral work, and also worked into it themes from unfinished projects, a Sonatina Quasi Sonata for Piano (BV 275), and a setting for baritone and orchestra of the poem by the great nineteenth-century Italian poet Giosuè Carducci, "Su Monte Mario" (BV 263). (The latter was in its turn originally intended as one of the "Songs of Four Nations," to poems by Carducci, Poe, Hugo, and Heine, conceived in 1914 immediately after Austria's declaration of war against Serbia, as an artistic gesture at uniting the warring nations. The *Rondò* and the subsequent opera, are permeated by a vivid awareness, laced with a bitter cynicism, of the impending catastrophe.) The *Rondò* is divided into four sections, as a kind of suite illustrating different aspects of Arlecchino's character and adventures, rather in the manner of Richard Strauss's tone poem *Till Eulenspiegel*. Although the *Rondò* had been indifferently received on its premiere in Rome, when it was performed soon after in Zurich it met with more perceptive appreciation. "Sometimes one senses that much of this motley bustle is only a mask concealing deeper, more painful things," wrote one reviewer shrewdly. Like Busoni's Piano Concerto, with its male chorus at the end, the *Rondò* surprised audiences with its tenor solo.

Influences, inspiration, and impulses behind the opera *Arlecchino* are many and varied. As we know from a long letter[18] to Egon Petri of June 19, 1913, written in Busoni's "thinking aloud" vein two days after the private performance of Schoenberg's *Pierrot Lunaire* in the Busonis's home in Berlin, that work and its subject matter had sparked off a train of thought that soon led to a first draft of the *Arlecchino* libretto. Busoni had also read extensively on and had occasional encounters with *commedia dell'arte*, knew Heinrich von Kleist's famous essay "On Puppet Theater," dating from 1810, and possibly Edward Gordon Craig's ideas on the *Übermarionette*. (Busoni owned a copy of Gordon Craig's *On the Art of the Theatre*, published in 1911, but no meeting between these two larger-than-life men has ever been recorded. Craig had lived in Berlin for a few months in 1907, and was living and working in Rome in 1916, when Busoni conducted his *Rondò*, and working on various projects involving marionettes.) There was also that childhood experience of puppet theatre in Trieste on the memorable evening when his father returned. Another impulse was Busoni's generalized ambition to "restore" Italian opera, that is, by returning for his inspiration to its origins in the seventeenth century, which for him, bore the same relation to nineteenth-century Italian opera composers as Gothic architecture to "Victorian Gothic." This makes his decision bizarre to write the libretto in German for an opera set in Bergamo, home of *commedia dell'arte*. But he knew the work would have greater chances of performance if written in German. (A decision all the stranger, nevertheless, in that he had also written to Petri in the above-mentioned letter, "It is unforgivable that the poems [of Schoenberg's *Pierrot Lunaire*] have not remained in their original French, which certainly comes closer to the 'esprit' of the content.—The longing for the native Bergamo doesn't sound right in German.")

Injected into *Arlecchino* too is a large dose of antimilitarism, and the venom distilled from Busoni's many frustrations, not only with the political situation of the time, but also its effect on his personal situation. And in the opera's merciless knockabout lampooning of all human values, it has much in common with Pulcinella, the anarchic Italian puppet character known in its English-speaking incarnation as Punch: "Let's lead the way," says the *Abbate* in *Arlecchino*, before entering the tavern, in an outrageous parody of self-interest parading as altruism, "and set a moral example of brotherly love to the nations." The opera's tone even managed to shock Busoni himself: "I read my libretto through for the first time in six months," he wrote[19] to Harriet Lanier in August 1915, shortly before returning to Europe, "and was a little anxious about the rather philosophical, biting tone of my 'Arlecchino,' who is an important character, 'and a grim friend of disagreeable truths.'" If read closely, it is a deeply disquieting work—and as if this were not enough, in the summer of 1918 Busoni was to write the libretto for a part 2, in four scenes, which was never set to music, but which contains perfectly vicious portraits of his parents, among others. In scene 2 of this text, "The parental home," after an exact description of the living room in Trieste and of Busoni's parents (the mother is even called Anna, and as the curtain rises she is playing a John Field Nocturne, which had been part of Anna Busoni's restricted repertoire), the father calls to the mother to hand him his handkerchief, which is lying beside him on the table—a scene that had shocked Gerda when she visited Trieste. The dialogue is wordy and totally unmusical—and bawdy: the father farts as he swears at all priests and soldiers. The fourth scene contains a flea circus, four cats, "The Author (in the costume of a traveling piano virtuoso) and even "The Dog Giotto Bernardoni." It can only be regarded as a personal document.

Arlecchino itself is nevertheless a performable work, with solid dramatic qualities not always evident in Busoni's operas—his attitude to the theater was ambivalent to say the least, and too encrusted with theory for sheer theatrical flair and intuition to flourish. The hour-long work contains the two principal characters of *commedia dell'arte*— Arlecchino (Harlequin) and Colombina—and other stock characters of the Italian stage: a priest (here the *Abbate*, who, however, appears to have ten daughters), a doctor, and an elderly tailor who is cuckolded by

Arlecchino in one of many stock situations. The action (like the *Rondò arlecchinesco*) is divided into four movements, showing Arlecchino as Rogue, as Warrior, as Husband, and as Conqueror. The score is through-composed, but with a few solo arias and ensemble passages.

Arlecchino is a spoken role, although parts of the singers' text are also spoken. (For the Zurich premiere, Busoni was fortunate to get the great Austrian actor Alexander Moissi (1879–1935), who acted for many years with Max Reinhardt's company at the Deutsches Theater in Berlin. Busoni had in fact written the role with Moissi in mind.) As the curtain rises, Arlecchino is alone on stage, and sets the tone: "It is not a play for children." After a very short musical introduction, Matteo the tailor is seen outside his house, reading his beloved Dante—he reads aloud, in Italian, from the story of the illicit love of Paolo and Francesca—ironically, because at an upper window Arlecchino is seen making love to Matteo's beautiful young wife, while the music quotes from Mozart's *Don Giovanni*. Jumping out of the window, and landing in front of Matteo, Arlecchino convinces him that war has broken out and "the barbarian is at the gate" besieging the city. He persuades Matteo to enter his house, then locks him in.

Dottore Bombasto and Abbate Cospicuo enter; after some conversation they notice that Matteo's shop is locked and call out to him. He tells them of the "siege," causing panic. They leave. Arlecchino returns as the Warrior and tells Matteo he has been called up. "What is a soldier? Something that gives up itself. A recognizable clothing. One of a hundred thousand. The artificial human. What is right? What one wants to snatch from others. What is the fatherland? Strife in one's own house." "Will you allow me to take my Dante?" asks Matteo. "No one shall say culture goes under in war," is Arlecchino's bitterly ironic reply. He has made a copy of the key to Matteo's house, and after the latter has been led off by two constables, Arlecchino is about to enter the house when his wife Colombina appears. He manages to slip away, and Leandro the troubadour enters, a parody figure of the ageing Italian operatic tenor (though in his first aria there is more than a hint of Wagner), and he soon begins to woo Colombina. Arlecchino, who has been secretly observing the scene, appears, orders his wife into the tavern and fights a duel with Leandro, apparently killing him.

It is now dark. Colombina, the Abbate and the Doctor emerge from the tavern; the Doctor falls over Leandro's body. They discover he is not dead after all, lift him onto a cart, and take him to hospital, to a four-part canon that turns into a Verdiesque quartet. Arlecchino is seen on the roof of Matteo's house. Annunziata, Matteo's wife, joins him and they disappear together. Matteo returns and finds a note from his wife saying she is at Vespers. He reopens his Dante and sits waiting. The curtain falls. In front of it, all the other characters cross the stage in couples: Leandro and Colombina, the Doctor and the Abbate, the donkey and cart, the two constables and finally Arlecchino with Annunziata. Arlecchino takes off his mask and recites a final, deeply cynical farewell to the audience. The curtain rises again and Matteo is seen, still reading and waiting.

The music is eclectic in the sense of erudite parody (as in *Die Brautwahl*), with echoes of Verdi, Mozart, and Donizetti—arguably Bergamo's most famous son. It is also in a deliberately startling mix of musical styles, reflecting Busoni's own broad-mindedness, as so eloquently expressed in his *New Aesthetic*, and the music of his contemporaries, including, of course, Schoenberg's *Pierrot Lunaire*.

The opera's cynicism shocked many.

> I have been reproached for *Arlecchino* because it is considered scornful and inhuman: nevertheless, this creation arose from an impulse completely opposed to such feelings—namely, out of sympathy for men who make life harder for one another than it should and might be, through egoism, through inveterate prejudices, and through convention when it is opposed to feeling. . . . After that of *The Magic Flute* (which I value highly) it is the most moral libretto there is. . . . *Arlecchino* is less than a challenge and more than a jest. . . . On the other hand, it has a tendency to ambiguity and hyperbole in order to place the listener, momentarily, in a position of slight doubt; it adheres consciously to the constant play of colour between grim jest and playful seriousness, and this is carried on throughout.[20]

Of Busoni's operas, it is the most performed, perhaps because of this intriguing quality, but also because of its acerbic wit and dramatic flair.

For his *Turandot*, Busoni based his libretto closely on Carlo Gozzi's 1760s play of the same name, and incorporated music from his *Turandot*

Suite, written between 1905 and 1911. Some of Gozzi's characters are either left out or merged; the link with Italian *commedia dell'arte* and Gozzi—a Venetian—is underlined by frequent references to Venice—gondolas, Saint Mark's, characters with names like Truffaldino, Pantalone, and Tartaglia, clearly incongruous in an opera set in Peking. The musical and literary style is cod-oriental, with—knowing Busoni's broad erudition—what must be deliberate mistakes: "Allah be praised," for example, is a sentiment scarcely likely to be heard in Peking. (Busoni looks westward at one point too: Act 2 begins, in Turandot's apartments, with the chorus singing to the tune of "Greensleeves" while the slave girls dance. This Western insert might indeed be unwitting: according to Egon Petri, Busoni had been shown the melody and gathered that it was an oriental tune; it was already in the *Turandot Suite* and reappears in the fourth of the 1908 *Elegies* for piano. However, it is difficult to believe that the ever-inquisitive magpie Busoni should never have come across the tune, particularly in view of his many and lengthy English tours. Furthermore, among his cryptic diary entries, for October 9, 1910, we find the entry in English: "The lady with the green sleeves.") This cultural jumbling, the German libretto, the frequent lapses into spoken text, and the fairy-tale characters often remind one of *The Magic Flute*, and indeed recall the operatic convention of Mozart's time for German-language operas of linking music with spoken text and not sung recitative, as in Italian opera. Composed seven years before Puccini's *Turandot*, and much shorter (it lasts only one and a half hours), Busoni's work is in music and mood in almost total contrast to the more famous version of his fellow countryman.

After a lively overture, very recognizably Busoni in its handling of strings and wind, with lots of brass, Kalaf enters and in a short aria sets the scene for us. The main differences in the story from the Puccini version are that the Liù character, Adelma, is vengeful: feeling rejected by Kalaf, she tries to engineer his downfall. And Turandot is softer, more willing to be conquered. There are some attractive and wittily written ensemble passages, such as the chorus of women mourners, with their "oh, oh, oh" refrain to throbbing rhythms, and a long aria by the eunuch Truffaldino, that remain in the memory.

Rehearsals began in the spring of 1917 for the premiere of the two works at the Stadttheater in Zurich on May 11. One of the dancers in

Turandot was a young Viennese dancer called Lotte Blamauer, soon to change her name to Lotte Lenya. Nine years later she was to marry Busoni's most famous composition pupil, Kurt Weill, and achieve lasting fame singing his songs. Lenya has left a brief account of the rehearsals in her own distinctive English:

> One morning we were called to rehearsals for Busoni's *Turandot*. When I arrived, Busoni was already sitting at the piano, and he played for the whole rehearsal. After it was over, he sat down on the floor and started talking about his opera. I remember very clearly how he held his feet close to his body: a Persian posture perhaps, but rather stiff, as if it wasn't an altogether easy position for a man of his age.[21]

The two operas were a great success in Zurich. There were soon further productions: in Frankfurt in October 1918 and in Cologne on January 26, 1919, the latter conducted by Otto Klemperer, who had been keen to bring about a German production since the Zurich premiere. In the summer of 1918 Klemperer had visited Busoni in Zurich, and they had discussed a Cologne production, among much else. Klemperer managed to see the dress rehearsal of the Frankfurt production in October, as he reported to Busoni in a letter[22] of November 21, 1918, ten days after the Armistice was signed. The letter begins with an excuse which—fortunately—cannot often be wheeled out: "I should have written long before, but what the last weeks have brought has been all too much, in truth world events made one forget everything else." Klemperer remained a champion of Busoni's work. The German productions were not a great popular success at the time; the current mood in the disastrous aftermath of the war was emotional, therefore the works were condemned as cold and cerebral.

In the summer of 1916 Insel Verlag had published in their Insel-Bücherei series a new edition of Busoni's *Outline of a New Aesthetic of Music*, first published by his good friend Carlo Schmidl in Trieste in 1907, together with the libretti to *Die Brautwahl*, and *Der mächtige Zauberer*. Busoni had revised and enlarged the *New Aesthetic*, which was published on its own, without the two libretti, in 1910, and an English-language edition of this version had been published by Schirmer in New York in 1911. Publication of yet another, extended edition of the *New Aesthetic* (though still only forty-two pages of text) had come about at the suggestion of the German poet Rainer Maria Rilke, who had first met Busoni in March 1914 in Berlin and was now living in Switzerland. The new edition was dedicated to Rilke. These slim, well-designed little Insel-Bücherei books were mainly by well-established authors and very popular—many have now become collector's items. Rilke's own narrative poem, *Die Weise von Liebe und Tod des Cornets Christoph Rilke* (The Lay of Love and Death of Cornet Christoph Rilke), of 1899, was number 1 in the series. It was to become a cult book during World War I, and countless romantic young German soldiers carried it in their knapsacks.

Although it had received attention from a specialist readership when it first appeared, after being published as number 202 in the Insel-Bücherei series, Busoni's *New Aesthetic* now reached a vast audience: after a large initial print run, yet another ten thousand were printed in the summer of 1917—quite astonishing in wartime for a theoretical work—and further print runs followed.

The *Outline of a New Aesthetic of Music* is part manifesto, part plea for openness toward new ideas, part summing up of Busoni's thoughts on music, theater, and the artistic process. On the verso of the title page of the Insel-Bücherei edition is a quotation from his libretto *Der mächtige Zauberer*:

"What seek ye? Speak! And what expect?"
"I know not, I want the unknown!
That which I know is limitless. I want
To go beyond. I lack the final word."

The text itself is headed by a quotation from the Austrian poet Hugo von Hofmannsthal, recounting his own search for a new language.

Busoni the cosmopolitan polymath introduces his book as notes which are the result of long-held and slowly matured convictions. He moves swiftly on to what might be called an open definition of a work of art: "The spirit of a work of art, the measure of feeling, the human element in it—their value remains unaltered through changing times; the forms these three took on, the means that expressed them, and the taste that the epoch of their creation poured over them, these are transient and age rapidly."[23] "The absolutely modern does not exist," he continues, "only what arose earlier or later, flourishing longer or fading more quickly."

This initial section gradually develops into a call for openness and experiment: unlike literature and the visual arts, Western music is scarcely four hundred years old, Busoni writes, and therefore still at the developmental stage, "perhaps in the very first stage of a still unforeseeable development, and yet we speak of classics and sanctified traditions!"[24] He aims a blow at these "traditions:" "'Tradition' is the plaster life-mask of which, in the course of many years and having passed through the hands of countless craftsmen, the similarity with the original can finally only be guessed at."[25] The "child" music should be free:

> Young as this child is, one radiant characteristic can already be recognized, which in particular singles it out from its older companions [i.e., the other arts]. And the lawmakers do not want to see this wonderful characteristic, because otherwise it would overturn their laws. The child—it is hovering in the air! Its feet do not touch the earth. It is not subject to gravity. It is almost incorporeal. Its matter is transparent. It is sounding air. It is almost Nature itself. It is free. Freedom, however, is something human beings have never understood nor fully felt. They can neither recognize nor acknowledge it. . . . Music is born free and its destiny is to become free. It will become the most complete of all reflections of nature through the unrestraint of its nonmateriality.[26]

"Is it not curious," Busoni asks a few pages further on, "that originality is demanded of a composer and that it is forbidden him in form? No wonder that when he is really original he is accused of formlessness."[27]

Beethoven and Bach are both beginnings on which others can build; "Wagner, a Germanic giant," on the other hand, "begins and ends with himself."[28] In orchestral sound Wagner reached far horizons, and did enlarge forms of expression, but brought it into a system (music drama, declamation, leitmotiv), and is not capable of further development owing to his own self-created limits. (This passage in particular was to draw the wrath of many in Germany on Busoni's head.)

Busoni also attacks "program music"—"a limited, primitive art!"[29]— and pours scorn on imitations of natural sounds: he calls the rolling of thunder, the rustling of trees, a degradation of sound (Klang) to noise (Schall). In this 1916 Insel edition he also aims a broadside at Italian verismo opera—in a sense an extension of program music in his eyes— and advocates a return to the old form of set pieces and arias, and to what

Brecht was later to define as the alienation effect on stage, and what Busoni himself advocated in his own operas, although it was viewed in his case as an adherence to the principles of *commedia dell'arte*.

> The sung word will always remain a convention onstage and an obstacle to all real effect: to emerge from this conflict honorably, an action in which the characters take part while singing, will from the beginning have to be based on the unbelievable, untrue, improbable, on one impossibility supporting the other in order that both become possible and acceptable.[30]

Verismo opera, in other words, is nonsense, a contradiction in terms, as in real life people do not sing, but speak.

Here Busoni himself, the advocate of freedom in this very work, falls into the trap of formulating rules. He becomes even more dogmatic when dealing with the future of opera: for him, music is indispensable onstage only for dancing, marching, singing—and the entry of the supernatural into the action. And the onlooker should always be aware that what is happening onstage is not reality; "artistic enjoyment should never sink [*sic!*] to human sympathy."[31] Shortly after, Busoni quotes a somewhat impenetrable text from E. T. A. Hoffmann's *Die Serapionsbrüder*, ending, "May the time of the fulfillment of our hopes no longer be distant, may a godly life begin in peace and joyfulness and music freely and powerfully exercise its seraphic flight, in order anew to begin the flight into the beyond, that is its home and from which comfort and salvation beam down into the restless breast of man."[32] It is amazing how Busoni, the admirer of Bach's disciplined world, could launch himself too into Hoffmann's obscure and uncontrolled anarchy. It is yet another Faustian contradiction in his character.

There follows some rather Jesuitical defense of musical transcriptions in a section on notation: "Any notation is already the transcription of an abstract idea. The moment the pen masters it, the thought loses its original form."[33] (Busoni's transcriptions often met with criticism.) He moves on to a highly personal treatise on feeling in music, comparing Italy, France, and Germany (time for another sideswipe at Wagner). Then comes a clear call for freedom:

> The creative artist should not accept on trust any handed-down law and consider his own creation a priori as an exception in regard to that law.

He should look for a suitable law of his own for his own case and after the first complete application of it destroy it again in order not to descend into repetitions of himself in a subsequent work. The task of the creative artist consists in setting up laws and not in following them. Whoever follows given laws stops being a creator.[34]

Busoni is prophetic in his advocacy of a music not restricted by the technical limitations of traditional instruments and how they are traditionally played—it was certainly this outlook that went to the heart of the young Edgard Varèse, who was influenced more by Busoni than by any other composer during his first stay in Berlin, from 1907 to 1914. (What Varèse found difficult to understand was that although Busoni advocated total freedom, this also entailed the freedom to choose one's particular path which, for Busoni himself, did not entail the radical experimentation Varèse followed.) Busoni calls for an open tonal system—that is, not necessarily keeping to the tone intervals common in Western music—and castigates the present system of defining harmony as "a pathetic pocket edition of that encyclopedic work [i.e., harmony]; artificial light instead of the sun.—Have you noticed how people gape at the brilliant lighting of a room? They never do so at the million-times stronger noon sunlight."[35] He then goes into a detailed exposition of different ways of breaking up musical sound, the possibilities of dozens of different tonal systems: "I have attempted to exhaust the possibilities of the arrangement of degrees within the scale; and succeeded, by raising and lowering the intervals, in establishing 113 different scales."[36] (In August 1909, in the first months of their correspondence, Busoni had sent Schoenberg a copy of the first edition of the *New Aesthetic*, which almost immediately provoked a long reply, concentrating—not surprisingly—on Busoni's ideas on notation, with Schoenberg suggesting some of his own.)

Busoni reports with some glee the invention of the "Dynamophone" in America by Dr. Thaddeus Cahill, "an electrical invention for producing scientifically perfect music," as it was described in *McClure's Magazine* in July 1906.[37] This machine, Busoni writes, "could allegedly transform an electrical current into an exactly calculated, unalterable number of vibrations. As the tone depends on the number of vibrations and the apparatus can be 'set' at any desired number, through it the infinite gradation of the octave is the work of a lever linked to the needle on a quadrant."[38] The machine could apparently also regulate the dynamics of each individual tone (a feat performable today in almost any recording studio). The possibilities offered by such machines filled Busoni with joy.

The book ends with a long quotation on the future of music from Friedrich Nietzsche's *Beyond Good and Evil*, advocating a free music, free of national boundaries, free of good and evil. On the last page there is a quotation from J. H. C. Kern's *Manual of Indian Buddhism* (1896): "Not all achieve Nirvana, but he who is from the outset gifted, learns everything that one should know, experiences everything one should experience, leaves what one should leave, develops what one should develop, realizes what one should realize, he achieves Nirvana."[39]

The final paragraph of the book:

> If Nirvana is the kingdom "Beyond good and evil," then a way to it is in-dicated here. Up to the gates. Up to the grating that separates man and eternity—or that opens to let in what was temporal. Beyond the gates is the sound of music. Not tonal art [*Tonkunst*].—Perhaps we must first leave the earth ourselves to hear it. But only to the wanderer who has learned on the way how to cast off earthly bonds, does the grating open.

More than one section in the book is rather over the top, but the sin-cerity of Busoni's belief in the power—and the future—of music is pal-pable. No wonder, then, that the book struck a chord in so many hearts—particularly among the young, and particularly in that second, 1916 edition. It was a time when hope was desperately needed. In spite of the occasionally hectoring, Fabian Society tone, a naive belief in the ultimate benefits of technological progress—both typical of the time in which it was written—and the odd burst of purple prose, the book is still worth reading today as a plea for open-mindedness, as an encour-agement to free creativity, and as a source of stimulating ideas on the very nature of music. Flawed though it is, the book can stand as Bu-soni's equivalent to Beethoven's "Heiligenstadt Testament," his own testament to intellectual and spiritual freedom, disregarding all na-tional and cultural boundaries.

Unfortunately, 1916 was also a time of feverish nationalism, partic-ularly in Germany; therefore no wonder too that, in addition to praise, the book's implicit rejection of national boundaries drew the fire of some critics in that country. None of the criticism was more vitupera-tive than that of Hans Pfitzner (1869–1949), a German composer with nationalist leanings and a conviction of his own conservative mission to carry the banner for German music: in his view, music in its highest form. (His nationalist leanings did not subsequently include National Socialism, which he detested, albeit at the end of World War II he had some trouble convincing the Allies of that fact.) In 1914, in the initial rush of nationalist euphoria, Pfitzner had written a poem beginning "All you swine that Germany has fattened," said swine being foreign artists who had fed on the rich harvest of German art—Busoni no doubt included. Busoni was a cosmopolitan to the very marrow, and loathed and despised national flag waving; this cosmopolitanism was the foundation of his agony during the war years, as he observed the re-sults of the insane hatred that swirled all around Europe outside the borders of neutral Switzerland like a particularly malignant virus.

Pfitzner's relationship with Busoni had been amicable hitherto—Busoni had conducted Pfitzner's music at his Beethovensaal concerts in Berlin, for example, and played in his Trio in F Major in Paris in 1914; and in January 1913 Pfitzner had conducted Busoni's Piano Concerto in Strasbourg, with the composer as soloist. It was not until some nine months after the publication of the Insel-Bücherei edition of the *New Aesthetic*, in May 1917, the same year in which Pfitzner's opera *Palestrina* was premiered (on June 12) in Munich, that Pfitzner made his reactions to the book public, in the pages of the *Süddeutsche Monatshefte*, under the title "*Futuristengefahr*" (The Dangers of Futurism). In some ways it could be viewed as a kind of prose backup to the main thesis of *Palestrina*—that Palestrina in Italy (and by clear implication Pfitzner in Germany) was the divinely chosen champion of national musical standards.

"*Futuristengefahr*" is a prime example of a polemic based on prejudice masquerading as rational thinking. Pfitzner chose to interpret the *New Aesthetic* as an onslaught on German music, and as an incitement to a rejection of tradition and civilization as he knew it. As the title of his attack suggests, he also chose to regard Busoni as belonging to the ranks of the futurists. (Apart from the fact that Busoni had strong reserva-tions about futurism, this assumption is based on a chronological im-possibility: the *New Aesthetic* was first published in 1907, whereas the first futurist manifesto was not published until 1909.)

Pfitzner's venomous and at times gratuitously personal attack on Busoni in *Futuristengefahr* makes unpleasant reading. He willfully misreads much of Busoni's text, in order then to demolish this distorted interpretation: where Busoni writes that what has been accomplished in music until now might just be the infancy of what might come, Pfitzner works himself into a lather on the false premise that Busoni is deprecating what has been composed until now—quite a different thing. There is much talk of "our classical composers"—meaning German composers—and tremendous scorn is poured on Busoni for admiring Liszt and Berlioz. "If they are so great," sneers Pfitzner, "why is that although they are played again and again, they never become really popular, their melodies are never passed on orally?" This is an argument based on a very dubious definition of musical greatness. There is much talk of "the heart," that unfailing standby of the rabble-rouser, and—a great giveaway on one of the mainsprings of Pfitzner's attack—he even quotes approvingly from Wagner's infamous essay "The Jews in Music": the music of these non-Germans "is incapable of producing 'that deep impression upon us or to move our hearts and souls,' . . . that every one of us 'has felt many times before, whenever one of the heroes of our art has—so to speak—merely opened his mouth to address us.'" (In this passage Wagner is in fact attacking Mendelssohn!) In the final pages of his attack, Pfitzner derides Busoni's alleged advocacy of a rejection of traditional musical notation, careering off on the hobbyhorse of his usual distorted logic to conclude, with some more unsavory racist overtones, that "Eskimos, Papuans, Swahili Negroes probably cannot distinguish major and minor either."

This is all argument at a shamefully low level, its only consistent element being that it is virtually all based on false premises, and it says much for Busoni's patience that he bothered to respond to it at all. His measured reply was published in the *Vossische Zeitung* of June 3, 1917 (reprinted in both English and German editions of *Essence and Oneness of Music*, under the title "Open Letter to Hans Pfitzner"). As so often happens in such cases, the attention drawn to Busoni's book by Pfitzner's attack boosted its sales and general popularity immediately. As also often happens, because Busoni remained the calm, urbane cosmopolitan, and Pfitzner lost his temper, Pfitzner ended up looking like a narrow-minded pedant, something of a Beckmesser—the peevishly pedantic town clerk, with his narrow ideas on what is musically permissible, in Wagner's *Die Meistersinger*. (In fact, mirabile dictu, once when the baritone singing Beckmesser in a performance of *Die Meistersinger* Pfitzner was conducting fell ill, Pfitzner stepped in and sang the role.)

"Germany is producing Martin Luthers of smaller and smaller stature, men who appear to be ardent reformers in the eyes of the bourgeoisie and who, at bottom, are quarrelsome and rigid sectarians," Busoni sighed in a letter to his Portuguese friend, the composer and pianist José Vianna da Motta, on May 29, 1917,[40] the same day in which he had written his reply[41] to Pfitzner's attack. (Vianna da Motta was another one of the "foreign swine" who had lived and worked for most of his adult life in Germany, and fled to Switzerland at the outbreak of war.) In his "Open Letter to Hans Pfitzner" Busoni began by refuting the title of Pfitzner's attack. "Already with the title 'The Dangers of Futurism' you are leading your readers astray, by heaping on my name, in the eyes of the public, all the weaknesses and faults with which you could possibly reproach a group of people—from whom I am far removed." Busoni's measured refutation, near the end of the letter, of Pfitzner's nationalistic appropriation of musical genius is gently ironic:

> But how do you describe the career of the "magic child" music? "After he had grown to a wonderfully vigorous and healthy baby with his Netherlands nurse, he spent happy times sojourning in Italy, and now for a hundred and fifty years, as a beautiful and strong youth, has been at home in our Germany, where it is to be hoped he will long thrive."
>
> Consider, honored friend, that in time even the most beautiful, the strongest youth will mature into an old man, and that for the maintenance of a sturdy race, cross-breeding is a proven expedient.

The Munich production of Pfitzner's *Palestrina* went on a short Swiss tour in November 1917, organized by the propaganda department of the German Ministry for Foreign Affairs, with performances in Zurich on November 23 and 24. "The German papers are treating me no better: that Teutonic genius H. Pf[itzner] is never mentioned without a dig at me," wrote Busoni to Egon Petri on November 20.[42] "On the 24th there is to be a performance of 'Palestrina.' For *this* reason, crowds of [German] people have been granted travel permits. . . . It seems the affair has been organized with special care. And again I shall find myself assigned a role against my will." It is not known whether Busoni went to the performance, but presumably not. Amazingly, even at this late stage in the war, the furor over Busoni's little book refused to die down, and on March 31, 1918, he wrote to the musicologist Hugo Leichtentritt: "meanwhile the misguided catchword of the narrow-minded Dr. Hans [Pfitzner] continues to have its effect and I can't even play a C Major chord without people going into paroxysms of Futurist hysteria."[43]

In the last year of the war, Busoni, like many others, was at a low ebb, wondering just how much longer the carnage could drag on. He filled his days, but found it more and more difficult both to cope with his situation of virtual imprisonment in Switzerland and to be artistically creative. During the years in Zurich, he wrote over five thousand letters; letters were a poor substitute, however, for the relaxed give and take of face-to-face creative exchange he had enjoyed with so many other artists and thinkers in his travels in Europe and North America. He acquired a thousand more books, but by late 1917 he had trawled the Swiss bookshops to exhaustion, and they were no longer being replenished. "Now I long for that traveling that once caused me so much suffering; but only travel to big countries and to big cities," he confessed to his old friend Jella Oppenheimer in Vienna. "I am tired of waiting."[44] Often the bizarre idiocy of the situation exasperated him: "In Berne (at my concert)," he wrote Petri in March 1918, "I could see high-ranking people, from countries hostile to one another, sitting side by side."[45] Busoni was still giving enough concerts in Switzerland to cover the family's material needs.

In the absence of virtually any letters from Busoni to Gerda during the war years, except for a few in the summer of 1918, when he resumed the old habit of remaining at home, albeit in Zurich, while she went away to Degersheim (although Lello remained with him), she remains an even more shadowy figure during this period. Edward Dent, in his great biography of Busoni, although writing with Gerda's full cooperation, mostly writes as though she never existed: "In the autumn of 1917 Busoni . . . took to spending his evenings at home with Giotto and his books"[46] is a typical example. Busoni himself nearly always wrote in the first person singular ("I leave New York tomorrow"), even when it is obvious that she—indeed, until they were adult, their sons as well—is included. But from his letters to her throughout his life, and from those tantalizing glimpses in accounts of their home by third parties, we know that her presence in his life was literally vital. His occasional infidelities—the casual infidelities offered by the aphrodisiac of public adulation to the virtuoso traveling artist—she certainly knew of, but was wise enough to ignore. To understand all is to forgive all, and Gerda's love delivered acceptance of this complex man, who had not only never had a childhood, but, owing to his early exposure on the lonely peak of world fame, had never fully mastered—or indeed acknowledged the existence of—the social mechanisms acquired in a life at ground level, as it were, as one among many. Others who loved him—and he was by all accounts an attractive personality—also accepted him.

Philipp Jarnach (1892–1982) was another cosmopolitan composer— his father was Spanish, his mother Flemish, and he was born in France—who "became" German (his wife was German). The young couple had fled to Zurich at the outbreak of the war, where Jarnach found a position at the conservatory teaching composition. He met Busoni there soon after the latter's arrival in the autumn of 1915 and soon became his "famulus," as Busoni dubbed him, preparing the vocal scores for both *Arlecchino* and *Turandot* and helping with rehearsals. For a while the Jarnachs shared a flat with James Joyce and his family, and the two men had become friends after Jarnach politely knocked at Joyce's door to request that the latter refrain from singing during Jarnach's working hours. Jarnach introduced Joyce to Busoni, but, as already stated, the two had little in common. Relatively straitened though the Busonis's circumstances were, they remained hospitable, and their home became one of Zurich's more stimulating meeting places.

One who had difficulties with Busoni's personality was his eldest son Benni, still in Boston. Contact with him had been fitful even before the other three family members returned to Europe in August 1915. ("Benni remains a lonely man and a foreigner to life," Busoni had written in English to an English friend on the eve of their departure from the United States. "He is super-critical and spoils many beautiful things by this unhappy tendency. . . . Now he stays—quite alone—at a country place, and I know very little of his doings." One suspects that Busoni made the common mistake with his children of overcompensating for his own parents' mistakes, and not only put no pressure on them, but went so far as to refrain from offering guidance. With Benni, this proved disastrous. Benni's unhappy love affair, with one Sibylle, was dragging on; he found himself in July 1917 with fifty cents left in his pocket, having tried unsuccessfully for weeks to get some kind of job, at the U.S. Navy enlistment booth in Boston. He was refused, even though the United States had entered the war on April 6, 1917; however, in February 1918 Benni, as a U.S. citizen, was called up for military service, but kept on the reserve list—a fact of which his parents were aware, so occasionally there must have been contact between them.

Two months before, on December 22, 1917, Busoni finished his Sonatina "in diem nativitatis Christi MCMXVII" for Piano (BV 274), first performed in Zurich on January 24 following. Busoni dedicated it to Benni. In all Busoni wrote six sonatinas between 1910 and 1921. It is not known why he called them "sonatinas," but the present writer is inclined to agree with Larry Sitsky, who writes in his *Busoni and the Piano* that using the word is "simply a quiet joke on the composer's part." They are not particularly short—this, the fourth, is a good eight minutes long—and they are certainly not lightweight. The fourth is, like its predecessors, a quiet, almost somber work, as is in keeping with its title, and also with its time of composition. As in all Busoni's works for piano, his own pianistic presence is palpable in the full, resonating sound.

In the spring of 1918 he wrote a Concertino for Clarinet and Small Orchestra (BV 276), which he dedicated to Edmondo Allegra, principal clarinetist in the Zurich Tonhalle orchestra, who gave it its first performance at the Tonhalle in December that year. It has an explorative character, with Busoni trying out many of the ideas he had been absorbing over the previous decade. It is consequently one of the least recognizable of his works.

That summer, while Gerda was in Degersheim, Busoni wrote a fifth sonatina, "Sonatina brevis 'in signo Joannis Sebastiani Magni' for Piano" (BV 280). It is part pastiche, part reworking and merging of four short works by Bach, to form a brilliant "interpretation" of Bach's original works. Its dedicatee was Philipp Jarnach. Lello again stayed with his father in Zurich; now eighteen, he was showing talent as an artist and was to have an exhibition of his pen-and-ink drawings at Tanner's art gallery in Zurich that September.

On October 15, 1918, the libretto of Busoni's last opera, *Doktor Faust*, was published in the German journal *Die weissen Blätter*, the same day the Frankfurt premiere of *Arlecchino* and *Turandot* took place, astonishingly because the war had only weeks to run. On November 11, 1918, what came to be known as World War I indeed came to an end. Military casualties alone, on both sides, came to over thirteen million. Large swathes of Europe were in ruins, borders were redrawn, the German population was in disarray and suffering severe food shortages. Travel within Europe was at first severely restricted, and, given the conditions, it is not surprising that for the time being the Busonis remained in the calm haven of Zurich.

In April 1919 Gerda went on a short holiday to Ascona, on the Swiss side of Lago Maggiore, where she received a letter[47] from Busoni telling her he had had a thorough examination by a doctor who decided "there is *nothing* wrong with me." If so, his improved health could only have been due to the more settled existence forced on him during the Zurich years. But the strains of touring, which had left him constantly exhausted before the war, were soon to take their toll again. In mid-September 1919, Busoni left Switzerland for a lengthy concert tour, first to Paris, then London and the British provinces—"my first attempt to fly," as he wrote[48] to Egon Petri. In April 1917 Petri had moved out of Berlin with his young family (a third child, Jan, had been born in early 1918) to Zakopane, a small town in the Tatra Mountains in southern Poland that he had often visited in the past. Busoni had received the program for the English part of the tour in July, while Gerda was away again, this time in Rovio. "My first concert will be in Liverpool on October 2. . . . I shall appear with Mme [Nellie] Melba—what miserable buffoonery! I shall demand a double fee."[49]

Just as Busoni was embarking on that first postwar tour, Benni, demobilized and having escaped active service, was embarking for Europe. He arrived in Zurich after his father had left. After a wretched and lonely time in America, for the unhappy young man it must have seemed like old times to arrive in the parental home and find his father absent. In Busoni's letters written to Gerda during this tour, there are tantalizing hints, obviously in reply to what Gerda was telling him in her letters, of the concern their eldest son, now aged twenty-six, was already causing: "Benni has not grasped yet that we have to thank others for the chief part of our means of existence and therefore we dare not repulse people, but we have to hold out our hands to one another," wrote his father[50] from faraway London.

In Paris Busoni himself had been depressed by the postwar atmosphere of want coupled with rapacity, anxious people "buying the necessities of life at exaggerated prices," and prostitutes with American soldiers who "walk by their sides without gaiety . . . simply because they believe it is the right thing to do in Paris. . . . All this is neither gay, fitting, nor moral; it makes me think of the last chapter in Dr. Moreau [*The Island of Doctor Moreau*, by H. G. Wells], where the animals fall down on all fours and behave according to their original nature."[51] Busoni met his friend Isidor Philipp (1863–1953), the Hungarian-born pianist, professor of piano at the Paris Conservatoire from 1893–1934, whom he had first met in early 1914, and with whom he had since regularly corresponded, and they had some long talks on Busoni's future. Philipp strongly urged that he return to Bologna. "His one idea is that my place, from now on, is in Italy," Busoni wrote[52] to Gerda. He could, of course, still continue to use Zurich as his base, but, grateful as he was for its generosity as a host, the years in the relatively small town had reinforced his conviction that the metropolis was his natural habitat— but which one?

He was in London by September 23, and relieved to discover it not so drastically altered as Paris. After a few days in the Savoy Hotel, which was very short on supplies, he moved to Maud Allan's apartment at West Wing overlooking Regent's Park, where he had often stayed in the past. One day during his first postwar visit to London Busoni had an experience that at the time, to his oversensitive nerves, carried Hoffmannesque overtones. He was returning to West Wing from a long walk when a thick fog suddenly descended. He managed to find his way to Regent's Park, but then lost his bearings. A man approached and Busoni asked directions to West Wing. The man took him by the arm and led him briskly to the house. As they arrived, by the light of a street lamp Busoni suddenly saw that his guide was blind. There was a quite rational explanation for this: the house next to Maud Allan's was now a home for blind war veterans.

At this time a massive public transport strike broke out, leading to the cancellation of Busoni's first concerts, which were all outside London. By October 7, however, the strike was over and touring could begin. It was on this tour that he shared the stage with Dame Nellie Melba, now aged fifty-nine, which he thought beneath his dignity—and hers:

> Although she is old and very rich, she cannot give up singing in public. It is a great strain for her now, but the production of the voice in her clarinet style is exemplary in its own way and enjoyable even now. Only, I can no longer understand this form of "art for art's sake" which makes the mastery of the instrument with the cheapest possible effect its sole aim. And this form is the only one the great English audience expects and demands and by which it is enchanted.

Busoni's first London concert, on October 15, was in his favorite venue, the Wigmore Hall (formerly the Bechstein Hall, its Germanic name changed during the war). He was moved by the welcome from the audience: he had to stand and bow three times from his piano seat before he could begin playing, and there was even more tumultuous applause at the end. Richard Cappel, the *Daily Mail* critic, wrote: "[Busoni is] far and away the greatest musical executant now with us; a commanding figure—more, a well-nigh awful one; a maker of music that is tremendous and statuesque; a steely and terrible power that regularly cows you as you listen, leaving you almost too humbled to admire."[53]

Benni was a continuing concern, and the more levelheaded Lello was also drawn in. "I hope that you, with your very sensible view of the cause and remedy for his contradictions, are right. I have no clear idea of what tone I shall have to adopt to talk to him," Busoni wrote[54] to his younger son. The uncertainties regarding the future of the whole family caused him disquiet. "I think of you so very much," he wrote[55] to Gerda on October 28, "even more than before. That is beautiful but almost painful, for I cannot always see the way yet, and feel that it is hard for you to bear. Everything might have been so good at this moment; put up with it patiently, meanwhile, with my love, till the better things come (and I believe they will come)."

On November 1 he reported[56] from West Wing on his first meeting with George Bernard Shaw:

> G. B. Shaw came to tea (which he did not drink). He is now sixty-three, very tall. . . . He talks too much and he cannot cloak his vanity. He began at once by shooting off one of his witty little darts. Maudi was saying that she had just come out of a nursing home. "I wonder that you are still alive," said G. B. S., "for in a hospital they throw you out into the street before you are half cured, but in a nursing home they don't let you out until you are dead." ("There's a remedy for that," I said. "You can stop paying.")

Busoni's canny eye saw through a lot of Shaw's bluster and coat trailing, but he enjoyed the cut and thrust of argument with him, twitting him relentlessly on the inconsistencies and shallowness of many of his pronouncements on music.

On November 9 Busoni played in a packed Royal Albert Hall, again in a program shared with Melba. The American baritone Augustus Milner, who had been in the ensemble of the Zurich Opera House since 1915, where he had sung in the premiere of *Arlecchino*, was now in Britain, singing Iago at Covent Garden among other things, and was very helpful to Busoni during this first postwar visit. A few days later Busoni spent a tortured few days in the recording studios, an experience he loathed, as the conditions of the time, with very restricted time limits, still did not allow for the seriousness of approach Busoni the perfectionist demanded of himself.

On November 22 Henry Wood conducted the British premiere of Busoni's *"Sarabande and Cortège"* (BV 282), which was to become part of his *Doktor Faust*, at the Queen's Hall. George Bernard Shaw was in the audience and wrote to Busoni immediately after. Busoni was touched by the appreciative and affectionate reception accorded him. London had always been a loyal audience, and his reception this time probably also had something to do with the relief at yet another sign—in this visit from one of the world's greatest musicians—that life was returning to normal.

Successful and feted though he was during this first postwar British tour, Busoni was weary and longed for the calm of home life. "Imagine, dear Gerda, I have an almost painful longing for Giotto; he would have had such a good time here and I should have had him with me."[57] And a paragraph in another letter[58] to Gerda offers a revealing metaphor for his own feelings of loneliness and alienation: "But there is always something remarkable to see in London. Yesterday, in the middle of heavy traffic, down the middle of Shaftesbury Avenue, trotted my dear, heaven-sent donkey [from *Arlecchino*], peaceful and innocent. All the cars had to swerve past him, for he went more slowly than they did. That went to my stupid heart."

He finally left Britain on December 11, writing Gerda a short letter[59] the day before (his forty-fifth to her on this trip), to tell her of a letter from the playwright and novelist John Galsworthy.

My playing, he writes, "is a lesson in the long task, which confronts us all, of expressing the utmost of emotion in forms perfect and *controlled*— the only indestructible art. One goes to one's work refreshed and inspirited." I was told that Galsworthy went to Spain yesterday morning. That he wanted to write a letter to me the evening before he started out makes me very happy.

In spite of the regretted loss of some of his old bookshops, Busoni still managed to accumulate fifty books during his two and a half months in Britain. His mind was also buzzing with ideas, on an "aesthetic of orchestration," among other things, which he "discussed" in long letters to Philipp Jarnach. Maud Allan accompanied him to Paris, where he made a brief stopover on his way back to Zurich, and where Maud was the innocent cause of what Busoni termed a humiliation. As her French was inadequate, he kindly accompanied her to an impresario with whom she was negotiating, Albert Carré. When they left, Carré more or less ignored Busoni, probably taking him for an interpreter from the Grand Hotel, Busoni surmised, and at which he took tremendous umbrage. "I shall never forgive myself for having taken this step," he lamented to Isidor Philipp.[60] "I think my visit to Carré should be *rectified* in some way. I am very *humiliated*." In spite of his triumphs in Britain, his fragile ego was still easily dented. The financial gains of touring were particularly welcome after the years of relative poverty in Zurich, but during those years he had had the time to compose and to meditate. "You ask me if I am happy," he had written to Isidor Philipp in October from London. "I confess that I am not. Starting again on this traveling circus existence [*cette existence de saltimbanque*] is an unbearable humiliation—at my age and at the moral and artistic point I have attained. And I see no end to it. Now I cannot work on my *Faust*."[61]

Sometime during that autumn an invitation had arrived from Berlin, via his former pupil Leo Kestenberg, now in charge of the music section of the Prussian Ministry for Culture, to take over a master class at the Prussian Academy of Fine Arts. Kestenberg (1882–1962) had long been a staunch socialist, and his idealistic political views had drawn Busoni's acerbic mockery on many occasions; however, in the brief existence of the Weimar Republic, beginning on July 31, 1919, Kestenberg's political allegiance had paid off. It also proved useful to Busoni, who should have been more grateful than he actually was: Kestenberg had had to fight stiff bureaucratic and political opposition to obtain the post for him. The terms were generous, and included six months' leave a year for touring. Shrewdly, Kestenberg floated the idea of classes being held in Busoni's home on the Viktoria-Luise-Platz: this would not only be congenial to Busoni, but would keep the housing commission at bay, who were requisitioning any spare rooms they could find, owing to the sudden dearth in housing in the city. (There was also a distinct possibility that the Busonis's apartment would be taken away from them entirely, if they did not return to occupy it.) Kestenberg's invitation was reinforced by a public appeal for Busoni to return, published in the *Vossische Zeitung*. Still Busoni hesitated.

A brief series of concerts in Milan in early 1920 was a disaster, the reviews hostile. *Il Secolo*, on February 2, 1920, hit hard, "with insults to which, with my name, and, unfortunately, at my age, I no longer wish to expose myself voluntarily," he wrote[62] the same day to Arrigo Serato, who had been trying to arrange concerts for him in Rome. Busoni had no desire at all to come to Rome now, he wrote. He claimed to be suffering from "influenza," his usual term for the indispositions that dogged him, and which probably made him even more irritable. The review, by Gaetano Cesari, had none of the respectful adulation he now considered his due, and attacked where it hurt most—his own compositions. After praising his Bach, Cesari went on, in the rococo style of the time,

The thermometer of success was to fall drastically, above all through the inclusion of three pieces by Busoni himself of rather questionable value.

The pianist has defended his music with the fervor of a father defending his own offspring. . . . But he did not succeed in gaining much sympathy for his creations born of the contact of a cold and sterile musical cerebrality with a pianistic nature which is first-class but eclectically impregnated with scholarly formulae, classico-romantic reminiscences and futuristic seeds.

After a hatchet job on the three Busoni works played, the Sonatinas nos. 3 and 4 and the *Indian Diary*, Cesari ended by dismissing Busoni's playing of Beethoven's *Hammerklavier* sonata as cold and unfeeling. It was not a very auspicious welcome for his first postwar Italian concert tour. Understandably, and particularly compared to the reception accorded him in Britain, this confirmed his decision to rule out settling anywhere in Italy—apart from the fact that he had not been offered a feasible position there.

At the beginning of March he returned to Paris, this time with Gerda, and immediately succumbed to yet another attack of "influenza," from which he recovered before his first concert. He gave nine performances, in five solo recitals and four orchestral concerts, at which he either conducted or played, and one of which included a performance of his Concertino for Clarinet given by Edmondo Allegra. Seven concerts had been scheduled, but such was the demand, with all seven sold out before Busoni arrived, that two more were arranged. In spite of performing, rehearsals, and meeting old friends, Busoni found time to write yet another sonatina, the "Sonatina super Carmen" (BV 284), the sixth, which he dedicated to Leonhard Tauber, the hotel owner and the Busonis's generous host in Paris.

He also continued work on *Doktor Faust*. The evening before he and Gerda left Zurich for Paris he had seen a visiting marionette theater from Munich perform an old version of the *Faust* legend. "It spoiled my departure," he wrote to Jarnach,[63]

> because it left me full of impressions and ideas. At that performance, which I followed as if it were a model for my own, it was touching occasionally to come across lines which appear in my libretto; it was satisfying to find it confirmed that my judgment had been sound in the question of what to retain or eliminate from the old "puppet play" in forming my own personal version.

The experience provoked the familiar sense of frustration: "I should have stayed at home and thrown myself into my work, stimulated as I was by what I had seen and heard. I wasn't at all surprised; it was as though I had often seen this play, the words were so immediately familiar, a proof of how conscientiously I had studied it." Would the puppet play still be running at Easter, when he got back to Zurich, he asked Jarnach anxiously? The Parisian concerts were a complete triumph. At one of them, devoted to his own compositions, "the end of the concert was indescribable, people stood up and shouted."[64] This must surely have expunged the "humiliation" unwittingly inflicted by Albert Carré three months before.

On March 31, at the Zurich Tonhalle, Volkmar Andreae conducted the premiere of Busoni's *Sarabande and Cortège* (BV 282), subtitled Two Studies for "Doktor Faust" for Orchestra, which he had written between December 1918 and January 1919. It was a valuable opportunity to try out some of his work on his opera.

In late June Busoni was in London again, with Gerda, where the decision to leave Zurich crystallized in his mind while writing to Volkmar Andreae[65]—a choice of recipient that somehow made the decision binding: Andreae had been his generous friend and benefactor throughout the Zurich years. Busoni had still not decided irrevocably *where* he was going, however. He was always ultrasensitive to slights, and after the disaster in Milan, he had learned in the spring that Serato had organized a concert there of contemporary Italian composers— and excluded his own Violin Sonata. (There could be several excuses for this omission.) In a letter[66] written on June 10 Busoni showed himself extraordinarily offended by this, and also by the fact that Serato did not seem to be answering his letters.

Writing[67] to Serato from London on June 27, Busoni begins by announcing that "until September" his address in Zurich will remain Scheuchzerstrasse 36. He then explains why he has rejected the idea of living in Italy. It is clear that he is focusing much of his sense of injury on Serato himself. The querulous tone is worthy of Hans Pfitzner. The strains of a divided self, lived out over so many years in Zurich, had caused cracks in his urbane self-control, through which a bitter malice seeped out. Serato claims he would meet with enthusiasm and full cooperation in whatever position he might assume in Italy, Busoni sniffs, but what are the realities? What Busoni is doing here is working up a lather of righteous indignation, in order to justify what he has in fact already decided—his return to Berlin. He has been offered the highest position there, of professor of composition. If Italy had offered a similar position, he would not have hesitated . . . Lucky Serato, who had a position in Bologna! Would he come and visit Busoni in Berlin? he asks ingenuously. The decision was made.

Much as he loved London, and cosmopolitan life, Busoni found the British capital simply too large, the atmosphere so overwhelming that it stifled creativity; one was bombarded by too many impressions (in spite of which, he recommended it to Benni). "One ceases to be and to feel as an artist. . . . If he had lived in England, Goethe would not have left us the legacy of his works," he observed to Philipp Jarnach,[68] after eulogizing springtime in London. (Goethe, whether Busoni realized it or not, was his ultimate example and ideal, and in a way his rival. Busoni obviously saw himself as an Olympian polymath in the mold of his great German predecessor. Comparisons are odious, but Goethe had the serene strength of character to make his choice and stick to it. The little town of Weimar might have seemed a strange habitat for such a great mind, but the results proved it to be the right one: a well-paid sinecure day job as minister for an extremely supportive grand-duke provided exactly the right environment for Goethe to flourish and to merit Napoleon's famous accolade after meeting him: "*Voilà un homme!*" Busoni, like his own Faust, was torn—and arguably destroyed—by unresolved decisions. Nevertheless, the two men shared many similarities, not least their ever-curious minds.)

During that summer tour in Britain, Busoni saw a performance of Puccini's *Trittico* in London, which he judged more positively than he had *Madame Butterfly* in Vienna years before. He observed that in the first of the three short operas, *Il Tabarro*, Puccini had really achieved what he had been trying to achieve in his previous works—*verismo* tragedy. At the beginning of July Gerda left London for Paris, where Ferruccio wrote[69] her that "the young man [William] Walton (who was at the Spanish Restaurant) sent me some manuscript music. He has a little gift for counterpoint. In other respects, they all write according to a formula: notes, notes, notes, all 'hither and yon,' without imagination or feeling." It is not clear who "they" are—probably young British composers.

That summer, Leo Kestenberg finally persuaded Busoni to return to Berlin—or rather, worked out the details. In addition to his teaching post, a production of *Turandot* and *Arlecchino* was promised at the Staatsoper for spring 1921. On August 21, Busoni gave a "modest farewell party," as he put it:[70] an orchestral run-through of his Divertimento for Flute and Orchestra (BV 285), composed in May. On September 9, 1920, he left, alone, for Berlin—by air to Stuttgart, then by train to Berlin—leaving Gerda and the boys to wind up affairs in Zurich.

Notes

1. Stefan Zweig, *Die Welt von Gestern* (Frankfurt am Main: Fischer, 1970; first published in 1944), p. 316.
2. Zweig, *Die Welt von Gestern*, p. 315.
3. Beaumont, *Busoni the Composer*, p. 201.
4. Beaumont, *Busoni the Composer*, p. 203.
5. Beaumont, *Busoni the Composer*, p. 203.
6. Elias Canetti, *Die gerettete Zunge* (Frankfurt am Main: Carl Hanser/ Fischer Taschenbuch Verlag, 1979), pp. 177–78.
7. Letter from FB to Egon Petri, May 13, 1916, MW, p. 255.
8. FB to Egon Petri, May 13, 1916, MW, p. 256.
9. Letter from FB to Hugo Leichtentritt, January 9, 1916, in Beaumont, *Letters*, p. 229.
10. Letter from FB to Hugo Leichtentritt, January 13, 1916, in Beaumont, *Letters*, p. 231.
11. Reprinted as appendix 4 to Jutta Theurich, ed., "Schönberg-Busoni Briefwechsel," *Beiträge zur Musikwissenschaft* 19, no. 3 (1977).
12. Letter from FB to Egon Petri, May 13, 1916, MW, p. 256.
13. This "plan" of Schoenberg's is reprinted as appendix 5 to Theurich, "Schönberg-Busoni Briefwechsel."
14. Letter from Arnold Schoenberg to FB, January 30, 1917, in Beaumont, *Letters*, p. 421.
15. Jutta Theurich, ed., "Briefwechsel zwischen Arnold Schönberg und Ferruccio Busoni, 1903–1919," *Beiträge zur Musikwissenschaft* 19, no. 3 (1977): 163–211.
16. Letter from FB to Egon Petri, August 11, 1916, MW, p. 259.
17. Letter from FB to Edith Andreae, June 23, 1915, in Beaumont, *Letters*, p. 203.

18. Letter from FB to Egon Petri, June 19, 1913, MW, pp. 214–15.

19. Letter from FB to Harriet Lanier, August 18, 1915, Beaumont, *Letters*, p. 212.

20. Part of this quotation originates from a letter to Margarete Klinckerfuss, written on May 19, 1918; the letter, and Busoni's other thoughts on *Arlecchino*, are included in the section "About Himself and His Works," in Busoni, *Wesen und Einheit der Musik*. The English edition, however, contains more of Busoni's thoughts on *Arlecchino* (pp. 62–70) than the German edition.

21. From autobiographical notes by Lotte Lenya contained in Lys Symonette and Kim H. Kowalke, eds., *Speak Low (When You Speak Love): The Letters of Kurt Weill and Lotte Lenya* (London: Hamish Hamilton, 1996), pp. 18–19.

22. Letter from Otto Klemperer to FB, November 21, 1918, StBB, Mus. ep. Otto Klemperer 8 (Bus. Nachl.) B.II.

23. Ferruccio Busoni, *Entwurf einer neuen Ästhetik der Tonkunst*, Insel-Bücherei nr 202 (Leipzig: Insel-Verlag, 1916), pp. 5–6. This edition can still be picked up relatively easily in secondhand bookshops in German-speaking countries. The present writer's own edition is from the "21st–25th thousand" reprinting.

24. Busoni, *Entwurf*, p. 7.

25. Busoni, *Entwurf*, p. 7n.

26. Busoni, *Entwurf*, p. 8.

27. Busoni, *Entwurf*, p. 10.

28. Busoni, *Entwurf*, p. 12.

29. Busoni, *Entwurf*, p. 14.

30. Busoni, *Entwurf*, pp. 17–18. This section on opera is also reproduced in *Wesen und Einheit der Musik*, "Von der Zukunft der Oper," pp. 61ff; English edition, pp. 39ff.

31. Busoni, *Entwurf*, p. 19.

32. Busoni, *Entwurf*, p. 21.

33. Busoni, *Entwurf*, p. 22.

34. Busoni, *Entwurf*, p. 31.

35. Busoni, *Entwurf*, p. 36.

36. Busoni, *Entwurf*, p. 41.

37. Ray Stannard Baker, "New Music for an old World: Dr. Thaddeus Cahill's Dynamophone, an extraordinary electrical Invention for producing scientifically perfect music," *McClure's Magazine* 27, no. 3 (July 1906).

38. Busoni, *Entwurf*, pp. 44–45.

39. Busoni, *Entwurf*, p. 48.

40. Letter from FB to José Vianna da Motta, May 29, 1917, StBB, Bus. Nachl. BI, 722.

324   Chapter Eleven

41. Busoni's "Open Letter to Hans Pfitzner," as first published in the *Vossische Zeitung* on June 3, 1917, is included in both English and German editions of *Wesen und Einheit der Musik*.

42. Letter from FB to Egon Petri, November 20, 1917, MW, p. 278.

43. Letter from FB to Hugo Leichtentritt, March 31, 1918, in Beaumont, *Selected Letters*, p. 270.

44. Letter from FB to Jella Oppenheimer, September 1917, StBB Bus. Nachl. BI, 752a.

45. Letter from FB to Egon Petri, March 1, 1918, MW, p. 281.

46. Dent, *Ferruccio Busoni*, p. 238.

47. Letter from FB to Gerda Busoni, April 19, 1919, StBB Bus. Nachl. IV, 949.

48. Letter from FB to Egon Petri, September 7, 1919, MW, p. 283.

49. Letter from FB to Gerda Busoni, July 23, 1919, StBB Bus. Nachl. IV, 950.

50. Letter from FB to Gerda Busoni, October 22, 1919, StBB Bus. Nachl. IV, 978.

51. Letter from FB to Gerda Busoni, September 21, 1919, Bus. Nachl. IV, 959.

52. FB to Gerda Busoni, September 21, 1919.

53. Review by Richard Cappel, *Daily Mail*, October 16, 1919.

54. Letter from FB to Raffaello Busoni, November 15, 1919, StBB Bus. Nachl. IV, 137.

55. Letter from FB to Gerda Busoni, October 28, 1919, StBB Bus. Nachl. IV, 981.

56. Letter from FB to Gerda Busoni, November 1, 1919, StBB Bus. Nachl. IV, 983.

57. Letter from FB to Gerda Busoni, November 17, 1919, StBB Bus. Nachl. IV, 992.

58. Letter from FB to Gerda Busoni, November 25, 1919, StBB Bus. Nachl. IV, 997.

59. Letter from FB to Gerda Busoni, December 10, 1919, StBB Bus. Nachl. IV, 1003.

60. Letter from FB to Isidor Philipp, December 13, 1919, StBB Bus. Nachl. BI, 313c.

61. Letter from FB to Isidor Philipp, October 17, 1919, StBB Bus. Nachl. BI, 309c.

62. Letter from FB to Arrigo Serato, February 2, 1920, in Sablich, *Lettere*, p. 418.

63. Letter from FB to Philipp Jarnach, March 4, 1920, StBB Bus. Nachl. XXX, 56.

64. Letter from FB to Philipp Jarnach, March 22–25, 1920, StBB Bus. Nachl. XXX, 57.

65. Letter from FB to Volkmar Andreae, June 23, 1920, in Beaumont, *Letters*, p. 311.

66. Letter from FB to Arrigo Serato, June 10, 1920, in Sablich, *Lettere*, p. 432.

67. Letter from FB to Arrigo Serato, June 27, 1920, in Sablich, *Lettere*, p. 433, abridged version in Beaumont, *Selected Letters*, p. 312.

68. Letter from FB to Philipp Jarnach, July 2, 1920, StBB Bus. Nachl. XXX, 62.

69. Letter from FB to Gerda Busoni, July 5, 1920, StBB Bus. Nachl. IV, 1009.

70. Letter from FB to Philipp Jarnach, August 13, 1920, StBB Bus. Nachl. XXX, 64.

~

CHAPTER TWELVE

Return to Berlin, *Doktor Faust*, Final Years: 1920 to 1924

Mephistopheles: Has this man met with an accident, perchance?

—Ferruccio Busoni, *Doktor Faust*, last line of last scene

Throughout the years of exile, Busoni had always carried the key to his library in Berlin with him, but it was only on September 12, 1920, one day after he had finally arrived back at the apartment on Viktoria-Luise-Platz, that he dared enter the room again. He was relieved to find everything still in place behind that reinforced door, although the huge Boccioni painting, previously hanging elsewhere in the apartment, had disappeared. (It must have been taken away temporarily for safe keeping, as its provenance in the records of the New York Museum of Modern Art, its present home, is given as the Busoni family.) Outside, much had changed—although some things had not: he met the singer Hans Herrmann in the street, who greeted him jovially, as though there had been no interim, with "Hello, Busoni, nice to see you. I want you to sign a fan for a lady!" "Is such a thing possible?!!!" Busoni wrote[1] wonderingly to Gerda. "You will see how things are," he told her in the same letter. "If this does not do, we must make another choice. But I am still convinced it will have to be tried. . . . I think I shall do a lot of work. I shall concentrate. I miss Giotto quite terribly. Yes, I am looking forward to work, even to experimenting at the piano again."

Thus the return, to the nearest thing to a home he was ever to know, of the "musical Ishmael." (Or, as he wrote[2] to Isidor Philipp three weeks after his return, "I am something between Don Quixote and the Wandering Jew.") In the first heady rush of being reunited with his books and other familiar objects, within four days he finished a Toccata for Piano (BV 287) he had begun in July, and then on September 19, to his own surprise and "for a joke," he wrote a *Tanzwalzer* (BV 288) which he immediately after set about scoring for small orchestra. "Officially" he was not yet back in residence in Berlin, and he seldom emerged from the apartment, except to go for a short walk; nevertheless, word somehow spread, and almost from the first day he had a stream of visitors. The *Tanzwalzer* had come to him during one of his short walks, when he heard the sounds of a Johann Strauss waltz coming from a coffee house. He claimed to have written it just to test his ability to write such a lightweight work, but it says much for his mood of elation at the time. (He dedicated it to the memory of Johann Strauss—the younger, one presumes.)

In Zurich, Gerda finished packing the contents of the apartment on the Scheuchzerstrasse, which were then sent off in a furniture van to Berlin. She herself preceded it at the end of September, leaving Benni and Giotto behind (Lello had gone to Paris to study art). Unsurprisingly, in spite of that initial elation, at first Ferruccio suffered considerable mood swings and depression, and was relieved to have Gerda with him again—although after the first few days she too became rather silent and unlike her usual cheerful self. This was the first time they had set foot on German soil since early January 1915—an absence of nearly six years. They knew they could leave, if the situation worsened, but by returning they had tacitly made a commitment to Berlin it would be psychologically difficult to break, and that knowledge was sobering.

The music journal *Der Anbruch* was devoting a whole January 1921 issue to Busoni, which he went through prior to publication, with some satisfaction. It contained articles on the main aspects of Busoni's work, as pianist and composer, by leading German and foreign experts, including Busoni's first biographer, the English musicologist Edward Dent ("Busoni as Composer"), and Gisella Selden-Goth ("The Goethean Element in Busoni"). The latter, another of the "caryatides," as the group of adoring women surrounding Busoni were known, had organized a public reading himself. These three Berlin concerts, in addition to being a further triumph, were enormously important to Busoni, who was anxious as ever to appear primarily as composer. The second concert contained the *Tanzwalzer*.

By early February 1921 Busoni was in London yet again, with the inevitable excursion into the hated but lucrative provinces. Gerda was with him part of the time, partly to take care of him. Already people were reacting with shock to his appearance—he had cancelled a planned trip to Paris prior to London, feeling he could not cope with so much exertion. Although he was still unwilling to admit it, by now the deterioration in his health, kept in abeyance in Zurich, was accelerating. Nevertheless, in April he was in Rome for five concerts in two weeks. While he was there, the title of *commendatore* was conferred on him, which caused him some amusement: he associated the title with the *commendatore* in Mozart's *Don Giovanni*. A ray of light was a visit to the marionette theater again, where this time he saw a performance of Rossini's *La gazza ladra*. In May there were more concerts in Berlin, and on May 19 a new production of his *Turandot* and *Arlecchino* at the Staatsoper, as promised.

On July 1 Busoni's academy composition class officially opened, and soon settled down to the routine of the pupils coming to him on Mondays and Thursdays, for an hour or so. "So far," he wrote[6] to Lello on July 15,

> there are four: a headstrong Russian [Vladimir Vogel] . . . ; a somewhat perfumed Croatian [probably Bozidar Sirola]; a very fine little Jew (who will certainly make his way and is already something of a factotum around the house) [Kurt Weill]; and finally a small pudgy youth who looks like an inflated tire, wears enormous glasses perched on his nose and is undoubtedly talented [Robert Blum, who left after three months owing to illness, and returned to Zurich]. The latter two are a source of pleasure.

In spite of the flippancy of Busoni's descriptions of his pupils—partly an expression of the relaxed and intimate relationship he always enjoyed with his youngest son, and certainly not intended for other eyes—the very choice of pupils is yet another proof of Busoni's sovereign disregard of national boundaries.

of the libretto of *Doktor Faust* in the Goethe House in Weimar in M₹
1920, for which Busoni had supplied her with some valuable commen₹
but he had not been present. (A year later she was to publish a whole v₹
ume on Busoni.[3] Subtitled "An attempted portrait," it is a gushing eulo₹
concentrating on his compositions, that in fact does Busoni few favors. ₹
Marc-André Roberge rightly comments in his *Ferruccio Busoni: A Bio-B*
liography, it is "written in an ecstatic style that gives the impression t₹
the book is a plea for the composer's beatification."[4] It has never b₹
translated into English.)

The changes in Berlin and in its people were shocking. Nearly t₹
years after the end of the war, the social and political upheavals of ₹
feat and the short-lived heady period of Spartacist revolution—the ₹
ter sparked off from the East by Russian example, and from the Wes₹
the desperate situation at the end of the war—were dying down ₹
Germany was settling back into a conservative status quo ante. ₹
Kaiser was gone, into exile in the Netherlands, but the imperial ir
tutions remained—and much of the mind-set. On June 28, 1919, ₹
ultimately disastrous peace treaty had been reluctantly accepted ₹
signed, polarizing public opinion. And a month later, on July 31, ₹
ill-fated Weimar Republic came into being, too pragmatic and rea₹
able to cope with the volatile situation created by the peace treaty ₹
the privations its punishing reparation clauses entailed. Inflation w₹
spiral out of control only in April 1923, but already it had begun, ₹
was exacerbated by shortages of all basic commodities. ("A poli₹
social reflection: I fancy it is fairly dangerous to ill-treat a starving ₹
wrote Busoni, astutely sardonic as ever, to his good friend ₹
Philipp.[5]) For the moment the Busonis were cushioned by Ferru₹
earnings in foreign currency from his recent tours abroad, and ₹
were able to help many of their Berlin friends in practical ways, su
inviting them for meals.

In spite of the grim circumstances in the city, concerts were r₹
theless soon planned for Busoni. At his first, a piano recital on N₹
ber 18, in the Philharmonie, to an audience of some three thousan₹
reception the Berliners gave Busoni bordered on mass hysteria. ₹
ond recital on November 28 was a similar triumph. In January he ₹
Hamburg, after the first of a series of three orchestral concerts in ₹
devoted entirely to his own works, the first two conducted by ₹

Although informal, not to say unorthodox, in method, these lessons were of crucial importance to these and other pupils. Kurt Weill had written[7] to his brother in February 1919, when the idea of giving Busoni a teaching appointment in Berlin first arose:

> Today I heard that one of the candidates for the job of director of the Hochschule is one of the most modern of modernists: BUSONI. Of course, the teachers and students at the Hochschule, that herd of old Teutonic, behind-the-times, idiotic goats, protest this with all their might. But he'd be healthy for this old dump, although I don't know if he's the right composition teacher.

Competition to study under Busoni was fierce; Weill only managed to get an interview with him through the personal intervention of the critic Oskar Bie. "You wouldn't believe how difficult it is to get close to Busoni," Weill wrote[8] his father in November 1920; "the doorman has orders to send everyone away. Nevertheless, I spent a tremendously interesting afternoon with him. . . . He is amazed at my youth [twenty years]; he kept my compositions but doesn't want to decide, because such big shots have already applied that there is almost no room for such a young fellow as me." But after that first meeting, Weill was soon frequenting the apartment on the Viktoria-Luise-Platz. On January 20, 1921, still six months before the official beginning of the lessons, Weill wrote[9] to Busoni:

> This afternoon, in my surprise, I could only hastily stammer my thanks that someone should so enthusiastically take an interest in me, and someone, at that, whom I hold above all others in such glowing esteem. . . . Let me assist you in whatever you might need me for in the future that I might be able to do. I would be very happy to be thought of always as your sincerely devoted *famulus*.

Busoni always had the ability to inspire this devotion, in his pupils and in a whole generation of young musicians, thanks too in large measure to his *New Aesthetic*, that clarion call for artistic freedom.

His Zurich famulus, Philipp Jarnach, was now in Berlin as well, and on Busoni's recommendation Weill supplemented his studies with intensive lessons in counterpoint with Jarnach. Later Busoni helped Weill by recommending him to Universal Edition, the Viennese publishers, who offered the young composer a ten-year contract.

The students were also always welcome at the frequent and distin-guished afternoon receptions in the Busonis's home, consistently with Busoni's maxim of giving his pupils a broad education. Musicians were generally in the minority at these gatherings, which were composed of painters, writers, poets, architects, scientists, and others, Busoni presid-ing and often delivering lengthy monologues, Gerda, that ever-kindly spirit, unobtrusively looking after everyone.

The students brought their own compositions to the lessons, where they were played, discussed, and criticized. As Kurt Weill later de-scribed it:

> He called us "disciples" and there weren't really any lessons as such, but he allowed us to breathe in his aura, which radiated into every sphere, but always led to music. . . . It was a mutual exchange of ideas in the best sense, without any attempt to enforce any opinion, without autocracy, and without the faintest hint of envy or resentment, and the recognition given to any work that betrayed talent and ability, was spontaneous and enthusiastic.[10]

This eulogy, written a year after Busoni's death by the twenty-five-year-old Weill, with its claim that "without being invested outwardly with any kind of powers, he had nevertheless become the invisible leader of European musical life," nevertheless offers yet another impression of Busoni's extraordinary power to inspire.

As Busoni himself expressed it in the letter to Lello quoted above:

> But *where* does one begin to teach? At the moment this is quite a prob-lem. They have great ability and yet are incapable of the simplest things, their forms are complex and yet not diversified, and they exercise the general right of today's youth to proclaim every crooked line as individ-uality and freedom. Where does one start? I can only bring them to rea-son gradually and patiently. Were I to "drive my point home," I would become ridiculous in their eyes and fail to convince them. Am I not one of the "leaders of modern trends"? Are they not fulfilling—this is what they feel—my boldest dreams?

That autumn of 1921 Busoni had an attack of illness that forced him to consult a doctor, and he discovered that he was gravely ill, his kid-neys and liver in particular seriously affected. He tried to hide it at first, even from Gerda—who of course *was* aware of it but went along with the deceit. In spite of this, in November he played in a concert with Egon Petri (since September resident in Berlin and now a professor at the Hochschule), and in December played six Mozart concertos in two evenings.

Although relations with Lello were always close and relaxed— letters to him from Ferruccio often beginning "Lieber Lellowitz," and Lello writing to his parents from Paris almost daily—Benni, remaining behind in Zurich, continued to make difficulties. He never wrote, and more than once his father was reduced to asking Volkmar Andreae if he had heard any news of him. At the beginning of 1922 Andreae wrote with some astounding news: Benni had become engaged. And on January 28 he married the twenty-one-year-old Henriette Rinderknecht, a Zurich dressmaker—it was said, because she was the only person Benni had ever met in Zurich who had never heard of his father. Benni was now thirty.

In late January 1922 Busoni was in London, again part of the time with Gerda, and again visiting the provinces—Glasgow, Manchester, and Bradford, among other places. Petri was also with him in London, Busoni doing his best to promote him, and the young violinist Josef Szigeti. With inflation in Germany gathering momentum, Busoni desperately needed funds in a more stable currency—the more so, as he was now aware he might not have long to live. He also endured some more recording sessions (Bach, Beethoven, Chopin, and Liszt). At the beginning of March he joined Gerda in Paris, where he was greeted at his first appearance on the concert platform with a ten-minute standing ovation. His program there included Saint-Saëns's E-flat Piano Concerto (Saint-Saëns had died on December 16, 1921), and Mendelssohn's G Minor Piano Concerto. With the latter, Busoni astounded his friend Isidor Philipp: he had not looked at the score for twenty-five years, but just borrowed a copy a day or two prior to the concert, to make sure of his entries.

Philipp could clearly see the state of Busoni's health, and for that reason tried to persuade him to accept an extremely lucrative invitation to Argentina extended personally by the country's president, who assured Busoni that he would be his personal guest. Busoni, whose repugnance to piano playing in public was now almost overwhelming, refused.

"Think of your wife and children," Philipp admonished him, causing Gerda to break down in tears. This made Busoni aggressive, his offensiveness toward Philipp only forgiven because the latter was aware of the gravity of his illness. Busoni had enormous respect for Philipp, which is possibly why he reacted so violently to his advice. Philipp was roughly the same age, a wise and balanced man who never succumbed to Busoni worship but offered honest friendship. (Although Egon Petri was now living in Berlin, the time of Busoni sharing his innermost thoughts with him was long past. They had simply grown apart, the main bond now the familiarity of a long-lasting relationship—which nevertheless still often included possessive demands and reproaches on Busoni's part.) Since before the war, Philipp had offered support while remaining his own man. "You are at this moment the only one of my friends who can listen to me with interest and understand me. Nevertheless, forgive me if I worry you with my confidences,"[11] Busoni had written to him from Bologna in June 1914. He trusted Philipp, and in letters from Bologna, New York, Zurich, and Berlin, over the following years, he had openly poured out his feelings, hopes, and fears, in addition to keeping Philipp abreast of what he was composing.

Gerda returned to Berlin after Paris, taking Lello back with her, and Ferruccio went to Hamburg to play a Mozart concerto in a concert that also included the *Sarabande and Cortège* from his *Doktor Faust*. Here there was another mood swing: a "man from New York" was there, "with big plans. Piano playing pleases me better again; I should still like to acquire yet another side to it; and I almost think that I shall do it!"[12]

By the end of the month he was back in Berlin, where the family was soon joined by Benni and his wife. Given Busoni's urbanity, and Gerda's saintly character, their daughter-in-law was most probably accepted without tensions on their part, if not on Benni's. (In early March Busoni had written[13] to his cousin Ersilia, "Benni, who has committed the stupidity of getting married on impulse to a girl I do not know, will probably also be coming [to Berlin], with or without the *other half*, who according to descriptions I have received on her figure represents more like *three quarters*.")

On May 29 Busoni played Beethoven's Fifth Piano Concerto in Berlin—his last public appearance as a pianist. Edgard Varèse, now based in New York, heard that Busoni was seriously ill, and that summer came back to Berlin with his second, American wife, Louise, expressly to see him. Through Busoni's secretary, Rita Boetticher, they found a room at a pension. Varèse always called Rita Boetticher "Busoni's Rigoletto," as she was slightly hunchbacked, and, according to Louise Varèse, "had the privileged role of king's jester. . . . In any case she was his accomplice, abetting him in his mocking gibes and adding her own malicious witticisms to his. Together they could be quite dreadful and dreaded by the timorous." Busoni's humor often had a cruel, or at least thoughtless, streak; for example, he was fond of playing with people's names—he nearly always called Vianna da Motta "Da," which was scarcely likely to cause offence, likewise "Ali Baba" for the Czech composer Alois Hába (1893–1973). Less pleasant (though the story could be apocryphal), is the incident related by Edgard Varèse: "I remember one evening at his house when a singer by the name of Frau Pissling came up to him to say good night, he took both of her hands in his and, keeping a very serious face, said, 'Dear Frau Pissling, every night before I go to bed I think of you.'"[14] And he shocked the young H. H. Stuckenschmidt during one of his first visits to Viktoria-Luise-Platz by referring to the conductor Hermann Scherchen as "Erschchen" (Ärschchen, or "little arse"), then pretending he had inadvertently mispronounced the name and apologizing.[15] Throughout his life he was fond of rather lugubrious and unfunny plays on words, which often feature in his letters too.

The Varèses found Busoni drinking milk, on doctor's orders, still very handsome but obviously ill. In November he was too ill to attend a concert featuring music by both himself and Varèse. From now on, he was to concentrate all his remaining strength on his masterwork, the opera *Doktor Faust*. Interruptions to his composing were henceforth not caused by performing, but by illness: that autumn and winter he was ill for four months. He had been due to go on another British tour in February 1923, but on the doctor's insistence it was abandoned. For part of the time he was too ill to do any work on the opera at all—although in March, "as fruit of my convalescence," as he wrote to Egon Petri,[16] he wrote three (eventually numbers 1, 3, and 5) of what were to become the Five Short Pieces for the Cultivation of Polyphonic Playing on the Piano (BV 296), the first public performance of which he offered to Petri (see below). Number 2 was written in May, and number 4 in July.

They are intended for advanced players. Again, the music is interwoven with prior and future works: number 3 contains a chorale containing the "Death motif" of threefold repetition of one note that had
appeared in the Second Violin Sonata and the Fantasia after J. S. Bach,
and which, as can be seen in the last sketch for *Doktor Faust*, was intended to be used in the closing scene of the opera. First published in
1923, they were also included in volume 9 of the second edition of Busoni's monumental *Klavierübung* in 1925.

In July 1923, on his insistence, Gerda had to go to Donaueschingen
to represent him at the music festival there, but in August he was able
to travel to Weimar for a series of concerts organized by Hermann
Scherchen, which was part of a weeklong *Bauhaus* Festival, at which,
on August 18, Petri gave the first performance of numbers 1 to 3 of the
Short Pieces for Piano, and Busoni sat next to Igor Stravinsky during a
performance of the latter's *Histoire du soldat*. In Switzerland during the
war years, Busoni and Stravinsky had not always seen eye to eye. They
never met during that time (Stravinsky lived in Geneva), but one day
it was reported to Busoni that Stravinsky had said he could not understand how such an open-minded and progressive man and musician as
Busoni could admire and rate highly the German classic composers
Bach and Mozart. Busoni retorted that if such an open-minded and
progressive musician as Stravinsky really got to know the German classic composers, he would rate, admire, and love them too. This was, of
course, immediately relayed to Stravinsky, but it is not known how he
reacted.

The concert in Weimar contained, in addition to Busoni's Short
Pieces for Piano, Paul Hindemith's *Das Marienleben*, Ernst Krenek's
Concerto Grosso, and, in the second half, Stravinsky's *Histoire du Soldat*, in Hans Reinhard's German translation. Stravinsky's first words on
meeting Busoni were: "Maestro, I love the classic musicians!" Busoni
was visibly moved by this openness, and shook Stravinsky's hand, saying in French, "Well, so we're in agreement today then!" The *Histoire
du Soldat* made a great impression on Busoni. According to Vladimir
Vogel, one of his pupils who was with him, he had tears in his eyes as
he came out of the theater, and said, "So he has succeeded in writing
an opera—without singing!"[17] (Busoni took four of his pupils, at his
own expense, with him to Weimar.)

By now, inflation in Germany was out of control, and the Busonis's situation too was affected: "Confined to the country on account of almost insurmountable legal restrictions, our movements are limited and we are obliged to subject ourselves to the general fate," Busoni wrote[18] Isidor Philipp in August. "My courageous wife has a daily struggle to find butter at 300,000 Marks a pound! (Everything else in proportion.) Often enough there is none to be had.—Even if one did leave: where would one go? . . . Anyway I would be in no condition to burden myself with new troubles and emotions."

Owing to the crippling reparation repayments, which led to a flight of German capital abroad, in turn causing obstacles to the revival of German trade, the financial situation in the country continued to worsen. The German government, in a misguided attempt to halt this situation, issued more money, leading to runaway inflation. During 1922, the exchange rate with the dollar fell from 4.20 marks to 160 marks, and by the end of the year it was over 7,000 marks. The year 1923 saw the culmination of this state of affairs, the mark falling from 160,000 to the dollar on July 1 to 4,200,000 [sic!] by November 1. On November 20, 1923, a new currency, the Rentenmark, was introduced in strictly limited quantities, but it took another year, and a stabilization plan agreed to by Germany and the Allies in August 1924, to bring the situation under control. Meanwhile, there was social unrest, localized revolt, and in general a very volatile atmosphere.

Nevertheless, possibly with Isidor Philipp's help, by late September 1923, Gerda and Ferruccio were in Paris, where they remained for six weeks. Philipp insisted on Busoni's being examined by a doctor there, whose verdict was that if he gave up alcohol and tobacco altogether he might live another four or five months, otherwise a month or less. In spite of much wavering on whether or not to move permanently to Paris, by mid-November Gerda and Ferruccio were back in Berlin. No longer able to ignore the fact that he was suffering a fatal illness, and with his strength ebbing drastically, Busoni's overriding concern now was to finish his *Doktor Faust*, for which he needed the environment he had created in his apartment. Dresden had already agreed to stage the world premiere, and that steeled his determination further.

The opera's gestation period was certainly lengthy. The basic Faust legend, of a man who sells his soul to the devil in exchange for earthly gain, had attracted Busoni for the whole of his adult life: the third of his *Racconti fantastici*, written around 1880 when he was in his mid-teens, was based on the story by Wilhelm Hauff (1802–1827), "The Cave of Steenfoll," in which a fisherman sells his soul to the devil in exchange for sunken treasure. The theme of an encounter with dark forces is found in Busoni's unfinished opera *Sigune*; in the libretto *Der mächtige Zauberer* (The Mighty Musician), published by Carlo Schmidl in 1907 in the volume containing the first edition of his *New Aesthetic*, but never set to music; and in *Die Brautwahl*. Around 1892, while living in Boston, he wrote sketches for an opera, *Ahasver*, on Ahasuerus, the Wandering Jew, the man who, according to legend, mocked Christ on the way to his crucifixion and was cursed with immortality. Busoni's version of the legend, from what can be gleaned from the extant fragments,[19] is particularly bleak: after the whole human race has been destroyed by another Ice Age, Ahasver is left alone, but is ultimately redeemed and allowed to die. At various times, Busoni had also toyed with the idea of operas on Merlin, Dante, Don Juan, Leonardo da Vinci, and Faust, drawn by a powerful sense of affinity to all these *âmes damnées*. His operas and libretti, completed or not, all in various ways contain a strong autobiographical element—one character with whom Busoni obviously identifies.

Leonardo was also the focus for that other recurring idea, the revival of Italian opera. ("For two days I have been pursued by an idea, stronger than any previous ones; that, as the natural result of quite fifteen years' development, I *must* write an Italian opera!" he had written to Gerda back in May 1908 from Vienna.[20]) This was an idea shortly to be buffeted by realities, when he toured Italy in September the same year, though it did return: "Dear Gerda: a great idea dawned on me this morning. I should like to give this Italy a national opera, as Wagner gave one to Germany, and which the Italians have not got yet."[21] This idea was, as we know, to come to nothing: none of his completed operas even had an Italian libretto. He was familiar with Giorgio Vasari's essay on Leonardo in his famous *Lives of the Most Eminent Italian Architects, Painters and Sculptors* of 1550, a book given to Busoni by his mother at Christmas 1886, and he also had the Russian Dmitri Merezhkovsky's historical novel *Leonardo da Vinci*, published in 1902 (significantly, one of a trilogy Merezhkovsky called *Christ and An-*

tichrist). Busoni had the Vasari and the Merezhkovsky with him in London in November 1908. Although he gradually realized the shortcomings of the latter ("It often reminds one of Baedeker"),[22] it nevertheless sparked ideas.

> I thought that he (Leonardo) might give me the wished-for figure for my Italian opera. The historical background of the Sforzas is great and one could make Leonardo the central figure of the action, like Hans Sachs in the "Meistersinger." The episodes, when he arranged the festivities at the court of the Sforzas and invented many clever mechanical devices for them, are quite reminiscent of the role of Faust in the puppet play by the Duke of Mantua, that Goethe also used in Part Two of *Faust*.[23]

Soon after, Busoni sketched out the text for two scenes of an opera on Leonardo. In 1912 he had discussed with Gabriele D'Annunzio collaborating on a Leonardo opera, an idea that simmered for another year before finally going off the boil. What remains is a tacit allusion to Leonardo's role as organizer of court amusements for the Sforzas in Milan, in Faust's similar role at the court of the Duke of Parma in his *Doktor Faust*.

Edward Dent had come to the *Die Brautwahl* premiere in Hamburg in April 1912, where Busoni discussed the Faust idea with him, whereupon Dent sent him Christopher Marlowe's *Doctor Faustus* in a three-volume edition of Marlowe's works. That same year the German playwright Frank Wedekind approached Busoni to write the music for his latest play, *Franziska*, a Faust parody, which, as related in chapter 9, Busoni declined, but only after much thought. In a letter[24] to Gerda that summer he listed pro and contra—as last of the latter, "It will spoil my own Faust idea for myself," though he only made his decision final after reading her opinion on it: "Your letter has strengthened me in my decision to let the 'Franziska' go. I knew I should!; and today I wrote to Munich to refuse."[25] Let no one say Gerda was mere background in his life.

The Faust idea was gaining hold: according to the dating of a text, "Basle, 31 August 1910," written on twenty sheets of headed letter paper of the Hotel des Trois Rois in Basle,[26] he had written the first scenes of a *Faust* libretto at that time, when he was giving a master class in Basle, based on the puppet play of 1846 by the literary scholar and poet

Karl Simrock (1802–1876), which in its turn is an amalgam of all versions of the legend. (We know from the catalog of Busoni's library[27] that he owned an 1884 reprint of the *Historia von D. Johann Fausten* published by Johann Spies in 1587—see below—and a collection of versions of the legend from the sixteenth century until 1884, the year before the collection was published, plus many other volumes either containing *Faust* versions, or secondary texts.) These scenes written in 1910 cover only Faust's despairing monologue in his study, the dialogue with good and evil spirits, the scene with Faust, his famulus Wagner, and the three students from Cracow, and a sketch of the pact scene with Mephistopheles. A diary entry for December 9, 1910, reads: "F[aust]? *Literarisch* too difficult, through Goethe-comparison. Or it would have to be something completely new." In Busoni's "On the Score of 'Doktor Faust,'" written in July 1922 and contained in *The Essence of Music*, he does not mention these early sketches: "As though in a fever, and in six days, I wrote the first sketch of 'Doktor Faust,' between the outbreak of the war and the preparations for an ocean voyage towards the end of 1914."[28] But from the diary entries for December 21–25, 1914, in which he records that while looking for his Leonardo sketches, he found the "F[aust] fragments," we know that he based the 1914 version on those earlier sketches:

> suddenly like a vision everything was together. Five movements. Study monologue cut out. G[retchen episode] assumed to be over; during pact Easter bells ring!—Garden party at court in Parma, Duchess betrays her love, Herod appears as picture. (Salome) John, with similarity: Duke, F[aust] three students from Cracow, beginning. Night watchman—end. Query whether Casperle—intermezzi in front of the curtain, without music, or not!

We see from this and from other diary entries that this version of the plot is essentially the same as the final one Busoni set to music. We also learn from his diaries that August Strindberg was the main catalyst for a resumption of work on Faust: the Swedish writer's play *Luther, the Nightingale of Wittenberg* (written in 1903), had its Berlin premiere at the Künstlertheater on December 5, 1914, and Busoni was there. In his diary of December 7 Busoni noted: "Strindberg's Luther impression— still excited after learning that Dr. Faust Luther's companion" (in the play, Luther and Faust meet). On the evening of December 26, 1914, he read the whole text to his family. (The diary entry for December 27 reads: "Luther [that is, Strindberg's play] was call [*Appell*] to the idea.")

During the following nine months in America, the only addition to the text was the spoken prologue, completed in June 1915. It was only when he was settled in Zurich that Busoni resumed work on the opera. The text, with further amendments, was first published in Zurich in October 1918 in the expressionist journal *Die weissen Blätter*; a final version was printed in 1920, when Busoni had returned to Berlin, and in May of that year, as recounted above, the actor Heinrich Devrient gave a public reading of the libretto in the Goethe House in Weimar. Shortly after, possibly oppressed by the weight of Goethe's play, Busoni deleted all mention of Gretchen: she was now referred to as "the girl." (Goethe was the first of all those dealing with the Faust legend to name her as Margarete, or Gretchen, and give her character.) This amendment was incorporated in a second edition published later that same year. There was another public reading in Berlin, in March 1921. Busoni's motive for publishing the libretto well in advance of an actual opera performance was to ensure that a future audience would (ideally) comprehend the work's philosophical meaning in advance of seeing and hearing a performance.

He began jotting down some initial ideas on the music while staying with the Marchese Casanova in Pallanza, in 1916, but then put *Doktor Faust* on hold while he completed the two operas *Arlecchino* and *Turandot* for Zurich. By the end of 1918, however, half the score was completed, including the *Sarabande and Cortège* (BV 282), which were written in Zurich during the period December 1918 to January 1919 and which, as so often with Busoni, were performed as separate pieces in advance of the completion of the opera. (They were premiered in Zurich at the Tonhalle on March 31, 1919, conducted by their dedicatee, Volkmar Andreae.) The outbreak of peace in November 1918 did not immediately affect Busoni's composing output—it was nearly a year later that he left Zurich for the first time, on that extended trip to Paris and London—but his energies were nevertheless gradually undermined both by the many indecisions regarding his future and by his deteriorating health.

By the end of 1920 he had still written only half the score, albeit interspersed with more of what Antony Beaumont terms "satellite works,"[29] all of which were eventually woven into the musical fabric of *Doktor Faust*, in addition to having independent lives of their own. Beaumont lists twenty-three of these, including a passage in the *Fantasia Contrappuntistica* (BV 256) of 1910, the fourth sonatina (*Sonatina in diem nativitatis Christi* MCMXVII, BV 274) written on December 22, 1917, various Goethe settings, the Concertino for Clarinet (BV 276) of March 1918, and the *Sarabande and Cortège*, which were actually subtitled "Two Studies for 'Doktor Faust' for Orchestra." In the summer of 1922 further work was accomplished on the score, interrupted that autumn by Busoni's serious illness, after which it limped on. On April 1, 1924—his fifty-eighth birthday—he drew up a plan for the final scene, but with his health now failing fast, he was unable to put this into execution himself.

The Faust legend is based on the life of a historical character who lived roughly from 1480 to 1540 in central Germany. It is possible that there were two men—Georg Faust and Johann Faust—with the same name, as both these names are recorded, or, quite simply, the one man had two Christian names: then as now, a common practice. By 1507, according to the Abbot of Sponheim, Johannes Tritheim, one Georg Faust had become a schoolmaster in Kreuznach, but was discovered to be abusing the boys under his care and fled. In 1509 "Johannes Faust" obtained a bachelor of arts degree in Heidelberg, and in 1513 "Georg Faust," "demigod of Heidelberg," was heard bragging in an Erfurt inn. Among other sightings: the account book of the Bishop of Bamberg in Bavaria records that on Friday, February 10, 1520, Dr. Faust received ten guilders for casting the bishop's horoscope. In 1528 "Dr. Georg Faust" was banished from Ingolstadt as a necromancer, and "Dr. Faust," "the great sodomite and necromancer," was refused a safe conduct by the city of Nuremberg in May 10, 1532. By 1540, shortly before his death, he appears to have been upgraded to "the philosopher Faust"; he had accurately prophesied "a very bad year" for a Venezuelan expedition. Although he studied theology, he also seems to have gathered considerable knowledge on medicine, astrology, and alchemy, very much the fashionable, frontier-pushing subjects of the time, and he was certainly a well-known, if not notorious, figure by the time he died.

His main field of operations was the central swathe of Germany running from the Rhine to the Elbe: Martin Luther country. Germany was in religious and political turmoil at this time, fomented by the energy and ideas floating over the Alps from Renaissance Italy, by the in-creasingly resented temporal power of Rome, and by a growing desire among a burgeoning middle class for greater justice and freedom. This was the rich mix that produced the Reformation. In 1517, Luther was to nail his ninety-five theses against the sale of indulgences on the church door in Wittenberg, thereby triggering a series of social, politi-cal, and religious upheavals that were to change the whole power struc-ture in Europe.

And Faust as concept was another product of these momentous up-heavals, which were to turn northern Europe in particular from a pas-sive theocentric society to an active, ever-questioning, and increasingly anthropocentric society; he was a kind of louche Martin Luther (or lit-erate Till Eulenspiegel, that other nonrespecter of authority). There were certainly others of that time and place to draw attention to them-selves with similar exploits, yet something about Faust, this maverick survivor and rebel, appealed to the popular mind; therefore, perhaps in-evitably, a mere twenty years after his death, the Church was upping the ante. Spin doctors spinning for those in charge were just as active then as today, and they made sure that their version of Faust prevailed: a dissolute quack, accused more than once of pederasty (a favorite slur put about by the Church to destroy reputations), and practicing black magic. According to these sources, Faust studied magic in Cracow (considered at the time, like Salamanca and Toledo in Spain, a center for alchemy, magic, and the beginnings of chemistry as a subject for se-rious study), conjured up spirits, foretold the future, and in Venice achieved flight; he was finally carried off by the devil, who had assumed the shape of a dog. (In fact the real Faust managed to die in his bed.)

But all this infighting—and Faust—would have quickly disap-peared from public consciousness had it not been for that other great promoter of political and social upheaval: the invention of the print-ing press by Johann Gutenberg in Mainz not long before Faust's birth. By the late sixteenth century, printing and book production had expanded from the production of Bibles and other religious works to scientific works, biography, and fiction, and the genie of universally accessible knowledge was definitely out of the bottle. In 1587, in Frankfurt, an enterprising printer called Johann Spies published the first book version of Faust's life, the *Historia von D. Johann Fausten* (author unknown), which became something of an international bestseller and an English translation of which inspired Christopher Marlowe's 1604 play. The book can obviously only very loosely be termed a factual biography, and is an amalgam of popular beliefs and trends of the time: anyone dabbling in "magic," or even with an inordinate thirst for knowledge, must certainly be in league with the devil, and be ultimately carted off by the latter in spectacular fashion. The title page makes the book's purpose clear: "History of D. Johann Faust, the notorious magician and necromancer/How he made a pact with the Devil for a declared time. What he meanwhile saw, himself instigated and undertook/until he finally received his well-deserved reward. Largely from his own writings/for all ambitious, inquisitive, and godless people as a terrible example." Much of the narrative is purloined from other sources, from Virgil to Roger Bacon, and presented in a crude, often naive manner. Nevertheless, the book has a primitive intensity, manifested in the author's genuine belief in his main God-fearing thesis, that ensured its survival and broad dispersion.

Reformation theologians, such as Luther and Melanchthon, were just as eager in their condemnation of too much freedom of thought as the Catholic Church they had broken away from. In ascribing all such freedom as of the devil, they continued to support the iron grip of Christianity on intellectual speculation that was only to slacken with the Enlightenment.

For most of the next two centuries the Faust legend was mainly kept alive in bowdlerized versions in plays, using puppets or actors, aiming with their mix of magic and broad comedy at providing popular entertainment with an undertow of cautionary tale. By the second half of the eighteenth century, the age of the Enlightenment and *Sturm und Drang*, and subsequently the Romantics, Faust was appropriated and remodeled, as an ultimately triumphant hero, the champion and pursuer of knowledge, daring like Prometheus to question the established order, in particular the received wisdom of the Church, which is treated with such supercilious contempt by Goethe through the mouth of his

Mephistopheles—a name, incidentally, most probably first invented by the anonymous writer of the 1587 *Faust* volume, although then spelled "Mephostophiles," the spelling Marlowe took over. And so Faust wandered through the nineteenth century, in the works of Byron and Lenau, not to mention the music of Berlioz, Spohr, Liszt, Boito, and Gounod, in a wide variety of guises but always, in some curious way, appropriated to contemporary concerns.

Busoni's Faust, in turn, in spite of being so firmly anchored in historical texts, embodies the confusion, despair, horror, and mourning for the loss of certainties that characterized so much of the twentieth century. His Faust neither achieves redemption nor defiantly faces damnation, but dies exhausted in the street, worn out by the struggle to make sense of it all. This bleak, bitter, and intensely personal vision was also in many ways hideously prophetic. At a deeper, possibly unconscious level, it was a return to the warning tone of the morality tale. And, surprisingly for a composer whose avowed intention was to revive Italian opera, it is difficult to think of a more German subject. One can only regret that Busoni never lived to read Thomas Mann's masterly novel *Doktor Faustus*, although it was perhaps a mercy that, unlike Mann, he did not live through the horrors of the two decades in Germany following his death. What Busoni did read, other than that first book version and Marlowe's play, was, as we have seen, primary and secondary literature not only on Faust, but on many other Promethean characters. His exhausting peripatetic life, in which his lively curiosity was so often frustrated by lack of time and energy, played its part in contributing to the negative shade cast over his *Weltanschauung*. (A particularly vivid illustration of so much of his daily life is provided by what he called his "office": in hotel rooms, he balanced his suitcase over two chairs and used the top as a desk. It sums up both his cheerfully enterprising acceptance of the discomforts of travel, and the less than perfect conditions under which much of his writing was done.)

The opera begins with a "Symphonia," with Easter bells, ending with a chorus singing "Pax—pax—pax." (This "Symphonia" was written over the period straddling World War I and its aftermath.) This is followed by "The Poet to the Spectator," in spoken verse, in which Busoni relates his desire to compose a work containing much of his life's philosophy; he considered basing the opera on various characters, ranging from Merlin

346 ～ Chapter Twelve

to Don Juan ("but Master Wolfgang succeeded too well, he has sung this song for all time") to Faust—the fateful three choices of folktales. This prologue is in ten octaves (plus a final couplet), in iambic pentameters with an extra foot, and a rhyming pattern a-b-a-b-a-b-c-c: exactly the same form as Goethe used in the *Zueignung* (Dedication) at the beginning of his *Faust*—which is likewise a personal statement, albeit, at four verses, somewhat more succinct than Busoni's ten. The opera is introduced as though it were a puppet play—which was, as we know, at one point Busoni's intention.

The first scene, "Prologue I," is in Faust's study. His assistant, Wagner, enters and announces three students, who want to give Faust a book: a key to magic powers. The students, who claim they are from Cracow, leave, mysteriously unseen by Wagner, who was in an anteroom and should have seen them passing. In the second scene, "Prologue II," Faust, with the aid of the book, calls on Lucifer, and six flames appear that, when questioned on their speed of action, are scornfully dismissed by Faust—except for the last, which claims to be as swift as human thought, and then appears in human form as Mephistopheles. Faust makes his demand: that for the rest of his life all his wishes be fulfilled, and Mephistopheles states his terms: afterward Faust must serve him. Faust rejects the pact, but when Mephistopheles points out that the brother of "the girl" whom Faust has seduced is looking for him, and priests and Faust's creditors are all banging at his door, Faust accepts by ordering Mephistopheles to kill them. (While the argument between Faust and Mephistopheles is going on, offstage the chorus sing the credo, and Faust exclaims, "Easter Day! The Day of my childhood," one of many autobiographical elements: Busoni's birthday, April 1, 1866, was Easter Day.)

In the next scene, "the girl's brother," a soldier, is praying before a crucifix. Mephistopheles, disguised as a monk, tries unsuccessfully to get the soldier to confess to him, then points him out to an officer and other soldiers as the man who has killed their captain; the soldiers kill him. This is followed by the Scenic intermezzo.

Now begins the main action—"Hauptspiel." In the First Tableau, the action has moved to the court of Parma, where the Duke of Parma's marriage is being celebrated. Faust arrives to perform his magic as part of the entertainment. He asks the Duchess who she would like to see and she names various characters from myth and history: she chooses Solomon and the Queen of Sheba, then Samson and Delilah. She then asks Faust to choose the next subject. He conjures up John the Baptist and Salome. Some of these characters resemble the Duke, the Duchess, and Faust himself. The Duchess and Faust fall in love, but are suspected by the Duke, who has arranged for Faust to be poisoned. Warned by Mephistopheles, Faust flees with the Duchess. Mephistopheles, in the guise of the court chaplain, advises the Duke to forget his bride and marry the sister of the Duke of Ferrara instead, to which the Duke acquiesces with the hideously ironic phrase, "Heaven has inspired you."

Here follows the Symphonic intermezzo, based largely on the *Sarabande*.

In the Second Tableau, time has elapsed and Faust is back in Wittenberg in a tavern, discussing philosophy with some students, who later divide into two factions, Catholics and Protestants, and begin fighting. Faust calls them and the strife is resolved by all singing Luther's hymn "Ein' feste Burg" in unison. Then, like Offenbach's Hoffmann, Faust is asked to tell them about his love affairs. He starts to tell them of the Duchess, when Mephistopheles rushes in to say she is dead and sends Faust the corpse of her newborn child as memento. Just as the students are about to seize Faust, Mephistopheles reveals that it is not a dead baby after all, but a bundle of straw, and sets fire to it, with incantations. The students creep away, and from the flames and smoke the figure of a beautiful woman emerges—Helen of Troy. When Faust tries to approach her, she disappears. The three students from Cracow reappear, demanding the book, which Faust claims to have destroyed. They warn him that at midnight his time will be up and he will die. He sends them away, and when alone he welcomes with relief his coming end.

The Final Tableau is a wintry street in Wittenberg. Mephistopheles enters as a night watchman, then Wagner, who has taken Faust's place as "Rector Magnificus," followed by obsequious students. Faust enters and looks up at his old house. At its door he sees a beggar woman with a child, and recognizes her as the Duchess. She gives him the child and disappears. Faust tries to enter a church but is barred by the apparition of the dead soldier. By the light of the night watchman's lantern, Faust sees a crucifix change into Helen. Faust places the dead child on the ground and bequeaths it his life and the future; the child rises as a youth and walks off. Faust falls and dies on the street. Mephistopheles enters, holds the lantern over Faust's body and comments, "Has this man met with an accident, perchance?"

It was Busoni's firm belief that an opera should use only matter that could not stand as a play, in other words, the music and the stage action made possible by the music were to be an integral part of the work; an opera should never be simply a play set to music.

> To me, the all-important condition seems to be the choice of the libretto. While for the drama there are almost boundless possibilities of material, it seems that for the opera the only suitable subjects are such as could not exist or reach complete expression without music—which demand music and only become complete through it. Therefore, the choice of subject matter for opera is strictly limited, according to my view of the musical stage of the future as something finer than we have yet known.[30]

The language of the text, Goethean in its measured, Olympian style, is meant to be savored as poetry in its own right—hence the publication of the libretto well in advance of the opera's completion. In *Doktor Faust* the sung passages are also broken up by the quite long intermezzi, during which Busoni had definite ideas of what should happen, and what the music was intended to convey. In its own way, the work is just as much a *Gesamtkunstwerk* as any Wagner opera.

> Before anything else it was necessary to sketch out the complete plan, the larger outlines of which were previously indicated by the words, to think over the choice, distribution, and employment of means and forms (forms in time and in movement). The principal thing for me to do was to mould musically independent forms which at the same time suited the words and the scenic events and which also had a separate and sensible existence detached from the words and the situation.[31]

The music represents the climax of Busoni's art; in spite of the long period of composition, there is a consistency in the writing that contributes immensely to the dramatic intensity. All those "satellite works" are closely interwoven in the score, with particular brilliance in the Parma scene of the First Tableau, which begins with a dance suite moving from a polonaise (opening of *Cortège*), to pastorale (Pifferata of the Fourth Sonatina), gallop (Pifferata again), waltz (*Tanzwalzer*), minuetto (last movement of Clarinet Concertino). The various scenes conjured up by Faust follow a similar pattern.

But this is not just a recycling of former works. Leitmotivs are also interwoven: a motif of thirds from the *Sarabande* for Mephistopheles, one of many for this character; strains from the *Nocturne symphonique* for Helen, and many others. Although Busoni worked on the score for over six years, some parts were written at great speed: the scene in the Wittenberg tavern with the quarrelling students was written in about ten days in the summer of 1921, a scene requiring large orchestra and double chorus in complex polyphony. As he wrote to Gerda, "It is, perhaps, technically the most perfect piece I have done in an opera. (At the same time very lively.)"[32]

The other long work dating from the last years of Busoni's life is his *Klavierübung* (Piano Exercise), written over a period of seven years. A first, five-volume edition was published before his death; a second, much fuller, ten-volume edition, which he managed to complete in 1924, was published in 1925.[33] The second edition is not a mere extension of the first; items are added to the five books of the first edition, others are removed altogether, and there is a general rearranging as well as the addition of much new material. The *Klavierübung*, like Bach's great work of the same name, is far more than piano exercises, and is intended for players of professional standard; it can be regarded as Busoni's testament as a pianist. It covers every aspect of the pianist's art, and draws freely not only on Busoni's own works, but from a startling variety of other sources, ranging from Bach's Goldberg Variations to Gounod's *Faust*. It builds up from scales, with fingering, to shorter and then longer pieces to focus on particular areas of expertise. The foreword[34] to the sixth book of the second edition, which can be regarded as the foreword to the whole *Klavierübung*, contains Busoni's passionately held credo on piano playing, which can be summed up as: no pointless athletics, a defense of his eclectic choice of music used in the exercises, and a plea that pianists should never forget that the study of art is "something to be enjoyed."

The first book, *Scales*, was written in three days, from September 10 to 12, 1917, with the exception of the final, sixth section, added a month later. After traditional scales, the exercises build up, using two excerpts requiring particular strength and speed: from Liszt's *Totentanz* and just one bar from part V of Busoni's own *Turandot Suite*, "Turandot's boudoir." Other volumes concentrate on trills and tremolandi, using passages ranging from Beethoven's *Hammerklavier* Sonata to the vision of Gretchen scene in Gounod's *Faust*. Staccato playing is dealt with at length; the fourth book of the first edition (eighth book of the second) is essentially a new edition of Busoni's transcriptions of Cramer études dating from the late 1890s; other studies are based on Chopin études and preludes, and more scale studies. The ninth book of the second edition consists of the Five Short Pieces (BV 296) written in 1923 as volume 8 of the Bach-Busoni edition.

In 1922 a volume appeared of essays by Busoni on a variety of aspects of music, *Von der Einheit der Musik* (On the Oneness of Music). (A new edition, with additions and omissions, was published in 1956 under the title *Wesen und Einheit der Musik*—Essence and Oneness of Music—and an English translation by Rosamond Ley, with some omissions, was published in 1957 as *The Essence of Music and Other Papers*.) The essays were garnered from articles published over the years in various journals and newspapers, from letters to Gerda and others, and the book also includes Busoni's two autobiographical fragments, dealing with his early childhood. There are sections on Bach, Mozart, Beethoven, and Liszt; on Busoni's operas and how they were composed; on piano playing and piano music; and on the future of music (this section contains the letter to Hans Pfitzner in reply to Pfitzner's attack). Two short sections deal with *junge Klassizität* (young classicity—translated too loosely by Rosamond Ley as "young classicism"), a term coined by Busoni himself around 1919 that was almost immediately misunderstood and misappropriated. By *junge Klassizität* Busoni intended a return to what he conceived to be the true purpose of music: a return to harmony, to melody, to "the most highly developed (not the most complicated) polyphony," and away from what is "sensuous," music as description, not "profundity, and personal feeling and metaphysics, but Music which is absolute, distilled, and never under a mask of figures and ideas which were borrowed from other spheres." He certainly did not mean by this a return to the styles of the past, but faithfulness to what he conceived as the higher purpose of music, "the conclusion of previous experiments." Inevitably, the concept was misunderstood—innocently or deliberately—by many, and the old feud with Pfitzner also became entangled in it, in the sense of advocates and opponents of that feud taking sides on the *junge Klassizität* issue along the same battle lines as the older controversy. To be fair, the matter was not helped by Busoni's particularly dense prose when writing on the subject.

For the winter months of 1923–1924 Busoni had been too ill to leave the house. The remainder of the score of *Doktor Faust*, as he wrote to his old Viennese friend Jella Oppenheimer, remained still "within the soul of the creator": the final scene was unfinished. (For the premiere of the work in Dresden on May 21, 1925, conducted by Fritz Busch, Philipp Jarnach completed the score. In 1984 the conductor and Busoni expert Antony Beaumont wrote an alternative version, which is often used today.) Throughout the spring of 1924, Busoni's health continued to decline. Kurt Weill, whose studies with Busoni officially ended in December 1923, immersed himself in work in an effort to forget the sight of the obviously dying composer, who had had to relinquish his teaching post and was succeeded by Arnold Schoenberg.

One side of Busoni triumphed to the end: his bitingly ironic sense of humor, which even extended to humorous notes to his doctor, some attached to specimen jars. In early June, too weak to write, he dictated his essay "The Essence of Music" (included in the 1956 edition of *Wesen und Einheit der Musik* and in the English translation). It was his final attempt to define the undefinable—the essence of music—in philosophical terms.

During the last weeks there were two nurses to provide around-the-clock care, and the faithful Gerda remained at Busoni's bedside almost constantly. He would drift in and out of consciousness; during a period of consciousness he repeated yet again what he had often said to his wife: "Dear Gerda, thank you for every day we have been together." Word spread in Berlin that he had little time to live, and his home was besieged. Except for close friends, however, particularly his young "disciples," as he called them, most of his admirers—including the strange band of adoring women who had followed him for years—had to be kept from him. He was unconscious for the last four days, and on 3:30 in the morning of July 27, 1924, he died. The official cause was heart failure, but the kidneys were also inflamed. In fact, he died of exhaustion: he had spent most of his life trying to reconcile the unreconcilable, the Italian and the German, the virtuoso performer and the composer, the wide-ranging polymath and the focused artist. Although he had never drunk to excess—except possibly during the Zurich years—he had always been a heavy smoker, and these indulgences, as we have seen, proved very false friends indeed. And now the restless wanderer had departed on his last journey.

Although half prepared, the world was nevertheless stunned. Busoni had been the very embodiment of the great pianist for so long, it was difficult to believe he was no more. The tributes, from all over the world, were fulsome, but—a fact that would have caused him distress—they largely concentrated on Busoni the pianist, and not the composer. The Academy of Fine Arts in Berlin had a monument erected over his cremated remains in the Schöneberg cemetery, with a bronze sculpture on the top by Georg Kolbe (which has since been removed). And in Italy, a group of friends and admirers, headed by Igor Stravinsky and the Polish pianist and (briefly) statesman Ignacy Paderewski, commissioned a bust from the Florentine sculptor Valmore Gemignani, which still stands facing the stairs in the main corridor of the Liceo Musicale in Bologna. Soon a plaque appeared on the wall of the house in Empoli where Busoni was born, and in Florence a street was named after him.

But the dark clouds hanging over Europe for the two decades following his death almost obliterated his memory. The great cosmopolitan was more or less airbrushed out of history by a virulently nationalistic epoch. For the Germans, he became an alien—Benni had trouble with the Nazi authorities in the early 1930s in being forced to prove, by the production of his father's baptismal certificate from Empoli (obtained with some difficulty), that he was not Jewish (in fact, it has since emerged, his great-grandfather, Giuseppe Weiss, *was* part Jewish). For the Italians, Busoni had thrown in his lot with the Germans, and he had no posthumous role to play in a Fascist state. His memory was kept alive by many of his "disciples" and other friends, but his music was seldom performed. In 1934 it was an Englishman, Edward Dent, who wrote the first—and until now the only—full-length biography. It was only in the last decades of the twentieth century that Busoni's music and his significance in musical history began to be rediscovered.

Within a few months of his death a halfhearted attempt was made on behalf of the Italian government to have Busoni's remains transferred to Italy. Similarly halfhearted was a plan for the Italian government to purchase his vast library. Both schemes came to nothing. At Busoni's death, Gerda was left in a difficult situation, mainly owing to Germany's economic problems of the time. Ten months after her husband's death, at the beginning of May 1925, she was forced to have most of his library put up for auction with the Berlin antiques dealer Max Perl.[35] Nevertheless, she passed over the whole of Busoni's music manuscripts to the Prussian State Library, for which Leo Kestenberg managed to obtain for her a special grant of 2,000 of the new marks. Others, including Edward Dent, made efforts to collect money for her.

There is a harsh truth in the opening sentence of the foreword to the auction catalog for the library, written by Julius Kapp, a member of Busoni's circle, to the effect that once the owner of a library has died, the library itself becomes a headless torso. The sentiment is also somewhat disingenuous. In addition to being an accurate reflection of Busoni's being, the library was an object lesson in the formation of an open, ever-inquiring, and cosmopolitan mind. Goethe would have taken his hat off to it, and recognized a fellow seeker. Books in English in the collection range from Blake, the Brownings, Burns, Samuel Butler, Byron, Carlyle, Dickens, through Kipling, Shaw, Shelley, Sterne, Thackeray, to Whitman, and many between. The German, Italian, and French sections are similarly comprehensive, and include Busoni's collection of "Faustiana"; several editions of Goethe, in complete editions and individual works; over fifty volumes on and by Hoffmann; sixty different editions of *Don Quixote* in various languages; and books on architecture, painting, history. . . . The dispersal of the library was an unwitting (to some extent) act of vandalism, which caused Gerda much pain and guilt.

Gerda spent the rest of her life in poverty, at first in Berlin; then during World War II in Lübeck, on the Baltic coast, whence the young Ferruccio had boarded ship for Helsinki fifty years before; and finally in Sweden. She lived on until 1956, dying at the age of ninety-three, looked after by her sister Helmi, cheerful, sweet-natured, and uncomplaining to the end. The keen eyesight that in her youth had enabled her to watch from the Brunnsparken in Helsinki as Ferruccio's ship shrank to a "black dot" and finally disappeared, was now extinguished: for the last years of her life she was totally blind.

In 1943 the house on the Viktoria-Luise-Platz was destroyed during an air raid. Many of the Busonis's possessions had been stored in the cellars, but these were subsequently looted of anything valuable, and many personal papers were destroyed, either by looters or the weather. Benni, who lived out the war years in Berlin, in spite of his American passport, did little to salvage anything, although constantly urged to do so in letters by his distraught mother. Nevertheless, many papers—letters and other material—did survive, some rain-damaged; these are now all in the State Library in Berlin, along with the lion's share of all other handwritten and printed matter by and pertaining to Busoni. Benni died in Berlin in 1976, difficult to the end. (A large collection of his letters, diaries, and other matter is also in the State Library in Berlin as part of the Busoni archive.) Lello emigrated to the United States in the 1930s, where he had a successful career as a book illustrator, and died in New York in 1962.

Notes

1. Letter from FB to Gerda Busoni, September 12, 1920, StBB Bus. Nachl. IV, 1013.

2. Letter from FB to Isidor Philipp, October 4, 1920, StBB Bus. Nachl. BI, 336a.

3. Gisella Selden-Goth, *Ferruccio Busoni* (Leipzig: E. P. Tal, 1922).

4. Marc-André Roberge, *Ferruccio Busoni. A Bio-Bibliography* (New York: Greenwood, 1991), p. 188.

5. Letter from FB to Isidor Philipp, October 14, 1920, StBB Bus. Nachl. BI, 337a.

6. Letter from FB to Raffaello Busoni, July 15, 1921, StBB Bus. Nachl. IV, 154.

7. Letter from Kurt Weill to Hans Weill, February 18, 1919, quoted in Symonette and Kowalke, *Speak Low*, p. 30.

8. Letter from Kurt Weill to Albert Weill, November 29, 1920, quoted in Symonette and Kowalke, *Speak Low*, p. 32.

9. Letter from Kurt Weill to Ferruccio Busoni, January 20, 1921, quoted in Symonette and Kowalke, *Speak Low*, p. 32.

10. Kurt Weill, "Busoni: Zu seinem einjährigen Todestage," *Berliner Börsen-Courier*, July 26, 1925.

11. Letter from FB to Isidor Philipp, June 22, 1914, StBB Bus. Nachl. BI, 299c.

12. Letter from FB to Gerda Busoni, March 26, 1922, StBB Bus. Nachl. IV, 1033.

13. Letter from FB to Ersilia Grusovin, March 9, 1922, in Sablich, *Lettere*, p. 478.

14. Quoted in L. Varèse, *Varèse*, p. 51.

15. H. H. Stuckenschmidt, *Zum Hören geboren: Ein Leben mit der Musik unserer Zeit* (Munich: Piper, 1979), p. 44.

16. Letter from FB to Egon Petri, May 29, 1923, MW, p. 305.

17. Vladimir Vogel, "Eine Begegnung," in Busoni, *Wesen und Einheit*, p. 251.

18. Letter from FB to Isidor Philipp, August 5, 1923, in Beaumont, *Selected Letters*, p. 369.

19. What remains of this libretto is now, untitled, in StBB Bus. Nachl. CI: Textbuch 16 (1892).

20. Letter from FB to Gerda Busoni, May 19, 1908, StBB Bus. Nachl. IV, 636.

21. Letter from FB to Gerda Busoni, September 9, 1908, StBB Bus. Nachl. IV, 649.

22. Letter from FB to Gerda Busoni, November 8, 1908, StBB Bus. Nachl. IV, 658.

23. Letter from FB to Gerda Busoni, September 13, 1908, StBB Bus. Nachl. IV, 654.

24. Letter from FB to Gerda Busoni, July 24, 1912, StBB Bus. Nachl. IV, 823.

25. Letter from FB to Gerda Busoni, July 29, 1912, StBB Bus. Nachl. IV, 825.

26. Now in the State Library in Berlin as part of the Busoni Nachlass.

27. *Bibliothek Ferruccio Busoni: Auktion 96 am 30. und 31. März 1925*, foreword by Dr. Julius Kapp (Max Perl, Antiquariat, Berlin). There is a copy of the catalog in the Potsdamer Strasse branch of the Berlin State Library, Signatur: 391093.

28. Busoni, *Essence of Music*, p. 71.

29. Beaumont, *Busoni the Composer*, p. 252.

30. Busoni, "The Oneness of Music and the Possibilities of the Opera," in *Essence of Music*, p. 7

31. Busoni, "The Score of *Doktor Faust*," in *Essence of Music*, p. 73.

32. Letter from FB to Gerda Busoni, July 23, 1921, StBB Bus. Nachl. IV, 1025.

33. For an admirably clear guide through the complexities of the two editions, the reader is referred to chapter 10, "The Klavierübung," in Sitsky's *Busoni and the Piano*, which also contains parallel contents lists of both editions on pages 164–66.

34. For an English translation of this foreword, see Sitsky, *Busoni and the Piano*, pp. 169–70.

35. *Bibliothek Ferruccio Busoni* auction catalog (see note 27).

~

Selected List of Compositions

I have used the Busoni Verzeichnis (BV) opus numbers also used by Marc-André Roberge in his *Ferruccio Busoni: A Bio-Bibliography*, as his list is the most complete, and also the most accurate. (Where details in the following list differ from those in Roberge, my changes are based on good evidence.)

Opus numbers BV 1–61, written before mid-1877 and consisting mainly of short works for piano, voice, and piano; two string quartets (BV 38 and BV 42, written when Busoni was ten); and other voice and piano combinations, are all unpublished; they exist in manuscript in the State Library in Berlin. (BV 9, *Marcia funebre in C Minor for Piano*, and BV 12, *La canzone del cacciatore in C Major for Piano*, have recently appeared on a CD of Busoni's childhood works, however—*Ferruccio Busoni: Early Piano Pieces*, played by Ira Maria Witoschynsky, Capriccio (10 546)—and other of Busoni's previously unknown works are regularly being recorded.)

BV 106–125 (except for BV 114, BV 120a, and BV 124) are listed in Roberge as "lost"; written between May 1879 and the end of that year, they may have been destroyed by Busoni himself, likewise BV 127 to BV 133 are also listed as "lost." It was toward the end of 1879 that Busoni began his course of study with Wilhelm Mayer, which could have led to the destruction of the works written over the previous year, which the family possibly had with them when they settled in Graz. This explanation can only remain conjecture.

In the list that follows, I have in general included only published works. I have chosen to list the works chronologically, rather than by category, as there tended to be an organic progression from one opus to the next in Busoni's composing. Publication dates are included for the first edition.

Original Works

BV 62 Scherzo in F-sharp Minor for Piano
Composed July 1877. Published 1882.
BV 67 Ave Maria: Antiphon for Voice and Piano
Composed October 1877. Published 1878.
BV 71 Five Pieces for Piano
Composed 1877. Published 1877.
BV 77 Minuet in F Major for Piano
Composed February 1878. Published 1882.
BV 80 Concerto in D Minor for Piano and String Quartet
Composed March 1878. Published 1987 (ed. Larry Sitsky).
BV 81 Suite campestre: Five Character Pieces for Piano
Composed April 1878. Published 1981 (ed. Franzpeter Goebels).
BV 85 Prelude and Fugue in C Minor for Piano
Composed May 1878. Published 1880.
BV 89 Gavotta in F Major for Piano
Composed 1878. Published. 1880.
BV 91 Ave Maria: Antiphon for Voice and Piano
Composed 1878. Published 1879.
BV 94 Lied der Klage for Contralto and Piano. Text: Otto von Kapff.
Composed 1878. Published 1879.
BV 98 Des Sängers Fluch. Text: Ludwig Uhland.
Composed 1878. Published 1879.
BV 100 Racconti fantastici: Three Character Pieces for Piano
Composed 1878. Published 1882.
BV 114 Album vocale: Four Pieces for Voice and Piano. Text: Ferdinando Busoni ("Il fiore del pensiero"); Michele Buono ("Il nonno dorme"); Lorenzo Stecchetti ("Un organetto suona per la via"); Arrigo Boito ("Luna fedel ti chiamo").
Composed 1884. Published 1884.

BV 119 Stabat Mater: Sequence for Two Sopranos, Alto, Tenor, and Two Basses and String Quartet.
Composed August 1879. Lost.

BV 124 Minuetto capriccioso in C Major for Piano
Composed 1879. Published 1880.

BV 126 Danze antiche for Piano
Composed 1878–1879. Published 1882.

BV 135 String Quartet in F Minor (no. 1)
Composed [1879?]. Unpublished.

BV 152 Gavotta in F Minor for Piano
Composed 1880. Published 1880.

BV 157 Prelude and Fugue in A Minor for Organ
Composed January 1880 (prelude), June 1880 (fugue). Published 1881.

BV 159 Three Pieces in the Old Style for Piano
Composed April 1880 (1), July 1880 (2), June 1880 (3). Published 1882.

BV 167 Two Songs for Voice and Piano. Text: Victor Blüthgen ("Wer hat das erste Lied erdacht"); Rudolf Baumbach ("Bin ein fahrender Gesell").
Composed October 1880. Published 1884.

BV 177 String Quartet in C Major (no. 2)
Composed January–February 1881. Unpublished.

BV 180 Prelude and Fugue for Four Voices in C Major for Piano
Composed April 1881. Published 1882.

BV 181 Twenty-Four Preludes for Piano
Composed May 1881. Published 1882.

BV 185 Una festa di villaggio: Six Character Pieces for Piano
Composed December 1881. Published 1882.

BV 189 Danza notturna in D Major for Piano
Composed June 1882. Published 1882.

BV 190 Ave Maria: Antiphon for Baritone and Orchestra
Composed June 1882. Published 1882.

BV 191 Primavera, Estate, Autunno, Inverno: Four Pieces for Soloists, Male Chorus, and Orchestra. Text: Francesco Dall'Ongaro.
Composed July 1882. Published 1882.

BV 192 Il sabato del villaggio: Cantata for Soloists, Chorus, and Orchestra. Text: Giacomo Leopardi.
Composed August 1882. Unpublished.

BV 194 Macchiette medioevali for Piano
Composed 1882–1883. Published 1883.

BV 196 Serenade in G Minor for Cello and Piano
Composed January 1883. Published 1883.

BV 197 Three Pieces for Piano
Composed [1882?]. Published 1884.

BV 201 Symphonic Suite for Orchestra
Composed 1883. Published 1888.

BV 202 Two Songs for Voice and Piano. Text (in German translation): Lord Byron ("Ich sah die Träne"; "An Babylons Wassern").
Composed [1883?]. Published 1884.

BV 203 Six Studies for Piano
Composed 1883. Published 1883.

BV 204 Sonata in F Minor for Piano
Composed December 1883. Published 1983 (ed. Jutta Theurich).

BV 206 Etude en forme de variations in C Minor for Piano
Composed [1883?]. Published 1884.

BV 207 Two Old German Songs for Voice and Piano. Text: Neidhard von Reuenthal ("Wohlauf! Wohlauf!"); Walther von der Vogelweide ("Unter den Linden an der Heide").
Composed [1884?]. Published 1885.

BV 208 String Quartet in C (no. 3)
Composed [1884?]. Published 1886.

BV 209 Second Ballet Scene for Piano
Composed 1884. Published 1885.

BV 213 Variations and Fugue on the Prelude in C Minor, op. 28, no. 20, by Frédéric Chopin for Piano
Composed January 1884. Published 1885.

BV 213a Ten Variations on the Prelude in C Minor, op. 28, no. 20, by Frédéric Chopin for Piano
Composed April 1922. Published 1922.

BV 215 Short Suite for Cello and Piano
Composed [1885?]. Published 1886.

BV 216 Two Songs for Low Voice and Piano. Text: Theodor Fontane ("Es zieht sich eine blut'ge Spur"); Ernst Freiherr von Feuchtersleben ("Es ist bestimmt in Gottes Rat").
Composed August 1885 (no. 1); March 1884 (no. 2). Published 1887.

BV 222 Five Variations on Siegfried Ochs's Variations on the Song "Kommt a Vogerl g'flogen" for Piano
Composed 1886. Published 1987 (ed. Jutta Theurich).

BV 225 String Quartet in D Minor (no. 4)
Composed June 1887. Published 1889.

BV 226 Fugue on the Folk Song "O, du mein lieber Augustin" for Piano Four Hands
Composed June 1888. Published 1987 (ed. Jutta Theurich).

BV 227 Finnländische Volksweisen for Piano Four Hands
Composed 1888. Published 1889.

BV 229 Four Bagatelles for Violin and Piano
Composed 1888. Published 1888.

BV 230 Concert-Fantasy for Piano and Orchestra
Composed 1888–1889. Unpublished. Revised as BV 240.

BV 231 *Sigune*: Opera in Two Acts and a Prelude after a Fairy-Tale by Rudolf Baumbach. Libretto: Ludwig Soyaux and Frida Schanz.
Composed December 1885–May 1889. Unpublished.

BV 234 Sonata in E Minor for Violin and Piano (no. 1)
Composed 1890. Published 1891.

BV 235 Two Pieces for Piano
Composed 1889. Published 1891.

BV 235a Two Dance Pieces for Piano
Composed 1914. Published 1914.

BV 236 Konzertstück for Piano and Orchestra
Composed 1889–1890. Published 1892.

BV 237 Kulsatelle: Ten Short Variations on a Finnish Folk Song for Cello and Piano
Composed 1889. Published 1891.

BV 238 Fourth Ballet Scene in the Form of a Concert Waltz for Piano
Composed [1892?]. Published 1894.

BV 238a Fourth Ballet Scene (Waltz and Gallop) for Piano
Composed February 1913. Published 1913.

BV 240 Symphonic Tone Poem for Orchestra. (Revised from BV 230)
Composed March 1893. Published 1894.

BV 241 Six Pieces for Piano
Composed 1895. Published 1896.

BV 242 Second Orchestral Suite (Geharnischte Suite)
Composed 1894–1885, revised 1903. Published 1905.
BV 243 Concerto in D Major for Violin and Orchestra
Composed 1896–1887. Published 1899.
BV 244 Sonata in E Minor for violin and Piano (no. 2)
Composed 1898–1900. Published 1901.
BV 245 Lustspielouvertüre for Orchestra
Composed July 1897, revised 1904. Published 1904.
BV 247 Concerto for Piano, Orchestra, and Male Chorus. Text: Adam
Oelenschläger.
Composed 1901–1904. Published 1906.
BV 248 *Turandot* Suite for Orchestra
Composed June–August 1905. Published 1906.
BV 248a Verzweiflung und Ergebung: Addenda to the *Turandot* Suite
for Orchestra
Composed 1911. Published 1911.
BV 248b Altoums Warnung: Addenda to the *Turandot* Suite for Orchestra
Composed 1917. Published 1918.
BV 249 Elegies for Piano
Composed September–December 1907. Published 1908.
BV 251 Nuit de Noël: Esquisse for Piano
Composed December 1908. Published 1909.
BV 252 Berceuse for Piano
Composed June 1909. Published 1909.
BV 252a Berceuse élégiaque for Orchestra: Des Mannes Wiegenlied am
Sarge seiner Mutter
Composed October 1909. Published 1910.
BV 253 Fantasy after Johann Sebastian Bach for Piano
Composed June 1909. Published 1909.
BV 254 An die Jugend: A Series of Piano Pieces
Composed June–August 1909. Published 1909.
BV 255 Grosse Fuge: Contrapuntal Fantasy on the Last and Unfinished
Fugue from the "Art of Fugue," BWV 1080, by Johann Sebastian
Bach, for Piano
Composed January–March 1910. Published 1910.
BV 256 Fantasia contrappuntistica for Piano (edizione definitiva):
Choral Prelude "Allein Gott in der Höh' sei Ehr" and Fugue with
Four Obbligato subjects on a Fragment by Bach
Composed June 1910. Published 1910.

BV 256a Fantasia contrappuntistica for Piano (edizione minore):
Chorale Prelude and Fugue on a Fragment by Bach
Composed July 1912. Published 1912.
BV 256b Fantasia contrappuntistica for Two Pianos: Chorale Varia-
tions on "Ehre sei Gott in der Höhe." Followed by a Quadruple
Fugue on a Fragment by Bach.
Composed July 1921. Published 1922.
BV 157 Sonatina for Piano (no. 1)
Composed August 1910. Published 1910.
BV 258 Die Brautwahl: Musical-Fantastical Comedy after a Tale by
E. T. A. Hoffmann. Libretto: Ferruccio Busoni.
Composed February 1906 to October 1911. Published 1914.
BV 259 Sonatina seconda for Piano
Composed June–July 1912. Published 1912.
BV 26a Die Brautwahl: Suite for Orchestra
Composed 1912. Published 1912.
BV 262 Nocturne symphonique for Orchestra
Composed September 1912–July 1913. Published 1914.
BV 264 Red Indian Fantasy for Piano and Orchestra
Composed April 1913–February 1914. Published 1915.
BV Rondò arlecchinesco for Orchestra
Composed April–June 1915. Published 1917.
BV 267 Indian Diary (First Book) for Piano: Four Studies on Motives by
American Indians
Composed June–August 1915. Published 1916.
BV 268 Sonatina "ad usum infantis" for Piano (no. 3)
Composed 1915. Published 1916.
BV Gesang vom Reigen der Geister: Study for Small Orchestra (Indian
Diary, second book)
Composed August–December 1915. Published 1916.
BV 270 Arlecchino: A Theatrical Capriccio in One Act. Libretto:
Ferruccio Busoni
Composed November–December 1914; November 1915–August
1916. Published 1918.
BV 271 Improvisation on the Bach Chorale "Wie wohl ist mir, o
Freund der Seele" for Two Pianos
Composed June–August 1916. Published 1917.
BV 272 Albumleaf in E Minor for Flute or Muted Violin and Piano
Composed 1916. Published 1917.

BV 272a Albumleaf in E Minor for Piano
Composed 1917. Published 1918.

BV 272 *Turandot*: A Chinese Fable in Two Acts after Carlo Gozzi. Libretto: Ferruccio Busoni
Composed December 1916–March 1917. Full score unpublished.

BV 274 Sonatina "in diem nativitatis Christi MCMXVII" for Piano (no. 4)
Composed December 22, 1917. Published 1918.

BV 276 Concertino for Clarinet and Small Orchestra
Composed March–April 1918. Published 1918.

BV 277 Altoums Gebet: Lied for Baritone and Small Orchestra
Composed [1917?]. Published 1919.

BV 278 Lied des Mephistopheles from Goethe's *Faust* for Baritone and Small Orchestra
Composed March 1918. Published 1919.

BV 278a Lied des Mephistopheles from Goethe's *Faust* for Baritone and Piano
Composed [1918?]. Published 1919.

BV 280 Sonatina brevis "in signo Joannis Sebastiani Magni" for Piano (no. 5)
Composed August 1918. Published 1919.

BV 281 Lied des Unmuts for Baritone and Piano. Text: Johann Wolfgang von Goethe.
Composed 1918. Published 1919.

BV 281a Lied des Unmuts for Baritone and Orchestra. Text: Johann Wolfgang von Goethe.
Composed February 1924. Published 1964.

BV 282 *Sarabande and Cortège*: Two Studies for *Doktor Faust* for Orchestra
Composed December 1918–January 1919. Published 1922.

BV 284 Chamber Fantasy after Bizet's *Carmen* for Piano (Sonatina no. 6)
Composed March 1920. Published 1921.

BV 285 Divertimento for Flute and Orchestra
Composed May 1920. Published 1922.

BV 286 Elegy in E-flat Major for Clarinet and Piano
Composed September 1919–January 1920. Published 1921.

BV 287 Toccata for Piano: Preludio, Fantasia, Ciaconna
Composed July–September 1920. Published 1921.
BV 288 Tanzwalzer for Orchestra
Composed September–October 1920. Published 1922.
BV 289 Three Albumleaves for Piano
Composed August 1917 (no. 1); April 1921 (no. 2); May 1921
(no. 3). Published 1918 (no. 1); 1921 (nos. 1–3).
BV 290 Romanza e scherzoso for Piano and Orchestra
Composed June 1921. Published 1922.
BV 291a Die Bekehrte: Song for Female Voice and Piano. Text: Johann
Wolfgang von Goethe.
Composed September 1921. Published 1937.
BV 293 Perpetuum mobile for Piano
Composed February 1922. Published 1922.
BV 295 Zigeunerlied for Baritone and Orchestra. Text: Johann Wolf-
gang von Goethe.
Composed March 27, 1923. Published 1923.
BV 295a Zigeunerlied for Baritone and Piano. Text: Johann Wolfgang
von Goethe.
Composed March 1923. Published 1923.
BV 296 Five Short Pieces for the Cultivation of Polyphonic Playing on
the Piano
Composed March–July 1923. Published 1923.
BV 297 Prélude et étude en arpèges for Piano
Composed January 29, February 12, 1923. Published 1923.
BV 298 Schlechter Trost: Song for Baritone and Orchestra. Text:
Johann Wolfgang von Goethe.
Composed February 24, 1924. Published 1960.
BV 298a Schlechter Trost: Song for Baritone and Piano. Text: Johann
Wolfgang von Goethe.
Composed February 1924. Published 1924.
BV 299 Lied des Brander for Baritone and Piano
Composed March [1918?]. Published 1964.
BV 303 Doktor Faust. Libretto: Ferruccio Busoni
Composed September 1916–May 1923; completed by Philipp
Jarnach (1924–1925) and by Antony Beaumont (1982). Pub-
lished 1925 (vocal score), 1984 (MS).

Works with No BV Number

Klavierübung in Five Parts
Composed October 10, 1917 (part 1); November 7, 1917–June 7, 1918 (part 2); December 31, 1919–March 10, 1921 (part 3); 1897 (part 4); May 8, 1922 (part 5). Published 1918–1922.

Klavierübung in Ten Parts
Composed December 1923–January 1924. Published 1925. Consists of some items contained in the Five Part edition, plus new material, the whole rearranged over the ten parts.

Cadenzas

Busoni wrote some twenty cadenzas for piano concertos and other works, by Beethoven, Brahms, Mozart, and Weber. They are numbers BV B 1 to BV B 19.

Transcriptions and Editions for Piano Solo

BV B 20 Bach: Prelude and Fugue in D Major for Organ, BWV 532
Composed 1888. Published [1890?].

BV B 22 Bach: Prelude and Fugue in E-flat Major for Organ, BWV 552
Composed [1890?]. Published [1890?].

BV B 23 Bach: Two- and Three-Part Inventions for Piano, BWV 772
Composed 1891, 1914. Published 1892, 1914.

BV B 24 Bach: Chaconne in D Minor for Violin, BWV 1004
Composed 1893. Published 1897.

BV B 25 Bach: The Well-Tempered Clavier, BWV 846–69, 870–93
Composed 1894 (part 1), 1915 (part 2). Published 1895 (part 1), 1916 (part 2).

BV B 26 Bach: Prelude and Fugue in E Minor for Organ, BWV 533
Composed 1894 at the latest. Published 1894.

BV B 27 Bach: Ten Chorale Preludes for Organ, BWV 631, 645, 659, 734, 639, 617, 637, 705, 615, 665
Composed 1898 at the latest. Published 1898.

BV B 28 Bach: Concerto in D Minor for Piano and String Orchestra, BWV 1052
Composed 1899 at the latest. Published 1899.

BV B 29 Bach: Two Toccatas and Fugues in C Major and D Minor for Organ, BWV 564, 565
Composed June 1899. Published 1900.

BV B 30 Bach: Concerto in D Minor for Piano and String Orchestra, BWV 1052
Composed 1900 at the latest. Published 1900.

BV B 31 Bach: Chromatic Fantasy and Fugue for Piano, BWV 903
Composed 1902 at the latest. Published 1902.

BV B 32 Bach: Eighteen Short Preludes and Fugues and a Fughetta for Piano, BWV 924, 939, 999, 925, 926, 940, 941, 927–30, 942, 933–38, 961
Composed 1914. Published 1916.

BV B 33 Bach: Four Duets for Piano, BWV 802–5
Composed 1914. Published 1915.

BV B 34 Bach: Capriccio in B-flat Major on the Departure of His Beloved Brother, for the Piano, BWV 992
Composed 1914. Published 1915.

BV B 35 Bach: Air with Thirty Variations (Goldberg Variations) for Piano, BWV 988
Composed 1914. Published 1915–1920.

BV B 36 Bach: Prelude, Fugue, and Allegro in E-flat Major for Piano, BWV 998
Composed 1914 at the latest. Published 1915.

BV B 37 Bach: Fantasy, Adagio, and Fugue for Piano, BWV 906, 968
Composed 1915 at the latest. Published 1915.

BV B 38 Bach: Chromatic Fantasy and Fugue for Piano, BWV 903
Composed 1915. Published 1917.

BV B 39 Bach: Three Toccatas in E Minor, G Minor, and G Major for Piano, BWV 914–16
Composed 1916. Published 1920.

BV B 40 Bach: Canonic Variations and Fugue from the "Musical Offering," BWV 1079
Composed 1916. Published 1917.

BV B 41 Bach: Fantasy and Fugue in A Minor for Piano, BWV 904
Composed [1917?]. Published 1917.

BV B 42 Bach: Fantasy, Fugue, Andante, and Scherzo for Piano, BWV 905, 969, 844
Composed 1917. Published 1920.

BV B 43 Bach: Sarabanda con partite for Piano, BWV 990
Composed 1921 at the latest. Published 1921.
BV B 44 Bach: Aria variata alla maniera italiana for Piano, BWV 989
Composed 1921 at the latest. Published 1921.

Busoni also wrote piano transcriptions to or editions of works by Beethoven (3), Brahms (1), Chopin (1), Cornelius (1), Cramer (1), Niels Gade (1), Goldmark (2), Liszt (19), Mendelssohn (1), Mozart (17), Nováček (2), Schoenberg (1), Schubert (9), Schumann (3), Spohr (1), Wagner (1), and Weill (1).

Of Franz Liszt, he also edited for the Franz Liszt-Stiftung in Weimar the Etudes en douze exercices, Douze grandes études, Mazeppa for Piano, published in 1910 (series 2, vol. 1); Etudes d'exécution transcendante, Grande fantaisie de bravoure sur "La Clochette" de Paganini for Piano, published in 1911 (series 2, vol. 2); Etudes d'exécution transcendante d'après Paganini, Morceau de salon, Ab Irato, Trois études de concert, Gnomenreigen, Waldesrauschen for Piano, published in 1911 (series 2, vol. 3); Grandes études de Paganini for Piano, published in 1912.

~

Bibliography

The vast majority of the manuscript letters drawn from are now in the Busoni Nachlass in the Music Department of the State Library in Berlin; full references are given in each case in the notes section. Likewise, the full references for articles in journals and newspapers quoted from are given in the notes section in the appropriate place. Other letters, in the form of typed copies, are in King's College Library, Cambridge, as part of the Dent Papers (EJD/2/1). A further manuscript source is the collection in the Centro Busoni in Empoli.

Allan, Maud. *My Life and Dancing*. London: Everett, 1908.
Applegate, Celia, and Pamela Potter. *Music and German National Identity*. Chicago: University of Chicago Press, 2002.
Beaumont, Antony. *Busoni the Composer*. London: Faber and Faber, 1985.
Bibliothek Ferruccio Busoni. Foreword by Julius Kapp. Catalog for Auction 96, on March 30 and 31, 1925. Berlin: Max Perl/Antiquariat, 1925.
Bird, John. *Percy Grainger*. London: Paul Elek, 1976.
Brendel, Alfred. *Nachdenken über Musik*. Munich: Piper, 1977.
Busoni, Ferruccio. *Briefe an Henri, Katharina und Egon Petri*. Ed. and annotated by Martina Weindel. Wilhelmshaven, Germany: Florian Noetzel, 1999.
———. *Briefe an seine Frau*. Ed. Friedrich Schnapp. Erlenbach-Zurich-Leipzig: Rotapfel-Verlag, 1935.
———. *Briefwechsel mit Gottfried Galston*. Ed. and annotated by Martina Weindel. Wilhelmshaven, Germany: Florian Noetzel, 1999.

———. *Entwurf einer neuen Ästhetik der Tonkunst.* Ed. and annotated by Martina Weindel. Wilhelmshaven, Germany: Florian Noetzel, 2001.

———. *Entwurf einer neuen Ästhetik der Tonkunst.* 2nd, extended ed. Leipzig: Insel-Verlag, 1916.

———. *The Essence of Music and Other Papers.* Trans. Rosamond Ley. London: Rockliff, 1957.

———. *Ferruccio Busoni: Lettere.* Expanded Italian edition of *Ferruccio Busoni: Selected Letters* (below), trans. and ed. Sergio Sablich. Milan: Ricordi/ Unicopli, 1988.

———. *Ferruccio Busoni: Selected Letters.* Trans. and ed. Antony Beaumont. London: Faber and Faber, 1987.

———. *Letters to His Wife.* Trans. Rosamond Ley. New York: Da Capo, 1975. First published London, 1938.

———. *Wesen und Einheit der Musik.* New edition, revised and augmented by Joachim Herrmann, of the 1922 ed. Berlin-Halensee: Max Hesses Verlag, 1956.

Busoni, Gerda. *Erinnerungen an Ferruccio Busoni.* Berlin: Afas-Musik-Verlag, 1958.

Canetti, Elias. *Die gerettete Zunge.* Frankfurt am Main: Carl Hanser/Fischer Taschenbuch Verlag, 1979.

Carley, Lionel, ed. *Delius: A Life in Letters; Volume I, 1862–1908.* London: Scolar, 1983.

———, ed. *Frederick Delius: Music, Art and Literature.* Aldershot, England: Ashgate, 1998.

Chamier, J. Daniel. *Percy Pitt of Covent Garden and the BBC.* London: Edward Arnold, 1938.

Cherniavsky, Felix. *The Salome Dancer: The Life and Times of Maud Allan.* Toronto: McClelland and Stewart, 1991.

Debusmann, Emil. *Ferruccio Busoni.* Wiesbaden, Germany: Bruckerverlag, 1949.

Dent, Edward J. *Ferruccio Busoni: A Biography.* London: Eulenburg Books, 1974. First published London: Oxford University Press, 1933.

Dieren, Bernard van. *Down among the Dead Men.* London: Humphrey Milford/ Oxford University Press, 1935.

Ellmann, Richard. *James Joyce.* Rev. ed. Oxford: Oxford University Press, 1982.

Ermen, Reinhard. *Ferruccio Busoni.* Hamburg: Rowohlt, 1996.

Feldhege, Claudia. *Ferruccio Busoni als Librettist.* Salzburg, Germany: Verlag Ursula Müller-Speiser, 1996.

Goethe, Johann Wolfgang von. *Faust.* Edited, annotated, and with an introduction by Ernst Beutler. Wiesbaden, Germany: Dieterich'sche Verlagsbuchhandlung, 1953.

Guerrini, Guido. *Ferruccio Busoni: La vita, la figura, l'opera.* Florence: Monsalvato, 1944.

Heyworth, Peter. *Otto Klemperer: His Life and Times.* Vol. 1. Cambridge: Cambridge University Press, 1983.

Hoffmann, E. T. A. *Die Serapions-Brüder.* 5th rev. ed. Munich: Winkler-Verlag, 1995. First published Berlin, 1819–1821.

Kraus, Gottfried., ed. *Musik in Österreich.* Vienna: Christian Brandstätter, 1989.

Leichtentritt, Hugo. *Ferruccio Busoni.* Leipzig: Breitkopf und Härtel, 1916.

———. *Music, History, and Ideas.* Cambridge, MA: Harvard University Press, 1958.

Leixner, Otto von. *Geschichte der Deutschen Litteratur.* Vol. 1. Leipzig: Otto Spamer, 1903.

Mahler, Alma. *Gustav Mahler: Memories and Letters.* 3rd ed. Ed. Donald Mitchell, trans. Basil Creighton. London: John Murray, 1971. First published 1946.

Mitchell, Donald. *Gustav Mahler: Volume I; The Early Years.* Rev. ed. London: Faber and Faber, 1980.

———. *Gustav Mahler: Volume II; The Wunderhorn Years.* London: Faber and Faber, 1975.

Op de Coul, Paul. *Doktor Faust: Opera van Ferruccio Busoni.* Doctoral thesis, Rijksuniversiteit te Utrecht, Groningen, 1983.

Prelinger, née Mayer, Melanie. "Erinnerungen und Briefe aus Ferruccio Busonis Jugendzeit." *Neue Musik-Zeitung* 1, 2, and 3 (1927).

Roberge, Marc-André. *Ferruccio Busoni: A Bio-Bibliography.* New York: Greenwood, 1991.

———. "Ferruccio Busoni et la France," *Revue de Musicologie* 82, no. 2 (1996).

———. "Ferruccio Busoni, His Chicago Friends, and Frederick Stock's Transcription for Large Orchestra and Organ of the *Fantasia contrappuntistica*," *Musical Quarterly* 80, no. 2 (summer 1996): 302.

———. "Ferruccio Busoni in the United States," *American Music* 13, no. 5 (Fall 1995): 295.

Sablich, Sergio. *Ferruccio Busoni.* Turin: E.D.T./Musica, 1982.

Sachs, Harvey, ed. and trans. *The Letters of Arturo Toscanini.* London: Faber and Faber, 2002.

Schebera, Jürgen. *Kurt Weill: An Illustrated Life.* Trans. Caroline Murphy. New Haven, CT: Yale University Press/Kurt Weill Foundation for Music, 1995.

Selden-Goth, Gisella. *Ferruccio Busoni.* Leipzig: E. P. Tal, 1922.

Sitsky, Larry. *Busoni and the Piano.* New York: Greenwood, 1986.

Stuckenschmidt, H. H. *Ferruccio Busoni: Chronicle of a European.* Trans. Sandra Morris. London: Calder and Boyars, 1970.

———. *Schöpfer der Neuen Musik.* Frankfurt am Main: Suhrkamp, 1958.

———. *Zum Hören geboren: Ein Leben mit der Musik unserer Zeit.* Munich: Piper, 1979.

Symonette, Lys, and Kim H. Kowalke, eds. and trans. *Speak Low (When You Speak Love): The Letters of Kurt Weill and Lotte Lenya.* London: Hamish Hamilton, 1996.

Tawaststjerna, Erik. *Sibelius.* Vol. 1. Trans. Robert Layton. London: Faber and Faber, 1976.

———. *Sibelius.* Vol. 2. Trans. Robert Layton. London: Faber and Faber, 1986.

Theurich, Jutta., ed. "'. . . wenn Sie doch auch hier wären!' Briefe von Kurt Weill an Ferruccio Busoni," *Musik und Gesellschaft* 3 (1990).

Toller, Owen. *Pfitzner's "Palestrina."* London: Toccata, 1997.

Varèse, Louise. *Varèse: A Looking-Glass Diary.* New York: Norton, 1972.

Vogel, Johann Peter. *Pfitzner: Leben, Werke, Dokumente.* Zürich and Mainz: Atlantis Musikbuch-Verlag, 1999.

Walter, Bruno. *Gustav Mahler.* New York: Vienna House, 1973.

Weill, Kurt. *Musik und Theater: Gesammelte Schriften.* Ed. Stephen Hinton and Jürgen Schebera. Berlin: Henschelverlag, 1990.

Wood, Henry J. *My Life of Music.* London: Gollancz, 1946.

Zweig, Stefan. *Die Welt von Gestern.* Frankfurt am Main: Fischer, 1970. First published in 1944.

———. *Tagebücher.* Frankfurt am Main: Fischer, 1988.

Index

~

About the Author

Like Busoni, **Della Couling** is more or less an autodidact. Having avoided the school of hard knocks, she entered the university of life on a traveling scholarship that literally took her around the world. This peripatetic polyglot career led to subsequent appointments teaching English in Munich, and German (as a teaching assistant) at the University of California at Berkeley. She then spent five years studying singing in Rome with Gino Berardi, subsidizing her studies by translating (from French, German, Dutch, Spanish, and Italian into English) for an information center attached to the Vatican. Since her return to England she has worked freelance over the last twenty-five years as a theater and opera critic (for the *Independent*, the *Times*, the *Financial Times*, *Opera Now*, *Classical Music*, various European newspapers and journals, and for numerous newspapers and specialist magazines in the Netherlands, Germany, and Italy), as a translator of books and plays, as a book editor for various publishers, and as an occasional lecturer. She also advises various opera houses around the world on repertoire and singers.